# The Making of a Pacific Citizen

## HUGH BURLESON II

To Ron + Judy —
May you enjoy reading
about an "alternative" FS
career.
        Hugh

authorHOUSE®

*AuthorHouse™*
*1663 Liberty Drive, Suite 200*
*Bloomington, IN 47403*
*www.authorhouse.com*
*Phone: 1-800-839-8640*

*First published by AuthorHouse 12/18/2007*

*ISBN: 978-1-4343-2208-1 (e)*
*ISBN: 978-1-4259-7108-3 (sc)*

*Library of Congress Control Number: 2007903991*

*Printed in the United States of America*
*Bloomington, Indiana*

*This book is printed on acid-free paper.*

To all who seek peace through
cross-cultural understanding.

# CONTENTS

# PART III: MIDDLE AND LATER CAREER

# PART IV: SILVER RETIREMENT

# INTRODUCTION

In fall 1960 at the United States Information Agency (USIA) in Washington, D.C., I was being "processed" by Personnel before leaving for Japan on my first Foreign Service assignment. A woman personnel officer scanning my file frowned slightly and said, "Hugh Burleson, you speak and read Japanese, you have a Japanese wife and a Japanese car; you've already lived in Japan for five years. Do you really know which country you represent?"

Her epitomization actually captured my rather extraordinary transformation over the previous 15 years. For, until age 18, I could be seen as a typical white American male. Born in a small Midwest town, son of a Protestant minister, my family on both sides Americans of northern European extraction for generations.

Of course, some of the changes that America underwent during World War II had drawn us into world affairs and so contributed to the changes in me. Those are alluded to in Chapters 3-8. In the late 1950's, the Foreign Service staffs of the State Department, Commerce, USIA, USAID and other American foreign affairs agencies were expanding to meet new US responsibilities abroad. So, I now would be one of hundreds of new American representatives overseas. Yet, I had already taken several steps beyond the career choices and altered outlook of many of my Foreign Service colleagues.

The ensuing narrative will explain my core theme: the impact that exposure to Japan from age 18 and into mature adulthood had on me. For, not a few Americans who were overseas shortly after World War

II had close Asian friends and enjoyed exploring East Asian culture—something that would fill my adult life and affect the lives of at least the first few generations of my descendants.

Those details will emerge after I sketch my mostly small-town-America boyhood, which contrasted so sharply with my later Asia-oriented adult life and career.

# PART I:
# YOUTH

# EARLY VITAE

In my earliest years, my father's employer, the Protestant Episcopal Church of America, and my father's health problems dictated where our family lived.

Born in Minnesota, in 1867, John Keble Burleson was the third son among eight children* of Solomon Stevens Burleson, a sometimes circuit-riding priest in Wisconsin and Minnesota in the second half of the 1800's. Theirs was an austere, but intellectually rich life. Solomon's five sons all followed in his footsteps by becoming Episcopal priests. Several, including my father, would earn Doctor of Divinity degrees.

After his ordination, John, my father, spent years in Michigan and North Dakota. Some time in that era, he fell passionately in love with a young lady who, however, would not marry him. After that heartbreak, he took responsibility for providing a home for his widowed mother and unmarried sister—major encumbrances for a minister who might wish to seek a wife.

After "the Great War," serving a parish in Rochester, New York, he met and in 1921 married Gwendolen English, daughter of mineralogist George L. English, then on the staff of Wards Natural Science Co. "Father John" was then 54. She was 30. By this time his next elder brother, Hugh Burleson, was Episcopal bishop of South Dakota. That

---

\* Eight survived to adulthood. A ninth died at six weeks when a locust plague in Minnesota poisoned the cows'milk.

and my father's wish to be a missionary priest to the Lakotas** led the newlyweds to leave the well-to-do Rochester parish for smaller locales in southeastern South Dakota: first Vermilion (where their first child Gwendolen Louise, was born in 1922), then in Sioux Falls and Springfield.

Their next four children—John (b. 1924), Mary (b. 1925), me (b. 1927) and George (b. 1928)—were born in Springfield on the South Dakota Missouri River border with Nebraska. There he was parish priest and head of St. Mary's Indian School close by our home. (I sometimes wonder if "imprinting" from being cuddled as a baby by Lakota girls from the school who often helped our mother had any bearing on my later deep affinity for an Asian girl.

All of this is second-hand memory, for while I was still a toddler we transferred to a parish—Porterville—in milder central California. My father's long years of service in the Dakotas had hurt his health and made that change advisable. Our journey in 1929 by train—my two parents with five young children from South Dakota to the San Joaquin Valley—must be a tale in itself; but I have no memory of that.

My earliest memory is of receiving a teddy bear on my 3rd birthday in January 1930, from Aunt Abby who was visiting from her home in southern California. The next memory, a month or two later: watching snow fall softly and melt into the green moss outside our dining room window. I had no recollection of the harsher Dakota snows.

In summer 1930, with Mother soon due to deliver her sixth child, Daddy drove brother George and me to Vista (in San Diego County) to spend a month with his sisters, Aunts Abby and Martha, thus easing life a bit for his expectant wife. In Vista, we enjoyed Aunt Abby's great cooking, the freedom to explore her 6-acre lemon orchard, the wild gully below the orchard and its patch of towering cactus nearby. On warmer days we cooled off in her lawn sprinklers, studied her fish pond a bit too closely and admired, from a safe distance, her collection of

---

** He had grown up during the Indian Wars in the West and had lived on the Oneida and Menominee reservations in Wisconsin as a boy.

6

Menominee and Oneida handicrafts on a dining room wall, received when her father Solomon served those reservations in the late 1800s. (Those artifacts later would be donated to the Denver Museum of the American Indian.)

Then George and I were back in Porterville and meeting new baby sister Katherine Ann (Kitty), whose arrival evened up the sibling roster at three girls and three boys.

Later Porterville memories: Being bitten on my bottom by a parishioner's German Shepherd. A scorpion that scampered up my pant leg when I disturbed him in the garage woodpile. (My pants were tight enough that he could not deploy his stinger; and I was able to shed pants and scorpion unscathed.) Being tearfully worried when Mary—a year older and precociously entering a tomboy phase—climbed onto the back of the old open truck of the Chinese vegetable man for a thrill ride as he drove off. "Mary's going to China! Mary's going to China!" I wailed, running into the house. A few years later I knew better: You must dig long hours through the earth to get to China. Also, a day trip into the Sierra foothills where a summer drought had nearly dried up the rivers, trapping many piteous fish in shrinking pools. And, harvesting almonds from a backyard tree.

We children enjoyed climbing the back fence to watch long freight trains pass by, hauling bountiful San Joaquin Valley produce. That is how I began learning to count: hearing my older siblings tallying the freight cars rumbling by, often over 100 even in those depression years. Now able to count, I could fully participate in games of hide-and-seek.

In Porterville, winters were mild, but the summer heat could be fierce, especially for Daddy, now 64 and still adapting to the "joys" of having six rambunctious children aged 1 to 9, while tending to the spiritual needs of his parishioners. So, out of concern for our father's health, the church again moved us, this time (1932) to truly milder Escondido in San Diego County, just 12 miles from our aunts in Vista and within range of the Pacific's cool evening fogs.

For two years, we lived at the rectory in Escondido next to my father's church. And of course, I began school. Just on the fringes of memory is an anecdote I heard later. I came home from my first day of school tearful because I had not learned to read as I had expected. (Hadn't Mother helped me overcome my trepidation about going to school by saying, "Now you're going to school to learn to read!"?) By the middle of 2nd grade I was avidly reading above my grade level, and so sometimes needed my pronunciation of new words corrected by older siblings: Orang outan is not read "orange outen," and "misled" is not past tense of a strange verb "misle" somehow akin to "baffle."

We boys happily went barefoot April through September, because that is what boys in southern California did in the early 1930's, but also because during the Great Depression a small-town minister's salary did not easily cover the cost of shoes for six fast-growing children. We took pride each spring in building up calluses that protected our feet from all but the sharpest or most unyielding hazards, e.g., nails, large rocks and cactus thorns.

In Escondido, we pursued the many fascinating activities of pre-TV America. We hunted crawfish along a nearby creek, played cowboys and Indians on still undeveloped hillsides and went to 5¢ Saturday matinee movies where, in lieu of store-bought gum, we chewed roofing tar from a vat alongside the newspaper office. In summer we cooled off in the Escondido plunge—also 5¢. Once I almost drowned there when an older boy pushed me in at the deep end. Maybe a year later, at Oceanside I almost drowned again when the backwash of waves sucked me into deep water and big brother John and a lifeguard had to save me. That was my third and last near drowning. The first had occurred, I am told, in South Dakota at a church social when, still a toddler, I checked out a big crock of iced tea and fell in head first while no one was watching. So, ice tea, chlorinated pool water and salt water! Who else in this world ... oh, skip it!

Other Escondido memories: Daddy taking me to a school music concert and on the way home singing old tunes from his youth (1870's and '80s). His paddling me with a hairbrush after I jumped on the back of his Model A Ford for a ride as he neared our home. Mother getting mired hip deep in mud while tilling our backyard vegetable garden, and her getting so badly scratched by a barnyard cat (a parishioner's gift) that she developed an infection. Brother John falling from a backyard tree and breaking his leg. Sister Louise being tilted out of a chair by aftershocks as she stood on it trying to find radio station KFI after the 1933 Los Angeles earthquake had knocked "Little Orphan Annie" off the air.

At school, I developed a crush on a girl in our 2nd-grade class, Hideko Sugita. I wince to recall my total lack of social grace one lunch hour in the pergola. Running past Hideko, I called out, "Don't ya know I love ya!" In those innocent days before sexuality so overtly permeated our society, such behavior was worth a giggle. I forgot the incident until much later, a few years into my long affiliation with Japan, when I was recounting my past associations with Japanese-Americans in southern California and the memory surfaced in face-reddening detail.

When navel oranges were in season, we could buy a 20-pound box full for 50¢--a fair boost to our nutritional needs. Brother John taught us how to make sidewalk scooters with the boxes: nail the box upright on a two-by-four, and nail your worn-out skates to the bottom. Zero cost, if you had the nails. Great recreation for a parson's kids in those years long before expensive manufactured skateboards and Razor scooters.

We certainly did not feel poor. Our college-grad parents made our lives culturally rich. My father had amassed a fair-sized library over the years, many books on religion, but also sets of Kipling, Dickens and the like. Mother also still had some of her college texts. One we never read but liked to chortle over as outrageously esoteric: Kant's *Critique of Pure Reason*. Mother's major was classical studies, including philosophy, Greek and Latin.

Each Christmas, well-off church families "back East" sent a large box of gifts for us—mostly slightly used clothes not in style in rough-and-ready Escondido. We boys groaned at having to wear the wool knickerbockers that were included. That hardly seemed to us like charity, since we—in return—helped Mother pick and mail boxes of fragrant and colorful pepper berries to people back East not fortunate enough to live amid the subtropical bounty of palm, avocado, citrus and pepper berry trees.

9

A rare event about then was a visit by my father's two elder brothers—Allan, down from his parish north of Los Angeles, and Hugh, the South Dakota bishop. This reunion of the three brothers with their sisters Abbie and Martha in Vista was unique. A highlight: The three dignified priests in their 60's went off to fish at Oceanside. When they failed to catch a single fish, they displayed mischievous humor by buying fish to bring back as their catch. The reunion proved sadly poignant, too. All three brothers died in the next few years: Bishop Hugh in 1933, my father in 1934 and Allan in 1935. Those losses were followed soon after by the sudden death of Uncle Ned Kelsey, Aunt Abby's husband, a lawyer who had worked on the California Indians' legal problems.

In winter 1934, my father was hospitalized in San Diego with pneumonia. He recovered and came home, but then died of a heart attack early on a February morning. He was 66. We awoke to find him gone and would only see him again lying peacefully composed at the funeral parlor. His remains were cremated; and a few weeks later, with eldest brother Allan officiating, we rode a small boat out of San Diego harbor to commit the ashes to the Pacific (a rite repeated with Mother's ashes almost 40 years later).

A year before, with money from Uncle Hugh and an acre of land split off from Aunt Abby's lemon grove in Vista, my parents had contracted to build a five-bedroom home. The plan included a chapel room that would be an Episcopal mission. In summer 1933, we camped for a time on our new "ranch" in the large tent our family had earlier used on vacations at the Episcopal campground in South Dakota's Black Hills. While work began on the house, we all helped to plant a mini-orchard of fruit trees. The house was still unfinished when our father died.

Now Mother decided she must teach again, as she had in her youth, to supplement the church's tiny pension. To update her teaching credentials, she would attend San Diego State Teacher's College (today's San Diego State University), while we children attended the attached training school. So, we moved to San Diego, renting out the Vista home when it was completed.

San Diego in the mid-1930's was a quiet little city where "big news" was the arrival or departure of US Navy units. It was the biggest city we had seen and had visited a few times to see the zoo, the Spanish mission, etc. Now we were living there and enjoying city life first hand. It happened that 1934-35 was the year of the San Diego International Exposition. We went several times to gawk at the chrome gadgets in the General Electric kitchen, Alfa the talking robot, the recreated Globe Theater of Shakespeare, the Ford Pavilion with its "spiffy" cars, etc. We boys were also naturally curious about the Sally Rand nudist show behind a high wooden fence at the expo. I found, regretfully, that the fence's knotholes were either too high for me or monopolized by bigger boys.

Anyway, I had keener interests. I would patrol our neighborhood to befriend local dogs or hike the wild ravines that cut deeply in among our neighborhood's streets. There I collected cacti, wild flowers and rocks, and pursued bird-watching—an interest my father had instilled in me. Once I found an arrowhead and once a rusty cannonball, presumably from a long-ago Navy training exercise.

All six of us were learning the difficult term "economize." The costs of rent and city living strained the family budget severely. One response we kids made: digging up narcissus bulbs from our back yard and selling them around the neighborhood.

But now a new problem arose: Mother's health. The strains of recent widowhood, her college studies, watching the family budget, keeping us children on track and undergoing a hysterectomy wore down this 44-year-old. Initially, she tried to cope by having an Escondido family's eldest daughter stay with us as a live-in maid; but that was an imperfect solution. So, one weekend we drove to Vista for a family conference with our two dear aunts there. The decision: We would return to Vista to live in our now completed house and try to get by on my late father's pension alone. Aunts Abbie and Martha promised to help, which they did generously over the next six years. We children pledged earnest efforts also in this more stringent life style.

So, in summer 1935 we moved to Vista, seven miles inland from Oceanside. Our fruit orchard was still too immature to bear fruit, but three large lemon trees from Aunt Abbie's grove had been left standing and bore two abundant crops a year. With some help from George and me, John built a chicken coop for 12-18 hens and a hay barn, milking shed and corral for a cow. We bought a Guernsey cow, Bossy, which Mother milked until she sprained her hand and John and I took over that chore. So, we had eggs, milk, cottage cheese, butter and lemonade. Among the fruit trees was space enough for us to grow many vegetables. Over the next few years, we took turns walking the neighborhood with a basket full of such produce from our acre, selling it to supplement the family income. We boys also earned pocket money by mowing peoples' lawns, etc.

Schools were within walking distance—the elementary school where I now began fourth grade and the junior high/high school that Louise and John attended.

So, we developed a routine of school, chores and family activity. Mother often read to us from such neo-classics as *Lorna Doone* and Kipling's *Jungle Book* and *The White Seal*. With her Cornell education and years as a teacher, she could offer enlightening comment.

George, 15 months my junior, was a bosom pal and playmate. Together we explored the nearby wild areas and with others sometimes took longer hikes into hills east of town. We also liked to fish and swim in Vista Creek's waterholes.

Some indelible impressions from those years: Waking at dawn to the sounds of quail calling through the thick sea fog that engulfed us many mornings, the Filipino pickers chattering in Tagalog among Aunt Abby's lemon trees, or Mr. Purvis* and his mule plowing that orchard. Also, going on summer days to a semi-public pool two miles away and, as we walked home, leaving a trail of orange peels from the bounty of the roadside orange groves. In truly hot weather we found the best thirst-quencher, though, was a half lemon with salt sprinkled liberally on it. (proto-Gatorade?)

---

* An uncle of the FBI's gang-busting Melvin Purvis.

Bossy, our first cow in Vista, sometimes gave us trouble. When in heat, that clever bovine would somehow escape from her barn and clop-clop past our house, sometimes at night in the rain, to look for a mate. We would groan, dress and go off with flashlights in search of her. It might take an hour or two to find her and bring her back. We then dealt with her needs by walking her the next day to a farm that had a bull. I think it was after her second calf that Bossy developed "milk fever" and died. We hired Mr. Purvis to dig a hole in the adobe hardpan near the corral and bury her huge body. We next bought a petite Jersey, Betsy. She gave prodigious quantities of milk for so small a cow. A year later, a county inspector came by on a routine check and found that she carried the TB bacillus and had to be destroyed. So, we got another Jersey—Betsy, too (Betsy II?).

My interest in birds and other nature studies increased in Vista's unspoiled environment. The fan palms lining Hillside Drive in front of our home attracted the beautiful orange-and-black Arizona Hooded Orioles, which hung their woven palm-fiber nests under the palm fronds in fair numbers. I often went off alone for bird spotting in nearby orchards, sagebrush hillsides or along Vista Creek. John, who enjoyed pragmatic do-it-yourself projects and such magazines as "Popular Science" and "Popular Mechanics," began ribbing me about this, arguing that a "science brain" was better than a "bird brain." He even nicknamed me "bird brain," which I learned to shrug off.

Speaking of magazines, an under-the-stairs closet in our home was chock-a-block with 15 years of "National Geographic" magazines and bound "Saint Nicholas" magazines dating from Mother's childhood. We spent uncounted hours, especially on rainy days, pouring over that trove, learning world lore and getting vast amusement from the droll Victorian humor of the "Saint Nicholas." (E.g., "There was an old man from Perth, who was born on the day of his birth. He was married, they say, on his wedding day, and died on his last day on earth.") From "National Geographic" maps and magazines as well as from my stamp collection, I gained a keen interest in geography.

Music enriched our lives, too. Mother had inherited her aunt's baby grand Steinway, and we had an old Victrola and some classical records.

Some folksier ones, too, like "Ol' Joe's Hittin' the Jug." We gave them all heavy use; and when the Victrola finally broke down, we had new fun spinning the records with our fingers to play them backwards. Mother encouraged us to join the school orchestra. Louise had a fine soprano voice, John played the flute and Mary had taken up the viola. In fourth grade I started on the cello; and soon after that George began on the violin. A few years later, 1939, at a school orchestra recital we five Burlesons performed "Londonderry Air" ("Danny Boy"), with Louise singing it beautifully. Kitty would later study piano and go on to major in music in college. For two years, I also played the bugle in the Vista Drum & Bugle Corps, which marched in such community events as the annual '49ers' Day Parade.

In the mid-1930's, I began noticing the news of wars far away—the Italian attack on Ethiopia, the beginnings of the Spanish Civil War and then Japan's invasion of China. And I heard Mother and our two aunts discussing those situations and the '36 presidential campaign. Our aunts were undaunted Republicans, while Mother retained the attachment she and my father had for more liberal causes. Some Norman Thomas socialists were her "dear friends." These political differences were always voiced gently; but they made me aware of partisan politics. I recall running about the schoolyard during the '36 campaign to ask students which candidate, Alf Landon or FDR, their families favored. My highly dubious polling technique showed a split so close that I became concerned about Roosevelt's chances. No matter: That same year the "Literary Digest" produced poll results so skewed that the journal disappeared from the face of the earth, while I went on—18 years later—to do political interviewing in the '52 presidential campaign that earned me an A+ on a political science paper; and a decade after that I would closely analyze Japanese opinion polls for our government's policymakers. But that's getting ahead of our story.

About this time, our street, until then a dirt road, was "paved" southern California style: The county's heavy road machines mixed used oil with the adobe dirt and then rolled that down into a near-asphalt surface. When it hardened, we could even roller skate on it. Late one evening in the bright light of a full moon, I went out to skate alone on the slope just above our home. On one descent, I was flying along with one skate

14

atop the other when a hole hidden in the shadow of a palm caught my skate wheel. Before I could react, my face smashed into the hard surface, earning me some beautiful bruises and a ban on skating after dark. Another form of recreation for us was playing "war" in nearby avocado and citrus groves using dirt clods and green fruit as ammo. Wild, wasteful fun.

I think it was summer 1937 that Mother's father, Grandpa George English, the Rochester mineralogist, came with his second wife for a visit. Already a rock collector myself, I was thrilled when he brought me some nice specimens and two small antelope skulls he had acquired in South Africa decades earlier while on a buying expedition for Wards Natural Science. We gladly showed him and Grandma Jane our subtropical paradise. They responded to the pleasant environment by buying a nearby building lot and starting plans for building a home there.

Sadly, for health reasons, they would never live there. During that visit, a conjunction occurred between the moon and two planets. I recall our cold shock when, presciently, Grandpa said he would not be alive for the next such occurrence 10 years hence. He did live to see his first book, *Getting Acquainted with Minerals*, published by McGraw-Hill. That, and his later more technical book would yield modest but very welcome royalties that came to Mother after Grandpa English died.

We boys enjoyed fishing for perch and blue gill in Vista Creek, but by the later 1930's we could afford to go to Oceanside to fish either off the pier (for free) or to pay $1 to fish all day on a 100-foot boat anchored about a mile offshore. We seldom caught much there, but were fascinated to watch men occasionally haul in giant sea bass in the 300-400-pound range. A few times we splurged, spending $2 or $3 to fish all day on a "live-bait boat" which cruised the coast in search of barracuda, yellowtail and rock bass.

In summer 1938, John and I camped for a week at the beach north of Oceanside's main bathing beach. We fished daily at the above venues and in the surf near our camp. One memorable time we returned from a day of live-bait fishing with a gunny sack filled with 80 mackerel and three sea bass. We kept the bass for ourselves, but spent an hour dragging the heavy sack through the campground trying to give the mackerel away. No takers. As a last resort, we dumped them in the lagoon behind the camp. The next day on the lagoon in rented kayaks (25¢/hour), we found hosts of crabs feasting on our catch.

Vista was home to a fairly large Japanese community. The best vegetables in the local market were grown by Issei and their 2nd-generation offspring. One of Mary's close friends was a classmate, Momoye Kinoshita; and several Nisei boys were among the classmates I played with during recess. The high school's star quarterback was Kenzo Ozaki. And, one team in Vista's amateur baseball league was the all-Nisei team, which usually did well in the night games at Vista Park.

A larger minority in Vista we called "the Mexicans." Some were families that had lived there hundreds of years, long before this was part of the U.S. One such family lived at the bottom of our hill. Sometimes as we walked past, the children would call out tauntingly, "Towhead, towhead!" For, the intense summer sun and swimming pool chlorine would bleach our brown hair a bit.

In those days, I was cursed by the foot-in-mouth disease of speaking on impulse—not thinking how another person might take my words. For example, when Japan invaded China in 1937, I was thoughtless enough to ask a Nisei schoolmate which side he wanted to see win—another embarrassing memory added to the cache I began amassing four years earlier in that Escondido school yard.

During summers we visited the Oceanside beach two or three days a week. As the morning sea fog retreated from Vista's orchards, the whole family would load into our big 1929 Packard and travel the seven miles to Oceanside. Our summer fun at the beach was amplified in those years when Aunt Abbie's daughter Mary and her family came down to visit from San Francisco, where whistling winds and chilly water discourage ocean swimming. We tanned "natives" enjoyed introducing—or re-introducing—Mary's children Alan and Judy to such beach arts as building sand castles, body surfing, fishing or simply beachcombing. During those same summers, our Episcopal pastor organized week-long summer camps which we joined, first at Dana Point south of San Clemente and then at Coronado's Silver Strand—the long sand spit that helps enclose San Diego Bay.

In those years the Great Depression caught its second wind, more people were jobless and more "tramps" showed up at our door asking for handouts or work. Highway 395 ran by the base of our hill, and our big white house on the hill must have appeared a good prospect for those drifters. We had precious little cash to offer, but sometimes shared with them the scant produce of our one-acre ranch in exchange for their doing odd jobs.

My bird-spotting hobby became a vehicle for my brief contact with a real (*not* " honest-to-goodness") Nazi spy. A Hungarian, the husband of cousin Mary's college classmate at Vassar years earlier, came visiting in 1939. That year, for a second consecutive season, it happened that a flock of wood ibises were summering at an estuary near Oceanside, far north of their usual range. The Hungarian asked me to guide him to see them; and I did. The day was uneventful, except for his nearly getting his rattletrap Plymouth stuck in mire near the estuary.

A short while later, we heard that the FBI had caught him trying to film US Navy facilities and aircraft plants near San Diego and had expelled him from the country. Clearly, our days of blissful innocence as children, and as a nation, were coming to a close.

# ADOLESCENCE

In 1938, another older cousin, Allan Willard Burleson, came to Vista, bringing his father, the youngest and sole surviving brother of the original five priests, to visit his sisters Abby and Martha. Uncle Ned (Edward), a parish priest in northern Idaho, had grievously wounded himself some 6-7 years earlier when a shotgun he was cleaning discharged and blew away part of his lower jaw. Imperfectly repaired in several years of plastic surgery (without anesthetic!), his lower face was partly hidden by a beard. His speech often was hard to understand because of damage to his tongue muscles; and his eyes had the watery look of someone who had endured great pain.

In summer 1939, Allan returned to Vista. I soon learned that this was no casual visit. He had come this time to discharge an obligation placed on him years before by Uncle Hugh: to see that I, as the bishop's namesake, received a good education. Allan (then a junior professor at the Episcopalian Hobart College in New York, my father's alma mater) now proposed to check out several prep schools in southern California to find one that would offer me a scholarship.

Most of our first cousins,* were PK's—preacher's kids— and lacked the kind of money it took to attend a prep school, even in southern California of 1940. Having scarcely traveled outside of San Diego County since we moved there seven years earlier, I found this a startling and exciting proposal.

---

* Because my father married so late, these cousins were all old enough to be our uncles and aunts. An exception to the above statement on financial means would be John E. Burleson, Uncle Hugh's son.

So, early one morning we set out in Allan's car, a 1930 Dodge touring car. It was an ambitious trip in those days before freeways and Interstates. We went up US 101 through Long Beach to Santa Barbara and then took a state road across the coastal range into the Santa Ynez Valley to visit a casual, country-style boy's school. We then doubled back to the Ojai Valley to check out the far more swank Thatcher School before returning to Vista. A few days later, we made a shorter trip to Claremont to see the Webb School. We ended the day with a trip into Los Angeles to see the Huntington Museum (home of "The Blue Boy" painting) and the Griffith Observatory, with its science exhibits and planetarium. A warm memory: Aunt Abby hurrying breathlessly toward us after she had wandered off and pushed a button on one exhibit that started circles of artificial lightning climbing a metal cylinder inside a glass case. She thought she had broken it.

Within months the decision was that I would attend Webb School on a partial scholarship after completing junior high in Vista in June 1940.

Meanwhile, war broke out in Europe. Suddenly countries I had known only from maps and their postage stamps were being swallowed up by Nazi Germany or being bombed. I got out a Geographic map of Europe and North Africa and began closely following the battlefronts, penciling in the ever-changing lines.

Starting high school in fall 1940 at Webb, 100 miles north of our Vista home, I entered a very different social environment from what I had known so far. I felt no homesickness, perhaps inoculated against that by the summer church camps and Boy Scout campouts. Also, headmaster Thompson and Vivian Webb worked hard to create a family-like atmosphere at the school, and the faculty also did their part in that.

Webb School of that era, with about 100 students, included many sons of Hollywood figures and southern California's wealthy (as in Getty) or near-wealthy nabobs. Such boys tended to set the tone at the school, easily taking material wealth for granted, but also assuming that high personal achievement was the norm and would mark their efforts in class, in sports and in a later career. Most expected to qualify for a good college. The few exceptions stood out as class clowns, jokesters or amusing oddities. One student from Canada was a chess whiz, but did poorly in his exams, emerging each time with a casual grin and a flip "Can't win 'em all!"

Webb is 30 miles east of L.A. at the base of the Sierra Madre range where, in those days, mountain biota yielded to miles of citrus orchards spreading west, south and east. The myriad housing tracts and choking smog that typified the area after World War II could not yet be imagined. So, for example, each fall I thrilled to see migrating snow geese in flocks of hundreds make their great downward spirals as they cleared the mountains and descended to about 1500 feet. Their bodies and wings flashed a brilliant white as they wheeled down in the bright California sun. With today's smog, I doubt that Webb students ever see them.

We students faced an outstanding faculty. Thompson Webb himself was the son of the headmaster of Webb School of Tennessee. He kept the focus on getting us superlatively prepared for our nation's best universities, as well as on building character. His influence was palpable every day at Webb. In the social area, we also frequently benefited from guidance by the vivacious Vivian Webb—a fine proxy mother there on campus.

The down-to-earth pragmatism of the Webbs and the faculty helped to suppress any sense of class or wealth distinctions among us students. As a scholarship student, I was asked —especially after labor became scarce in 1943 and 1944—to do chores in the kitchen (like sectioning grapefruit) and gym (mopping the floor of the basketball court), or to take incoming after-hours phone calls for other students, as we had no dorm phones. Yet, we scholarship students were never made to feel second class. My first room-mate, John Marin, was the son of a film director; my second, Charley Skouras, was the son of the owner of the Fox West Coast Theaters chain. I became close with both.

During my freshman year, I grew 10 inches—an awkward time when I was adjusting to the new environment, playing intramural sports and upping my sights academically. I enjoyed a physical geography course with Mr. John Vedder, a fine science teacher of laconic humor who stressed hands-on experiments as much as possible. Sometimes in class we would ask, "But, sir, what makes it run?" His stock answer: "Oh, you just hire a little boy." He also had us regularly monitor the on-campus weather instruments.

In summer 1941, Mother decided that, with Louise and John nearing college age, but with family finances too tight to support them at college away from home, we should move to Berkeley to be near the university. So, she sold our '29 Packard, bought a '37 Plymouth. Then she and Louise left to house-hunt in Berkeley.

Before leaving, Mother asked a poultry dealer to come and buy our six geese, 10 ducks and 12-14 chickens. When the man offered just 5¢ a pound for them, she balked, saying they were worth more than that to us as food. So, after she left and with Mary as chef, we began devouring them. Kill a duck, goose or two chickens on Saturday, roast and eat it Sunday, eat the leftovers Monday and Tuesday, make it into soup for Wednesday and Thursday, and restart the fowl cycle on Friday or Saturday.

We had barely dinked the flock when Mother and Louise returned some three weeks later, having bought a house in Berkeley. So, John found a school buddy to take the surviving birds to live (happily ever after?) on a 2-acre "ranch" with a pond next to Vista Creek. Of course we sold the cow. And, we sold our home to a piano teacher who had been using our living room to give lessons on the Steinway baby grand.

In mid-August, a Bekins van from San Francisco arrived to load our household items for Berkeley. As the men worked in the warm sun, I was shocked to hear one complain, "I'll be damned glad to get back to the San Francisco fog!" Pure blasphemy to a southern California sun-lover. Raised my doubts, too, about life in Berkeley.

Yet, we were thrilled some days later to arrive in the Plymouth in the Bay Area, cross the Bay Bridge, in thin fog, and finally see Berkeley. Our home in north central Berkeley was not as spacious as our Vista home, but met our basic needs. We had a whole new environment to explore; and even that cooler climate supports some types of palm trees.

In my sophomore year, we had a great biology teacher, Raymond Alf, who taught with dramatic flair and infectious enthusiasm. At that time, he was working on a Ph.D. in geology; and several of us delighted in joining him on weekend hikes into the mountains, where he collected rock specimens relating to his thesis on the geology of the Sierra Madres.*

In biology class we often used microscopes, especially to study the varied microscopic life forms in pond water. I will never forget Mr. Alf's reaction one day when I was examining a euglena (one-celled protozoan) under the microscope, and he kept urging me to say what the one outstanding trait was of this creature that no other pond critter had.

Finally, I said, "Well, he has a round spot like an eye behind that long cilium."

"Yes! But, what color is it?" Mr. Alf fairly shouted in frustration and with his usual dramatic vigor.

"I don't know, sir."

"You don't know? It's red! Red, isn't it?"

"Oh. Well, I'm red-green color blind, so I couldn't say," I answered.

His emotions imploded and he apologized profusely for making such a to-do over my seeming obtuseness. He remained one of my favorite teachers then and in succeeding years when I took plane and solid geometry and trigonometry from him.

Our English teacher, Gordon Wilson, was also one to inspire us to strive for an ever better command of our native language, to look deeper into

---

* Raymond Alf continued his association with Webb for another half century. A 10/4/99 "Seattle Times" obituary called him "a teacher who inspired students with his unusual teaching styles and founded the Raymond M. Alf Museum of Paleontology"—the only such accredited museum on a US secondary school campus. He was 92 when he died.

Shakespeare and to become familiar with noted poets of the past. One fall while we were studying "Macbeth," he developed appendicitis and suddenly was hospitalized for surgery. We sent him a get-well card and received a return note making light of his experience. It included the line: "Just as I was going under the ether, I heard the surgeon exclaim, 'Who would have thought the old man to have had so much blood in him!'" We recognized the line from "Macbeth."

Our Latin teacher was the spitting image of the bust of Caesar pictured in our textbook, and his classroom manner was similarly imperious. Doze off or make a disturbance in the classroom, and he would peg a bit of chalk at you. Really goof off or fail to pay attention, and he would saunter over and place a loaded wastebasket over your head. He made sure that we well understood the extent to which Latin underpins English—a real boon for one's later vocabulary building.

Sobering events impinged on my sophomore year: Pearl Harbor and our nation's plunge into war. One night early in 1942 we heard distant air-raid sirens and, a bit later, the muffled booming of anti-aircraft guns, lasting some 30 minutes. The news the next day spoke of a false sighting of enemy planes over Los Angeles. A second air-raid alert sounded about a month later when a more concrete threat appeared: a Japanese submarine shelling oil derricks up the coast near Santa Barbara. The first crude US radar was sparking these alerts, but we had not yet heard of radar. (In summer '44 I attended an impressive demonstration of radar and anti-aircraft guns in U.C.'s football stadium.)

During 1942, Thompson Webb completed his years of hard, dedicated labor on the adobe walls of a new school chapel. The bricks were mostly made right on site; and Mr. Webb cut a memorable figure in his muddied work clothes and topi hat as he sweated the 50-60-pound bricks into place. Occasionally, we boys would pitch in to help. Then it became a custom that each boy would lay at least one brick in the walls during that phase of the construction; but Mr. Webb took great pride in laying most of the bricks himself.

Some of my classmates kept horses at the school stables, and I often jogged along with them when they rode into the foothills behind the school. Such training helped get me in shape for the track team; and I began entering the mile events. That also gave me the wind for distance swimming in the school pool. I would dive in and swim for 1½-2 hours non-stop. I also began practicing underwater swimming, useful for exploring rocky seashores. Otherwise, I was still mostly doing intramural touch football, soccer and basketball.

The influence of the Webbs, the fine faculty and our wartime sense of being bound together in an earnest national effort created a fine spirit at the school. That, in turn, made being so far from home (now 450 miles away) quite bearable. For my remaining years at Webb, I would get home only at Christmas, summer vacations and Easter.

On some school holidays or weekends when most boys returned to their homes in the L.A. area, I was invited by the Vedder family (one of whose three sons was a classmate) to go with them to their home at Laguna Beach, one of the gem spots of the California coast. There we snorkeled, spear-fished and used tire irons to lever abalone off the rocks in 6-10 feet of water. One February weekend was so warm that we could swim (briefly) in the ocean. The following week brought a cold snap that had us hiking the next weekend through deep snow on Cucamonga Peak.

Santa Ana winds sometimes whipped through Claremont and once sparked a brush fire that swept past the school. We were allowed to volunteer to help homeowners near the campus fend off the flames. One highlight of 1942: a dance that Webb held for the girls of Northridge School, which Shirley Temple was attending; and the young star came. I did not attend the dance, being still a bit awkward socially and on a restricted allowance. The mandatory corsage would have taken nearly half of my monthly pocket money.

During summer 1942, the Berkeley YMCA (where John worked part-time) mobilized a bunch of us boys to help pick pears in Cupertino (now part of "Silicon Valley"). Poor coordination between the YMCA organizers and the orchard men, however, meant we often had no work and earned very little money.

Earlier that summer I had become smitten with "an older woman," saucy, red-headed Ellen, a classmate of Mary's. I was hoping to get a date with her before returning to Webb. So, I asked permission to leave the fruit camp; but the camp managers were trying to hold the project together and asked me to stay. After two more days of no work, I quietly left, hitchhiking to San Jose, where I caught a bus to the East Bay. I felt pangs of guilt, but was convinced that we boys had been let down.

That weekend I did get a date with Ellen: took her to a movie and held her hand! Yet, as I dropped her off at her home, she told me she was getting serious with an older fellow, a Navy man from Treasure Island (whom she would marry a year later). During the next school year, I corresponded with Ellen. My infatuation grew, but alas ... Ah, youth!

Starting my junior year at Webb in Fall 1942, I made the varsity football team, playing left guard. One game we won 13-12, which I got credit for. The school paper reported: "Hugh Burleson, using his head, thwarted their effort at a field goal"—meaning that I had jumped up to block the kick and took the football right in the face.

That year, with the new chapel all but finished, Thompson Webb brought in a diminutive Scottish woodcarver to work on the interior décor. A Webb tradition was that each Sunday evening we boys attended "vespers" in the library. Twice that year the gentle old Scotsman delighted us with talks on Scotland and Bobby Burns, whose poems he recited at length *from memory* in his soft Scottish burr. Another Sunday evening the speaker was Alfred Noyes, the British poet, who gave us a dramatic reading of "The Highwayman" and other British poems. We also had a French speaker who compared French and English modes of expression. He held that French is more mellifluous than English, but admitted that English does have some lovely phrases, like "cellar door." (I got the joke only after students taking French explained that it sounds like "I adore you" in French.)

In this junior year, I finally began going to the school dances, and was surprised that some girls showed more than passing interest in me, even girls from families with money (e.g., a Burpee Seeds daughter). Being

25

from a family of no means, I often felt I was sailing under false colors as a Webb preppie and so did little to encourage such girls.

That was true, too, when classmate Jack DeMott, from a well-off Santa Barbara family, arranged to meet me during Christmas vacation at San Francisco's Mark Hopkins Hotel for an evening at Top of the Mark dancing with his sister, whom I had met at a school dance. The girl apparently had a crush on me, but I (1) saw no future in it and (2) was finding that I did not relate well at a deeper level to such girls. That may have been partly defensive. I knew I could not entertain them in ways they would expect, and I sensed differences in our value systems and life experiences. They would carry on about their vacations in Hawaii or Florida or summers at their family's home at Tahoe or Big Bear Lake. I had no subject matter relevant to such a life style.

One girl, a cousin of the Vedder boys, really caught my eye, though. I met her also at a school dance. In a February '43 letter to "my confidante," sister Mary, I confessed a fair infatuation with this girl; but after a few dates, she seemed to lose interest in me. With hindsight, I can guess that I was too self centered to be interesting to any girl for long.

I remained keenly interested in nature studies and amassed a collection of butterflies and other insects. I continued with my stamp collection and with the cello, playing in a trio that a Claremont music teacher put together. I joined the school glee club—now as a bass. We had some joint concerts with choruses from other prep schools. A memorable one was held with three other prep schools—some 100 voices together—at Cal Tech. And, on my Geographic maps on my dorm room wall I continued to follow the now faster moving battle lines in Africa, Russia and the Pacific.

That year, I bought a pair of white rats during Christmas vacation in Berkeley. Not allowed to keep them in the dormitory, I made a pen for them in an empty horse stall. By Valentine's Day they had a litter of babies, and by Easter vacation I tallied a rat population of 50. Before leaving for home, I arranged for a helper in the school kitchen to take them scraps. But, back from vacation, I found they had all escaped. End of rat tale. (I promise another from 38 years later.)

All summer in 1943 I worked at Durkee Famous Foods, a food-packing plant in west Berkeley, helping to load cases of pickles, mayonnaise, cooking oil and the like onto trucks or boxcars, often stenciling the cases for delivery to military depots or overseas. That was my first experience with being a member of a labor union—Harry Bridges' ILA—with membership mandatory to work at Durkee.

Back in Claremont for my senior year (1943-44), football was a prime interest. Early in the season we played San Dimas High, whose star player of the previous season, Glen Davis, was headed for West Point. He had spent the summer at San Dimas making up credit deficiencies and so played that one game against us. Grayer heads that yours, dear readers, will recall that Davis was an outstanding star at West Point in the late 40's along with "Doc" Blanchard; but we held his high school to a tie in that game in 1944. I won my second varsity letter that year, and in track and field did a bit better running the half mile than the mile, often placing second or third.

That year, three other boys (including Jack DeMott) and I lived, not in a dorm, but in a small house beside the football field. Besides two bedrooms and a bathroom, we had a living room with a fireplace and record player. And, I had my dog Clown with me for company. Pleasant living.

As seniors, we of course were all focused on college and beyond. I had locked onto attending Cal Berkeley, while other classmates were applying to colleges across the US, including Harvard and Princeton. A Webb tradition was that each senior carved a wooden plaque to be installed on the walls or doors panels in the school library. I did one of the Cal Campanile.

At a late spring dance, I met a young lady of unique background. She had grown up in Chengdu, China, the daughter of American missionaries from the famed New England Phelps family. Dating her once more in Claremont, I learned that her grandparents lived in Berkeley and she would visit them soon after graduation that year.*

After our Class of '44 graduation, the first in Webb's completed chapel, I went home to Berkeley and arranged to start my freshman year at Cal in the summer quarter. I sold my ¾-size cello, now too small for me, to pay for a new suit that would serve me for my freshman year, along with my navy-blue blazer and gray flannel slacks from Webb. As it turned out, I would not touch a cello again for nearly two decades.

In late June, I contacted the girl from Chengdu and we dated twice. I found her ever more fascinating, but soon she was off for New England. We corresponded until a final letter came from her in which she spoke glowingly of a special young man she had met at a church camp. Curtains for my chances with her.

At Cal, I took a job in the university's photostat lab, where I could work between classes of German, English, chemistry, physical anthropology. ROTC (where I played the bugle again in our marching drills) was mandatory. Ignoring the warning I should have gotten from not seeing the euglena's red eyespot, I thought I wanted to be a medical researcher and so made a special effort in chemistry. But, chem. lab became a problem when I had to note the colors in chemical reactions. Fellow students could help somewhat, but my handicap should have been obvious to me.

An inability to see subtle shades of red also handicap a fellow when he would benefit from knowing if a girl is blushing (or green, for that matter, in case the problem is jealousy). As I joined in frosh activities, dances, etc., that may have contributed to my uneven record with girls. Another of sister Mary's friends, the vivacious Helen Davies, attracted me and, on a second date, was apparently ready to be kissed; but I had to hear that after the fact from Mary. One girl at Cal took special interest in me, even inviting me sometimes to dances at her dorm. I never warmed up much to her, though. Her voice had an odd timbre, like a

---

* My recent study of family records shows that we had a triple-great grandmother from that family.

28

permanent falsetto, that rasped on my ears. Another time I blind-dated a girl whom Louise had met at San Jose State College. She was bright and pleasant, but because she was on the heavy side, I did not really warm to her. Still far too self centered, maybe even narrow minded.

With the war taking ever more men off to Europe and the Pacific, guys on campus were thinned out, making coeds more available for dates. So, I dated several, perhaps trying to make up for my limited experience so far. I had my first kiss, but got no farther than that because, a few days later, the girl told me she had only dated me to spite her regular beau, with whom she had now made up. So, I learned more about feminine psychology during my brief freshman year than I had during all four years at Webb. Slow learner?

That fall, Mary got married, and I took over her job at the Lawrence Radiation Lab on campus, tending to lab rats and specimen kilns. The lab's 40-inch cyclotron was being rebuilt the whole time I worked there; but substances irradiated by the larger cyclotron on the hill above campus were being used to learn how radiation affects animal tissue. We found it amusing when the two "mystics" (chemists) at the lab would put their hands under a Geiger counter during coffee breaks and make it buzz furiously. Only later would we know what that might mean for their health later on.

At the University YMCA, I became acquainted with a couple of unique fellows: Hans Baerwald and Don Helm—unique in that they spoke Japanese fluently and had grown up in Japan. Helm, in fact, was part Japanese. I note this here because I would cross paths with both again and because, with the war in Europe heading toward a conclusion, our focus would soon shift to Asia and the war with Japan.

That fall, too, I heard about ASTP—the Army Specialized training Program. By signing up immediately, a college student could go into that program and avoid being drafted for combat duty. But I thought I preferred the Navy, dredging up memories of the fleet in San Diego, a Boy Scout trip to the Navy training center there and happy hours on fishing boats out of Oceanside. Problem: the Navy was uninterested in color-blind men. Then I heard of an eye doctor in Oakland who reportedly could correct color-blindness. So, I started going to him to exercise my eyes with the flashing colored lights he had rigged up in a darkened room. After three or four sessions ($59) and no improvement, I quit and decided to take my chances with the draft. I would be eligible in January 1945. By the time my freshman year ended that January, I had my draft notification and so did not re-enroll for the next quarter. But, I continued at the lab for another month.

Over the 1944 Christmas holidays, I again dated Helen Davies; and we agreed that I would be her date at a Valentine's Day dance at Claremont Women's College, which she was then attending. Wartime gas rationing had deterred me from learning to drive; and I did not wish to put out bus or train fare for the Claremont trip. So, I opted to hitchhike.

Starting from Berkeley one early February morning two days before the dance, I quickly found that gas rationing was making hitchhiking a tough way to go. Few vehicles were making long hauls; and after five or six rides I had only reached San Jose. Two more hops got me to Gilroy, north of the Salinas Valley at about 2 PM. The last driver suggested I might do better on the San Joaquin Valley route, 50-60 miles shorter than Highway 101 down the coast.

So, I next caught a farm truck taking the state road that cut through San Juan Batista to the Valley. Just five miles up that road, the truck dropped me off. No more rides came along for over an hour. I decided to return to 101. By early evening, I had made it to San Luis Obispo—less than half way to Claremont. Two more rides took me to Santa Maria in the wee hours. I gave up and went to the Greyhound Bus station to sleep until the next L.A.-bound bus would leave. It was mid-afternoon of Valentine's Day when I arrived in Claremont. I contacted Helen and found a place to freshen up before dinner and our date.

At the dance, Helen's friends should have been impressed that I had come 500 miles to be her date; but my mode of travel somehow left them unimpressed. During the evening I began to sense that Helen might have acquired a new beau, a Claremont boy who now could be her real interest. And, by evening's end I was almost sure she was sorry that I had held her to our holiday agreement and had come down for the dance.

With hindsight, I can see that I was no great date for any girl in those years. Unskilled at the repartee needed to be amusing, and more interested in my own hobbies and interests than in theirs, I probably was something of a bore. If I should ever again meet any of the girls I dated 1943-45, I would want to apologize sincerely for so wasting their time.

The next day, I made the long trip more worthwhile by stopping at Webb School to see friends there before heading home. Then I took a bus to L.A. and managed to hitch a ride in an old Willys with a sailor on leave and headed for San Francisco. (Servicemen could get a special gas ration.) He had hoped I would share the driving with him, but I had to tell him I was still unlicensed. Besides, the Willys had a carburetor problem that needed skilled attention just to keep it rolling along.

In the few weeks I now had left as a civilian, I explored San Francisco some more, and hiked the hills around Point Reyes, where the San Andreas Fault slices through behind the Point, creating some interesting topography.

# IN THE ARMY NOW

On 22 March 1945, I reported to the Army induction station in Oakland, along with 20 or so other young men. After being sworn into the Army, we were bused to Camp Beale in the Sacramento Valley for processing and assignment to training. There, in uniform and dog-tagged (39434019—"Memorize that number, soldier, until you can spit it back even in your sleep."), we learned to get around the camp, saw movies at night, training films during the day and ate that abundant Army chow.

Aye, there was the rub! After about four days, the rich, fatty diet aggravated hemorrhoids that had occasionally troubled me for a few years. I saw a base doctor, who deemed the problem severe enough to require surgery. So, into the base hospital. I spent over a week waiting for surgery, about eight days for recovery, and then was back in the barracks ready for assignment.

During this time, we heard the sobering news of FDR's death and soon after that the news that Germany had surrendered. The war was clearly moving into a new phase, focusing on the Pacific Theater where the brutal battle for Okinawa was raging. At Beale we witnessed some fighting, when several hundred Nisei men from Hawaii came through, and reacted strongly when anyone called them "Japs." There, too, we were bemused to see that German POWs were serving us in the chow line. Adjustments!

So, it was late April before I received orders for training and was off on a troop train bound for Camp Hood, Texas, where we would undergo

17 weeks of Infantry basic training. Our troop train arrived at Killeen station in the first week of May.

Our "cycle" was a feisty mix of Texans, Oklahomans, Louisiana Cajuns and us "California bastards." The colorful, metaphor-rich speech of the Texans fascinated me; and we all got a bang out of our Cajun buddies. E.g., pulling guard duty one night, Private Babineau challenged a figure approaching in the dark: "Halt and reconize yousef!" It turned out to be the company commander. I was intrigued also to find that in the mess hall chatter I could pick out the Berkeley High School speech cadence: an idiosyncratic rushing of phrases that I had heard Mary and George acquiring at that school after we moved to Berkeley.

There deep in the heart of Texas, I was also fascinated to see marine fossils all over the ground in the company area—shells, small corals, etc.—signs that this was once the bed of an ancient seabed. Not that geologic history made the increasing heat any easier to bear. We West Coast types now learned about humid southern summers as we worked with Browning automatic rifles and machine guns while lying prone on the Texas earth, scorching hot much of the time, steaming hot after the frequent thunderstorms.

We also learned the risks of raising a hand when a non-com asked a question, like: "Who can tell me how soap is made?" Any hand that went up was soon deep in mess-hall soap suds doing KP. Fortunately, when I raised my hand after a question on who had past military training, I was made a squad leader—even though my nine months of ROTC at Berkeley had taught me little more than close-order drill and some Army bugle calls.

Being squad leader gave me a taste of leadership. I enjoyed it, despite my being no great shakes at squad leading. I recall one exercise when the company commander called us squad leaders together to instruct us on firing from a skirmish line. I was seconds late getting the target identification. So, by the time I got back to my squad, the other squads were already firing and my squad could not hear my shouted orders. We scored at the bottom in that exercise.

33

Another time, after an overnight bivouac we all helped police the area and then burned our trash. As we stood waiting for trucks to pick us up, a blank round suddenly exploded in the fire. As we looked to see what had happened, I suddenly felt blood streaming down my neck. A piece of brass casing had gone right through my ear.

I must have looked mortally wounded as I left by ambulance, because my squad members were amazed when I returned from the hospital three days later, hale and hearty. And, I was surprised that they greeted me warmly, saying they were fed up with the "California bastard" who took over in my absence. "But, I'm a California bastard, too," I reminded them. "Yea, but you're an *okay* California bastard," they responded.

We could get only day passes while at Camp Hood—like 8 AM to 9 PM—just enough time for short visits to places like Waco or Austin, but not adequate time for exploring the farther reaches of that big state. Some men did manage to get home to "San Anton" when the weather was right.

Besides the fossils, I became quite familiar with living Texas biota: mesquite, chiggers and armadillos ("Hoover hog", the Texans called the last, for in the Depression needy Texans had caught and eaten those homely beasts in lieu of pork). We also learned during field operations to look out for another kind of live thing: unexploded artillery shells left behind by armored units from North Camp Hood during their maneuvers.

The training and vigilance of the non-com cadre kept our cycle nearly injury free. Besides the dinging of my ear, one man in our company caught a grenade fragment in his upper arm during training with live grenades. Otherwise, all we suffered were chigger bites, sunburn and a few heat prostration cases.

During a week-long bivouac in late July, we were given a classified briefing on balloon-borne explosives being lofted from Japan to the West Coast, where they occasionally killed civilian hikers or started forest fires. The information was secret because if the Japanese had learned where their balloons were landing that might have allowed them to launch them more effectively. We also were told of the Potsdam Declaration to Japan.

During a second bivouac in August, a far more stunning briefing told us of the atom-bombing of Hiroshima and Russia's entering the war against Japan. Mulling over the implications of the bomb, I wondered how much our Berkeley cyclotron might have been involved. Our briefers said Japan's die-hard military still might try to fight on, so that we could not ease up on our final days of combat training. When we arrived back in camp came the news of Japan's surrender. Years later, I liked to joke, "If I were a proper megalomaniac, I would claim that the Germans surrendered when they heard I started basic training, and the Japanese quit when they heard I had finished."

Now we had no idea what military tasks might await us. We were quickly disabused of any idea that we might be quickly demobilized. After our end-of-training ceremony, we received orders for a month's leave, after which we would report to either an east coast or west coast facility for onward assignment. Wartime secrecy was still in effect, but the cadre said we could tell from those orders whether we would be going east to Europe or west into the Pacific Theater. I was ordered west to Fort Ord, California.

So, in late August we boarded a troop train, California bound. The long hot haul behind a coal-burning locomotive made it hard to keep our uniforms looking decent. Especially for me, after I bought a can of grape juice when we stopped in Barstow on the Mojave. No pull-tabs in those days. I used a can opener, and the purple juice when phhht! all over my khakis. My only change of uniform was already filthy from 2½ days of rumbling through Texas, New Mexico and Arizona with the windows open. So, I was a colorful sight when I arrived in Berkeley the next morning to start a 30-day furlough.

That leave with the family passed uneventfully and too quickly. One memory from that was saying goodbye to Mary as I left for Fort Ord and remarking, "If I end up in Japan, maybe I can find a missionary's daughter there to marry." The girl from Chengdu must still have been

35

in the back of my mind. But why was an 18-year-old thinking of marriage anyway?

Soon I was in barracks again, on the sandy hills of Fort Ord, overlooking Monterey Bay. We began a week of refresher training on things like map reading that we had studied *ad nauseum* at Hood. The only new things were range-firing the new carbine and the "grease gun"—a crude submachine gun so called as it looked more like a mechanic's grease gun than a battlefield weapon. Each day we tramped through the sand from one training site to another. As we settled down for a demonstration or lecture, the cadreman would announce his subject and then add, "But first, does anyone know any good jokes?" Meaning ribaldry. On our second day, one man in our group turned out to be a walking encyclopedia of bawdy jokes, poems and ballads. That day's actual training probably totaled 10 minutes.

We were told we would be at Ord for 7-8 days before shipping out, and were allowed only 8-hour weekend passes. For most, that meant a half day in Monterey; but I guessed that I could get to Berkeley and maybe spend three good hours at home before returning.

So, that first Saturday, I hitchhiked from Ord (It worked better now that I was in uniform and gas rationing was being eased.) and arrived in Berkeley in time for lunch. Problem: About mid-afternoon I developed a fever that felt like the flu. After a quick consultation by phone, John took me to the Oakland Army Hospital. Checking in, I asked that Fort Ord be informed.

Four days later, I was okay again and returned (by bus) to Ord. There I found myself listed as AWOL. The hospital's message had not been received. However, once my story was corroborated and since I had returned voluntarily, I was reinstated on the unit roster. Our group was preparing to leave by train that afternoon; so I had to pack quickly.

Again on a troop train, we made the long haul through northern California, winding around impressive Mount Shasta and into the cool evergreen empire of Oregon and Washington. Our new home was Fort

Lawton, a lushly wooded base in a remote corner of Seattle. (Now the site of Discovery Park and Daybreak Star Indian Center.)

During our four days there, the post had little for us to do, and we were given no passes. Also no one could tell us where we were going in the Pacific area or what to expect when we arrived. We heard lectures and saw training films on topics like Asian VD. Finally, on a mid-October morning we packed up and boarded trucks bound for the port. The morning air was nippier than on Monterey Bay, but our sense of anticipation kept us from feeling the chill. A short ride through the city and we were on the docks and then plodding up the gangway of the "General Weigel," a Navy troop ship.

"Where are we headed?" I asked a lieutenant checking our names as we boarded. He grinned. "It won't be Hawaii, soldier. Somewhere in the western Pacific." No one seemed to know any more than that.

The ship got underway in the early afternoon, steaming slowly north up Puget Sound toward the Strait of San Juan de Fuca. After dark some hours later, the ship began to pitch as it met incoming Pacific swells. I was lying on the uppermost bunk of a tier of three, reading a book and chewing a large wad of gum. One by one, men nearby began getting seasick. Having acquired "sea legs" long before on the southern California bait boats, I felt immune even in that increasingly rancid atmosphere.

Yet, I began to feel queasy and then queasier. "Am I going to be seasick finally?" I wondered in dismay. I sat up and abruptly released a huge belch—air swallowed over two hours of chewing gum in a prone position. I immediately felt fine, but went up on deck anyway for some fresh air.

On the second day, headed north-northwest, we were called out on deck. A captain explained that wartime secrecy had required that our sailing orders be opened only after getting out to sea. He said we were bound for Nagasaki. "What's the deal?" a man near me muttered, "Nothing there but atomic ashes!" So, maybe we're to be the cleanup detail I thought to myself, recalling my cleanup work on irradiated rat parts at UC's Lawrence Lab.

We still knew nothing of what we would face in Japan, little information having yet filtered back other than that the first Allied Occupation troops had moved in peacefully and unopposed.

Half way across the Pacific, a lookout spotted a floating mine. Our ship began circling it while Marine guards on board tried to explode it with pot shots from their M-1's. A mine's "triggers," however, are the protruding horns, which are exceedingly hard to hit with 30-caliber bullets. So, after half an hour, we sailed on. A crewman later told us the mine's position was radioed to Honolulu for someone else to deal with.

By the time we crossed the International Date Line, our gabfests on deck had about exhausted our small talk—where we were from, training experiences, etc. We began to speculate more on Japan, now not so far over the horizon. In that 100% male society, many typically speculated about Japanese women and whether we could "fraternize." When the GI talk turned too seamy, I would often leave and go stand at the rail and study the ever-changing sea.

One afternoon the ship entered a stretch of extraordinarily calm water, almost flat and free of ripples. As the sun slowly sank toward the horizon, the lazy surface motion of the water began catching the reddening hues of reflected light. That led me to recall that for the past 2½ years, this area had witnessed fearsome air and naval battles and submarine warfare. I let myself fantasize that the red color on the sea was blood from the casualties, concentrated by winds, much as the trade winds concentrate seaweed in the Sargasso Sea. Then, again whimsically, I noted that it was Halloween.

Early the next day—November 1—we saw islands to the west, and before noon our ship had rounded the southern tip of Kyushu and turned north toward Nagasaki. By mid-afternoon we were close enough that on some islands we could see villages, temple roofs and pagodas.

I was amazed at how closely those scenes resembled the miniature landscape trays from Japan we used to see before the war.

Just before evening mess, the ship anchored at Nagasaki Bay, where hills screened the ruined city from our curious eyes. Nearby were several US Navy ships, and small fishing boats were coming and going, some propelled by rear sculls, some by sails and a few by smoky, two-cycle engines. That evening, I went out on deck again. Now many of the fishing boats had mounted burning torches, using their light to attract fish. A very exotic scene for a Californian. Even moved me to write a poem, which I've since refined.

For a whole day, we sat in Nagasaki Bay. Occasionally an LST made a run between our ship and the shore. Then we were told we were going instead to Nagoya. Someone had goofed in typing or reading Nagasaki as our destination. So, we spent another day rounding Kyushu again and heading up to Ise Bay and Nagoya's port, Atsuta.

Docked at Atsuta for one last night on board, we were enjoying a final movie on deck when suddenly an explosion shook us and a fireball burst skyward, close enough that we could feel its heat. Something had set off a fuel drum on the dock close by. We began to wonder if Occupation duty in Japan might, after all, require some of our combat training.

Yet, all was peaceful after lunch the next day, November 4, 1945, as we disembarked. Shouldering our duffel bags, we marched through rubble from our intensive incendiary bombing raids and soon reached a railhead where a troop train awaited us. Typical of military "hurry up and wait" operations, we then sat on the train for perhaps two hours without moving.

Small Japanese children in grungy clothing gradually approached the train. "Chooing gamu? Chocoleto? Shigaretto?" they called to us, and soon were scrambling for the goodies we showered on them. After 10 or 15 minutes, a Japanese policeman appeared—black uniform, peaked hat, high leather boots and a sword at his side denoting his authority. He barked commands to the kids, who reluctantly scattered back into the rubbled neighborhood from which they had emerged.

Finally moving, our train rolled through several miles of bombed-out factories before we began seeing undamaged small towns, fields and rice paddies. These first close-ups of Japan were quickly adding dimension to the impressions I had of this nation from maps, postage stamps and photos. As dusk fell, I was struck by how dimly lit were the stations and towns we passed through. Fuel for power plants clearly was in very short supply.

Our train moved along slowly—never over 30 miles an hour—with many stops on sidings to let regular passenger trains pass. At about 8PM we finally reached our destination. We were marched perhaps a mile through the murky streets of a small city and into a military camp. There at the barracks, a supply sergeant issued us not army cots, but (culture shock!) thick stiffly bound straw & reed mats—*tatami,* I later learned. Another non-com showed us to our barracks where we laid these odd beds on the floor and prepared for our first night ashore in Japan.

We shaved and washed in cold water the next morning, then went out to find the mess hall. Second culture shock: all through the camp were Japanese men in uniforms stripped of any insignia. They met us with smiles, calling out, "Ohayo, ohayo" (good morning). We called back, "No, California! Texas! New Jersey!" At the mess hall we heard that these men would be our mess attendants, houseboys, laundrymen, etc. The prospect of using any combat training in the Occupation faded rapidly toward zero.

After chow, a cadre corporal called us out for calisthenics and a briefing. "You are in Camp Otsu. You'll be readied for duty in this here Allied Occupation and then sent to your assigned units. So, no leaving the post at any time; but you'll be here just 4-7 days."

Later that same morning came another call for us to fall out. This time it was a sergeant who clearly had been enjoying the local beer—large bottles of it. He swayed and rocked as he spoke, "You men, glad to see ya! "'Cause now me n' my buddies c'n get the hell outa here. Been fight'n all the way up the west Pacific. Three goddam years! New Guinea, Halmahera, the Philippines. Now here. Onliest thing I'll

40

miss is the beer. Best damn beer in the Pacific. So, like I said, glad to see ya. Real, real glad."

By this time the corporal had showed up and persuaded the sergeant to yield command so that we could be put through some marching drills. In fact, that turned out to be the last close-order marching I would do in the Army.

"No leaving the post" proved to be a hollow constraint, as the gate guards were very lax. Regular cadre could leave freely, and we easily mingled with groups exiting without our IDs being checked. Also, the tattered fence around this onetime Japanese Army post was very permeable. So, we got out into the town almost daily for sightseeing or whatever. I took one daylight walk down to the Otsu waterfront of what I later learned is Lake Biwa, Honshu's largest lake. The boats there showed severe wartime neglect, like much else that we had seen so far. A nation's defeat in war shows up in many little things.

We were not allowed to exchange US dollars for Japanese yen, but had to exchange all our dollars for "scrip" yen issued by US Forces at fifteen yen (¥15) per dollar so that we could buy sundries at the tiny PX. Some Japanese in camp had things we desired, like Japanese flags, but we were not supposed to trade with "the enemy." So, a black market barter trade had sprung up: a Japanese flag for so many chocolate bars. Or we traded cigarettes, etc., for real Japanese yen at 20-30 per dollar to use in town.

One evening I slipped off post with a cloth bag of chocolate bars (about two pounds) that I had accumulated and began looking for a buyer. Soon I saw a man coming down the dimly lit street. I slowed down, but he passed me by. I started on, but then he called out, "You, cigarette, chocolate?" I turned toward him. "Yes, chocolate," I said and held up my bag. He approached in the gloom. I grew uneasy as he furtively reached into his coat; but he pulled out a paper bill. "How much?" he asked. I had no idea what this candy was worth, but said, "Two hundred yen?" He felt the bag and asked to see the contents. In the dim light he showed me a paper bill with "500" printed on one corner. I nodded quick approval, and we made the swap.

41

Elated with my great luck, I later showed the bill to a non-com. He looked at it and said, "Hell, that's no yen note." It turned out to be 500-yuan scrip from the Japanese Army in China—worthless. A harsh, but relatively painless way to re-learn that a deal too good to be true is likely a bad deal. Another evening I found a man with Japanese postage stamps, and exchanged some chocolate for them. I still have them in my collection.

After six days at Camp Otsu, I was assigned to an Infantry unit in Nishinomiya, between Kobe and Osaka. Riding with two other GIs in the back of a big "six-by" truck, we went through Kyoto to Osaka, where the driver stopped at a 6th Army office for directions. Whereas Kyoto was all but untouched by the bombing* and its unique houses and stores were a quaint architectural feast, Osaka was heavily damaged. Rubble and twisted metal stretched for miles as we drove through the city and into Nishinomiya.

We finally pulled into a factory compound and stopped. The factory itself was gutted and roofless, but the adjoining worker barracks were untouched. These would be our home for the next three months: Company K, 123rd Infantry Regiment, 33rd Division, 6th Army.

At the supply room, we were issued sleeping bags, mess kits and unit shoulder patches. The company sergeant showed me my barracks and told me I would be a bugler, with alternating guard duty. The battalion's mission was rounding up Japanese war materiel: weapons, gas masks, swords—all of which came piling into the battalion area as teams returned from day-long forays. This was Japan's demilitarization up close.

Between guard shifts, I spent time with other company buglers learning and practicing calls in the remains of the one-time factory. In a letter

---

\* We had avoided bombing Kyoto proper. The Japanese guessed that was due to the influence of Dr. Otis Carey, who taught at Doshisha U. in Kyoto before and after the war; and they planned a statue there in his honor. Carey adamantly refused the credit and the statue. Investigations later proved the real credit belonged to Secretary of War Stimson, who had honeymooned in Kyoto long before WWII.

home, I described some of the men in our squad: our squad leader from West Virginia, a private who carried on about coon hunting in Texas's Brazos bottoms, PFC Willy Horton from New Mexico, etc.

The company had a liberal policy on passes, and from a commuter train station close by we could go southeast to Osaka or northwest to Kobe. Sometimes I went alone and sometimes with a few buddies. On one solo trip to Kobe, I noticed western-style homes on hills nearby. So, I got off there to explore. From those heights, one overlooked much of the city; and now I could better see the wide devastation from our bombing. It looked as though a titan had simply gone through flattening everything with his fists—all except the train lines, which ran oddly intact through the rubble.

In Osaka, too, most areas I walked through were just wreckage. Japanese living there had pulled together rough shelters of scorched corrugated steel sheets and other scrap from the ruins. Here and there they even had planted flowers, and children were at play in those grim surroundings.

On one trip, I saw a sign in English: "Osaka Zoo." I decided to seek it out. En route, a uniformed student came along and identified himself as Taizo Hachioka, a medical student. He wished to practice his English and was glad to guide me to the zoo. We found many cages empty, and Taizo explained that dangerous animals were destroyed when the bombing began, lest they escape and imperil the public. Near the war's end, other animals were killed because the zoo could no longer feed them properly. A few domesticated animals remained.

Kobe and Osaka each still had one major department store open, but with little to sell. In Osaka I bought a writing brush for 45 sen (less than ½ yen), and in Kobe, a carved jade signature seal for ¥250 (then about $12). With other GIs I once went to an Osaka dance hall where ¥10 bought a few dances with a Japanese girl. Other than faint smiles, little communication was possible, so that this form of recreation quickly palled on me.

In December, the division USAFI (US Armed Forces Institute) officer arranged for Japanese classes to be taught on post. I promptly signed up. Our teacher, an amiable Japanese gentleman, took a liking to me and once invited me to his home after duty hours. I arrived and sat on the wooden entry step of his modest house while his wife prepared tea. That was my first green tea; and its somewhat bitter taste led me to ask casually for sugar. My host seemed surprised, but asked his wife to fetch some. Perhaps 20 minutes later, she returned with coarse raw sugar. Only later did I learn that (1) green tea is *never* drunk with sugar and (2) the woman probably had to go to the black-market to find it in those early postwar days, paying a pretty price for such a scarce commodity.

A few entertainers on contract to the USO also visited our unit. Most memorable were two Japanese men who treated us to a running banter in broken English with comic gestures while they busily folded paper and cut it with scissors. We cheered them and applauded enthusiastically when, finally, they would unfold their paper to reveal complete cutout scenes, such as a house with a cat on the roof and people inside sitting at a table. "Now no food, so just talk," one commented. When we went out on pass, we could readily guess, from the prevalence of adult and child beggars that, indeed many had little food. Conditions were getting tough as the first postwar winter approached. That made me think twice as the ample fare in the company mess boosted my weight—up to 195 pounds!

Before Christmas 1945, the regimental chaplain arranged for two local Christian colleges —one for men and one for women—to hold a joint Christmas concert with us. I signed up, even though it was now almost two years since I had sung in the Webb glee club. We had an all-GI rehearsal at regimental headquarters in Takarazuka, and another with the Japanese students at the Takarazuka Theater, the home stage of Japan's famed all-girl musical theater troupe, which had performed at the 1939 San Francisco World's Fair. On Christmas Eve we gave a heart-warming concert of carols for the GIs of the regiment—some 50 GIs and 100 Japanese singing together on that huge stage. After our concert, the Takarazuka girls treated us to a full performance of "Pinocchio." Years later James Michener would use a fictionalized Takarazuka as the focus of his novel "Sayonara," about an American officer's romance with a Takarazuka girl. That became the movie starring Marlon Brando and Red Buttons, except that the novel's downbeat ending was flipped in the movie to a Hollywood ending—Brando gets the girl. (Michener himself had a Nisei wife.)

Between Christmas and New Year's Day, we GIs were also treated to a special program of Japanese performing arts in Osaka: samples of Kabuki, Noh, Joruri puppet theater, Japanese classical music and dance and a short skit by the Takarazuka troupe.

On New Year's Day 1946, I went out to explore Nishinomiya a bit more and set out for the nearby seashore. En route, I found a large stadium standing open and deserted. I went in and saw it was a baseball stadium. Walking onto the field, I noticed a plaque on one wall of the bleachers and went over to read: "Here on October 11, 1934 [I'm not sure of that date, but about then.], Babe Ruth hit a home run out of this stadium." I later learned it was Koshien Stadium, now much modernized and the home of a pro baseball team and the venue for semiannual national high-school baseball tournaments.

Continuing toward the sea, I passed a small airfield where I saw half-dismantled planes. Two were all white, and I recalled reading that, in arranging for the surrender, the Allies had Japan send its envoys to the Philippines in an all-white plane. To thwart die-hard militarists' efforts to block the surrender, all-white planes were deployed to several fields in Japan. So, no telling whether these planes were used in the surrender process. Past the airfield, I reached the shore, a rough sand beach where I saw distant islands and a stretch of the coast of this inland sea. I beach-combed for shells and then returned to camp.

One day the war materiel brought to our battalion included many gas masks. We were allowed to pick a few non-lethal items from among the incoming items, and I had already acquired a Japanese Army bugle. Now I chose a pristine, new gas mask from among those in the latest stack. Months later, when I had close Japanese friends, I learned why this one mask was unused: The number "42" was stenciled on its carrying bag. One way to read 42 in Japanese is "shini,"—a homonym for "death."

By mid-January 1946, the main mission of our division was complete; and it was clear that the Occupation could continue with fewer combat units. So, the 33rd Infantry was slated for deactivation. We green replacement troops were told not to think this meant we would soon return to the USA. Instead, by late January, we were readied for transfer to Signal Corps units in Yokohama.

The afternoon of our departure, the company adjutant called me to the orderly room and said I must perform one last task as an Infantry bugler. The Army had a field hospital in Kobe, where GIs occasionally died. So, I unpacked my bugle and was taken by jeep to a temporary US Forces cemetery, where I played "Taps" as a casket was lowered into a grave. An hour later, I was on a troop train bound for Yokohama. Taps for my 9-month Infantry career, too.

After an overnight trip on hard train seats, we arrived in Yokohama and were loaded onto Army trucks for a brief, cold ride along the waterfront. Some Western-style buildings still stood undamaged, interspersed by blocks of bomb devastation. Later, we would see that the city core away from the waterfront was so totally burned out that our Army Engineers could simply bulldoze and roll flat wide swaths of the downtown rubble with graders (no demolition required) in preparing extensive Quonset-hut villages for us.

For now, though, we were trucked to warehouses below a bluff south of the main harbor, where we were quartered while awaiting our assignments. Here, too, passes were handed out liberally and we could spend much time exploring our new surroundings.

Over the next few days, I saw many fellow infantrymen leave to become phone linemen or motor pool drivers. So, I was relieved when— February 3, 1946—I was assigned to the Central Film and Equipment Exchange (CF&EE), which handled training and entertainment films and projection equipment for Occupation Force units.

Arriving at the CF&EE, chief sergeant Finney told me I was assigned to the unit's photo lab, as my personnel file showed I had worked in UC's photostat lab. The photo sergeant informed me that he was mainly a photographer and wanted me to do all of the darkroom work. I had to tell him that my darkroom experience was very limited, as I had simply helped run student records through the developer and wash tanks; but he asked me to give it a try and to help him on photo assignments.

About a week later we landed a big one: covering the Yokohama visit of Army Chief of Staff, General "Ike" Eisenhower. We tagged along as the general inspected 8th Army headquarters units, a USO theater and local units.

Shortly after that, I was relieved when I was shifted instead to clerical work, joining the small front-office staff: Sergeants Finney and Greenberg and Corporal Kogel. I became a T-5 (corporal). We mainly handled requests for films and projection equipment. Next door was our C.O., Captain Irwin Reif, a young, good-natured non-career officer from St. Louis. Beyond him was the office of his secretary, Miss Ina.

The Film Exchange occupied the upper three floors of the 4-story Shizuoka Bank, located on a freight canal just a block from the main shopping street, Isezaki-cho. We handled a big inventory of projectors, parts, training film and Hollywood movies. About half of our staff, Japanese and GIs, did projector repair & maintenance; and we had a few jeeps and light trucks in our motor pool. The other GIs soon initiated me into the unit by showing me a Medical Corps training film on amputations—in color.

Just west of our building was the new Quonset-hut village where we now were housed, about 20 men to a hut. An oil-burning stove in the center of each building provided heat; and larger Quonset huts served as mess halls, laundries, company offices, etc. Latrines and showers were in separate buildings. A barbed wire fence surrounded the compound, and guard posts monitored each of three gates.

The Army already had entertainment and educational facilities in place for us. It had appropriated a major Yokohama Theater, Odeonza, for movies and USO stage shows; Yokohama's baseball stadium, renamed Nile Kinnick Stadium; and office space for USAFI classes, where I learned to type. Of course, GIs will find their own entertainment.

47

Some enjoyed going out "sanju-yenning" (¥30 then being the going rate for a fling on the tatami with a "pom-pom" girl). The very hard six months since the war's end had put many women on the street as a last-resort way to feed themselves and family members.

Only slowly did goods worth buying appear in the shops: cheap silk kimonos and low-end pearls at the Yokohama PX (a former department store), etc. On city blocks now emptied of war rubble, Japanese men in partial military uniforms hawked things they had "liberated" from the Imperial Army or Navy after the surrender. That was how I acquired a pair of good Japanese Army binoculars, trading ¥1000 and a carton of cigarettes for them. By then the street exchange rate had risen to about ¥50/dollar.

At the Film Exchange, the scrounging talents of Captain Reif and the supply sergeant began assembling a 4th-floor lounge where our whole staff—American and Japanese—could relax and enjoy occasional parties for dancing and movies. We helped equip the party room with a Coke machine, record player, wicker easy chairs and sofa, and its own 25-seat theater.

That was important to us, as Occupation policy discouraged "fraternizing," citing the legality that the Japanese remained enemy aliens until a peace treaty was signed. In fact, in the ever more relaxed atmosphere at the street level, most Americans and Japanese got along famously. Though defeated, the Japanese interacting with us were enormously relieved that we were turning out to be benign occupiers. Many friendships blossomed between the two peoples, some based on newfound respect for each other, others based on economic self-interest and still others on outright passion *cum* acquisitiveness. I.e., in those early postwar days, with basic necessities hard to come by, a Japanese female might agree to attach herself to an American as his "only" in return for food and PX items that GIs and US civilians working in the Occupation could easily get.

My upbringing as a PK (preacher's kid) kept me from any such an arrangement, although I saw no harm in such petty black-marketing as bartering cigarettes for binoculars. The military "legal eagles" could argue against "trading with the enemy," but was not the PX system doing just that? In any case, we "Occupationaires" increasingly saw the Japanese as America's wards and even our colleagues. Throughout Occupied Japan, Americans were "doin' what comes nacherly," the refrain of Doris Day's pop hit of that era.

Of course, the situation was very *un*natural in many ways. Most American facilities were staffed with Japanese: houseboys, maids, boiler men, typists, etc. Most Americans there had more money than ever before and had made a quick transition from the Depression to war, with its shortages, rationing, etc. Now some were petty overlords in exotic Japan—a heady change of circumstance that made some lose their sense of values, even their self respect. So, not far into the Occupation era, the saying, "Never had it so good!" became the unofficial slogan of many Americans.

Inevitable inflation in Japan's battered economy raised the value of our dollars, even as better goods slowly became available on PX shelves and in the shops of the Ginza district.

In early March, I heard of an enchanting seaside islet—Enoshima—that was easily reached by train. So, one Saturday I set out to find this rumored site. A first train got me to Ofuna in about 30 minutes. There I got directions for taking another train to Kamakura,* where I could connect to the Enoshima train. In Kamakura I walked a mile to the two-car Enoshima trolley—my first solo walk in a smaller city since Otsu five months earlier. Few GIs were around, so that I attracted the attention of children curious about a lone GI on foot. Soon I was on this quaint trolley and off along the seacoast.

I got off one station before Enoshima, as the rocky coast looked interesting. Close by, I saw a tide-pool area and a young Japanese man with a fishing spear. As I watched, he speared octopus and other critters.

---

* The capital of Japan's first shoguns in the 12th & 13th centuries, and so full of historic sites.

Just offshore rose a piney islet that the spear-fisher confirmed was Enoshima. A sand spit stretched seaward toward the island; and a rickety-looking wooden bridge spanned the tidal wash that made Enoshima an island only at high tide. Reaching the island, I entered a narrow shop-lined street running up the slope. Soon I began seeing seashells for sale.

A shell collector from childhood, I began buying shells at amazingly low prices. Then I found a shop that was a collector's paradise: shells of endless varieties and sizes from all over the western Pacific. By the time I began running low on yen, I had all I could carry for a total outlay of ¥500-600 ($10-12). Hauling all that treasure back to my barracks in Yokohama gave me achy shoulders.

# ENCHANTING DESTINY

About this time, my interests at the Film Exchange took a new tack: Ina-san ("Miss Eena")—the captain's secretary.   As you will see, not just my interest, but in fact my entire life would change course from this point on.  Miss Ina was constantly in and out of our office, serving as the hour-by-hour interface between each section and the captain.  Her bright vivacity and feistiness enlivened our days almost as carbonation lends zest to plain water.

I began paying closer attention to her the first or second time she got into a sharp debate with Corporal Kogel.  Kogel was pure Brooklyn and had his own form of feistiness.  He liked to debate the Japan situation we all were experiencing: the black market, such major Occupation policies as democratization, responsibility for the war, the coming war crimes trials, etc.  One day he picked an argument with Miss Ina about who started the war, goading her about Japan's militarists, Pearl Harbor, etc. She kept insisting that Kogel did not know the whole story, including the Japanese side of such matters.  He would not yield an inch, always insisting that Japan was in the wrong on every point.

Finally, Ina-san's *samurai* temper broke through.  Her eyebrows arched and she threw back something at him in Japanese as she stormed out. (Later, I would understand: "Ignorant barbarian!")  Kogel was delighted at the reaction he had sparked and after that sniped at her almost daily.

Ina-san was unusual, first in having office skills much needed by Occupation offices: English typing, shorthand dictation and good conversational English. Quizzing her in the office, we learned that she had attended the top Catholic girls school in the city, where her teachers were mostly British and French nuns. During the war, using English was taboo in Japan; and that had caused her fluency to deteriorate some. So, another game that Kogel played was aping the Japanese and British accents in her speech. She would always fire right back, insisting that British pronunciations were best and our American accent inferior.

Most striking was her lively, upbeat personality and overall sociability. Other Japanese on staff clearly admired and liked her. That came out clearly in a late February 1946 incident. Food was so scarce that winter in Japan's devastated cities and the rationing system was so ineffective that most people had to go to black markets even for staples like rice, paying exorbitant prices. Capable Japanese employees were so valuable to Occupation offices that special ration allotments were provided for them. In March, with rice absent even from the black market, we drove a Film Exchange truck to Kawasaki, perhaps 15 miles each way, to fetch bread from a bakery for our Japanese staff. It turned out to be a coarse dark brown bread made from imported flour.

Captain Reif reacted to the sight of that bread by contacting acquaintances who had access to C Rations by the case lot and soon had set up an unofficial allotment of C rations for our Japanese staff. C-ration biscuits did not suit the Japanese palate; but the canned meat, coffee, sweets and cigarettes were precious to them. The captain put Ina-san in charge of doling out these rations. For a while it ran smoothly. Then some cases were missing; and a rumor in the GI grapevine held that Ina-san's committee had black-marketed them.

When Ina-san heard that, she marched into the captain's office in a cold fury. In rapid fire, she asserted that her committee had nothing to do with the shortfall, that she had heard some of our GIs were involved, that as commanding officer he should better control his GIs, and anyway she was quitting because of the distrust the rumor revealed.

Standing in the doorway while this slim "enemy" samurai girl told off our burly C.O., I watched Reif's expression change from perplexity to amazement to sympathetic amusement at her animated vitriol. He stood up and assured her that he fully trusted her, that he would check into the problem and that she should defer any thought of resigning.

Word of this got around and won Ina-san even warmer affection and respect from the Japanese and grudging admiration from some GIs. From that time on, I began engaging Ina-san in conversations, curious to know more about her and her kind of Japanese —so utterly different from the Pacific enemy portrayed by our wartime propaganda. I learned that she was working at the Film Exchange not because she needed the pay, but because Japanese friends in 8th Army Personnel had persuaded her that her skills were much needed and that she could help avert problems between the two peoples.

I became intrigued by her bright intelligence and lively personality, not to mention her pretty face framed by soft dark hair. In late March, some of us were chatting when the subject of Japanese food came up; and Ina-san asked me if I had ever tried *sushi*. I had not, as Occupation rules kept Japanese food and eating places off limits to us, due to sanitation concerns. Night soil—human waste—was being widely used on Japanese farms; and some diseases endemic in Japan were types that our pampered gastro-intestinal tracts had never confronted.

Spontaneously, Ina-san invited me for a sushi dinner at her rooming house, the Yanagi Hotel, the following Friday. I eagerly accepted. So, a few evenings later, we went together by streetcar to a northeastern area of Yokohama. In the intervening days, my youthful imagination had fantasized a romantic interlude. So, when she casually told me, as we climbed the stairs to her room, that her roommate would share the meal and evening with us, I suffered abrupt fantasy collapse.

I was still recovering as Ina-san introduced me to Midori-san, her roommate. Midori-san also worked in an 8th Army Office, where— because *midori* means green—she was called Greenie.* Now Greenie told Ina-san that the rooming house bath would close at 8 PM due to

---

* We would later learn that Midori had a communist boyfriend and, still later, that she had joined the Japanese Communist Party. So, we lost contact with her.

the fuel shortage. So, Ina-san quickly collected her bath supplies and exited, leaving me awkwardly trying to make small talk with the rather spinsterish Greenie for what seemed like over an hour.

Finally, Ina-san returned, her cheeks glowing from the warmth of the bath and her walk through the cool March evening to and from the fish shop where she bought ingredients for the sushi. Now she wore a simple cotton kimono, with a blue-and-white pattern of sandpipers—the first time I had seen her in non-Western dress. As she chatted with Greenie, her high musical voice filled the room; and I seemed to be seeing her for the first time, really seeing her and willy-nilly falling under the spell of her effervescent charm.

Putting aside my past ideas about raw seafood, I managed the sushi well enough and decided to skip a joke with the punch line, "Either eat or cut bait." Departing later that evening, I only vaguely sensed that I had made a crucial transition. No longer was Ina-san just an interesting office acquaintance, She now was *the* girl I must know far better. Our differences of race and culture seemed to be not barriers but portals to a fascinating new world.

It must have been the next Friday that I resolved to ask her for a real date; but when I went to her office, there sat a typist from another section. While she could not yet know of my growing interest in her colleague, my face must have betrayed something when I asked where Ina-san was. She hesitated and then said that Ina-san had left for a weekend at Hakone, a mountain resort.

On the way back to our quarters after work, I heard two Film Exchange GIs talking about Captain Reif's weekend—with Ina-san! As they speculated salaciously about what might go on at that mountain retreat, my tension rose. Finally I broke away and began a long, moody walk through Yokohama's byways. I tried to convince myself that the GIs' ideas did not square with the Ina-san I knew; but nagging doubts would not leave me for the entire weekend. After all, I had but limited experience with the opposite sex and near zero with Japanese girls.

54

The following Monday, Ina-san was back at her desk, poised and chipper as ever. I began wondering if I had taken my acquaintance with her too seriously. Whatever had transpired in the Hakone Mountains was none of my business. Watching her come and go nonchalantly that day only confused me more. At the day's end, almost as a test, I went to her desk and abruptly asked her to be my date at the next Film Exchange social. She seemed puzzled by my manner, but accepted.

So, on a Friday evening in late March, I heard talk and laughter when I knocked on her door at the Yanagi Hotel. After a long moment, Midori-san opened the door and invited me in. There stood Ina-san in an elegant silk kimono, so stunning that I was briefly tongue tied. She apologized for keeping me waiting and said with a radiant smile, "I don't often wear real kimono now and Midori must help me."

Our arrival at the Film Exchange lounge created a stir as the GIs and their dates took in Ina-san's attire. Soon enough, though, the general hubbub resumed and the (78 rpm) record player filled the room with dance music. I nearly monopolized Ina-san's time, feeling highly privileged all the while. I found her a superb dancer, light and graceful. Later, we went in to enjoy the movie with the others. I held her dainty hand and laid my arm across the back of her chair.

Once when she leaned forward laughing at a funny scene, my hand dropped under her arm and suddenly into an opening under her kimono sleeve, touching the side of her breast before I knew it. Surprised, I pulled back, but Ina-san did not react. When the film ended and the lights came up, our eyes met; but her expression told me nothing.

After the party, a Film Exchange jeep was to take her and another girl home, as it was after hours for streetcars. So, she and I went down to wait in the rear of the jeep for the others. We kissed for the first time. She was light hearted as we talked and laughed; but her warm kisses burned deep into my heart. Never had I known so utterly enchanting a girl. From that time, we began dating often. And, I soon learned that she had taken an older friend with her to Hakone to chaperone her quite platonic sightseeing weekend with Captain Reif. And, I learned that her given name was Kimie (KEE-mee-yeh).

About this time, two dormitories opened for Japanese employees of the 8th Army—one for women and an adjoining one for men, just a 15-minute walk from the Film Exchange. So, Kimie began walking to work from there; and I began going a few times a week to her dorm, the Momijisaka Hotel to see her and her many friends, all fluent in English.

That meant immersing myself more and more in a Japanese environment and spending ever less time with other Americans. It was not long before I began hearing other GIs using the terms "gook lover" and "gone Asiatic" in talking about me. Water off my back!

Associating with my new friends at the dorm, I was gaining new knowledge and insights into their culture and thinking. This and my observations of Japan and its people over the preceding half year showed me how very slanted our wartime propaganda had been.

By this time, mid-Spring 1946, Japanese reactions against the war and bitter defeat had led them to begin rejecting many of the values, beliefs and leaders that had taken them into war against the West. As if blinders had fallen from their eyes, the public began a 180° turn that would lead them to embrace pacifism and democracy. This tectonic shift in attitudes was helping to facilitate truly amicable relations between them and us Americans in the Occupation—at least at the level I was observing.

The few who seemed unhappy with this trend were some U.S. Regular Army volunteers now arriving to replace outbound draftees. Such new men came with chips on their shoulders and sometimes nasty tempers, as though they felt cheated to have arrived after all the fighting was all over. Soon enough, we who had come earlier persuaded them to ease up and accept that they, too, "never had it so good!"

Miscreants there were, though. One rainy April night, I was riding a streetcar when a rock came crashing through a window. Two Japanese women were cut in the face by the flying glass. I saw three GIs run off laughing. Occasionally, we also heard of rapes of Japanese women by GIs—one by a not too bright MP sergeant whose uniform and tattoo made him easily identifiable. But, overall the level of violence between occupiers and occupied was amazingly low. I never felt in danger as I came and went, day or night.

By mid-April 1946, I felt increasingly that I, especially, never had it so good. I was beginning to grasp how very special Kimie was. We found that we shared many values and common interests. She, too, was a seashell collector and enjoyed classical and popular western music. We both had a good sense of humor. The attraction we now felt grew ever stronger. But, we had many ups and downs.

For, it was not all sweetness and light. The obverse of Kimie's vivacity and bright mind was a quick, fiery temper. I could make some insensitive remark, and she would stay angry with me for days at a time. The shallowness of my experience with the opposite gender and my vestigial foot-in-mouth problem worked against me. I had to learn the hard way when and how to ease up and concede arguments to avoid setting off her hot anger and how to back off and let her pique burn itself out.

On Easter Eve (April 20), we had a particularly sharp argument. Still tense and disturbed about that on Easter morning, I chose to go for a pre-dawn walk. Eighth Army had imposed a midnight-6AM curfew early in the Occupation. So, I went over the barbed wire fence to avoid the gate guards of our Quonset-hut compound. I set out walking, but soon a cruising MP patrol jeep spotted me and picked me up for violating curfew. Along with another such major criminal, I was taken to a nearby MP station for booking.

At the front desk, a sergeant was busily booking GIs previously brought in. Soon the two MPs who brought me in left. With no one actually watching me, I sidled to the door and slipped out. As I darted into a narrow lane between Japanese shanties, I heard shouts from the MP station; but I was not going to let my Easter sunrise walk blacken my so-far spotless record. I faded into the landscape; and minutes later the curfew was over. I made my way to Kimie's dorm to begin reconciling. (In my letters home I still referred to her as Ina, perhaps hoping that would sound less exotic to my family than Kimie.)

As warmer weather arrived, we began taking weekend trips with our friends, to hot spring resorts and the Hakone Mountains. Although two men among our friends had showed great interest in Kimie, they now accepted the fact that we were a pair. On one such trip with several friends, to the port/hot spring resort of Ito (on the Izu Peninsula) during "Golden Week" (serial holidays April 29-May 5), our relationship blossomed into total commitment. On May 4, 1946, we agreed we should consider ourselves engaged.

I gave Kimie no engagement ring at this point, as the Army discouraged serious fraternization. We knew not what obstacles we might face, but did not really care. We were totally in love, and everyone knows that "love conquers all things." I was 19 years, 4 months and 2 days old. Kimie had indicated she was about four years older than I.

Now I began going to her dorm every evening except on the weekends when she went home to her family. Kimie had a double room and a roommate. She and her friends, especially Sato-san ("Sugar," because Sato is a homonym for sugar), were in and out of each others' rooms constantly. We often passed time in the dorm lobby, too, where the residents held impromptu dance parties, playing old phonograph records that had survived the war, like "La Cumparsita," "Blue Moon" or "Colorado Moon."

One weekend, Kimie was visited by a prewar acquaintance, Jimbo-san, then living in Nagoya. I arrived at the dorm that evening to find Kimie with the usual group, dancing in the lobby. She introduced me to Miss Jimbo. At one point, Jimbo-san and I were alone in a corner of the lobby. She said that she was concerned about Kimie. I assured her that I was as concerned as she about Kimie's welfare, as Kimie was my fiancée.

"Oh, so you know then that she was married and has a child," Miss Jimbo said.

I felt like a combined tornado and earthquake had hit me. I answered weakly that I knew that, but guessed that my face was telling her the truth. For, Kimie had told me only that she had been engaged early in the war. Later that evening when finally we were alone, I asked Kimie about it.

She turned away and, in a disconsolate voice, said she had been married on paper to Takemitsu Ina after he was drafted and sent to China before they could live together. She said a woman who claimed she was Takemitsu's girlfriend later visited her, with her baby girl. She said the woman asked her to take the child, as she could not properly care for her. Later in 1942, a cable arrived informing them that Takemitsu had died in China of typhus. He had been a great music lover who spent his off time visiting Chinese villages to share music with the people. Apparently he contracted typhus on such a visit.

Soon after this revelation, I began gently urging Kimie to let me meet her family: her Ina in-laws and the Yamadas—her own family. But, I left it to her judgment as to when.

Twice I was sent on TDY to an Occupation Forces R&R hotel in Kawana on the Izu Peninsula to take movie films and help screen them for the GIs there. I disliked the separation from Kimie, but enjoyed the easy duty during these 3-4-day stints. In a letter home I wrote, "When I called her on the phone, she teased that I must be having fun with the Japanese girls here. Neither of us has any real doubts about the other, though. She knows how lonely I am; she feels the same way. It was really good to hear her voice ... so pretty, musical, sweet." I have sometimes wondered if our new C.O. had gotten wind of my interest in Kimie and tried to cool that off by sending me off to Kawana.

In late June, the 8th Army ordered all GIs to get encephalitis-B (sleeping sickness) shots, because of an outbreak in Japan. Within hours of getting mine, I had a slight fever and headache. I went to the dispensary for aspirin, but the doctor there would not accept my self-diagnosis of a reaction to the shot. He ordered me straight to the 155th Station Hospital nearby. No detour to the Film Exchange. I would be there for 10 days. Kimie came to see me the day after I was hospitalized, very worried about what had happened to me. On her other visits during that time, she became friends with a young Nisei girl, Amy Baba, working there. We would see more of her later.

59

Letters from home at this time indicated that they considered me simply too young to be getting serious, especially across ethnic, cultural and national lines. I sought to counter their suggestions that I was "living in a dream world" by writing, "I realize the great difficulties ahead. *I do not fear them.* ... I know that many people let themselves be unnecessarily hemmed in and controlled by the limitations of society's checks and balances. They do not take what freedom they can have." I said I hoped to become a writer and English teacher in Japan. My ideas about my future obviously were in transition or, shall we say, vague and uninformed.

I began adding snapshots of Kimie to my letters so that the idea of a Japanese in-law might seem less bizarre. The one most critical of the situation was Charley James, then engaged to Louise. A Guadalcanal Marine vet, he remained bitterly anti-Japanese.* I wrote: "Doesn't he realize you can't judge a people by their army, their military clique, by the wartime propaganda you've heard? ... His kind of thinking is not the thinking for 'One World.' ... Will the rest of the world think we are sincere when racial and even religious intolerance are as widespread as they are in the United States." Thus wrote the worldly wise (?) 19-year-old.

As the summer heat set in, I worried about possible spoilage of the food Kimie kept in her room. So, together we went and bought an ice chest (3 cubic feet) to cut that risk.

Meanwhile, I had learned to drive, and had the daily duty of picking up Film Exchange mail from 8th Army Headquarters, about a mile toward the port area. I was approved to drive by a very irregular process. One Saturday night after a Film Exchange party, the motor pool sergeant was told to drive some of the Film Exchange Japanese staff home, as public conveyances did not run that late. Somehow I was chosen to "ride shotgun" in the ¾-ton truck, as the sergeant seemed pretty high. So, off we went, threading our way through Yokohama's dark streets as we tried to follow the uncertain directions of our Japanese passengers, who

---

* Charley would later live many years in Hawaii and become a good friend of many Japanese and Japanese-Americans.

60

normally traveled by train or streetcar. The sergeant began sideswiping power poles along the narrow lanes, obviously getting ever drunker. So, for self protection, I persuaded him to let me take the wheel, even though I had never before driven a truck and had only driven a jeep inside our small motor pool. But, with the sergeant's half intelligible hints, I somehow made it.

That experience led him to give me private driving lessons. After about a week, I asked the C.O.'s deputy about getting officially licensed. He said, "Well let me see you drive." So, I drove around our tiny motor pool while he watched from a third-floor window. By the time I got back upstairs, he had signed my license.

About mid-July, the compressor at the ice shop near Kimie's dorm, broke down, meaning no more ice. I found another source about four miles away. Now, twice a week when I went for the mail, I detoured to that ice shop, bought ice and dropped by the dorm to pop it into Kimie's icebox.

One day in mid-August, Captain Seeburg, our new commanding officer, called me into his office. He said he had noticed that some days I was gone on mail runs much longer than on others. "I've checked into this and found you're running some kind of errand for Miss Ina." As it was not black-marketing, I did not expect him to make much of it. So, I tried to downplay it. His voice became strained. "Corporal, you are at least misusing US Government property. Now, you're one of our brighter men here, and I hate to see a man like you get into trouble over his involvement with a local girl."

That caught me off guard—his switch from misuse of Army property to my relationship with Kimie. I tried to mollify him, insisting it was "entirely honorable."

"Then it's hard for me to understand what's going on," he said. When I told him we were serious about each other, he had me sit down and asked about my future plans. I was not at all clear on that, especially with all the uncertainties about Kimie. We did establish that I expected to get back into college eventually.

"So, wouldn't it be best not to get over-involved—break it off before things get too complicated," he suggested.

I stared at him, seeking to devise a reply that would divert him from such questions; but he seemed to think my silence meant he was convincing me. "Now, it's one thing to play around a bit with girls easily available for that purpose. That's as old as the Army itself, and I don't take issue with it. But, for a man who's college material to get in deep with a girl of the *Mongol* race—a race that's our recent enemy, too, well—"

That infuriated me. He stressed "Mongol" as if it were a synonym of "mongrel" or otherwise pejorative. So, I shot back at him, "So, you're saying it's okay to screw 'gooks,' but not to treat them as fellow humans. Correct?"

Captain Seeburg reddened and blew his top. "Now see here, Corporal, goddam it! I'm your commanding officer, and I'm trying to set you straight! Watch your attitude!"

I stood and told him that I flat out rejected his kind of advice. His jaw muscles were working. "Is that all, sir? May I go?" I asked.

"No, you may not!" he shot back, rising to his feet also. "Corporal, I wanted to set you straight, but you won't take it straight. So, I'm transferring you right out of here, to the battalion in Tokyo." He ordered me to get ready to take a courier truck to battalion headquarters that afternoon.

I saluted and started for the door, then turned to face him. ""Captain, this'll only make me more determined to marry her—some way or another," I asserted.

In a tense voice, he snarled, "Don't you know about our law barring Orientals? You can't take a Jap girl back to the States. Now get outa here!" His words chilled me, for at that time I had little idea of the legal obstacles.

So, my 6+ months at the Film Exchange abruptly ended; and I went off to 3186th Signal Battalion headquarters, 20 miles away in southwest Tokyo. The battalion was housed in a beautiful 3-story stucco building appropriated from the Hoshi Pharmacy College. Instead of a stairway between floors, a spiral ramp led to the 2nd and 3rd floors. On the walls lining the ramp were painted murals showing a progression of landscapes from lowlands to uplands and finally alpine views at the 3rd-floor level. On the campus around this architectural gem sprawled our olive-drab Quonset huts housing enlisted men and battalion support operations.

I was assigned alternately to supply-room detail and night guard duty. That reduced the frequency of my trips to the Momijizaka to about three a week. To reach Yokohama, I had to ride three train lines, but with only 60-70 minutes total travel time. The net effect of my Tokyo exile was to tighten the bond between Kimie and me as we faced this challenge.

# WHO WAS THAT WOMAN...?

Early in my courtship of her, Kimie fudged the facts on our age difference, perhaps fearing the truth would drive me away. She had implied we were about four years apart. Likewise, the story of her daughter's parentage, which had to be the accepted version for the next seven years. In the first year of our relationship, Mother feared that Kimie might be "a very clever little actress," while Kimie feared that I might yet leave her in the lurch —another Madame Butterfly. Obviously we all had problems of trust to tackle.

In a September 1946 letter to Mary, I described Kimie as "sociable, vivacious, fiery, motherly and loved by all" (which would accurately describe her for the rest of her life). In the same letter I admitted, "Only recently have I seen clearly how much she loves me. It is a beautiful thing" of which I felt "awed."

Since my life would thereafter focus on Kimie, I should fill in the picture on this special person. The details of our early years draw on a long epistle that I wrote to Mary in 1947 and include some facts Kimie and I had both forgotten over the decades.

She was born on October 2, 1919, in Yokohama (two years before my parents were married). In her usual, ebullient manner she liked to say, "I was born in Yokohama, by mistake." Her father, Kōjiro Yamada, was an architect for a construction company that, before the war, built major public works such as railway stations, tunnels and airfields. When his wife, Kise, was in her 9th month, Kojiro was at a Yokohama construction site, and she went down to be with him. That weekend she went into labor with Kimie, her first child. It was a difficult labor that squeezed Kimie's skull so that, for her first few months, it had steps in it. (In early 2001, Kimie was sitting in a chair and rubbing the top of her head. "It's still pointy and has steps!" she exclaimed.)

The Yamada home was then in the Uguisudani section of Mejiro in Tokyo. Hence Kimie's birth in Yokohama "by mistake." On September 1, 1923, the Great Kanto Earthquake and ensuing fires devastated wide areas of Tokyo and Yokohama, killing over 140,000 people. The Yamada home was not significantly damaged, but Kimie recalled being carried piggyback past some of the quake wreckage. Not long after, the family moved a few miles north to Ikebukuro. Today a bustling, densely urban center, Ikebukuro then still had some open fields and cow pastures. Nearby was Rikkyo Daigaku—St. Paul's University, founded by the Anglican Church.

From age three, little Kimie displayed a strong will. Once, taken along on a shopping trip by her mother, she so stubbornly resisted going that she had to be dragged, skinning her little knees, which earned Kise a scolding from Kōjiro.

In the mid-1920s, for the convenience of her father's employer, the family moved to northeast Yokohama—no "mistake" this time. As she grew, Kimie became a real tomboy, playing baseball with the boys, climbing trees, hunting tadpoles and showing no interest in dolls. At age 80, she once remarked, "Say! I just realized that I never see children today with skinned knees or elbows. When I was that age, I always had a scab on a knee or elbow." At around 10, she had a like-minded girlfriend who at least matched her: That girl liked to raid wasp nests with Kimie and eat the larvae, which she said were "sweet." Kimie abstained.

Her strong will and other strengths notwithstanding, Kimie developed some odd phobias, some for reasons mostly forgotten. She disliked lifelike dolls as they reminded her of the body of a young cousin she saw at a funeral at an impressionable age. One phobia that we traced to its origin was caterpillars. (What's the Greek for that?) A novel she read while young vividly described a boy who had no arms or legs and so "slithered along like a caterpillar." In her youth, another cousin drowned in the sea; and when his body was found, he was snagged on something underwater. She only heard about it, but retained so sharp an image of him that forever after she refused to dive into water or put her head under water.

Those phobias point to another unique trait: She had total emotional recall. Anything that reminded her of a traumatic experience would bring back all the associated emotions undiminished. E.g., in 1946 I accidentally cut the palm of my hand as she was watching me. *Fifty-two* years later I had a similar slip-up. She immediately cried out, "You did it again!" So, it would always be unwise for me—when we were having an argument—to refer to a previous spat, as her emotions of that past moment would return full force and intensify her current feelings.

Kimie was one of five siblings: brother Toshio born in 1921 and sisters Fusae (1924), Sumie (1927) and Hiroko (1930). The family's Yokohama home had a smallish backyard, but space enough for fruit trees, a good-sized carp pond and a grape trellis over a well. Kimie's favorite was a fig tree. In season, she would climb it and lick the figs she wanted for herself and then go tell her siblings.

As a sixth-grader, Kimie attended a Protestant Sunday school to be tutored in English. Secondary school in prewar Japan was a five-year "middle school," combining what we call junior and senior high. Kimie's parents wanted her to attend the American-run Ferris School; but her best friends had opted for the more costly Koran Girl's School, a Catholic mission school staffed by British and French nuns. Kimie chose to go there.

Our strong-willed Kimie soon ran up against school rules she disliked. Such as, the girls were required to wear their hair in braids, which Kimie detested. So, she instead bought human-hair braids that she clipped on as she entered the campus and pulled off as she left each day. French was a required course, along with English. But, Kimie was so repelled by the haughtiness of the French nuns (most from the French nobility) that she became a lifelong Francophobe. She claimed to have slept through some classes—geography, French and history—then crammed enough to ace her exams. For the rest of her life, she refused to visit France; and only in the 1990s did she show enough interest in Japanese history to absorb some of it from historical dramas on our TV-Japan satellite service. She would always be weak in geography, insisting that maps could not be trusted or were printed upside down. She described herself as *hōkō-onchi*—having no sense of direction—and so needed a dry run to learn the way to any new destination. She made no excuses, but simply said, "That's the way I am."

In her mid-teens, Kimie metamorphosed into a *mo-ga*, the Japanese abbreviation for "modern girl" or flapper. She loved to dance, including the Charleston, which reached Japan about a decade after it was the rage in the U.S. She dressed stylishly and collected the latest hit records. Ever the autocrat, her father disliked many of her records and sometimes smashed them. Kimie would go right out and buy replacements.

After high school, Kimie continued at Koran (now Yokohama Futaba Jogakuin, a sister school of the Tokyo Futaba which Japan's current Empress attended) in its business college. She learned Japanese and English typing, Pittman shorthand for dictation in English and other office skills. To pass the English typing course, she had to achieve 90 words a minute—no mean speed on a manual typewriter in a language not your native tongue. She also took a special course in Chinese cooking, taught by chefs from Yokohama's "Nanking-machi" (China town). Her mother had to pay the costs of that from her household accounts.

After completing her college work, Kimie took an office job not far from her home at the Victor Company (today's JVC—the Japan Victor Company), where her boss was an American. A fringe benefit was meeting and socializing with such pop singers as Haida Katsuhiko, whose records she had long been collecting.

In her upper teens, Kimie met a man four years her senior, Takemitsu Ina, eldest son of the family that owned Yokohama's prime music and phonograph store, Yokochiku. They both loved music (classical and modern), dancing and going to college baseball games.

But, now war impinged on her life. Takemitsu was drafted (1939) and sent to Manchuria. In less than a year, he returned and was discharged. They might have married then, but Kimie contracted pleurisy— inflammation of the diaphragm—and needed most of a year to recover from that.

When "the Pacific War" began in 1941, Takemitsu again was drafted and was to go to China, where Japanese forces had been fighting Chiang Kai-shek's Nationalists since 1937. Now, the young couple did marry, a few months before he shipped out. Kimie became pregnant.

Not long before daughter Ritsuko was born in August 1942, a cable came informing the Inas that Takemitsu had died. Even though Kimie had been scrapping with Takemitsu (by mail) over evidence of an infidelity, she was devastated and cried every day for a year, she told me. During the remaining war years, she mainly lived with the Inas, but often went with little Ritsuko to visit her own family.

After Pearl Harbor, most Americans in Japan, including Kimie's boss at Victor, were interned to await repatriation. Ignoring the camp guards' hostile stares, she sometimes took relief items to him—food, mittens, scarves against the coming winter cold, etc.

The Japanese Government now insisted that women show solidarity with the war effort by shunning Western dress and instead wear working-class attire of baggy pants (*monpei*), loose cotton blouses and *zori* sandals or wooden *geta* (clogs). Not our Kimie: Through the war years she continued to wear Western dresses, silk stockings and high heels. Even though, thus conspicuous, she sometimes attracted the attention of "special" police. They would stop her aboard trains or in train stations and interrogate her about her nationality and family background. Each time, they let her go with a warning to dress more appropriately. She never did.

The Yamada home was situated between the local Yokohama Line and the main Tokaido rail line (Tokyo-Osaka). In 1942, after the Doolittle raid on Tokyo and other nearby cities, the government ordered all houses between the two lines razed so that the railroads would not be blocked by burning homes after any future raids. The family found another house a few miles away. In early 1945, our incendiary bombs destroyed that house. All the family's possessions were reduced to ash. One of Mr. Yamada's friends then sold them a small house in Kozukue, in rural northwest Yokohama.

In the massive May 29, 1945, raid on Yokohama by our B-29s, the Ina's record shop and the home above it also burned. Kimie watched that raid from an Ina home on a hill near the city's edge. As her city was being incinerated, a fighter plane came by strafing, so close that its 50-caliber bullets hit in the garden right in front of her and she could clearly see the pilot. She was furious. That house was spared, however.

In that raid, Mr. Ina was lost. For days afterward, Kimie gamely searched in vain for his body in makeshift morgues full of burned bodies. Ghastly images from that experience gave her nightmares for years afterward. Decades later, when visiting Yokohama, Kimie would sometimes see a face resembling that of her lost father-in-law and wonder he had somehow survived and taken on a different identity.

Kimie's last few possessions were destroyed along with the record shop. That loss was so traumatic for her that, in the later 1940's when she was really angry with me, she would sometimes scream, "Give me back my records, my kimonos, all the things your bombers destroyed."

By late July 1945, food was in very short supply in Yokohama and other major cities. Until then, both families had found black-market food to supplement what they could get through official ration channels. So, Kimie, her mother, Fusae and Sumie took a train north to rural Tohoku to buy rice and other essentials directly from farmers. (Mr. Yamada had been drafted—with the rank of colonel—and was awaiting orders for overseas duty (which never came), while brother Toshio was in Manchuria and also being drafted. The women found the farmers hostile and demanding exorbitant prices. People in that area had suffered terribly over the decades in years of crop failure, enduring famine, crushing rents from absentee landlords and, in the worst years, had to sell some daughters into prostitution so that the rest of the family could survive.  Now city people were coming to them for food.  The cumulative bitterness naturally welled up.

The Yamada women found most of what they needed, however; and Mrs. Yamada and Sumie started back first, while Kimie and Fusae stayed a few more days to make more purchases.  When they had all they could carry, they went to the Koriyama train station to buy their tickets home.

Suddenly air-raid sirens sounded.  The two girls hurried to a shelter to wait out the raid.  Re-emerging, Kimie did not see Fusae and so went to the station waiting room, thinking Fusae had preceded her there.  Then she heard the high whistle of another bomb coming.  It exploded in the middle of the waiting room.  When Kimie came to, people all around her were dead or gravely wounded.  Close by, a woman cradled her husband to comfort him, too much in shock to grasp that his head was gone.  Kimie told me that she had only minor cuts; but in Spring 2003 Sumie told me that Kimie returned with her head covered in bandages.  The date: August 6, Hiroshima Day.

Soon Fusae re-appeared, and they made their way back to Yokohama without further incident.  Six or seven years later, in Berkeley, we extracted from Kimie's knee a piece of glass about the size of a rice grain that had worked to the surface of her skin, undoubtedly a fragment from Koriyama station.

When the war ended, rumors began flying of terrible atrocities the arriving Americans would commit.  Younger women and girls began seeking refuge in remote rural sites.  Kimie went to the far-off home of a family friend in Tochigi for several weeks. Until, in September, they began hearing that all was well and they could safely return.  Years later, I would tease Kimie, noting that only she among the four sisters had fled the Americans and only she had married one.

In November 1945, a friend who had taken a job at 8th Army Headquarters persuaded Kimie to take a job with U.S. Army censors at the Tokyo Central Post Office.  It was a translation job: all day translating selected Japanese letters.  She developed headaches from the work and quit after a week without collecting her pay. A few weeks later, the same friend persuaded her to take the secretarial position at the Film Exchange, where I would meet her three months later.

# SETTLING IN

In early fall 1946, the Allied Council for Japan, which set broad Occupation policies, ruled the demilitarization phase of the Occupation completed. That allowed the Allied Forces to begin a fast reduction phase, especially by cutting back combat units in Japan. Many of us with just a year of overseas service became eligible for return to the U.S. for demobilization.

In June, *Pacific Stars & Stripes* had reported that military personnel could be discharged in Japan to take jobs as Department of Army civilians with Occupation Force units. By August, determined not to leave Kimie, I applied at 8th Army and landed a clerical job at the Quartermaster Depot in Shinagawa, south Tokyo. I also was offered a higher-ranked position with a Military Government team in Nagano, but turned it down because of Kimie. ("That's okay; I'll go there with you," she had insisted. But her family would be far away, and she knew no one in that area.)

So now—mid-October 1946, just three months after my exile to Tokyo—I found myself with other GIs from the Signal Corps battalion en route to the Zama Replacement Depot. So many were being processed just then that it took four days for my paperwork to be completed. As I would be remaining in Japan, I managed to secure a pass while waiting for my discharge, but on condition that I had an "on limits" place to stay overnight. So, I arranged to bunk in the civilian billet at the QM Depot. Then I proceeded to Yokohama.

At the dormitory I found a somber Kimie. She had convinced herself that, instead of getting discharged to work in Tokyo, I would let the Army send me back to the States. Nothing I said could convince her otherwise. The following Monday, I received my discharge and final pay. Only when I returned to Kimie as a civilian and showed her my discharge certificate would she tell me how deep her doubts had been. That made me realize that many of the tensions between us had been rooted in her nagging doubts. So now we entered calmer times, about eight months after our first meeting.

And how different was my outlook now from that of a year earlier. Then, just arriving in Japan, I had expected to be there for a brief time and then return home and re-enter Cal. Now I felt I had barely scratched the surface of so many things about Japan that intrigued me. I had bonded tightly with one of Japan's supreme cultural achievements—a cultured Japanese lady. Yet, not every day was sweetness and light; I still was learning how to appreciate this fine, but feisty girl who loved me. Often in later years, I have wished I could repeat those early years and apply the understanding of her that I so slowly acquired over the succeeding half century.

At the QM Depot, my job was detailed record-keeping on incoming subsistence items, mainly food for Occupation Force mess halls, and for commissaries, too, now that American dependents were arriving. As the troop levels steadily dropped, we inevitably built up surpluses. I had to keep the planners updated on how Depot stock levels for each item compared to estimates of what was needed for the next six months. That was long before today's electronic gadgetry arrived on the scene. We mostly used little hand-cranked calculators to do the math.

Most nights I stayed at the Depot barracks reserved for the 30 or so American civilians working there, but each evening rode the train to go see Kimie at the Momijizaka Hotel. On some weekends we would join our friends on jaunts out of the city.

As winter approached, the trip to Yokohama could be pretty nasty. So, I bought a very used jeep, civilianized by replacing its canvas sides and roof with a plywood cab. It was clunky but kept out most of the cold air. The mobility it gave us was a welcome change from constantly riding and transferring between trains, street cars and buses when we wanted to go somewhere.

By then, I had met the Inas a few times at their rebuilt Yokochiku store on Yokohama's main shopping street. And, I began pressing Kimie to let me meet her own Yamada family. She said she still needed time to prepare them for the idea of an American boyfriend.

We finally made that first trip to Kozukue [KOH-zoo-kway] on New Year's Day 1947. I parked my jeep on a main road, as it would have blocked the narrow lane to the Yamada house. Then typical of rural homes, the water supply was a well in the yard beside the house. Later, many improvements would be made; but in early 1947 it was a very basic home. (Occupied today by brother Toshio and his family.)

After some lessons from Kimie on the rudiments of Japanese etiquette, I met her parents, three younger sisters, and 4-year-old Ritsuko, the totally adorable child of Kimie's late husband. My use of Japanese was still rudimentary, too. So, I relied on Kimie to interpret for me. That meant she could filter out any awkward remarks or questions from me and so keep this first meeting with her family on an even keel.

After listening to this for a while, little Ritsuko climbed into Kimie's lap and whispered into her ear. Kimie burst out laughing, then explained that Ritsuko had said, "Hugh-san speaks very good English, doesn't he!" She had heard Kimie tutoring Sumie and Hiroko and so recognized how it should sound.

Kimie's mother and sisters had prepared the traditional New Year's dishes. The family seemed to assume that, being acceptable to Kimie, I might pass muster as a prospective family member. They had long since learned not to cross her. New Year's Day is the prime annual holiday in Japan and entails some formality—special greetings and wishes for the coming year, exchanges of gifts, etc. I had brought a few PX items. So, in any case this could not have been a totally casual social call.

Near the end of 1946, Kimie had a verbal spat with the Film Exchange C.O. who had exiled me; and she quit. Now she was working at the 155th Station Hospital for the mess hall officer there. GIs there were attracted to her, not knowing of her commitment to me, and tried to compete for her favor by giving her things. She cured them of that by simply—right in front of them—passing their gifts to other Japanese in the office. Nothing indirect about my girl!

While at work there, Kimie deepened her friendship with Amy Baba, the Nisei girl whom we had met earlier and who was stranded in Japan during the war. Kimie helped her contact the American consulate to start the process of confirming her citizenship. In the same time frame, we also befriended other stranded Nisei, especially Ken Kaneda and Roy Iwaki, who became a threesome with Amy and sometimes took weekend jaunts with us—to the beach, ski slopes, etc.

In fact, my first skiing experience was with Ken and Roy at Echigo-Yuzawa in southern Niigata Prefecture in winter 1947. And, what an experience! Ken was a crackerjack skier who would several years later be on the U.S. Army's ski team in Europe. So, on the first morning I followed him straight up a steep slope, herringboning my way up. No ski lifts would be in place there for another couple of decades.

Near the top I turned and looked down, and it dawned on me that I might break a leg skiing straight back down. So, I began a shallow zigzag course down. On my second zig, another skier cut across my skis, knocking one loose. I watched in dismay as that lone ski slid smoothly to the bottom of the hill. Now my only way down was to sit on my remaining ski and sled down.

Next time, I took a roundabout route away from the main slope. There local children were skiing—little tykes with dried mucus under their noses, wearing straw ski boots on stubby skis and kept warm by padded conical cotton hoods over heads and shoulders. Now, this stalwart American was wearing Army OD pants and Ike jacket, both recently dyed blue, with GI combat boots on 6-foot skis. Naturally, he was going to whiz past the kids, right?

But, I did not know how to turn or to stop without on collapsing my derriere. So, I began to make short runs, plop down, get up and slide again—all the way down. Looking back up the hill, I saw that my dyed pants had left a trail of *blue* sitzmarks. The little kids were zipping by and laughing at my unorthodox performance. But, hey! There's more than one way to ski, you know.

That afternoon I followed Ken up another slope, shorter and less steep. He gave me some pointers on how to deal with the slope; but I chose to loop around its gentler perimeter. Near the bottom, I saw that I would have to navigate a narrow gap between a haystack and a small stream. To avoid the risk of sliding into the creek, I chose the haystack—head on—and bounced off. I could hear laughter from the top of the hill.

Next I scouted an even gentler slope just below that. Its snow terraces promised some easier schussing. So, I gave that a try. Suddenly I came to a snow bridge and a drop-off. The snow bridge collapsed, and I found myself hanging upside down by my skis over a muddy rice paddy that a snow bridge had hidden. Fortunately, Ken saw me disappear and came to help me get out without sampling the paddy mud. That evening I had my first beer. It tasted great after that dramatic first skiing day.

As winter yielded to spring in 1947, Kimie and I found some pleasant places to spend weekends together—in Atami, Odawara and Yugawara— to truly deepen our bonds away from roommates and "the madding crowd." Odawara was two hours by car from Yokohama on a highway paralleling the Tokaido line down the coast. For centuries Odawara was a castle town strategically located where travelers on the old Tokaido Road had to leave the coast and tackle the steep Hakone Mountains. The castle was dismantled in the mid-1860's, but its moats and some stone walls still remained. On one visit, we rented a rowboat there and enjoyed the serenity that had overtaken this place where Kōjiro Yamada's samurai forebears once served the *daimyo* (feudal lord).

About this time, seeking more privacy, we found a room to rent in the home of the Nishios, an elderly couple in Myōrenji, a quiet middle-class suburb in north Yokohama. This would be our home for the next two years. I still kept my assigned room in the QM Depot's new civilian billet in south Tokyo. That same year, I bought John's 1929 Model A Ford Roadster, arranging with the Army to ship it to me. I sold my Jeep to a Depot sergeant, who promptly wrecked it while driving drunk, seriously injuring himself.

The Model A should have meant a better commute between Myorenji and Shinagawa; but every second or third weekend I had it in the PX garage with a carburetor problem. Also, the car had rigid brake rods that tended to snap when I hit the brakes on the washboard roads making up half the commuting distance. Fortunately, Japanese car-part stores had the rods. So, I kept spare rods in the trunk and became adept at replacing broken ones.

I earlier mentioned my contact at Cal with two Japanese-speaking fellow students: Hans Baerwald and Don Helm. They now were Army officers in GHQ; and we saw each other sometimes in Tokyo. Hans was later a USC political science professor, and Don would graduate from Berkeley and work for decades in the family business, Helm House, in Yokohama. He is now deceased, but his two sons are successful businessmen in Seattle, and his widow recently moved to Seattle to be near them.

In early 1947, Kimie's brother suddenly came home. Toshio had gone to Manchuria in 1940 to study architecture at the University of Dairen. His desire was to be a musician, but his father had insisted that Toshio follow him in the field of architecture. Toshio finally agreed, but on the condition that he go away for college. Near the end of the war, Mr. Yamada had visited Toshio in Manchuria. In about June 1945, the family heard that Toshio had been drafted. Then silence. In August, Soviet forces swept through Manchuria in the war's final days, capturing over a million Japanese—military and civilian. By the end of 1947, about 300,000 had come back to Japan, but another 300,000—mostly soldiers—never returned from the Siberian *gulag* system. So, Toshio was one of the lucky ones. He had been sheltered part of the time by Chinese friends and now arrived back with a wife and only what they could carry on their backs. I was able to help him a little in getting more clothes.

# COMPLEXITIES

I should have explained earlier why Kimie and I did not marry soon after getting engaged in May 1946. In fact, it was impossible, as Captain Seeberg had said in August '46.

For half a century, "the yellow peril"—Chinese and Japanese immigrants—had been a hot issue, especially in California. White workers and their unions feared the impact of Asians willing to accept low pay; and farmers in California had watched the Japanese market cheaper and better produce. In the 19th century, immigration of Chinese labor was banned. In the early 20th century, the Hearst press, the nativist Sons of the Golden West, labor groups and politicians had pressured Congress and the White House to stop Japanese immigration. In 1923 a new U.S. immigration law—the infamous "Oriental Exclusion Act"—halted the influx of Japanese labor. That and similar state laws barred Japanese immigrants from citizenship or owning real estate. That was the law until 1953.

Because Japanese could not enter the U.S. for permanent residence, Occupation Force regulations barred unit commanders from approving any marriage of an American to a Japanese. Marriages in Japan, for anyone, are legalized by registry at local government offices. So, the same regulations forbade Japanese registrars from recording American-Japanese marriages. Check mate! Maybe.

By mid-1947, pressure had built up on Congress to enact some relief, especially for the Nisei serving in the Occupation who had found that special girl. The heroism of the all-Nisei units in Europe during World

War II had become more widely known and had begun to change American attitudes towards them. In early July, the *Stars & Stripes* reported that Congress had enacted a "GI Brides Act" temporarily suspending the effects of Oriental Exclusion and Occupation regulations against American-Japanese marriages. It allowed any American who married a Japanese between July 23 and August 21, 1947, with proper military permission to take that spouse to the USA for permanent residence.

The *Stripes* also spelled out procedures for getting such permission. Applications and letters of recommendation would go to the unit chaplain. Japanese police and military investigators would check on the prospective Japanese spouse. Unit chaplains would interview the couples and give commanding officers their recommendations.

Getting our paperwork ready immediately consumed me. The actual application was simple enough; and we easily got good recommendation letters from two of Kimie's friends. Also, we had become acquainted with a consular officer in Yokohama, Douglas Overton.* So, naturally, I got a recommendation from him. Warm letters of welcome came from Mother and my siblings to Kimie. John wrote: "...You will find that our family will be very eager to know you and to love you ... and I hope you will often eat at our table and grace our fireside." John was then studying for the ministry at the Pacific School of religion.

We got our forms in, including Mother's approval, since I was four months shy of legal adulthood. Kimie's bright personality and English ability impressed he the Depot chaplain; but he focused on my age and our plan to live in California—in his mind still a hotbed of anti-Japanese feelings. He called Kimie in a second time and tried to convince her she would be miserable in California. The red warning flags were flying!

---

* Overton had taught before the war at Rikkyo University. Through him I had arranged for Mother to send my father's books on religion to Rikkyo, helping restock their library. Active in Yokohama Anglican circles, Overton met us through Ken Kaneda and Roy Iwaki, who worked at the consulate. Doug knew of Uncle Hugh and so could assure Kimie that I came from a good family.

Worried by the chaplain's negative approach, I consulted with Overton about what we could do alternatively, for we were sure that if any match ever is "made in heaven," ours was. In his consular capacity, Overton could not advise taking any course contrary policies of the U.S. Forces. As a friend, he unofficially suggested trying an end run around the Occupation: Before the law expired, get married in a Christian ceremony at Christ Church on Yokohama's Bluff. Then send a copy of our marriage certificate to the Immigration Service in the USA, asking that Kimie be granted entry to the U.S. based on our marrying within the law's 30-day grace period. He thought that the Occupation's limitations on Japanese sovereignty might lead the INS to see our marriage as legal in the U.S. and therefore meeting the law's conditions. A test case, obviously.

By August 20, several Depot men had received approval to marry their Japanese fiancées. I had nothing. When I told Kimie we should assume the worst and activate our end-run plan, she reacted *bitterly*. "But, I don't want such a marriage!" she cried out in distress, a cry that echoes painfully in my memory even now.

Nevertheless, on August 21 we had a simple ceremony at Christ Church, with a few Japanese and American friends as witnesses. From the Japanese priest we received the crucial certificate dated August 21, 1947. I mailed it to the INS. In late September the response came back in a plump envelope. I held my breath as I opened it, hoping to find forms to fill out. But, it was our certificate, along with a stonewalling letter suggesting that I ask GHQ for help. The INS had ducked the issue. Failure of gamble and test case. Check mate! Almost.

The only solution now appeared to be getting U.S. immigration law changed to end the blatant racism of "Oriental Exclusion," that ugly relic of our past phobias. It of course tied into the panoply of attitudes that had led to US-Japan alienation and contributed to the war in the Pacific. Falling in love with my Kimie had put me on the "wrong" side of that law—on the receiving end of all the injustice and racial bias it embodied.

I quietly grew bitter; and because that was contrary to my nature, I developed some reactions that, with 50+ years of hindsight, now look pretty odd. First, in the racist parlance of the day, I "went Asiatic," strongly and uncritically identifying with Japanese culture and society, associating ever less with fellow Americans, and communicating less with my family "back Stateside."

Second, feeling betrayed by Occupation officials, who had rejected our marriage request, I did some petty black-marketing. I allied with a Japanese PX clerk who simply did not punch my PX card when I bought rationed items so that I could buy extra items. I shared some things with him and sold the others. My conscious motive was improving our living standard. I did not consider it immoral, because it helped the Japanese, Kimie and me; and no one was hurt.

Meanwhile, Kimie and I had honeymooned in Nikko, the famed tourist site where the Tokugawa shoguns had built gorgeous shrines in the mountains, with many hot-springs nearby. We stayed at the highest part of Nikko—Nikko Yumoto with its sulfur hot springs above Lake Chuzenji with steep cliffs rising behind. That was before we received the turn-off from the INS and before we knew what obstacles we still faced or what hot water we could be in if we were not careful.

I again consulted with Doug Overton on what to do next. He said our best remaining option was to campaign for Congress to change US immigration laws. He also said that, even under the just expired temporary law, we would have had a problem: It would not have allowed Ritsuko to go with us to the USA, even if I adopted her, as she was not my natural daughter. We would need either a revised immigration law or a private law that covered Ritsuko also.

So, in fall 1947 we began a long campaign. Much of the political pressure on Congress had eased after over 800 marriages (3/4 Nisei) took place under the 30-day law. We might be just a few lonely voices. Certainly, we heard no rising chorus of demands to end Oriental exclusion. The Nisei, back from the battlefronts or internment camps and trying to put their lives back together, were focused on proving to other Americans that they were 100% American, not special advocates for Japanese issues. But, in the next few years I learned that their Japanese American Citizens League was pushing for their parents' right to become citizens, which would require immigration law reform.

I now enlisted my family in writing to Congress, and they were quite supportive. Their first letters and mine went to Congress before 1947 ended. I also intensified my study of Japanese language and the culture so that I would not be merely marking time in Japan.

# GLIMMERINGS OF HOPE

## (1948-1950)

In 1948, the Nishios, from whom we were renting our room, moved out to live with their son. Now we rented the whole house; but, facing an indefinite sojourn, we wanted our own place, something more modern. So, we began consulting with Kimie's architect brother, Toshio, about designing a two-bedroom house for us, in the $2000 range.

That same spring, a new crisis: Kimie developed tuberculosis, mild at first, but by early summer the bug suddenly invaded her throat. Her physician warned me that, unless somehow checked, the infection would become life threatening. He heard that new anti-TB drugs were now available in the U.S. Kimie was losing weight, her eyes lost their sparkle and the pain in her throat muted her ringing voice. I became seriously worried.

Using a new overseas phone center for Occupation personnel in Tokyo, I phoned Mother to ask her to try to get the new drugs for us. She responded quickly and with loving concern. Soon we had the vital drugs—streptomycin and PAS (para-amino-salicylic acid) which together promised to help halt the disease. Indeed, within a week of starting the treatment, Kimie was better, could speak more normally and eat solids. But, it took until January 1949 before her doctor felt confident that the TB was truly stopped.

To help boost Kimie's morale during her convalescence, I bought her a new record player, the first new LP player to show up in our Depot PX, plus some classical records to go with it.

At the QM Depot, I won a promotion to CAF-7, a grade equivalent to 1st lieutenant.

In South Korea, the "democratic" government of Syngman Rhee was installed under UN-supervised elections, and most U.S. combat forces were withdrawn. Large amounts of commissary and troop supplies were shipped over from Korea to our QM Depot, where we had just finished liquidating excesses generated by the force cuts in Japan since 1946. Our office now was stuck with finding ways to get rid of these new excesses. We even had, for a time, some 20 barking K-9 guard dogs nearby—also evacuees from Korea.

From Yokohama and Berkeley, our letter-writing to Congress went on, focused ever more on the Senate Judiciary Committee, whose early responses gave me little optimism. In 1948, Congress was preoccupied with the Berlin Airlift, presidential elections, China's imminent fall to Mao's armies, imperiled democracies in Europe, etc. We Americans in Japan seeking "mixed" marriages with Japanese girls seemed a low priority.

So, another year passed and 1949 dawned. When Toshio's carpenters had completed the frame of our house, we threw a party for him and his men—a traditional rite, with sprigs of bamboo and *sakaki* branches on the ridgepole. At Toshio's request, I provided bottles of scotch. Unfamiliar with scotch, the carpenters chugged it down as they usually did sake, which is only 1/4 as strong. Most did not make it home that night, sleeping wherever they passed out.

In spring 1949, the family in Berkeley began getting responses from Judiciary Committee senators, including Chairman Pat McCarran. In May, Mother wrote to another senator, Bill Langer of North Dakota, ending her letter with a note about the service of my father and his brothers in North Dakota in the early 1900s. I followed up with my own letter to him. In mid-July, he sponsored a general bill to erase the racial bar to Asian immigration; and I had good letters from Hubert Humphrey and McCarran about that bill.

Then, July 22, 1949: a letter from Senator Langer saying, "I have decided to introduce a private bill" that would cover both Kimie and Ritsuko. Finally, a real cause for hope!

That fall he sent me a copy of the bill; but it did not move out of committee. In early 1950, I again wrote to Langer and Chairman McCarran about "our" bill and the more general bill that would lower the anti-Asian barriers in U.S. immigration laws.

In early 1950, I jumped at a chance to buy a two-year-old Nash from a departing Depot officer, and so sold the Model A. The newer car was better suited to transporting Kimie as she recovered. I paid for it with proceeds from the Model A and some money from an education fund Uncle Hugh had set up for each of us. To make that transfer of funds, I placed a call home, with Kimie at my side.

That was her first chance to talk with my family directly. In a March '50 letter home I wrote:

> "She said after the phone call that your voice is very sweet. She was pleased and excited to talk with each of you. Before, she had feared she might not get along well with you, recalling the problems she has had with Army officers here. She used to insist she would not go to the States and would jump off the ship if I tried to take her. Now her attitude is the reverse, and we talk about 'when we go' without her stubborn nature kicking in."

In May, Mother heard from Senator Langer that our bill finally was moving and, in June, that it was cleared for a vote on the Senate floor. He added that cousin Allan Burleson, had visited him to inquire about the bill. (Two years before, Allan had cabled his congratulations when California repealed its "anti-miscegenation" law, thus removing one legal barrier.) A decade after he had helped to get me into Webb, my cousin was in there pitching again!  On June 9 came a cable from Mother that the bill had passed the Senate.

June 25, 1950—war in Korea!  The sudden invasion by Kim Il Song's Soviet-backed forces.  President Truman persuaded the UN that troops must come to South Korea's defense, and he moved the 25th Infantry from Kyushu across to Korea.  A few weeks later, I and others from our office were called for an emergency meeting at 8th Army in Yokohama.  The gist was that most of the excess supplies shipped from Korea a year or two earlier had to go back to support allied forces mounting a defense against the north.

We worked overtime for days getting the shipment on its way.

A week later, another emergency call from 8th Army: The entire first shipment had been captured.  We had to come up with a replacement shipment.  Now we had only excess commissary supplies, not mess hall or field rations.  So, we got out our little hand-cranked calculators and began busily churning out figures.  How many 4-oz. jars of maraschino cherries equal a #10 can of fruit cocktail?  Can we substitute 20-oz. boxes of Bisquick for 20-lb. bags of whole-wheat flour?  And so on.

When we were done, we had cut below the normal 6-month stock level for both troops and commissaries in Japan.  That soon became immaterial as ever more troops were being pulled out of Japan and sent to Korea to help man the "Pusan perimeter."  We began getting orders even to select individual GIs from our Quartermaster units to go fill gaps in Infantry units.  That was tough for young men with little or no combat training who had been enjoying "never had it so good" duty in Japan.  Some had to say quick goodbyes to Japanese girlfriends and head for the front lines in Korea.

From one, we received a bitter letter, saying things like, "It's not hard to stay awake here at night.  If you fall asleep the communists sneak up and drop a grenade in your foxhole."

From the 155th Station Hospital we heard of a truck company sergeant, an Afro-American from our Depot.  A few weeks before, he was spiritedly leading cheers for the QM Depot football team. In Korea, his truck convoy was shot up and he was seriously wounded, escaping only by hiding in a farmer's liquid fertilizer tank (human waste).

In a letter home, I wrote, "Kimie and Ritsuko are weeding my garden for me, as the only time I'm free to do it is late evenings, when I'd need a flashlight." I also noted that I had only part of July 4th off, just long enough to meet Kimie at Shinagawa Station and drive with her to pick up paint from her aunt's house in north Tokyo—paint that the aunt's son would apply to our Myorenji house. When it was finished and we moved in, Kimie's mother came to help keep house while Kimie regained her strength.

In mid-summer, we went to Tokyo's Meiji Park for a trade festival. At the Victor Record exhibit Kimie met an old friend who once worked with her at the Yokohama Victor plant. Kimie was now strong enough that she tired very little during that half day in the park; but Mother was still sending Kimie's medicine to us.

In Washington, Senator Langer's private bill for us finally cleared Congress! President Truman signed it into law on July 26, 1950 (while still preoccupied with getting a better UN response to the Korean crisis). On August 12, I received copies of Private Law 666. In it, Langer described Kimie as my fiancée, to avoid revealing that we had married in '47 without Army permission.

In a file I have kept on our entire campaign to get Kimie and Ritsuko to America is a chronology of the sequel—something I had entirely forgotten. Hoping to get the Army to cover the cost of sending Kimie and Ritsuko to the U.S., I tried to get the Army to agree that our law would allow us to marry in Japan since it overrode the immigration laws that were the basis for barring American-Japanese marriages. I went around to several GHQ offices and the Yokohama consulate on the matter. I persuaded the GHQ chaplain to approve the marriage. (I was now 23.) Unresolved was whether Kimie could enter the U.S. as my wife, as "our" law defined her as my fiancée and said we must marry within three months of her arrival in the U.S. So, the snag now was not the Army, but GHQ lawyers who foresaw Immigration Service officers in San Francisco having a problem with this legal point.

In the end, the GHQ Diplomatic Section—in the person of one Jack Webb (the youngest son of Thompson and Vivian Webb of Webb School in Claremont!)—confirmed that Kimie had to arrive in the U.S. as my fiancée.

So, after what had seemed an eternity, we three—Kimie, 8-year-old Ritsuko and I—were free to go to the USA. In the following weeks, we went through the red tape: physical exams and proper documents for my two girls. As Japan was under Allied occupation and not fully sovereign, the Yokohama Consulate General issued official IDs for them in lieu of passports and a U.S. visa. (Signed by Consul General U. Alexis Johnson, whom we would later know as our U.S. ambassador in Tokyo.)

Then I arranged transportation for them. I sold the Nash and used the proceeds to book passage for them on the APL liner "President Wilson," leaving Yokohama on November 9, 1950. The Army owed me my return transportation to the U.S., so that I would fly back separately.

Together with her mother, brother Toshio, sister Sumie and husband Takeo Takeuchi, we started walking from our Myorenji home to the train. Kimie seemed only mildly excited, but a few blocks along she suddenly exclaimed, "The tickets, the tickets! I left them on my bureau!" That little oversight corrected, we continued to the station and took a train to downtown Yokohama. There we needed three taxis (which were small in those days) to get to South Pier, where the trans-Pacific liners docked. It was a classic sailing, with tears, ticker tape and the PA system playing "Auld Lang Syne."

Two days later, I boarded an Alaskan Airlines DC-4 (Army-chartered to meet Korean War needs) at Haneda Airport in south Tokyo. My first ever air travel! Thus would end my first sojourn in Japan: 5 years and 8 days. I had arrived a slightly starry-eyed teen-ager on his first trip overseas. I left a bit more mature and a serious family man.

Such a long flight! Leaving Tokyo in mid-afternoon and heading north to Shemya, the westernmost of the Aleutians, we arrived at some ungodly dark hour for breakfast in a military mess hall. Then on eastward. Through gaps in the cloud deck over the Alaskan mainland I could see frozen lakes and endless, seemingly uninhabited expanses of that great land. We finally arrived at Elmendorf AFB outside Anchorage for a 2 PM lunch, and were off again at 3:30 PM (already dark!), headed for Seattle. I think it was 10 or 11 PM that I checked into a Seattle hotel. My final leg home would be by train from there.

# HOME IN BERKELEY

## (1950-54)

From Seattle, I had alerted the family of my arrival time in Berkeley; and they were waiting at the station when I alit on hometown soil. One of their first comments I heard was, "Hey, where'd you get that Texas accent?" A Texas drawl was so pervasive in the Army that apparently my six years around the Army had infected me, too.

In the days remaining before the "President Wilson" would dock with my Kimie and Ritsuko, I prepared our space in the family home in north Berkeley, checked on re-entering the university and investigated used-car prices.

Then the big day: welcoming Kimie and Ritsuko to America. Several of us went to the American President Lines pier in San Francisco and watched the liner dock. We stood outside a steel fence as passengers came down the gangway headed for customs and immigration clearance. When my two precious ones came in sight, I choked up as I called to them. That long-awaited moment was total happiness; and I had to struggle to hold back tears. Once inside the large covered pier we finally were together, my family, Kimie, Ritsuko and me. A warm, warm meeting and reunion with smiles all around.

Kimie introduced me to a Mr. Wilson who had sat with her at the captain's table (!) on the voyage. He had been a forestry advisor in Korea, but had to leave due to the war. One of Kimie's many instant admirers, he said he "wanted to make sure that the young American she had chosen was good enough for her." I guess I passed. We exchanged Christmas cards for years, keeping him updated on how Kimie was faring in America.

En route to Berkeley, Kimie described the highlights of the 13-day voyage. She had been seasick the first several days, but finally took motion-sickness pills and thereafter enjoyed the fine shipboard cuisine. One day the sea was so rough that people in the dining room slid across the floor in their chairs. When they stopped in Honolulu for a day, Kimie contacted Amy Baba, our Nisei friend who had earlier returned there from Yokohama. Kimie and Ritsuko spent a day with her family, who taught Kimie how to make *kimchee*, Korea's fiery pickled vegetable condiment.

Kimie said that as they approached the Golden Gate Bridge, she was sure the ship's rigging would snag the great structure. Apparently, the tide was low enough that they managed to clear the bridge and arrive safely for our dockside welcome.

Now in the USA, our first task was getting married *again!* Ten days later, December 3, we re-tied the knot, at St, Marks Episcopal Church near the U.C. campus. After that, we would celebrate that second anniversary, too, reconfirming how closely bonded we were. In later years, we joked that if we ever were to divorce, we'd have to do that twice, too.

I arranged to re-enter Cal in the spring semester, starting in late January 1951. (Spring comes early in California.) And, Mary helped me land a job at the East Asian Library (EAL) on campus. Soon I was into the heavy labor of helping to move that collection of some 80,000 books from the Main Library to EAL's new home in Boalt Hall, the former Law School. Boalt Hall was old enough not to have elevators. So, we had to carry the books up three or four floors to the stacks. Over the next five years I would haul thousands of books, including heavy tomes, up and down those stairways. In good weather I supplemented that exercise by walking three miles from home to the campus.

The job was located close enough to my classrooms that I could often work between classes. It also helped my study of written Japanese, giving me invaluable practice on the Chinese characters in book titles and the character classification system used for filing catalog cards. Also at EAL I met grad students in Asian studies with whom I sometimes crossed paths in later decades, as well as faculty members who would be my teachers for the next several years.

Four decades later, in 1998, EAL staff members of that era held a reunion in Berkeley. They asked me to emcee the party. I opened by saying, "I was going to propose a toast to old friends and nostalgia; but, seeing all the gray heads here, I'll instead propose a toast to nostalgia and neuralgia."

The EAL job also meshed nicely with my changed academic major. A few years before, when she had discovered that I was red-green color-blind, Kimie convinced me to forgo any medical science major. So, after five years in Japan, with a good start in learning Japanese and with a Japanese family, I now had a new focus. The war with Japan was the cause of Kimie and me meeting. So, now I would be seeking a career allowing me to work for better US-Japan relations so that our two nations might never again be enemies. Our Nisei friends had showed us the pain of families divided by war.

So, I switched from pre-med to social sciences. Cal's Political Science Department offered a "regional group major on Japan and East Asia." The term "area studies" had not yet been coined, nor were there yet enough solid materials on Japan alone to support an exclusively Japan major. I went for the group major, and focused on political science, international relations and courses on Japan and East Asia. Poli Sci Professor Robert A. Scalapino, just eight years my senior, would be my faculty advisor.

On the home front, an early concern was getting Ritsuko into school. She stubbornly resisted our efforts to teach her English at home. As long as she could rely on her mother to interpret, why bother? I would ask Kimie, "You tell her …," and that sounded to her like the Japanese *yutte yo* (say it), and she would beg her mother to interpret. After nearly two months of little progress, we went to Thousand Oaks Elementary, two blocks from our home with Mother and Kitty. The school said they had done very well with such cases by assigning another student to help the newcomer learn the language and make the adjustment.

Ritsuko was assigned to a Belgian girl who had grown up in the Congo and just a year earlier had come to Berkeley and begun learning English. That worked beautifully; and they became best friends. Soon we heard that Ritsuko was speaking English at school, even though still insisting on Japanese at home. It was not until Easter vacation, when her friends came over to play, that she transitioned to using English at home.

At the university, I was taking cultural anthropology, some poli sci and such required courses as economics and English, which was mainly writing and lit. The English teacher was an inspiring woman who had been on the *New Yorker* staff and was very good. That was lucky, because my English teacher at Webb had been so excellent. A few years later, we heard the very sad news that that woman had signed up to teach in Burma but was killed in a plane crash en route there.

Meanwhile we had a very troubling new situation. In February we had joined Kitty and her fiancé Boyd Weeks on a skiing trip in the Sierras. The return trip was very cold, and Kimie developed what seemed like bronchitis, with a cough persisting for weeks. At the same time, we discovered she was pregnant. So, we began going alternately to a gynecologist, Dr. Terashima, and a GP, Dr. James Harkness, the Cal football team doctor who was trying to diagnose her cough. In late April or early May, he confirmed his suspicions: Kimie's TB was back.

We were scared! TB on top of a pregnancy—a bad mix! Incompatible in those days because today's powerful anti-TB drugs were still unknown. Dr. Harkness urged that Kimie go to a sanitarium to get intensive care and protect the rest of the family from exposure. But, the cost seemed beyond our means. So, he referred us to a state Social Services office. The big question: could Kimie safely continue the pregnancy? Dr. Terashima gave us the pros and cons. Dr. Harkness said the pregnancy would tend to compress Kimie's lungs—just what was needed to help the TB lesions heal. On the cost of a sanitarium stay, the Social Services office proved very helpful. As I was a veteran and college student, the social worker there* was able to arrange a reasonable rate at Arequipa Sanitarium across the Bay in Marin County.

So, in early June 1951 I took Kimie to the sanitarium, where the women patients were a mix of nationalities and races—an introduction for Kimie to America's ethnic diversity. Each weekend I visited her, sometimes on both Saturday and Sunday. But, because beginning Japanese (which I needed to get into the written language) had not been offered in the spring semester, I was taking intensive (4 hours a day for 12 weeks) Japanese in the University Extension that summer, besides working half days at the library. So, weekday visits were out.

One Saturday in July, I could see Kimie only for about an hour: I had a horse trailer in tow behind our 1940 Mercury. The horse was Kitty's. The story: Ever since she was a little girl in Vista, Kitty had loved horses. Now earning a salary (in the same job I had at the UC Radiation Lab before I was drafted six years earlier), she had bought a horse, and *another* horse—the second one for Boyd so that they could ride together. Now she was moving temporarily to Mendocino County on the north coast to assist a friend who was expecting a first child. I agreed to haul one horse, while Boyd would take the other horse up there later.

I had never before towed a trailer, much less a loaded horse trailer. After leaving Kimie, I headed north on US 101—the easy part. Ninety miles from San Francisco, I had to turn onto State Highway 128, which runs northwest some 60 miles through redwood country to the Mendocino coast. Redwoods meant logging trucks coming my way with BIG loads, sometimes on hairpin turns on steep grades. Very unequal kinetic forces! A few times I lost forward momentum while slowing to make way for a big rig on a curve and had to fight a balky transmission to get going again. I made it okay (as did the horse), but the car's transmission was never quite the same after that.

About a month later, George got married. A year before, with a UC YMCA group, he had visited an "intentional community"—a group

---

* She had been born without arms and typed and wrote with her feet!

of families sharing all worldly goods and similar philosophies—on a farm in Modesto in the San Joaquin Valley. There he had met Vonnie Kramer, who was just graduating from high school. Over the following year, their attraction matured into all-out love. So, on a summer weekend I attended their wedding in a glade in upper Yosemite. The officiating pastor was the Rev. Kramer, Vonnie's father. About a year later, George quit his post-graduate studies in UC's School of Social Welfare and joined the Modesto community.

In my summer Japanese class I had two most interesting teachers. One, Mrs. Togasaki, had come to the USA as a "picture bride"* in 1930 to marry an Issei businessman whose first wife had died. This second Mrs. Togasaki had taught English in Japan. The other teacher was Brooks McKinnon, who had left his Boston home at age 19 to teach English in Japan. When the war erupted, he was separated from his Japanese wife and interned. Their three children were in college in the U.S. His wife died during the war. He could be quite American or very traditionally Japanese when he wished.

Mr. McKinnon's role was to teach us the Chinese characters (*kanji*)**. One mnemonic he used helped us learn the *kanji* for cherry tree. First, a few *kanji* basics. Unlike our alphabet, kanji started as pictographs, not unlike early Egypt's hieroglyphics. Over time they evolved to represent abstractions by adding other pictographic or phonetic elements. So, sometimes they are called ideographs, which is sometimes valid. Let's just say that in Japanese one or more kanji together can represent a thing or a concept. To create order among the thousands of characters, one

---

* Due to our immigration restrictions, only "picture brides" could come here after 1924. Most Issei men came here as bachelors to earn a fortune and return to Japan. So, with few eligible Japanese women here, men would have relatives in Japan find a prospective mate, and the two would exchange photos and letters, then have a marriage legalized by registry in Japan. The woman could then come to the U.S. to join her husband.
* The Japanese became literate via China's writing system in the early centuries of the Christian era, and then adapted that to work better in their language. Character dictionaries list up to 14,000 kanji, but ordinary literacy today requires knowing "only" 3000-3500.

part of the kanji is treated as a classifier that indicates the categories of things represented (trees, people, disease, animals, speech, etc.).

So, for example, a Chinese scholar, maybe 3,000 years ago, invented the character for cherry tree, by writing the tree kanji on the left and on the right appending a character pronounced like the Chinese word for cherry. So, the cherry tree—*sakura* in Japanese—has the 4-stroke tree symbol on the left, plus a group of right-side elements. That cluster consists of two "seashell" characters (7 strokes each) and one "woman" character (3 strokes). So, 21 strokes to write cherry tree. Daunting?

To dissuade us from that conclusion, Mr. McKinnon gave us an intriguing mnemonic. In Japanese, two shells can be read *nikai*, which is a homonym for second floor. So, he suggested, you climb the cherry tree to the second floor to see your woman. The 21 strokes are but a small obstacle with that prospect in mind!

One character that surely is politically incorrect today is a 9-stroke cluster of three "woman" characters. It can mean noisy, debauchery, adultery or simply mischief. A very ancient character? Or one based on bad experiences?

About September first, after three months in Arequipa, Kimie was allowed to come home. She was due to deliver in three more weeks, and the sanitarium had no maternity ward. She was much improved and looked wonderfully healthy, even quite transformed. Whereas she had been 100 pounds and small busted, now she weighed 125 pounds and needed a large bra. I had a brand new wife! And, we were ever more deeply in love.

Ultrasound was unknown in 1951, so that we did not know the gender of our baby, but decided to name it Christopher if a boy.

On September 25, Kimie went into labor. Dr. Terashima had arranged for her to deliver at Highland Hospital in Oakland. So, I drove her there and stayed with her into the middle evening. In those dark ages, a father-to-be was not allowed to be present for the delivery. I was unceremoniously sent home.

About 6AM the next morning, the hospital called to tell me we had a son. When I arrived, Kimie said she had decided to name him after me—Hugh Latimer Burleson III.

He was already registered that way so that there was no point arguing. A first impression of the newcomer: My, what a big nose you have, and what a lot of hair! Don't worry. I'm 7 pounds 14 ounces and quite healthy, thank you.

Kimie later told me she had kept to her samurai standard of not crying out from the pain of contractions. So, the nurses did not know she was about to deliver until just before she did. She had to call them to roll her into the delivery room!

Now Kimie faced new ordeals. First, due to the risk of infecting the baby with TB, she could have no direct contact with little Hugh ("Hugh-ko" = Hugh junior). And, because the baby's upward pressure on her lungs was gone, Dr. Harkness came to the hospital just hours after the delivery to start a new treatment: pneumothorax: (1) deaden the skin and subcutaneous tissue, (2) punch a large needle through the chest wall and (3) pump air in to reduce the expansion of the lungs. That would help keep the TB bacillus trapped in their calcium prisons. This treatment would continue about weekly for over a year, and then be replaced by pneumoperitoneum. Same principle, but pump air into the stomach cavity instead. My stoic samurai lady never complained, even though the treatment would spoil her up-to-then svelte figure by stretching her tummy.

An interesting occurrence during Kimie's second day in the hospital: In the next room was a Chinese woman who spoke no English. Her doctor knew she was in pain, but needed specific information. He came to Kimie and asked if she spoke Chinese. She did not, but told the doctor that if the woman could write down her symptoms in Chinese, Kimie might understand. That was done and Kimie was able to give he doctor the information he needed. The *kanji* are shared, if not the language.

For Hugh-ko's first year, his primary caregiver was my mother. Having had six babies herself, she knew the routines well and had an infinite capacity for love. I often helped with the details. Like putting him to sleep by singing his favorite tune, "Rudolph the Red-nosed Reindeer" over and over for as long as it took. After his first few weeks, the rest of his face caught up with his out-sized nose and we had as adorable a baby as one could hope for. Very good natured, too.

A year after Hugh-ko's birth, Dr. Harkness declared Kimie free of active TB. So, finally she could hold and care for our boy. Both made the transition nicely; but Kimie, with her acute sense of smell, found diaper-changing a tough chore. She would tease him about how smelly his diapers were, saying to him in Japanese. *Ah, kusai, kusai!"* (O, so stinky!) Soon he was giggling and imitating her: "Ah, tai tai!"

About this time, I discovered that Kimie had a talent I had been totally unaware of. We had some old illustrated Japanese books. In one was a black-and-white print of horses that Kitty just loved. We were reluctant to spoil the book by cutting the picture out. So, Kimie offered to copy it for her. Not expecting much, I brought Kimie some Japanese paper, *sumi* ink and the brush I had bought in Osaka seven years before (for half a yen). She reproduced the picture free hand—perfectly, down to the minutest detail. We all were stunned, and Kitty was delighted. A decade later, Kimie would further expand her previously hidden artistic abilities, always to my delight and amazement.

Back on campus, I was doing well in my studies, keeping a roughly A- average. For one political science course in fall 1952, I helped with a door-to-door opinion survey of voter preferences in the presidential campaign. My essay on that earned me an A+ and the professor's suggestion that I submit it in a national competition! I let that go by, for it seemed to me that my academic advantage was due mainly to the maturity I had gained during my six years away from Cal.

Advanced Japanese courses in the Oriental Languages Department focused on Japanese literature, especially medieval lit. My interest was in the social sciences, the keys to understanding today's Japan. So, I took just main-line courses that would help me the most. Prof. Boodberg's course on kanji classification was required. For that he led us through some Chinese classical poetry. That helped me appreciate

Chinese sentiment; and my growing familiarity with the kanji was immediately useful on the job at the EAL.

Boodberg, incidentally, had an interesting background. Ethnically "white" Russian, he and his family had escaped Bolshevik Russia after World War I, fleeing through Siberia and eventually making their way to the USA. In the mid-1920s, he was a grad student on the campus when a great fire swept over the Berkeley hills. He described that scene to me: While students and faculty hurried about the town in a panic, he was sitting quietly under a tree studying. A newspaper reporter approached and asked whether he was not concerned about the fire. He replied that he found his books more interesting. A true scholar!

The federal GI Bill was paying for our most basic needs; and my library work plus living at home (I chipped in maybe $40/month) enabled us to get by. In 1952, we replaced the '40 Mercury with a '46 Ford and a few years later replaced that with a '48 Studebaker, each vehicle bought on credit.

Those cars let us access the many Bay area amenities: zoos, parks, fishing lakes and the Bay itself. In September 1954, when Hugh-ko was 10 days shy of three, we were fishing on a rickety jetty in the Bay. I was catching nothing on my 9-foot bamboo pole with cheese on the hooks. So, when someone nearby hooked a fish, I handed Hugh-ko the pole and went to see what had been caught. Seconds later, Hugh-ko called out excitedly, "Daddy, Daddy!!" He had a 12-inch striped bass on the line. He has loved fishing ever since. Is that "paternally induced piscaphilia" or what?

We often visited San Francisco's Golden Gate Park, its aquarium and museums. Also Muir Woods's stunning redwoods, Playland at the Beach and Cliff House, a petrified forest and Geyserville in Napa County. During two summer vacations we sent Ritsuko by train to Modesto to spend a week on the co-op farm with George & Vonnie and their little girls. In 1954, we picked Ritsuko up after her week there and drove on to Yosemite to see its natural wonders.

On weekends in spring 1953, I began teaching Kimie to drive our stick-shift '46 Ford, practicing on a road encircling Berkeley's Aquatic Park by the Bay. She initially had trouble coordinating the shift and clutch and that made the car buck. Riding in back, Hugh-ko (18 months old) enjoyed that and would laugh delightedly, "Mommy go bum*pity*, bum*pity*!" Verbally precocious he was. We never spoke baby-talk to him, and he responded by quickly learning to speak clearly. A year later, he had picked up the meaning of "also" and began using it often. So, we would tease by calling him "Hugh also" instead of Hugh-ko.

I side with the majority in advising against a husband teaching his wife to drive; but we could not afford the lessons. And, Kimie soon was able to drive around town and to her doctor appointments. She never had a good sense of direction; but in Berkeley one can almost always orient from Bay and city views or the hills that rise steeply behind the city.

At the end of most days, she came to the campus with Hugh-ko to pick me up. While they waited, they picked fresh watercress in Strawberry Creek. Also, pineapple guavas had been planted as decoration near Boalt Hall; but the northern Californians did not know they were edible. So, we would take a few for ourselves. Likewise, a large persimmon tree in front of the president's mansion. Fine Japanese persimmons were dropping to the ground and being left to rot. We made sure that some were eaten.

A bit later, Kimie and I went through a difficult period. She now was strong again after beating TB a second time and felt more self assertive. During the long months of her illness and convalescence when she was confined to bed, Mother had tried to help her morale and draw closer to her by spending much time chatting with her. Kimie appreciated that, but Mother overdid it. Kimie's Japanese sense of etiquette required her to keep smiling. The problem was cultural differences in communication styles. Where we tend to elaborate on subjects ad infinitum, the Japanese way is understatement, purveying meaning with a few phrases. In a word, Mother was talking Kimie to death.

I was so preoccupied with school, work and my studies that I did not fully grasp the situation until Kimie began taking her frustration out on me. Also, we were very pinched financially. So, we had some heated spats. After some months of that, I consulted with Mary about the problem. She was sympathetic and said that, if it came to that, she would support me on getting a divorce and knew that Mother would, too.

That was like ice water in the face. I wanted sage advice, not a divorce. I was totally committed to Kimie; yet it seemed my family was willing to turn against her. Sobered up, I looked into renting an apartment where we would be more on our own, but soon realized that with car payments, Kimie's medical expenses and the costs of raising our two children, we could not afford a decent place. Part of our problem was that Kimie had never before experienced such tight family finances. I was working all possible hours at the East Asian Library, but earning only about $2000 annually. Besides the GI Bill, a $150 scholarship from the University helped me to continue.

About this time, eldest sister Louise asked Mother to join her in Indiana, where she and Charley James now had four children. Louise needed Mother's help, and we in Berkeley needed more elbow room psychologically. With sister Kitty now in her own apartment, this meant we would have the Tacoma Avenue house to ourselves.

# FINAL BERKELEY YEARS

## (1954-56)

In 1952, Congress finally passed the long-overdue revision of U.S. immigration law, the McCarran-Walters Act, liberalizing Asian immigration and enabling Japanese with permanent-resident status to gain citizenship. The Japanese-American Citizens League (JACL), especially its man in Washington, Mike Masaoka, had lobbied long and hard for this, as it would finally permit the Issei to become U.S. citizens. Kimie would be eligible to apply three years after the law's enactment. I had decided to try for a career as a Foreign Service Officer (diplomat). In that era, a candidate's spouse had to be a U.S. citizen. So, Kimie signed up for a citizenship course for adults at a local high school to assure her passing the citizenship test.

On March 22, 1955, exactly ten years after I was drafted, she became a citizen. Ever after, we celebrated March 22 as our "double anniversary." Of course, we already had two wedding anniversaries: August 21 and December 3. Checking my files while writing this biography, I re-discovered two more dates for us to celebrate: February 11, when we first met, and May 4, our engagement date.

In January 1954, I completed my undergraduate work "with highest honors" and was voted into Phi Beta Kappa. I also took the Foreign Service exam for the first time, but decided to go for an M.A. degree to keep my options open, on the advice of my advisor, Professor Scalapino, who by then was one of America's prime Asia specialists.

In Spring 1954, EAL's Japanese bibliographer, Betty McKinnon (yes, the daughter of my 1951 kanji teacher) went to Japan to finalize a large EAL purchase: some 30,000 volumes from the Mitsui family library. Many would prove to be rare manuscripts and books hundreds of years old. I was one of a team from EAL that spent much of summer 1954 helping to sort through that collection. I now could read enough Japanese that I could be fairly helpful. In the semester just ended, for a Japanese course I had done a book report on a Japanese philosophy book (*Zen no Kenkyu*, or a study of goodness by NISHIDA Kitaro). That spring, with Kimie's help, I also translated for a fellow poli sci student a Japanese Communist Party article.

One of the interesting grad students I met at the library was Hans Bielenstein, a Ph.D. candidate in Chinese studies. We worked together most of that same summer on the Mitsui collection. A Swede, he had previously studied in London and Peking (pre-communist era). As a teenager he had fought as a volunteer helping the Finns repel the Russian invasion of 1940. He had endless amazing experiences to relate. Later, he would help Canberra University start up its Chinese studies department. A Swede with an American Ph.D. heading Chinese studies in Australia—how international can you get?

Others whom I knew at the EAL: a double major in math and Chinese studies who was snapped up by the CIA, a Mormon specializing in Mongolian studies, an avid specialist in Tibetan Buddhism—one of a tiny number of Americans who could read Tibetan, and several specialists in Japanese medieval literature who would play central roles in that field in the 1960s, '70s and '80s. At the library, I also met senior scholars whose books were the standard in their fields at the time. An interesting community of brains!

Back on Tacoma Avenue in 1955, an old problem cropped up. Kimie had her US citizenship, but she also had to renounce her Japanese citizenship. We applied to the Japanese Consulate General in San Francisco for help; but the Consulate had to verify her citizenship from her Family Register—the document that in Japan records parentage, births, marriages, deaths, etc. In my letter accompanying that document, I reported, as Kimie had told me, that she was Ritsuko's foster mother, not her natural mother. As I was finalizing these papers, Kimie began to get nervous; but she always had become tense when dealing with government authorities.

Soon we had an inquiry back from the consulate: The Family Register showed Kimie was Ritsuko's natural mother, contrary to what my letter stated. Now Kimie grew very agitated and wanted to stop the whole procedure. But, she had to shed her Japanese citizenship for me to be eligible for the Foreign Service and to certify Ritsuko's deriving US citizenship from her mother's naturalization. That situation remained unresolved for several days.

One Saturday afternoon, I was mulling over this puzzle while weeding a lady's garden (for pay). Then it struck me that the only explanation was that Ritsuko was in fact her own daughter—something she had hidden from me since 1946, fearing that the truth would scare me off; and since then she had been too ashamed of her white lie to undo her story. I confronted her as gently as I could with my new perception of the truth, and she did not deny it. Now the legalities were quickly resolved and we became an all-American family.

In fact, resolving this matter helped in Kimie's further Americanization. For, Japanese social etiquette says one must carefully avoid telling someone anything that may be upsetting or that they may not want to hear. So, Kimie's elaborate fib was a natural way for her to deal with the facts on Ritsuko back in 1946. Ending that fiction in 1955 helped rid Kimie of a burden she had been carrying and let her become the more open, confident and sociable person that her true nature was impelling her to be.

By now, Ritsuko was a teenager, in the Girl Scouts and entering junior high school. Hugh-ko was four and big boy enough to start pre-school. Kimie began attending pre-school mothers' classes at Thousand Oaks Elementary at the co-op pre-school where the mothers took turns helping out.

After Mother left to Indiana, Kimie told me some very intriguing things. She said that when she first entered our house back in November 1950, she felt an eerie chill, despite the warm welcome she was receiving. And, while in bed recovering from TB and childbirth, she had repeatedly seen, while on the edge of sleep, the figure of a man who stood at the foot of the bed and said, "This was my house; I lived here." Never in a threatening way, though. Also, when she went down to the basement laundry room, she felt the same cold chill and sensed that someone had died there with great loss of blood. So, she always tried to take our dog Clown down there with her. (Yes, the same Clown I had with me at Webb in 1944.)

We talked over these experiences; and Kimie decided to ask Mrs. Badger about it—our next-door neighbor who had lived there since before our house was built. Kimie asked her if she knew anything unusual about the previous homeowners. Mrs. Badger told her that one night when those neighbors were holding a party, the husband went down to the basement and slit his own throat—in the laundry area.

Then I asked Kimie if she had ever before had such an otherworldly experience. Matter-of-factly, she said:

> "When I was about 10, I was playing near our house one afternoon when I saw Grandmother coming to visit. I greeted her, but kept on playing. When I went inside, I did not see her and asked where she was. No one had seen her. Soon after, we received a phone call that she had died a few hours earlier in Tokyo. So, I guess her spirit was coming to say goodbye to us."

Now I was in grad school. My federal GI Bill eligibility ended, and I went onto the California GI Bill, which paid slightly less. So, I took an evening job at the Campus Theater, which ran classical and art films. I was assistant manager, with the manager located at another theater nearby. I supervised the cashier, candy-bar clerk and usher, welcomed patrons and changed the marquee signs (every two or three weeks). The pay was about $100 a month, more than making up for the switch to the state GI Bill. Of course, I continued working at the East Asian Library, took a full course load and began research for my M.A. thesis.

One could do that in the days before cable TV, computer games and the Internet.

In fall 1954 I fell while changing the marquee sign. The ladder slipped out from under me and I dropped 10 feet to the sidewalk, banging a hip and pulling a ligament in one elbow. For the next 10 years I would periodically have severe hip pains as a result.

That fall, too, I did my first translation job from an outside source—a government research station article on plant diseases. I could not have handled it without the EAL's special dictionaries and some help from my Kimie. Over the next 18 months I translated several more such articles. Not big pay, but every bit helped.

Now the State Department informed me that I had passed the Foreign Service exam, and in fall 1955 I met with an oral panel in San Francisco. The session went well until an examiner, noting my Japan focus, asked my opinion of the Tokyo War Crime Trials. I said that the trials were inevitably seen by the Japanese public as "victor's justice," while the Allied prosecutors showed a very Occidental bias on Japanese motives and actions. So, I concluded, it would have been better to wait until the Japanese people themselves were ready to try their military leaders for having led them on such a disastrous course.

That viewpoint was politically incorrect, of course, in those years. Just a few years before, Berkeley had its "loyalty oath" crisis; and McCarthyism was just then beginning to die down, while colonialism still held sway in many parts of the world. Sympathy for non-Western viewpoints aroused doubts. Needless to say, the panel did not pass me.

One of my most memorable graduate seminars was Scalapino's "Colonialism in Asia." Bob Scalapino himself was always thought provoking and highly knowledgeable. Mid-way through the course, he had to take a trip to Asia and got as a substitute teacher a former British colonial administrator from Malaya. In that class were two remarkable students. One was a brilliant Israeli, who later would be a senior diplomat in his nation's Foreign Service.

The other was a Kenyan from a Kikuyu village in the area where Mau Mau terrorism was then rampant. He got a mission-school education in Nairobi, *hitch-hiked* to England for more education, then made his way to Baltimore for graduate study at Johns Hopkins University, earning his way in part as an elevator operator. Communication between poli sci professors brought him to Berkeley on a scholarship. He and the Israeli often got into intense discussions with each other and with Scalapino, making the whole seminar truly lively. Soon after, the Kikuyu was speaking before public groups in the Bay area. Of course, he completed his Ph.D. A few decades later, he was Kenya's education minister.

After Scalapino returned from his absence, I became directly involved in the product of his trip. He had been scouring Japan for socialist and labor union journals, mainly from before World War II. He had them put on microfilm in Japan. Now, at the EAL I got the job of cataloging the two cartons of microfilm reels. A priceless archive of material.

In Fall '55 I began writing my thesis. Most poli sci grad students in international affairs were working on such topics as the Cold War, colonialism and communism. My sense about Japan was that, as active as domestic and foreign communists were in trying to influence Japanese policies, the Japanese public would forever see communism as foreign—alien to their cultural values—and so would ultimately reject it. I decided to study the nativist ideology of the ultranationalists whose ideas had led Japan into empire building (1895-1945) and so into confrontation with the European colonial powers and the United States.

One aspect of the Allied demilitarization of Japan (besides confiscating the military gear I saw coming into our battalion in Nishinomiya a decade earlier) was the ban on right-wing and ultranationalist books. Those were confiscated and sent to our Library of Congress. Any extra copies were meted out to universities with Asian studies programs. A fair number came to our East Asian Library at Cal. So, I knew we had good raw material for the topic I now chose for my thesis. Much of it was in antiquated Japanese and so a tough read. For another Scalapino seminar I had used some of those sources to write a 32-page paper, "Some Preliminary Notes on the Ideology of the Kokuryūkai."

The Kokuryūkai was a major ultranationalist society in Japan 1900-40 and had caught the attention of foreign correspondents in prewar Japan as the fountainhead of much of the ideology then inspiring Japan's hostile policies. They translated the name as "Black Dragon Society" and called its members black dragons—good sensationalist copy for those times. But, Kokuryū is the Japanese reading for Heilung, the Chinese name (meaning black dragon) for the Amur River that forms much of the boundary between northeast China and Russian Siberia. The "black dragons" chose that name because they considered the Amur, or Heilung River, a natural northern limit for an expanded Japanese empire on the Asian continent. Their hard-cover books were embossed with stylized dragons, and so encouraged outsiders to focus on the dragon in their society's name.

I got heavily into studying the Society's publications, and things were often quiet enough at the Campus Theater after about 9 PM that I was able to do much of my study on this sticky subject while standing at the candy bar.

In Spring '56 I again took the Foreign Service exam, and passed again; but now I had heard of the U.S. Information Agency (USIA) and knew it was part of State Department until 1953, after which it became an independent Agency—one of our government's new foreign affairs agencies. When USIA recruiters came to San Francisco to interview for their Management Intern Program, I jumped. I soon was accepted for this agency that was "telling America's story to the world."

Being accepted by USIA was not contingent on my completing the M.A. work; but I was determined to finish. Urged on by Kimie, I redoubled my efforts to finish the thesis, now titled "The Kokuryūkai in Northeast Asia," by June '56. I did that and the faculty review committee (including Scalapino) approved it. And I aced my last seminar with an A grade. I was done.

I have continued my interest in rightwing ideology in Japan ever since and keep books on that topic in my library. For, it is no fossil topic, even if today's groups are on the fringe of politics. Sound trucks of rightwing groups have regularly cruised Japan's cities for decades, blaring extremist messages. Assassinations or attempted assassinations by rightwingers punctuated Japan's domestic politics into the 1960s and '70s; and rightwing influences on Japanese school texts have regularly roiled Japan's relations with its Asian neighbors, who are ever on the alert for a revival of the nativist ideology.

My study at Berkeley in the '50s helped to temper the overly pro-Japan bent I developed in the years that Kimie and I were battling the anti-Asian bias of U.S. immigration policy. Through objective study of international relations in Asia before and after World War II, I had a clearer picture of the interactions between Japanese and American values and policies that had contributed to the outbreak of war between our two nations.

Also, Senator Langer's help in getting Kimie and Ritsuko to America and the lessened bias of the 1953 immigration law showed us that our system can correct its errors. So, where I had once seen the government as an adversary, I now was ready to become part of it, in a career with USIA that I hoped would give me a role in helping to build better and stronger US-Japan ties, and to pursue our mission to help insure that Kimie's family would never again be considered part of an enemy nation.

*Family in 1928*

*Hugh and Brother George - 1932*

*My first day in Japan - 1945*

*Already a Tech-5*

*Kimie's ID photo*

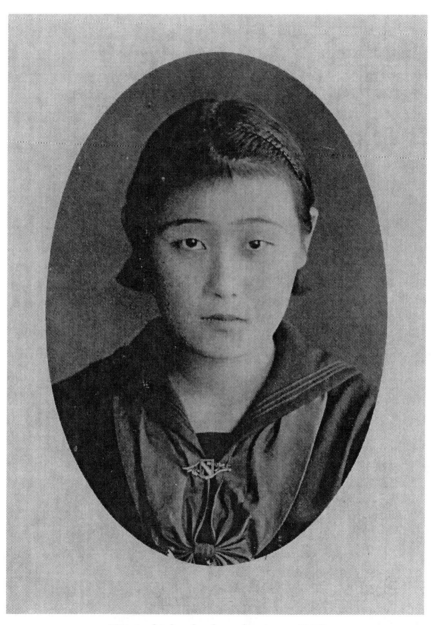

*Kimie: high-school graduation - 1937*

*Spring in our Berkeley yard*

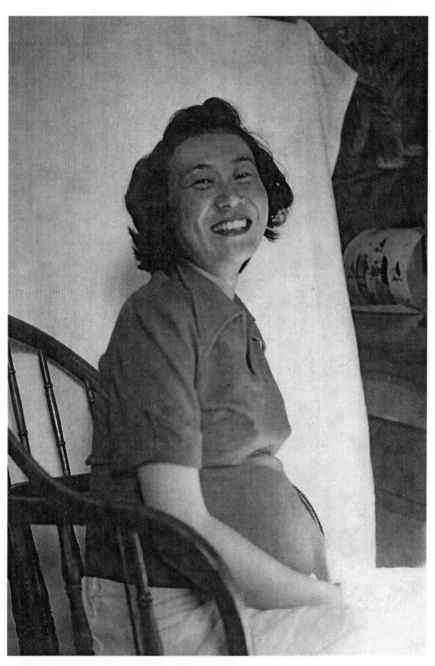

*Kimie - 10 days to go*

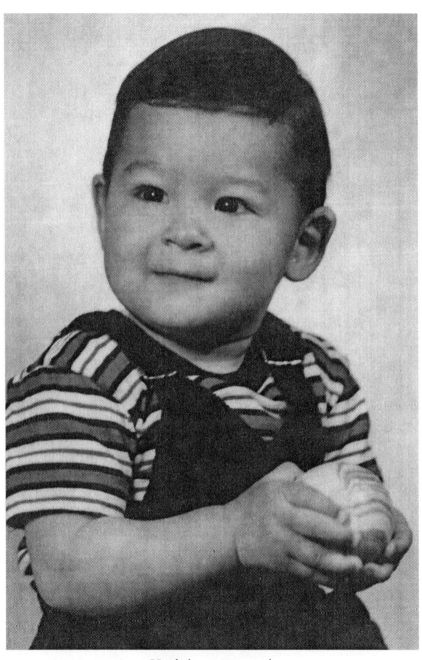

*Hugh-ko at 18 months*

*Studio pic of Kimie*

# PART II:
# EARLY CAREER YEARS

## WASHINGTON AND POINTS WEST

# A CAPITAL BEGINNING

## (1956-60)

So, I had a job waiting for me at USIA in Washington, D.C., as one of the agency's five management interns for 1956. With no home there and almost no acquaintances in that area, we decided I should go first, get set up with USIA and begin looking for a house. Kimie and the children would remain in Berkeley and come when I gave the signal.

On an early August weekend, I flew east into terra incognito. I had never been east of the Mississippi; and even my parents had not been east of the Mississippi since 1920. So, as the plane came in over the Potomac to land at Washington National, I took in the aerial view of this new territory with keen curiosity.

Before leaving Berkeley, I had arranged with a college friend to stay with his sister and her family in Hollin Hills, Alexandria VA. So, I collected my bags and took a cab to that pleasant suburb. Arriving at the sister's front door, I found no one home. I went next door to inquire. I was told that the family was on vacation for the next 10 days and had left the door key with that neighbor. As my explanation was reasonable, they gave me the key and I moved in, using one of the children's bedrooms.

On Monday I reported to USIA Personnel, where I met fellow interns Jerry Inman from Stanford, Bob Speck from Chicago, John Clyne and Stan Silverman from the Bronx. Stan had attended Cal, so that we formed a kind of bond.

After spending years in Berkeley's cool summers, I experienced climatic shock in adjusting to the capital's steamy heat. When I went outside after working in air-conditioned offices, the humidity instantly fogged my glasses. Not all offices were air conditioned, so that one had to adjust to changing environments.

We were to spend three months being oriented in various USIA offices, then three months each in its administrative divisions to complete our intern year. We received training ranks of CAF-7; but since I had left the QM Depot as a CAF-7 six years earlier, I began at the stratospheric level of CAF-7 Step 2. I found it ironic that five additional years of college were worth just one step increase within grade; but we were to be promoted to CAF-9 after our training year.

Of course, I communicated often with Kimie and the children, but was busy enough getting my bearings the first several weeks that I did no house hunting.

After I had spent 10 days based in Hollin Hills, the family came home. They were totally shocked to find a stranger living there! It turned out that my college pal in Berkeley had not followed through on getting his sister's approval for me to stay in their home. They had not expected me at all. I had to vacate post haste. So, I took a cab into Washington and checked with the YMCA, just two blocks from USIA. They were able to give me a room for just one night, but referred me to a nearby rooming house. I went there the next day and found a shared room at $40/month that would be adequate. As the other boarder worked evenings, we rarely saw each other. Now I was better based for starting a house hunt.

In September, I contacted a cousin, Oliver (Ollie) Popenoe, who worked nearby at the Executive Office Building beside the White House, and sought his advice on where I might house-hunt. He promised to ask around and contact me.

A few weeks later, he called back to tell me about a house in his neighborhood that had just come on the market and might fit our needs. Its owner, a State Department officer, planned to move to Herndon, a quiet rural area of northern Virginia.*

The following Saturday I met Ollie in the Maryland suburb of Silver Spring and went to see the house. It was a two-bedroom "Cape Cod Rambler" with one bathroom plus an unfinished sub-floored attic. It would do; and I immediately called Kimie and got her tentative okay to proceed. Our cash reserves were minimal and would be needed to get my family across the country. So, I (a) applied for a "GI Loan" to cover a mortgage of some $9000 and (b) called my uncle in Madison, Wisconsin, who had in the past helped my older siblings in similar financial situations. He agreed to lend me a down payment of $2000. I told him the one drawback was that the property backed up against the right-of-way of the B&O Railroad's line between Washington and Chicago.

When I relayed this information to Kimie (apparently forgetting to tell her that trains would run through our back yard), she was thrilled. We began planning for her and the children to come east. She contacted sisters Mary and Kitty and arranged for Kitty to take over the house on Tacoma Avenue. Kimie had to dispose of some of our things and arrange for the rest to be packed and shipped. She began handling these and other details with the same competence she had displayed a decade earlier as chief factotum for the Film Exchange's commanding officer.

In USIA, our initial three months of training ended with our debriefing by a personnel officer who had supervised our training. To emphasize how lucky he considered us to be, he told us of his early years. He said (in so many words),

I grew up on a Midwest farm; and whenever I went into town, I could see that we farm boys didn't get much respect. But, I noticed that college men were respected. So, I began asking my parents about college. Eventually, I went to college and got my degree. I came

---

* Several years after the man moved there, plans were announced for building Dulles Airport in that vicinity, putting him under the path of the jets and SSTs using Dulles. Truly, "the best laid plans ... "!

back and got a job in town. But, somehow I still didn't seem to get much respect. My parents were proud of me and would take out my diploma—a bit bug-eaten by then—and talk about my career. Then I noticed that government men were respected. So, I decided to try for a government job. The New Deal was in full swing then, and I was able to land a CAF-3 position. You young fellows will get your CAF-9 at the end of this year and could easily get a CAF-11 a few years after that. So, sometimes I still wonder if I'm getting any respect.

We had a hard time keeping straight faces during this recitation.

After my first few months at USIA, I learned something the USIA recruiters in San Francisco had not made clear: USIA's civil service and Foreign Service were distinct and separate. The Management Intern program was civil service. Getting a Foreign Service position was another matter. I was advised to remain as a Management Intern and see later about transferring into the Foreign Service. About that time I received State's invitation to meet with an oral examining panel again. I liked what I had seen of USIA and so declined.

My first training assignment was with USIA's Finance Division. After just a week there, I was asked to join an inspection officer for a week in New York, reviewing control procedures at USIA's warehouse in Brooklyn, focusing on their controls for books and other cultural materials bound for USIA posts abroad. So, I was to have my first visit to New York. The inspector and I took hotel rooms in Manhattan and daily rode the subway into Brooklyn to work at the warehouse.

In the evenings we worked on our report draft, but also did some sightseeing or went to movies. A memorable experience was going to a 50¢ movie house on lower Broadway to see Humphrey Bogart in "Left Hand of God." Part way through the movie we noticed a man squirming a bit in his seat two rows ahead of us. Finally, he turned around and said to the man behind him, "Will you quit breath'n! You're makin' a cold wind on my neck!" Ah, New Yorkers!

On the weekend sandwiched into our stay in New York, my colleague went back to Washington to be with his family. I went to the Natural

History Museum, the Metropolitan Art Museum and the UN Building. And, I phoned Kimie.

She was feeling the stress of preparing to leave Berkeley after six years and even said maybe she would just stay in Berkeley and not come east at all. She could so easily out-contrary "Mary, Mary, …"! By the end of the phone conversation, though, I had talked her out of that frame of mind.

Before I left Berkeley, we had bought our first new car ever: a 1956 Studebaker Sky Hawk. I was glad Kimie would not be driving an older car across the country with the two children. She had Bekins movers pick up our meager possessions—meager because, living on Tacoma Avenue, we had mostly used Mother's major furniture pieces. So now, Kimie packed the Sky Hawk full with our remaining things—such that 5-year-old Hugh-ko had to sit atop some of them all the way across the U.S. Kimie had gone to AAA and gotten maps and advice on motels for her long drive. This was, after all, the era before the Interstate system was built.

So, they set out, just after Thanksgiving 1956. My intrepid samurai girl, who had arrived from Japan just six years before and learned to drive just 3½ years earlier, was starting a long drive across the U.S. We had visited the San Joaquin Valley and Yosemite, so that she had a good idea of how to get from the Bay area to the "Big Valley." She had AAA's maps, but this was the girl noted for being "directionally challenged" and not trusting maps. So, the trip would test her courage as much as her driving skills.

To avoid any chance of her getting lost in the Middle Atlantic States, we had agreed that I would take a bus to whatever place she designated for a rendezvous. So, each night of the final days of that drive, Kimie called to update me on her progress.

She easily made the connection from old Highway 99 in the lower San Joaquin to Route 66 at about dusk of the first day, but didn't realize how long and lonely the transit of the Mojave Desert would be. It was late at night when they finally saw the lights of Needles on the California-Arizona border—their first stopover.

The second day, they drove into Arizona. At one point, Kimie pulled into a small-town gas station for an oil change. There Indians were lounging around and looking at her curiously, as if trying to guess which tribe she was from. She had known of Indians only from movies in which Indians were always the bad guys. So, she had Ritsuko and Hugh-ko stay in the car as it was hoisted on the lift for the oil change and grease job.

On they went, through Albuquerque, across a corner of Texas and into Oklahoma. She called me the first time from Tulsa. By then, she was getting a real feel for how vast the USA is. At Joplin, on the Missouri side of the border with Oklahoma, the Rte. 66 signs were confusing and she took a turn to the northwest instead of continuing northeast. A kind service station operator there set her straight.

When Kimie phoned from her Indiana stop, we agreed to meet the next morning in Cambridge, Ohio. I prepared to leave Washington that evening after work. Problem: It was a Friday, and many federal employees recruited from states north and west of the capital had flocked to the Greyhound depot to go home for the weekend.

So, at the bus station I found long lines and could not board the first bus leaving for Pittsburgh. After a 1½-hour wait, an older bus rolled up and took on us leftovers. The trip started uneventfully, but just as we reached the Pennsylvania Turnpike snow began to fall. Then we heard a banging in the motor. The driver stopped and went out to find the trouble—a broken piston, he told us. In the cold he opened up the engine and removed the broken parts. That consumed over two hours on the highway shoulder. When we got going again, we all cheered the driver.

About ten minutes later, POW! A tire had blown. We all groaned. As the weary, chilled driver was changing the tire, a Highway Patrolman stopped to offer help. But, by then the driver was nearly finished and ready to go on. Snow was still falling; and the motor was running very

126

rough due to the missing piston. So, some 100 miles east of Pittsburgh nearly at midnight, the driver pulled into a service area and phoned for a replacement bus. Some hours later, we saw that bus arrive, on the other side of the Turnpike. He was not allowed to cross over without a Highway Patrol car to lead him across; but the Patrol now was helping cars that had crashed or slid off the icy highway.

Now we Greyhound passengers began bumming rides from motorists who pulled into the service area. About 4:30 AM, I caught a ride with two newlyweds bound for Michigan; but their route ran north of Pittsburgh. So, at 5:30 AM I found myself standing in slushy roadside snow thumbing a ride. I finally was picked up by a couple of steel workers going to work. They took me to within a few blocks of the Greyhound station. I was resigned to missing my bus, scheduled to head west from Pittsburgh at 6:30 AM.

At the station, however, I learned that the snow had delayed most buses, and mine now was scheduled to leave at 9 AM. I called Kimie at the motel and explained my situation. I finally got to the designated motel in Ohio about noon, but was told that Kimie had checked out! Now what to do?

I started walking away from the motel, mulling that over when I met Kimie and the children returning to the motel in the Sky Hawk. They had gone out for lunch. It was a most joyous reunion after four months of separation, the longest that Kimie and I would ever be apart.

The early December snowfall had not lingered long in the mid-Atlantic lowlands and our drive into D.C. went smoothly. We stayed at a downtown hotel for the next several days, while we bought furniture and awaited the arrival of our Bekins van. About a week later, we had made our new home habitable and prepared to spend our first night there, with Ritsuko and Hugh-ko in bunk beds in the second bedroom.

About 11 PM a B&O train rumbled by. Kimie nearly leaped from the bed. "What was that!?" she cried out. That was when I realized I had not told her about our proximity to the rail line. Over time she learned to ignore it, if not accept it.

Not only was the B&O right behind us, but also a spur line branched off close by. On many a Sunday morning, a B&O locomotive would sit out on the spur, tooting signals to the B&O station, a mile away—a sure cure for sleeping in on Sundays. The sole fringe benefit of the railroad's proximity was that for decades its crews had burned off weeds on the right-of-way up to our back fence. That had created good compost nearly a foot deep. We mined that over the next several years for the vegetable garden we put in each spring, on our side of the fence of course.

A little backtracking (no railway pun intended). A friend at the East Asiatic Library in Berkeley was a Japanese woman whose cousin, Shotaro Takahashi, was a Japanese diplomat now assigned to the Japanese Embassy in Washington. We knew that initially my salary would barely cover our basic expenses and mortgage payments. So, I had contacted him about a job in the Embassy for Kimie. Early in January 1957, he called to ask when she could start work. We had put that off while getting settled; but now I took her to meet him and arrange for her to start as a typist/receptionist.

Ritsuko enrolled in the junior high school a few blocks away, with no streets to cross. Hugh-ko went to kindergarten at the primary school next to Ritsuko's school. We also arranged for an older couple across the street to care for Hugh-ko after school until one of us got home from work. So, we had a viable living arrangement. That is, until June's muggy weather set in.

I tried to persuade Kimie that she would adjust; but, accustomed to Berkeley's cool clime, Kimie would not accept stifling in the steamy Mid-Atlantic summer nights. She went right out and bought a window air conditioning unit, getting a loan from a bank secured by her own salary. The unit was powerful enough to make our small house relatively comfortable.

In the '56 presidential campaign, Congressional Democrats were angered by the political speeches of the GOP-appointed USIA Director; and in the next budgeting season they retaliated by sharply pruning USIA's budget. So, as our training year ended, the Agency had few interesting management jobs to offer me. On my own initiative I lined up a job in USIA's Office of Research, as Japan/Korea research officer. Bob Speck decided to leave USIA and took a job with IBM. Jerry Inman made the switch to USIA's Foreign Service and was assigned to Korean language training in preparation for a Korea assignment. That left only Clyne and Silverman in the management field. Silverman would later serve as USIA's chief budget officer for several decades. Clyne split his Agency career between management jobs in Washington and administrative positions in our overseas posts.

Now I was working again in the Northeast Asia field. My job: to review and analyze a wide range of documents (many highly classified) on Japanese and Korean opinion trends, media commentary and opinion polls and to draft weekly summaries of public opinion trends in Japan and Korea for USIA and other foreign affairs agencies. My studies at Cal had included quite a bit on Korea, and of course I had closely followed postwar events in Korea and so had some background on Korean affairs.

After some four months on the job, I noted in many intelligence reports on Korea a trend of growing student unrest. In early 1958 I included in one weekly trend report a few paragraphs that noted this. A week later, a "zinger" came back from the Political Section of our Seoul Embassy vigorously protesting this item and asking where USIA got the authority to do political analysis. I had considered it an analysis of social psychology.

My boss had cleared the item before it went out and defended me, pointing out that I had merely seen an apparent opinion trend between the lines of reporting by the intelligence sections in our Embassy. The problem: the Political Section in Seoul had not reported any such trend. Less than a year later, students in Seoul launched massive riots that ultimately led to the overthrow of President Syngman Rhee. A short time later, Korea's generals staged a coup that would begin 30 years of rule by military dictators.

Things were calmer in Japan; and I enjoyed analyzing Japan's more familiar trends.

On the home front, Kimie settled into her Embassy job well. Her bright intelligence and outgoing nature made her a popular staff member and her near-bilingual use of both languages made her valuable in many ways. Japan's diplomats, at best, had experience dating only from 1952, when the Occupation ended and Japan regained full sovereignty. The diplomats' wives, too, often arrived with little English or knowledge of how to manage a household in our very strange land.

So, most of the diplomats turned to Kimie for advice and help with a myriad of problems: renting and equipping their homes, getting their children into school, arranging medical care for their wives, dealing with their many traffic accidents (as their driving experience also was quite shallow), etc. Kimie also became the Embassy's interface with dealers in office supplies, duty-free liquor and so on. We sometimes got phone calls from the Japanese diplomats at night when a child or wife suddenly took sick, asking Kimie to meet them at a hospital to interpret between the American doctors and their Japanese patients.

One night about midnight we had a call from the Silver Spring police, who explained that they had stopped a Japanese man for drunk driving who claimed diplomatic immunity. We dressed and drove the two miles to the police station. It turned out that the man was the son of Japan's UN Ambassador Toshikazu Kase. He had driven down from New York and had an overly liquid dinner along the way. In those days, local police were not clued in on the niceties of diplomatic immunity. So, it took some persuasion from us to convince the police that his diplomatic status indeed should be honored.

A perk of Kimie's job was that, in compiling the embassy's orders for duty-free liquor, she was given a commission each time of a few bottles for herself. So, over the years we built up a fair-sized liquor collection. At BYOB parties with friends and co-workers, we were never short.

Neither of us drank much, however. Kimie did go out with other Embassy staffers sometimes for lunch and cocktails. At a party with the other USIA interns, she once showed her drinking inexperience by asking for a scotch and tonic.

One of Kimie's Japanese Embassy co-workers was Mary Eary (whom we liked to call Eary Mary—the Japanese word-order for personal names). She had grown up in a poor area of Washington, D.C., where her family had no indoor plumbing. At a party one evening, she told us her life story. As she gaily related the tale—like one by Faulkner—I began mentally kicking myself for not having brought a tape recorder.

At the end of WWII, still a teenager, she married a handsome Marine whose spiffy uniform had bowled her over. About then he was discharged. For their honeymoon, they took a train from Washington to West Virginia to visit the groom's family. Getting off at a rural station, Mary expected the family would have a car waiting for them.

No car. No one from the family. They started walking, carrying their own luggage.

Before descending into the hollow where the family lived, the spiffy bridegroom stopped, took off his GI boots, slung them over his shoulder and rolled up his pant legs before going on to the family's two-room house, which also had no indoor plumbing.

On Sundays, the mother would boil up a big pot of pinto beans, the entrée for the following week's meals. On Saturdays, the pot was washed out and everyone used it for taking their sponge baths. The newlyweds' main daytime recreation on that honeymoon was shooting rats from atop the chicken coop.

After a few weeks, his separation pay running out, the ex-Marine found a job in a nearby town, working graveyard shift in a mill. He rented a basement apartment in the town; and every night as he left for work, he locked the door from the outside, warning Mary to stay put—to keep the neighbors from bothering her, he explained.

She had noticed that the neighbors upstairs *were* noisy, sometimes even rowdy.

By now, Mary's expectations were being seriously short-changed. They had fights.

Then she learned that the whole building—minus their apartment—was a "cat house." Though pregnant, she made up her mind to leave. One night she broke out a window and went home to D.C. Over the next several years, they alternately lived together and separated. And, produced two daughters. Whenever her husband failed to send the child support, she had him jailed. She found jobs in Washington and so somehow got by.

Eventually, she got divorced and found work at the Japanese Embassy.

Shortly after this recitation on her life, she married an embassy chauffeur (attracted by the uniform?). Last we heard, the couple was happy and the two girls were doing well.

About this time, Kimie bought a 1950 Plymouth from a departing diplomat, so that she would have her own transportation. I usually commuted to work by bus, as parking at USIA, two blocks from the White House, was very limited.

In 1958, Kimie's reputation for intelligent efficiency induced the Japanese Embassy's military attaches to offer her a more responsible position in their office. She turned the offer down. Because I was in a Government position that required a security clearance, she explained. She could foresee possibly awkward situations since she was bilingual. So, she remained a receptionist/typist, helping people visiting or phoning the embassy, typing the ambassador's speeches, etc.

The job had other interesting aspects. When Prime Minister Kishi came in 1959 for talks with President Eisenhower on trade and the bilateral security relationship, he brought a fishing pole as a present for Ike. His aides forgot to take the pole to the first meeting; and Kimie was asked to rush it down to Blair House where the two leaders were.

Innocently she drove up and parked in front of Blair House (the official guest house). Guards and Secret Service men instantly closed in to shoo her away. She had to explain about the pole and get one of the Secret Servicemen to promise to take the gift pole right in.

That same year, the first politically hot postwar US-Japan trade dispute was simmering: stainless steel flatware. Japanese tableware was flooding the U.S. market and sending major American tableware makers screaming to Congress and the White House for relief.

In fall 1958, a Japanese delegation came to Washington—trade officials and representatives of the Japanese manufacturers. It seemed that 90% of Japan's flatware was made in one small town, Tsubame, whose Mayor Tamaki was in the delegation. Most had never before been in the United States; and Kimie, with her usual charm and efficiency, gave them valuable tips about getting around, dealing with their hotels, etc.

The outcome of the meetings between the two sides was an agreed-on quota for imports of the Japanese tableware, a far better outcome than the embargo or steep tariffs the Japanese had feared might be imposed. So, they left in good spirits and thanked Kimie profusely for all her help with social and logistical matters.

By this time, I had been promoted to GS-12. (The GS [general service] designation had replaced the old CAF). So, our finances were now less straitened. We could take day trips to some of the area's sights, Chesapeake Bay beaches and, with Hugh-ko and Ritsuko, to the zoo and Smithsonian museums. We made a trip to nearby Lily Ponds in rural Maryland where we bought a lovely long-tailed goldfish whose voluptuous movements led us to name it Marilyn Monroe. We mounted the tank in a living room wall where we could watch Marilyn during TV commercials.

A few times we went to the Patuxent River near the Chesapeake Bay to fish for crabs. We would buy some chicken necks, rent a rowboat, go out in the river and lower the chicken necks on a string to the bottom. After a while, we would gently raise them. Extra weight meant a crab was hanging on. With a dip net we would scoop up the crab and then lower the bait again. We often got 10-12 crabs and sometimes a few dozen in two or three hours on the water. Delicious experience! One time we took the Takahashis from the Embassy with us. (In subsequent years we socialized with them several times in Washington and Japan.)

We also discovered the shad runs on the Potomac. One could go down to the rocks along the river and net several gallons of the fish—with their roe—in an hour or less. The parts we didn't eat made excellent fertilizer for our vegetable garden.

From early 1957, I had resumed free-lance translating in my free time and had a fair amount of such work coming to me from a U.S. Government translation service. At times, when deadlines were tight, I would set up shop in the attic, which I had insulated, and work all night with a big mug of coffee to sustain me.

In fall 1958, Kimie took a trip to Japan to see her family, for the first time in eight years. She was gone for two weeks.

In early summer 1959, we had a call from my elder brother John. He was now a Methodist minister in a small town in western Washington State. He loved to fish and camp in his free time. He was calling to invite Hugh-ko for a two-week fishing and camping trip on the San Juan Islands in Puget Sound north of Seattle. At first, Kimie and I thought it was impractical. Hugh-ko was not yet 8 years old. How would he fly safely across the continent? But, after we had talked it over and consulted with the airlines, the proposal did not seem so odd. We put Hugh-ko on a plane in the care of the cabin crew; and John met him at the other end to take him to the islands that would, forever after, be Hugh-ko's idea of Eden. He had done some pup-tent camping in our back yard and was an enthusiastic Cub Scout. So, he had a fantastic time, and caught, among other things, a 17-pound ling cod about 2/3 as long as he was.

An embassy visitor whom Kimie charmed in 1959 was Douglas MacArthur II, nephew of the general, who dropped by the embassy for a courtesy call prior to leaving as our next ambassador to Japan. He was a career diplomat, but was casual and sociable in Kimie's office—shooting the breeze for a while with her before meeting with the embassy's top officers. We also met him at two Japan-America Society events before he left.

I believe it was fall 1959 that brother George, his wife Vonnie and their four children dropped by for a few hours' visit. They were transferring from a co-op community in north Georgia to a more economically sound one in New York state. In '57 or '58 I had driven Ritsuko down to north Georgia to visit the co-op farm for a few weeks, just as she had in Modesto several years earlier. So, we had had recent contact; but their visit was a very welcome chance to update those ties.

In spring 1960, USIA announced new procedures making it easier for officers in civil service positions to transfer into the Foreign Service. I immediately applied, for my aim all along had been the Foreign Service.

In Japan meanwhile, left-wing forces were rallying against their government's plan to renew the US-Japan Security Treaty. The Japanese public's postwar antipathy to things military and their affinity for pacifist causes lent wide support to the anti-Security Treaty camp. The White House had planned a grand Asia tour for President Eisenhower, ending in Tokyo to celebrate the Japanese Government's ratification of the renewed treaty (and to cap Ike's eight years as President). Kishi promised Ike that his Liberal Democratic Party (LDP) would get the Japanese Diet (national legislature) to ratify the treaty. But, the massed labor unionists and students kept escalating their daily demonstrations around the Diet and elsewhere in Tokyo and other cities.

A decisive event occurred at Tokyo's Haneda airport when Eisenhower's press secretary, Jim Hagerty, arrived with an advance team to check on the arrangements for the visit. Radical students massed at the airport and mobbed Hagerty's car as it tried to leave. Clearly, security could not be guaranteed if Eisenhower were to come. So, his Japan visit was canceled—hugely embarrassing the LDP, which nevertheless went on to ram treaty ratification through the Diet. Kishi resigned to take responsibility for the fiasco and was replaced by Hayato Ikeda, an economist whose promise of "income doubling" for the average citizen within a decade effectively diverted popular attention from defense issues to the economy and individual welfare.

In late spring 1960 we learned that Ritsuko, now 17, was going steady with "an older man"—Bill Geoghegan, who was attending Catholic University in the capital. We met him briefly when he came to take her on dates.

About this time, Nissan was trying to get a foothold in the Middle Atlantic auto market; and a sales representative came to the Japanese Embassy with a package deal: Datsun Bluebirds for $1000 each if 10 Japanese diplomats would buy one. Nine signed up. To round out the ten, Kimie was offered the same deal. We debated that for about one day and then jumped at it. We then had three cars, including the 1950 Plymouth, used mainly by Ritsuko. It was still running fine.

In June, my transfer into the Foreign Service was completed when first I, and then Kimie faced State-USIA oral panels probing our suitability. Just a few years earlier, it had been Foreign Service policy not to assign an officer to a country that was his spouse's native land. That policy now was junked. Kimie was nervous about facing the panel; but her strengths impressed the panel, and we both passed handily. My views on US-Japan relations were now—five years after my first paneling— not so off-the-wall.

In mid-summer I was offered a position in Japan: Branch Public Affairs Officer (BPAO) in Niigata, some 170 miles north of Tokyo on the Sea of Japan. The officer who had been there had not passed his home-leave physical, opening up the position unexpectedly.

Normally, an officer assigned to a substantive position (in contrast to an administrative job) in Japan must take two straight years of intensive language study before taking his post. I was tested at the State Department's Foreign Service Institute and rated 3 Speaking and 3 Reading (on a scale of 1 to 5)—quite adequate. I would have done better, but faced an awkward situation during the testing. I knew the examining teacher socially and felt I should not reveal that to the monitor, whom I assumed knew Japanese, too. It turned out that the monitor knew no Japanese and I could have been much more relaxed.

Now a thunderbolt: Bill and Ritsuko wanted to get married! She had just graduated from high school; and naturally we considered her much too young. We argued in vain. Bill's family was in favor; Bill and Rits (as she now preferred to be called) were adamant. We finally gave our approval and attended the wedding. But, it was hard to think of leaving our Rits as we prepared to leave for Japan.

We would also leave behind Choji, our personable beagle and Hugh-ko's pal of the past three years. We had taught Choji ("long ears" in Japanese) to sit up and beg, for which he was rewarded with food. Now we learned that he had been exploiting that trick. Even after we fed him, he would tour the neighborhood in the evening, bang on front doors with his paws and be sitting there begging for food when the door opened. His gluttony ran him up to almost 40 pounds; and we could not afford to fly him to Japan at that weight. So, we found him a rural home as we began winding up our affairs.

We also found a buyer for our home in Silver Spring, getting about 10% more for it than we had paid four years before. We deeded the '50 Plymouth to Ritsuko. USIA hired movers to pack our things and divide them into items for U.S. storage, items for surface shipment to Japan and the things for our accompanied luggage. We decided the Nissan Bluebird would be great for Japan, even though equipped with left-hand drive—opposite to the standard in Japan. We had dubbed the car "Hidari Jingoro," the nickname of the famed left-handed artist who had carved the three moneys and sleeping cat at Nikko's Toshogu Shrine, where we honeymooned 13 years earlier.

This, dear readers, brings my story to the point where it opened, November 1960, with the query by the lady personnel officer about where my loyalties lay. She did have reason to be curious about me.

# NIIGATA
## (1960-61)

After saying goodbye to Rits and Bill, we three—Kimie, Hugh-ko and I—flew first to Los Angeles. I had not visited California's southland since that last date in February 1945, unless we count my transit of the Mojave by train to and from Texas.

So, it was a shock to see, as we flew over the San Jacinto Mountains dividing the deserts from the citrus orchards and coastal clime, that L.A.'s notorious smog extended all the way to those mountains. The brown blanket obscured most landmarks, including Webb School. Only as the plane descended into the airport would we see such details as the Hollywood hills, the backyard swimming pools and the palm trees.

Staying aboard the plane at the airport, close by the Pacific, we watched the sun sink into the sea as the pilot waited for clearance to take off. We began taxiing just as the last bit of the sun's disk disappeared, and then watched fascinated as the sun rose out of the ocean again as our plane climbed. It set a second time as we flew north to San Francisco. Two sunsets in an hour! It was the eve of Election Day 1960, when Richard Nixon would experience his first political sunset.

We overnighted in the Bay area, long enough to see the family in Berkeley, and then flew off to Hawaii. Arriving in Honolulu in the early evening of Election Day, we were met by sister Louise and Charley James, now living across Oahu on Kaneohe Bay. In those days, we travelers wore suits and ties—totally out of place in Hawaii. So, at their home the family hurried to dress us in appropriate aloha wear. Hurried because they were having an Election Night party with friends and did not want it known they had such square relatives. In 1961, Charley James became administrative aide to Hawaii's first appointed senator, and they went to live in Washington, D.C., where suits are worn.

We stayed in Hawaii long enough for Louise to take us on a round-the-island tour, past pineapple fields and to Sea Life Park at the south end. And long enough to learn that JFK had squeaked by Nixon. After two days, we flew on to Japan, arriving there almost 15 years to the day after my 1945 landing at Nagoya and 10 years since we had returned to the USA.

In Tokyo, there were many changes to behold. We got our first look at the Tokyo Tower, taller than the Eiffel and completed only two years before—emblematic of Japan's firm intent to rise again to world prominence.

I had about three days in Tokyo for briefings and orientation in USIS offices and other embassy sections. One diplomatic ritual for a newly arrived officer was a courtesy call on the ambassador, the same Douglas MacArthur II whom we had met in Washington a year earlier. Except now, as I was introduced, he gave no sign that he had ever seen me before. He was all business. This was less than half a year after the "Security Treaty riots." So, we discussed the need to work with university students and labor union leaders—the moderate ones—in the area where I would be representing the United States, the prefectures of Niigata and Akita.*

On our second day in Tokyo we went for lunch at a noodle shop near the Ginza. When we heard the familiar slurping sound all around us— normal etiquette for Japanese signaling appreciation of the cuisine—

---

* A prefecture, the administrative level below the central government, is run by a governor and so equates to a state. But, since Japan is about the size of Montana and has 53 prefectures, a prefecture is closer in size to one of our counties. Prefectures include counties (gun), cities, towns and villages, so that we settle for equating them to states.

Kimie and I smiled broadly at each other. We knew we were truly back in Japan again, despite all the changes.

This was Hugh-ko's first exposure to Japan, and during our walk on the Ginza after lunch he was all eyes. He noticed, for example, that many Japanese were wearing the gauze masks they then favored to keep from spreading or catching a cold. Hugh-ko took this all in and finally blurted out, "Mom, why does Japan have so many doctors?"

Over the preceding few years, we had tried to teach Hugh-ko some Japanese; but he had resisted. "Dad, you didn't begin learning Japanese until you were college age," he argued, "So, I'll wait until I'm college age, too." We later would learn that children typically resist anything that marks them as "different" from their peers, including language learning. (Six years later, as we were arriving back in the U.S. on home leave, Hugh-ko warned Kimie, "Now we're in America again, Mom. So, no more Japanese.")

We visited Kimie's family in Yokohama, but soon were on a train bound for my first Foreign Service post. I would be "*kancho*" (director) of the American Cultural Center in Niigata City (pop. ca. 300,000), but responsible for our cultural and information programs in the two prefectures, with a total population of some 4 million.

This was one of 12 American Cultural Centers (USIS branch posts) in Japan. Started by the Occupation as "Civil Information & Education Libraries," 23 such CI&E libraries were turned over to USIS as the Occupation ended. Nine were converted into binational "Japan-America Cultural Centers" (JACCs) subsidized by USIS but staffed and operated by local civic entities and America-Japan societies. That left 14 American Cultural Centers (ACC's) run directly by USIS. In the late 1950's two more were converted to binational centers. So, in 1960 USIS had branch posts in Sapporo, Sendai, Niigata, Kanazawa, Tokyo, Yokohama, Nagoya, Kyoto, Osaka, Kobe, Hiroshima and Fukuoka.

We arrived in Niigata about November 10 after a 7½-hour train ride from Tokyo, across the Japan Alps and onto the plain of the Shinano, which flows into the Japan Sea at Niigata, making that a river-mouth port. We were met at the station by three of the ACC Japanese staff, a vice mayor and local America-Japan Society members. The deference shown us was surprising after being just one more Civil Service family in Washington. Now we would be our nation's chief representatives there for the next three years.

We first stopped to see the ACC, on the third floor of a downtown building. On the second floor were 13 "stand bars," tiny bars whose customers mostly stood while drinking and where my predecessor, Charley Magee, had damaged his liver enough that he failed his physical. So, these bars had contributed to our presence there. After being shown around the Center, we were taken to our official residence, a sizable 2-story house that once was the home of a president of Niigata University. His widow lived in a separate suite of rooms at the back.

As we entered the house, we immediately picked up the smell of cat urine. Magee had left his pregnant Siamese cat and Irish setter "Rusty" at the house in the care of his maid; but the maid had no experience with managing a house cat. So, one of the first tasks we gave our administrative assistant was to arrange for the living room carpet to be replaced and the curtains to be thoroughly cleaned. It was that bad!

The house was furnished, including the loan from USIS-Tokyo of a "hospitality kit"—bedding, linens, pots and pans, etc., to tide us over until our household items arrived from the U.S. The holdover maid had some food items in the refrigerator for us; but Kimie immediately went out with her to a grocery to augment our supply.

The house stood on a long dune hill on the city's west side facing the sea, but partly shielded from sea winds by a Shinto shrine, Gōkoku Jinja, and its associated pine woods. The beach was about 400 yards away, close enough for us to hear the surf during a storm.

After a comfortable first night, Kimie and I arose to the sounds of the maid in the kitchen. Hugh-ko's bed was empty, and the maid said she had not seen him. We checked outside, but saw no sign of him or Rusty. We called around the immediate vicinity and got no answer.

He'll be back for breakfast when he and the dog return from their walk, we thought.

After breakfast the ACC's driver picked me up in the big Chevy Carryall and took me to the Cultural Center for my first day at work: messages from Tokyo to read, receipts to sign, people to meet. I was briefed on the library. About four years earlier, a major fire had swept through the city and burned out the original Cultural Center with all its books. So, our current collection was about 80% hand-me-downs from other ACCs, making it a pretty motley collection. I would later help the librarian cull the collection by about 30% as we pressed our new-book budget to its limit.

At mid-morning, Kimie called, her voice now very anxious. Hugh-ko still was not back. I had Public Affairs Advisor Minoru Fujita quietly ask the police to begin checking the area. By noon there still was no sign of him or the dog; I went home for lunch and to give Kimie emotional support. She was now tense and very nervous, but keeping "a stiff upper lip." And trying her best not to imagine worst-case scenarios, as she usually did.

Rain began to fall, and we asked the police to step up the search, since a 9-year-old who had eaten neither breakfast nor lunch could well be in real trouble. And, I went back to the office.

About 2 PM, Kimie called. Hugh-ko and Rusty were back! Wet from the rain, but undamaged. Where had he been? Beach-combing. But, the police had searched the beach! Well, some fishermen had invited him to go out with them in their boats to lay down their nets. How could he communicate? The only Japanese he knew was *neko*, *inu* and *sayonara* (cat, dog, goodbye). Gestures, body language and smiles had sufficed. But, he had nothing to eat! The fishermen fed him some raw shrimp (our first introduction to ama-ebi, the sweet tender raw shrimp that now costs dearly at sushi bars). And Rusty went out on the boat, too? No, he waited on the beach, but the police had somehow missed seeing him.

That affair ended when Kimie took a bottle of scotch to the police station to express our appreciation and apologies for the trouble caused them.

The house furnishings included a TV set; and Hugh-ko was delighted to find that many of the same cartoons he had seen over and over in the USA were on Japanese TV—with sound tracks in Japanese. So, he knew the dialogue; and this now became a way for him to learn Japanese—that plus talking with the maid and, soon, playing with Japanese children in the neighborhood. Local American and Canadian missionaries had organized a small grade school nearby, and we enrolled Hugh-ko there.

Thanksgiving was close upon us, and Kimie went the butcher shop to buy turkey. She came back with their biggest—about 13 pounds. By the big day, she had found most of the other ingredients for a proper Thanksgiving meal and had invited a few professors and some of the ACC staff to join us.

An hour after the turkey went into the oven, we began smelling fish. Kimie went to the kitchen to see if the maid was cooking fish. She was not. The only possible conclusion: the turkey was causing the smell. Turned out it was fattened on fish meal! So, we had to discard the skin and fat, where the odor was concentrated, and proceed with the meal. A few weeks later, Kimie went back to the butcher shop to order a "non-fishy turkey" for next year. We got it, all right, but were tripped up by the fact that the Japanese language has no articles—definite or indefinite—and no singular or plural noun forms. So, her order for a 9-10 kilogram turkey resulted in 1961 in our getting 20 pounds of turkey—distributed between two birds! No fishy smell, though.

Being the official American in town meant forming cordial relations with the area's movers and shakers, from the prefectural governor and city mayors through all categories of community leaders. I would learn that we in USIS were privileged to work with the most interesting people in the societies where we are posted: opinion leaders in all walks, educators, college students, labor unionists and government officials who influence local and national agendas. That was true also in Niigata.

I could have started on the wrong foot with the editor of the daily *Niigata Nippo*. After a few weeks of trying to adjust to the Siamese cat whose odors had greeted us when we arrived, we made it known that we would be glad to give it to any cat-lover who could give it a home. The wife of the *Nippo* editor gladly accepted the cat, and reportedly loved it dearly ever after. The editor himself sometimes mentioned the gift cat with a wry expression.

A *Niigata Nippo* report of our arrival brought in Kimie's friends from Tsubame, which turned out to be just 30 miles south of us, to pay their respects and renew their friendship with my lady. Mayor Tamaki, the town council chairman and the metal flatware export association's Namba greeted us warmly and urged that we visit their town soon.

I had been Director of the American Cultural Center in Niigata just a few days when I was visited successively by two professors of Niigata University: Professor Ninomiya of the Humanities Faculty and Prof. Tatsuma of the Education Faculty. Both were returned Fulbright scholars and quite friendly. They would help me understand the dynamics of the university and get USIS-sponsored American speakers onto the University campus for lectures and discussions. Also, I soon met the retired senior advisor for the ACC, Dr. Naganuma, noted as the translator of Walt Whitman's *Leaves of Grass* and a great old gentleman.

On New Year's Eve 1960 we ate out with some of the Japanese staff and then brought them home for drinks. But, since snow had begun falling heavily, they left early—long before the stroke of midnight. The next morning (1/1/61) we awoke to see thick snow still falling, with about two feet already accumulated.

The west side of Japan is *yukiguni*, snow country. For, prevailing winter winds sweep from bitter cold Siberia across the Japan Sea, there pick up moisture and then dump that as heavy snow when they make landfall.

At that time, the only transportation open from Niigata to Tokyo in winter was the railway. Southern Niigata Prefecture gets the heaviest snow—10-12 feet of snow *pack* during a winter—*even near sea level.* Stores and homes in strip villages along main roads were built right up to the sidewalk or the street. As the snow fell, people had to shovel their roofs to avoid their collapsing, usually dumping the snow on the street. That blocked roads with packed snow up to eight feet deep. They then leveled that to make roads passable. Corrugated-steel arcades sheltered the sidewalks, so that people could walk along the near-tunnel in front of stores. To get down to normal sidewalk level, residents cut steps in the snow. To get to the opposite side of a street, they would climb up the snow steps, cross the snowed-in street and descend snow steps on the other side.

This snowstorm continued through New Year's Day and into the evening. The next morning it had stopped, with 40 inches accumulated! The ACC's Chevy Carryall was buried beside the concrete fence in front of our house, as we had no overnight parking for it near the Cultural Center. Fortunately, I had a snow shovel and was able to clear a path to the vehicle and out to the road, which was impassable. Fortunately, too, we had two well-stocked refrigerators, as our official duties included giving parties for up to 25 people. So, food was not an immediate concern. Fortunately (#3), Hugh-ko had a sled; and over the next several days we used it to trek several blocks to the nearest cleared road. After two days, I also used the sled to get to work. (In Japan, the first several days after the New Year are a holiday; and U.S. offices in Japan observe both American and Japanese holidays, because of their large staffs of Japanese employees. So, I had not missed any work.

Over the next week Hugh-ko and neighborhood kids had great fun practice-skiing on the short slope below the shrine, with the crashing surf just 100 yards away.

Perhaps on the second day after the snow ended, our maid took a call from a Japanese general. She came to Kimie in shock. "He didn't ask for Mrs. Burleson; he asked for Kimie-san!" she blurted out. It was the officer who, as defense attaché at the Japanese Embassy, had offered Kimie the job she turned down. They had been good friends, such that when he was promoted to full colonel and she congratulated him mischievously on becoming a "chicken colonel," he got a big laugh out of it. Now a brigadier general, he had brought Self Defense Force units to help clear the rail lines of snow.

On the third day, I had my staff ask the city when our road would be cleared. No one knew. So, Fujita, Fukui and I began shoveling the road from the house. After clearing one lane of heavy meter-deep snow for about 80 yards, we were exhausted. Now we made a more urgent request to the city for a plow. The next day, the city plow came and cleared the 400 yards we had been unable to handle. That freed the Chevy Carryall and put us back in business, as the main downtown streets now were clear, too.

During our first three months in Niigata, Kimie was fairly busy arranging and equipping the house to our taste, hiring and training another maid, etc. Together with the inclement weather, that kept her from making many social contacts; and the ladies of Niigata, for their part, were preoccupied with their existing social obligations. So, in February Kimie took a train to Yokohama to visit her family for about a week.

The social climate began changing for Kimie when, through our Cultural Center staff, we arranged for Hugh-ko to have piano lessons, hoping to continue the progress he had made in Maryland. In 1958 Kimie had bought a heavy old upright piano from a Japanese Embassy officer leaving Washington; and Hugh-ko then had lessons from a teacher in Silver Spring. We shipped that piano with our household effects to Niigata.

Because our things had arrived in Tokyo just as the big snowfall hit in Niigata, the Embassy had held them in Tokyo until freight shipments into the snow country could be assured. So, it was perhaps mid-February before our things came, including the piano. Unfortunately, the packing crates had been stored outdoors and rain had soaked in and damaged some things. The piano came through safely, however.

The teacher recommended to us was Mrs. Kimi (her last name), a graduate of a major Tokyo music academy, the wife of an M.D. heading the public health section of the prefectural government, and a key social figure in Niigata City. Through Mrs. Kimi, our Kimie began to meet and charm the ladies of Niigata society and soon was involved in several handicraft-cum-social groups. Soon she was making some very good friends.

About then, I began getting tutoring to further brush up my Japanese skills that were under-used in Washington. This was okayed by my boss in Tokyo, Frank Tenney.* In May, Frank came up on an official visit. It happened I was giving a speech at a Rotary Club while Frank was in town. Hearing my Japanese, Frank blew the whistle on any further tutoring. "I can't justify spending the funds when you can do that well," he said.

That spring, I made my first visit to Akita, some 150 miles up the coast. The scenery en route is mostly rural and very picturesque. Farm women working the rice paddies wore unique clothing. Anil-dyed cotton *kasuri* cloth with endlessly varied patterns made up their baggy pantaloons and blouses. Rubber sandals and cloth-strip leggings shielded their legs from insects and other hazards. On their heads they wore broad-brimmed hand-made reed hats held in place by cloth ties. Cotton scarves shielded their necks and most of their faces so that only their eyes, nose and mouth were exposed.

Akita City is a former castle town** and major hub for its area. The prefectural government ran the Japanese-American Cultural Center (JACC) there. So, on such visits I called on the Superintendent of Education whose staff manned the Center. From our ACC or from Tokyo, we provided periodicals and some books for the library. And we sometimes sent cultural programs to Akita to be presented under the Center's auspices. In my second year in Niigata, I went to Akita to

---

* Frank, now retired in Vermont, is the son of American missionaries, who in the early 1900s, founded Kanto Gakuin, an important college in Yokohama. Raised in Japan, he speaks Japanese fluently and translates Japanese literature. Just a few years ago, I discovered that we are 4th cousins.
** Under the feudal regimes of about 1220-1868, each local lord (daimyo) maintained a castle from which he ran his domain; and around these grew new towns, most of which now are cities.

judge an English-speaking contest at the Center; and during my third year we held a retreat for Fulbrighters in Japan at a hotel on Akita's Oga Peninsula.

An amusing incident: Perhaps six of us, Americans and Japanese, were talking at the bar in Japanese and giving the girl bartender our drink orders, also in Japanese. Suddenly she suddenly blurted out, "It's just too weird to hear foreigners speaking in Japanese!" We offered to switch to English, but warned that then she would not understand our orders.

Until recently, with foreigners fluent in Japanese appearing more often on Japanese TV, Japanese never expected foreigners to be fluent in their admittedly difficult language —as if it were only genetically transferable. We used to hear the tale, ostensibly true, of a U.S. diplomat who stopped at a Tokyo police box and, in flawless Japanese, asked a policeman standing there for directions. The policeman stared a second and then went inside and brought out an English-speaking officer to talk with him.

A fascinating locale in my "domain" was Sado Island. About 25 miles west of Niigata, it was accessible then only by a 2+-hour ride on a passenger ferry. Today one takes a plane or a speedy surface-effects vessel. Sado has an interesting history. In the middle ages, political prisoners were exiled there. In that era, political intrigue and rivalries among court families led to a period when the official line of emperors was challenged by a collateral line. The tombs of two such "failed" and exiled emperors are well preserved on Sado. Lesser prisoners did hard labor, some in a primitive gold mine on the island. Today that mine is a tourist attraction: a rounded hill with a pie-slice wedge cut from its summit over the centuries of mining there. A museum close by has exhibits of the tools, ladders (logs with notches for steps) and models of workers in the cramped mineshafts.

On my first trip to Sado in spring 1961, local officials guided us. Sado's population, then about 30,000, lives mainly in the eastside shipping port of Ryotsu and westside fishing port of Aikawa. Paddy and upland fields are scattered wherever soil and terrain permit. At the south end is the picturesque port of Ogi. In its harbor the local dingy traditionally was a large round flat-bottomed wooden tub and was still seen there in the 1960s.

At one point, we passed a paddy where a farmer was dusting his crop with DDT (not yet banned anywhere), using a hand-cranked duster. In the next field, no DDT—just a tall bamboo pole among the rice plants, with a cord tied at the top to bend it into a simulation of a bow, with an arrow strung on it and pointing skyward to deter the evil spirits which, as everyone knows, bring rice diseases and insect pests.

Nearby and close enough to the seashore to be subject to damaging salt spray was a small unplanted paddy. There an impoverished-looking young farmer was marking the mud for his rice seedlings by walking along on snowshoe-like wood frames set with pegs to make holes for the plants. He used straw ropes to lift the frames awkwardly with each step.

Now (1961) we entered our first summer in Niigata. The beach was fine for swimming and fishing. Our Cultural Center driver was an avid angler and sometimes took us out on his friend's boat for early-morning angling for *kisu*, a smelt-like fish. As the summer warmed up, we found that the sea here supports phosphorescent sea life.* As the waves break in the night, the disturbed zooplankton make the churning water glow. Or, if you dive in or swim underwater, people watching will see you as a glowing, ghost-like form in the water due to the plankton you disturb.

In July, Niigata's gregarious Mayor Watanabe invited Kimie and me for lunch at his private home on the edge of the city. He proudly showed us his strawberry patch. He had searched three continents for strawberries best suited to Niigata's alluvial soil and changeable climate. For dessert we feasted on strawberries and local watermelon.

In August, we saw our first Niigata Port Festival**, two days of parades and fireworks. The parades mainly featured folk-dance clubs, each

---

\* Part of the tropical current that washes Japan's Pacific coast also flows into the Japan Sea, bringing the plankton. In summer, southerly winds blow over those currents to keep Japan warm and humid.

\*\* Celebrating Niigata's designation as a port for foreign trade by the 1858 Treaty of Shimoda in distinctively patterned *yukata* (cotton kimonos), and all dancing in unison to folk music on a P.A. system along the parade route. The local radio/TV station broadcast the parade live. On the first morning, Kimie and I were invited guest commentators at the open-air broadcast booth as we observed the parade live on camera for over two hours. So, all in the prefecture who were watching saw that the ACC had a director who spoke their language and had a charming Japanese wife.

For the Port Festival fireworks, we were invited to sit in the mayor's box in the viewing stands to watch the spectacular show, every bit as great as in any major American city.

In summer 1962, we were invited to a fireworks show down prefecture in Nagaoka*, also on the Shinano River. Kimie could not go, but Hugh-ko and I went. Nagaoka used the river's flood plain for launching its aerial displays. The highlight was to be a firework not seen before or since: a three-foot diameter ball. In the train station was displayed a steel tube—8-feet tall and an inch-thick—that would launch the monster ball.

The show progressed that evening from many one-foot diameter balls exploding in the air to maybe a dozen 2-foot balls, whose bright explosions shook the sky. The three-footer was the finale. It was announced, shot into the sky and exploded with a dull shock wave and rather dull glow. We groaned in disappointment; but then dozens of balls that had been packed inside exploded simultaneously across a 75-degree arc of sky, the most stunning firework ever. The shock wave slammed into our bodies with total authority. About 34 years later, Japan's Consul General in Seattle was from Nagaoka and arranged for Seattle's July 4th fireworks to be supplied by Nagaoka's firework factories. A great show; but without the yard-wide ball.

In 1962, Mayor Watanabe told us of his wish to find an American sister city for Niigata. In 1956 President Eisenhower had proclaimed his People-to-People Program, aimed at helping to rebuild grass-roots ties

---

* Incidentally the hometown of Admiral Yamamoto Isoroku, who planned the Pearl Harbor attack.

among peoples that the wars of the '30s and '40s had frayed or broken. Sister-city programs are a continuing facet of that. Mayor Watanabe was focused on Long Beach, California, as a potential sister city because Niigata and Long Beach are port cities and shared a common problem: land subsidence. Long Beach had been sinking due to oil being pumped up from below; and its engineers had had some success in slowing the land sinking by injecting sea water under pressure to replace the oil. Niigata, especially its port area, had serious land subsidence from pumping natural gas from under the Shinano delta silt. Some jetties and wharves had sunk as much as six feet by 1961. And the rate was increasing.

Niigata had another problem, too. A diversion channel had been cut from the Shinano to the sea 20 miles down-river and was opened during high water to avoid flooding the densely populated city and vital port area. An unintended consequence: Some silt that normally came down with the high water and was deposited on Niigata's beaches now exited through the diversion channel. That silt had offset beach erosion by storms and so kept the beaches fairly stable. Now much tax money had to go into erecting sea walls and setting up huge concrete tetrapod barriers against the encroaching sea.

During the winter of 1961-62, that erosion began chewing up an old coastal dune with a former city dump in it. Enterprising souls used wire-mesh clam rakes to sift out antique bottles, old coins, etc., from the sand and make a bit of cash from this coastal calamity. That was just half a mile from our house.

On official trips, we traveled widely in Niigata Prefecture, which stretches 140 miles along the Japan Sea west of the Japan Alps. Sometimes with ACC staff members and sometimes with personal friends, we visited perhaps a dozen smaller cities and towns. I often arranged with local English teachers to visit their classrooms. Once we went to the Snow Festival at a Tokamachi high school where students had labored for days building a stage of packed snow in the schoolyard—4 feet high, 35 feet long and about 15 feet deep, with a sculpted snow backdrop rising up 15 feet. There was music, singing by the nationally known Dark Ducks quartet and a kimono fashion show. Delicious food was sold at half-dome snow stalls along the route to the festival site.

Another time we visited the river town of Shirone to see the annual kite contest, with kites unlike any we had ever seen before. A local schoolyard was used for making up the kites. That much space was needed as these kites averaged 10 feet by 7 feet and were flown by crews of 4-6 men who played out the half-inch rope and sometimes were lifted into the air by the tug of the huge kite. We were told that the kite festival grew out of a dispute over a lost kite between villagers on either side of the river. So, the lively but peaceable contest was instituted. The point was to fly your kite so that it forced an opponent's kite into the intervening river. We saw that done over and over. Each time the frame of the swamped kite would be pulled from the river and rushed back to the schoolyard to be re-papered and flown again.

# MUSICAL INTERLUDES

While in Niigata, besides bringing in American academicians to talk with local audiences about economic and political issues, we (USIS-Japan) featured some musicians. The first that we hosted were a pianist and singer—a husband (Czech pianist) and wife (American soprano). They did three concerts—one in Niigata's Prefectural Citizens Hall and two at Sado Island high schools. Near the end the first concert, while the duo was performing, a smallish rat trotted across in front of the footlights, stopped and sat up to look at the singer before continuing off to stage right. (Maybe her high voice made him feel a kinship.) The singer did not stop, but said later she was ready to leap onto the piano if the rat had moved in her direction.

On Sado, our musicians first spent an afternoon on a grassy slope facing the Sea of Japan as a contract film crew filmed them for a documentary on the Fulbright Program in Japan. Despite a warm sun and a moderate wind, they enjoyed being interviewed and sharing a scene with kimonoed dancers performing to local folk music and accompanied by *taiko* drummers beating huge wooden drums. At the Aikawa High School gym that evening, wild life intruded again: With no air conditioning, the windows were open for ventilation; and large moths had a ball dive-bombing the lights, the audience and our performers. The following night at Ryotsu High School, we again were in a ventilated gym, this time under attack by mosquitoes from the surrounding paddies. I tried to time my swatting of those biting through my slacks to musical crescendos so that the slapping sound would not disturb the musicians or audience. Again the singer was a target: once she nearly swallowed a mosquito when she took in a deep breath.

Another musical duo that we toured: a young pianist (Bernstein, but not Leonard) and a lady violinist from New York. Traveling by train, they discovered the charm of the green tea sold at stations along the route. In those days, it was sold in little one-cup ceramic pots made by local potters. Each pot was unique and charmingly folk-crafty. By the end of their Japan tour they had a nice collection.

Again, we programmed them first at the Prefectural Hall. That was a cliffhanger. The day they arrived, we heard of a typhoon blowing across Kyushu. By the next morning, the typhoon was approaching along the Sea of Japan. We began to discuss canceling the concert. By early afternoon, the forecasters said the typhoon's eye would either pass outside Sado or come right by Niigata. Then it was too late to get word out of any cancellation; and our musicians were game to proceed. By concert time, we had rain and gusty winds, but the audience was arriving.

During the concert, we could hear the wind picking up and were told the storm's eye would soon be just offshore. In the middle of one duet the power went out. Quickly the hall staff hurried in with large Japanese paper lanterns lit by candles. They placed two on the piano and two on the stage wings. With that much light, pianist Bernstein could see the keyboard. He announced he would play Moussorgsky's "Pictures at an Exhibition" (the original piano version) and proceeded to enthrall us with the piece's crashing chords, often accompanied by the crash of windows being blown out on the upper floors of the building.

With the concert over, the storm's fury had abated; but the bus service was out. So, we helped to ferry audience members home in the Chevy Carryall. Bernstein later wrote up the experience for the Asian edition of *Time* magazine, where his friend was music editor. He entitled it "Playing up a storm." We also took the duo to a music school in Takada in southern Niigata Prefecture, where Kimie's mother's ancestors were educators of the local daimyo's offspring. (Takada is now re-named Echigo City.)

154

An equally interesting musical event, but with less drama, involved a U.S. Marine Corps band from Iwakuni Air Base. Junior Chamber of Commerce members from nearby Shibata came to us one time to ask for a U.S. military band to play at ceremonies dedicating the town's new civic auditorium. In the following days we tried the Air Force and the Army, but could get no commitment. Then we contacted the U.S. Navy and were told they would try.

A week or so later, the bandmaster of the Marine band at Iwakuni (near Hiroshima) called to say they would come. Our Shibata contacts were delighted and began working on the plan with us.

On the big day, senior advisor Fujita and I accompanied two Shibata JC's to the Niigata airport. As the band members filed off the plane in their green uniforms, one of the Shibata men remarked wryly, "Well, those uniforms look familiar!" Turned out he was a veteran of a Shibata battalion that had fought our Marines on Guadalcanal two decades before. Unlike some veterans of Western nations, the Japanese were nursing no grudges so long after the war. They usually simply said, "That is war." They had put it behind them.

The JC's had hired a tour bus to transport the band and a truck for their instruments. In Japan, with a tour bus you also get a girl guide trained to sing the local folk songs. So, our guide began her usual routine. Except that she was a poor singer and off key. Soon the bandleader came to me and asked me to tell her that his musicians were tired and preferred a bit of quiet.

As we neared Shibata, we found that the JC's had us booked into a hot-spring hotel at the edge of town. It being midweek, the inn had no other guests. We got our room assignments and then had dinner, all paid for by the JCs. After dinner, the hotel staff urged us to take baths, the usual routine in Japanese inns. The baths were in one spacious room, large and medium pools filled with steaming, sulfurous water. Per age-old custom, men and women here used the same baths, but of course modestly covering private parts with their washing towels when bathing.

No one else was in the baths as the Marines went in, and they had not been told of the dual-gender tradition here. Just as they were getting out and toweling off, the hotel maids came in to take their baths. Immediately, many of the Marines realized they were not yet clean enough. They did an about-face and went back in to scrub some more and chat amiably with the maids in neighboring pools. Cleanest Marines ever seen, I'm sure!

The next morning, while I made a courtesy call at City Hall, the Marines played in a downtown parade. That afternoon we gathered in the new auditorium to enjoy their indoor concert, undoubtedly more spirited than usual, due to the JCs' great hospitality.

As we said goodbye to the band at the airport that afternoon, the bandmaster urged that we ask for his band if we ever had such a request again. He was roundly seconded by the cheering bandsmen.

Niigata was no musical desert, of course. I have mentioned finding a first-rate piano teacher for Hugh-ko. After his second year, Mrs. Kimi held a public recital by her students, including Hugh-ko, at the Prefectural Hall. Niigata had an active association of Suzuki-method violin teachers also. We twice enjoyed Prefectural Hall concerts by their students, from pre-school tots through high schoolers, all playing impressively, especially in large ensembles.

Niigata also had an amateur orchestra, the Niigata Symphony Orchestra, which offered public concerts once or twice a year. One year they had as guest artist a local violinist, Wanibuchi, by then a nationally known concert violinist. (The name Wanibuchi puzzled me. It means "crocodile pool"; yet Japan has no crocodiles!) We had become friends with several of the musicians and so were included in their convivial after-concert party for Wanibuchi-san, who had brought with him his lovely daughter, Haruko, a budding movie and TV star.

At the party they asked Wanibuchi his opinion of the orchestra. He smiled and said tactfully that they were making progress, but that he had heard some "strange sounds" from the horn section. There I also learned the members' humorous nickname for their orchestra. Japanese commonly abbreviate long organizational names, using the first syllables of key parts of the name. But, to spoof their amateur group and its "strange sounds," they called it Gata Kyō--the Gata from Niigata and the Kyō from Kōkyō gakudan (symphony orchestra). But, Gata Kyo can also mean "rattletrap orchestra."

From the group's cellist, I borrowed a cello to see if I could resume playing the instrument I had not touched since 1944. After a few weeks, I realized that it was like starting all over again and that I really did not have time to pursue it with proper concentration. So, I returned the instrument to its owner with regret.

Sadly, about a year later one of these musicians came to a tragic end. On his way home after an evening in Niigata's many bars, he fell into one of the canals running through the city. The tide was low and he landed head first in oozy mud and suffocated. His body was found only in the early light of the next morning. (The canals have since been filled in to become wide boulevards.)

Many devotees of Japan's traditional music are active throughout Japan. I have mentioned the folk dance troupes on Sado and in Niigata's port festival. Kimie's gynecologist in Niigata was a master of the *shakuhachi* (bamboo flute) and sometimes played in concerts. So, when Kimie asked about finding a teacher of *koto* (horizontal harp or Japanese zither), which she had studied before the war, friends introduced her to Mrs. Miyake, a fine performer and former student of one of Japan's foremost composers and *koto* masters, MIYAGI Michio. After a year of brush-up study, Kimie performed twice in koto concerts at the Daiwa Music Hall. I became interested, too, especially in the 17-string koto, which is to the standard 13-string koto what the cello is to the violin. I took a few lessons from Miyake-sensei, but again my busy schedule interfered and I had to suspend the lessons. I later sold my instrument in Tokyo.

# NIIGATA BYWAYS

## (1962-63)

One unique experience was our visit to the island of Awashima, about three miles long by one mile wide. The island school's English teacher invited me there. The trip involved an hour's train ride to Murakami in northern Niigata Prefecture, a taxi to the port and a voyage across 10 miles of water by a passenger packet boat.

Kimie, Hugh-ko and I arrived on a Sunday about noon and were met at the dock by the teacher and a few students. They escorted us to a small *ryokan* (Japanese inn) that had but 6-8 guest rooms. The island (pop. about 800) had no vehicles other than a motorcycle at the school and one at the town office.

After we had lunch, the students gathered in our room and gave us a slide show on their life and activities through the seasons. We learned the island economy depended 90% on fishing and 10% on harvesting bamboo, with some subsistence farming on the scant arable land (maybe 20 acres) on the island's lower level and its rounded hills. The students' time was filled entirely by studying and helping their parents. A major late-winter school event had all students spending a day making wooden crates for the island's fishermen.

After a few hours with the students, Kimie sat back and asked them, "So, what is the one thing that you want most but do not have?" (I am sure she was thinking of something material that we might send to them.) Several of them in unison shot right back, "*Jiyu!*" (freedom).

Kimie persisted, "Well, there are many kinds of *jiyu*. What do you have in mind?" After some discussion, we found they meant free time, time to pursue their own interests. Of course, the parents were just as *jiyu* deprived as their children.

Early the next morning the English teacher took us on an hour's cruise around the island. Completing the circuit and nearing the island's tiny harbor, we found we were trailing a fleet of fishing boats just bringing in their catch. They had made a big haul and so were flying colorful banners from their mast heads. Much of their catch turned out to be large *fugu* (puffer fish), known for their delicately flavored white flesh, but also for their highly toxic gall bladders. With great skill and caution, licensed specialists remove the livers and gall bladders before the fish can go to the chefs.

After a seafood breakfast we went to the school for morning assembly in the gym. Some 100 students were already seated in rows on the gym floor. Our arrival stirred a murmur among them. The principal introduced us and then asked that I speak to the assembled students. When I asked whether I should talk in English or in Japanese, the English teacher said, "Oh, in English. I will interpret."

I had no sooner said, "Good morning, boys and girls," than the smallest children in the front rows began giggling. They had never seen a *gaijin* up close, nor heard English spoken by a native speaker. The principal shushed the kids and I went on with my short talk, rather awkwardly interpreted by the teacher. Kimie fidgeted and later said, "I could have interpreted much better!" And, she could have.

After lunch, we took the boat back to Murakami and returned to Niigata. A few days later, I received a postcard from one of the students with whom we had spent that Sunday afternoon. She wrote that she had so wanted to go down to the boat to wish us goodbye; but she had to work in the kitchen and so could merely crane her neck and watch as we departed. We hope that life on Awashima has become less rigorous since then.

Traveling around Niigata and Akita prefectures to visit schools, libraries and the like gave me a broad feel for this part of Japan, then called "*ura Nippon*"—in effect "Japan's outback." In recent decades, better transportation and communication links and economic development have made the term obsolete. But, in the early 1960s the area was fairly rustic and isolated, especially in winter.

One winter day, I met with English teachers in Sanjo in central Niigata Prefecture for a Saturday seminar on English. Afterward, we all went to a nearby ski slope. That area's poetic and euphonic name intrigued me: Fuyu-dori-goe (winter bird pass).

Speaking of picturesque names: At the south end of the prefecture, the Japan Alps crowd down to the shore, making the seacoast extremely rugged, such that today's coastal railway there is forced into a series of long tunnels. But in olden times only a rough trail skirted its steep cliffs and narrow coves. Travelers passed that way only at great peril. They gave this coastal strip the name Oyashirazu-Koshirazu. Literally, "don't know my parents/don't know my children," the implication being that it was so perilous that parents and children might abandon each other to save themselves when passing there.

One warm friendship we made in Niigata was with the Kijuro Saito family. Once major landowners in the hinterland behind Niigata city, the Saitos had to give up most of their farmland under the Occupation-era land reform, retaining only hilly land unsuited to farming. One fall Mrs. Saito invited us for a mushroom hunt on a piney tract of hills they owned. Not just any mushrooms, but the savory *matsutake*—as treasured in Japan as truffles are in France and for which, in some mountain areas of our west coast, people sometimes are threatened by those protecting favored gathering areas.

We found few matsutake, but enjoyed the outing. It was on that day that we saw first-hand a bit of rural lore. The caretaker who lived in a hut on one of the hills had a liter bottle of sake into which he had placed a live snake. The idea: by letting a snake die in the sake the liquid captures its essence—its strength and vigor—which you then drink. One hears tales in Japan of people using the poisonous mamushi (a pit viper) this way and getting bitten on the lip when trying to swig the sake before the poor critter has expired.

During one of Kimie's visits with Mrs. Saito at their downtown mansion (since then donated to the city as a historic site), Mrs. Saito gave Kimie some exquisite gifts: an 8-panel screen of sumi paintings created in 1927 and two fine antique stacked lacquer box sets. I now treat these as heirlooms for our descendants.

The Saitos' son Joe (actually Kuranojo) became one of Hugh-ko's friends in Niigata. Joe and Mrs. Saito encouraged Hugh to take up horsemanship at facilities at the Niigata racetrack. Joe Saito would later spend several years in Virginia training to join Japan's horsemanship team at the 1980 Moscow Olympics. Of course, the West and Japan boycotted those Games because of the Soviet invasion of Afghanistan. Joe later spent some years helping to manage an Alaskan resort owned by his mother's family, the Tsutsumis, one of Japan's wealthiest. He now manages parking facilities in Niigata and Tokyo.

From Bunny (Bunjiro) Saito, a nephew of Mrs. Saito, we learned more local lore. He lives in a large country manor east of Niigata city. It was partly converted into a "Hoppo Bunka Hakubutsukan" (Museum of Northern Culture), which held treasures from Japan's Edo period (1603–1867). Also intriguing to us was Bunny's "pad." Right in the middle of the old manor's 2nd floor he had fixed up for himself a very modern, Western-style suite of rooms, complete with expensive stereo equipment, a luxury bathroom and all.

Bunny was then recently divorced from an American woman whom he had met on one of his foreign travels. We would later meet her in Tokyo, where she was a columnist for an English-language daily. Bunny owned a number of homes near the U.S. Navy's base at Yokosuka and rented them to our Navy officers. A most interesting man, still (2003) active and vigorous.

We made other interesting friends in Niigata. Through her koto lessons, Kimie had met a daughter of the Miyao family (pronounced "meow"). Her father was a prominent ear-nose-throat physician. Generations of

161

the Miyao family had lived in Niigata's Nekoyama (cat hills) section. No comment.

A young Niigata socialite whom we also met through Kimie's contacts had a unique family name: Nakashizuka ("inner serenity"). We did not get to know her well enough to find out whether that trait resided in her genes. She seemed a bit of a play girl and spent much time in Tokyo. And, my other senior advisor at the Cultural Center was Yasutomi-san. One of the local missionaries liked to tease that the name translated as "cheap riches." A kinder translation would be "easy wealth." Now retired in Tokyo, Yasutomi-san and his wife enjoy the arts. Both paint; and the husband is an excellent photographer. They travel abroad frequently.

Early in our Niigata sojourn, I called on the Prefectural Government's division chiefs. I have already mentioned Mrs. Kimi, Hugh-ko's piano teacher. Her husband headed the Public Health Department and would become governor in the '70s.

At the Agriculture Department, I was shown a documentary film they were still editing. It depicted rice cultivation in the Shinano River delta as it was practiced before the government built drainage canals and pumping stations to convert marshy areas there into more readily usable paddy fields. The footage showed the extraordinarily grueling labor needed to raise and harvest rice in that area from ancient times.

Farmers and their wives were struggling through water and muck chest deep to plant and tend the rice. At harvest time, they were again in deep muck, cutting the rice with their sickles at chest level and lifting it *up* into small boats in which they then floated the crop out of the marshes. After the threshing, those same boats took the rice through the city's canals to market. The farmers then spent the chilly fall dredging mud from uncultivated areas and floating it by boat to their submerged fields to gradually raise their level.

About a year after I saw that film, an international meeting of irrigation engineers was held in Tokyo. Some of the attendees came up to look over the areas now properly drained by the pumping stations. I was slightly puzzled when Governor Tsukada invited me to his reception for the visiting foreign engineers. Puzzled, that is, until the middle of the party when he took my arm, led me to the podium and asked me to interpret his message of greeting. I had never before attempted oral interpreting, but got through it without major gaffs.

A visiting delegation that became my total responsibility was a 5-man U.S. trade mission. Frank Tenny called from Tokyo one day to tell me the delegation would visit Niigata and asked that we plan their three-day visit. Fortunately, Fujita-san and others of the staff had experience with such planning and greatly assisted me with the myriad details—all the logistics, whom they should meet in government offices, private companies, etc.

On Tokyo's instructions, our final plan had the delegation tour together only half the time and separately the rest of the time to maximize what they could accomplish. Of course, the plan included Kimie and me holding a reception for the delegation and key Japanese contacts at our home. Kimie always did a beautifully smooth job of planning and hosting such parties and making people feel relaxed—as if it were in her blood to do so.

We decided that two men in the delegation would visit Tsubame, the stainless flatware-producing town from which the delegation had come to Washington in 1958. Because the Tsubame movers and shakers remained so warmly cordial toward her, we included Kimie in the Tsubame visit. She was my best emissary there.

We drove down in the Chevy Carryall and two rented vehicles. As we approached Tsubame, it seemed incredible that so compact a town amid the rice paddies of the Shinano River plain could inundate the Western world in tableware. But, entering the town, we began to hear the hum of machinery, almost from every other building it seemed. During the next four hours we would learn how it was all done.

After being greeted and feted by Mayor Tamaki at City Hall and by the chamber of commerce, we began visiting factories. Most were small to medium size, and some had dirt floors. We winced inwardly when we saw workers using tongs to carry red-hot steel around with only rubber sandals on their feet.

We learned that this region had had a cottage industry in metal ware for centuries, once forging swords and more recently making tools and such decorative products as fine copper vases hammered out by hand from flat discs. Before World War II they got their start in tableware when the Imperial Navy contracted with them for flatware for its officers' messes. We saw that Tsubame still was producing both traditional metal wares and modern tableware, but now was getting into golf clubs and a wide range of items for the globe's more affluent consumers.

A fact that amazed us: The final polishing of the flatware was not done in Tsubame's factories. Instead, all that production was trucked across the Shinano plain to hill towns for farmers' wives to polish, usually at night, after their main chores were done. Then it was trucked back. That was less costly than keeping polishers on staff to do that.

We saw an example of the problems of overseeing trade agreements. The bilateral agreement defined the flatware as 100% stainless steel items. One factory owner proudly showed a trade mission member his latest innovation: flatware stamped with a small indentation on the handle which, when finished, would be filled with a dab of decorative plastic. No longer 100% steel, it would be exempt from the quota, he thought. The American delegate urged him to reconsider.

In fall 1962 our Tokyo Embassy asked us to host a visit by the Deputy Chief of Mission (DCM—the embassy's #2 officer), Mr. John Emmerson. He had studied Japanese at the Embassy before World War II and served under then Ambassador Joseph Grew. During the war, he was posted to China as a liaison between the Nationalists and communists. The early '50s Nixon/McCarthy hearings on alleged communists in the State Department caused severe damage to the careers of some of our diplomats in China at that time, even though no disloyalty was proven. Emmerson should by now have been an ambassador, but was in Tokyo as DCM mainly because Ambassador Reischauer had asked for him.

I had met John Emmerson during one of our periodic Center Director meetings in Tokyo, when he hosted a party for USIS officers. There we witnessed one of his talents besides the diplomatic. He was a superb piano player, and had a couple of acts that he did on the piano. One was to play music from "Peter and the Wolf" as a Russian, an Italian and a German would perform it. The other act: a little boy who is supposed to play a piece for four hands with his sister at a recital. But, sister gets sick at the last minute. The boy goes to the piano to play his part solo; but it does not sound right. So, he kicks off his shoes and plays sister's part with his feet. Eternally memorable to see that dignified, white-haired diplomat playing the bass part with his stocking feet!

Now Emmerson would come to Niigata on an official visit on a Friday, flying in from Tokyo. (We now had twice a day service by air! In good weather.) We began contacting the usual local dignitaries. One of the DCM's requests was that we include an unofficial weekend trip to Sado Island, which he had never visited.

Niigata city had earlier suffered embarrassment when a visiting European diplomat's vehicle had an accident—no injuries, just much delay and awkwardness. So, the local police insisted that our plan accommodate a police escort during Emmerson's stay. But, the Sado trip would be treated as unofficial, they stressed, since it was simply a weekend excursion. No escort vehicle therefore.

Finally, the Embassy emphasized that the DCM must catch the Sunday PM plane back to Tokyo, as Emmerson was to attend Reischauer's dinner for John Glenn. Working on the schedule, we saw a problem. The ferry returning from Sado would dock at 3 PM, but the plane was scheduled to fly out at 3:20. In the Center Carryall, I tested three different routes from the ferry dock to the airport. In normal traffic none could be covered in under 20 minutes; and there was always a possibility of rough seas slowing the ferry.

Fujita-san then contacted the president of the ferry company; but as a regularly scheduled ferry, it could not leave Sado Island early. So, we had decided our best hope was have the Carryall at the dock ready to go, and then simply press the speed limit going to the airport. Then

Fujita-san talked to the ferry captain, who said he could speed up on the return voyage to cut 5 or 10 minutes off the time. I relaxed, just a bit.

The Friday office visits went well. Kimie outdid herself in throwing a party at our house for Mr. Emmerson and invited dignitaries. We had a great visit on Sado, with the central government representative on Sado as our "unofficial" guide. On Sunday the ferry did reach Niigata 10 minutes ahead of schedule and the Carryall with our driver was waiting with the motor running. But, surprise! A police escort jeep was also waiting. They had decided after all not to risk another diplomatic accident. And, Fujita-san was at the airport checking on things there. So, we rushed through the ferry terminal into the Carryall and followed the police jeep across the Shinano toward the airport.

About half way there, we saw the plane coming in to land. Plenty of time, we thought. But, then our police escort turned on its siren and the passenger-side officer frantically waved for us to speed up. We were totally puzzled, but could only comply. As we arrived at the air terminal, the manager and Fujita-san were at the front door. Instead of leading us to the check-in counter, they gestured urgently that we hurry straight through, non-stop to planeside for a quick goodbye to an equally puzzled John Emmerson.

Only then did I have time to turn ask Fujita, "What gives?" He said that a weather front was closing in. So, the plane had departed early for Tokyo, while we were still on the ferry. Fujita-san saw that happening and protested vigorously to the airport manager: This was America's DCM, second only to Ambassador Reischauer, and he must get to his dinner with world-famous astronaut John Glenn. The plane was called back; and that was when we saw it flying in over our heads.

So, we had accelerated the ferry, turned an airliner around and got Mr. Emmerson to his date in Tokyo. Talking with Mr. Emmerson in Tokyo the following year, I found that no one had told him those details. In 1964, after I had relocated to USIS-Tokyo, he tapped me to accompany him and Mrs. Emmerson on a trip to the Kurobe Gorge and its hydropower dam, just south of Niigata Prefecture.

The circle of Niigata ladies with whom Kimie was closest invited her, Hugh-ko and me on a Spring '63 cherry-blossom viewing party, in style. Instead of merely going to a park to socialize under the blossoms, they organized a multicar caravan to Shibata, where we boarded two river boats and floated down the Kaji River between rows of glorious cherry trees blooming on each bank, with snowy mountains as a backdrop. Some two miles down river we stopped at a riverside beach for a relaxed picnic lunch. A waiting minibus took us back to our cars. We then drove farther inland, heading for a hot-spring hotel in the hometown of two in our group who were mid-level prefectural officials.

As our procession approached a T-intersection near the town, a policeman sitting there on a motorcycle flagged us to stop. He sauntered authoritatively over to the lead car and stared in surprise at the two hometown fellows. *"Ah! Omera-ke!"* (Ah, you guys!), he exclaimed in the local dialect. He had been a classmate of the two men and was merely curious about our unusual convoy of vehicles. Now he hopped on his Kawasaki and escorted us into the town. There we had relaxed baths and a light dinner at a hotel before returning to Niigata City after dark.

A unique sidebar to our time in Niigata was the Korean repatriation. A Korean minority had long lived in Japan; and during the '30s and '40s as more and more Japanese men went into the armed forces, the Japanese brought in Koreans, willing or not, as labor for Japan's mines and factories to assure unflagging war production. A few returned to Korea after the war; but conditions there in the late '40s were bad enough that most stayed on in Japan, despite blatant discrimination and being denied the right to Japanese citizenship. After the Korean War and during the '50s, propagandists in Seoul and Pyongyang vied for the allegiance of these Japan-resident Koreans.

After the Korean War North Korea had too few skilled laborers. So, in the later '50s Kim Il Sung began appealing for Koreans in Japan to return "to the motherland" to help build a socialist "paradise." The heavy propaganda worked with many, and political pressure led to a pact among North Korea, the International Red Cross and Japanese

167

Red Cross to send to the north any Koreans who applied to go. Niigata was chosen as their exit port.

Swiss Red Cross representatives supervised the entire process. They hired local Japanese to serve as interpreters; and the best interpreters in Niigata just happened to be returned Fulbrighters, good friends of ours at Niigata University. They were always discrete about what they told us of the goings-on at the repatriation center beyond the airport. What we heard from them was already reported in the media and by the Swiss Red Cross people, whom we had as guests at our house a few times. It was quite clear that North Korea and its agency in Japan (Chosen Soren) were supplying funds to the repatriating families to buy and take with them quantities of consumer goods that North Korea needed.

We also heard that families who went had a code to inform Koreans remaining in Japan whether the north's bright promises and glowing reports were true: If true, the repatriates would send postcards back written in ink; if false, they would write in pencil.

In early fall 1962, Kimie, Hugh-ko and I spent a memorable three-day weekend in Fukushima Prefecture's Bandai National Park. We were accompanied by botany professor Funabiki of Niigata University, who knew the area and could guide us as we drove our Bluebird east into the mountains.

The main attraction was Mount Bandai, a dormant volcano that erupted early in the 20th century. Like Mt. St. Helens in the Cascades, it had blown its top explosively toward the north; but whereas the St. Helens' blast nearly destroyed a lake (Spirit Lake), Bandai's dammed a valley to create a new lake and many ponds. Venturing out from our hotel on the north side of Mount Bandai our first morning, we followed signs pointing to the "five-colored ponds" (Go-shiki Numa). Reaching the ponds one by one, we saw that they were indeed five different shades of turquoise, blue green, etc., stained by copper and sulfur compounds leaching down from the volcano rising behind them.

Dr. Funabiki led Hugh-ko and me on a hike up the 5600-foot mountain, with a good trail making the climb relatively easy. Two thirds of the way up was a soft-drink stand. From there we saw steam rising at various places in the multi-hued half crater.

At the top was a snack stand, not particularly necessary for us, as we had brought lunch with us. So, we sat and ate while taking in 360 degrees of panoramic scenery. Endless mountains to the north and west, a valley and break in the mountains to the east toward the Pacific and just south of us a large lake, Inawashiro. Our scholar/guide said the lake to our north, created by the eruption, covered several villages; but people who survived the eruption had had time to evacuate before rising waters drowned their villages forever.

Before starting back to Niigata the next day, we visited the town situated between Mount Bandai and Inawashiro Lake. At one shop I found the distinctive hand-woven reed hats that local farmers and their wives wore when working in the rice paddies. They had the usual wide brims, but turned up front and back, like conquistador helmets. I added one to my collection of varied Japanese hand-made farm hats. (Most of these I turned over to a delighted Smithsonian Museum curator about 20 years later). I like to imagine that the brims of these Bandai hats were upturned to let the wearers more readily watch for another eruption of the volcano towering above them.

During our two years so far in Niigata, Hugh-ko had become a regular beachcomber on the nearby beach and developed a keen interest in marine biology, almost equal to his love of fishing. He made friends with a marine biologist at the university's Science Faculty just a few blocks from our house. So, when he found something unusual on the beach, he would take it to his scientist friend for identification. Twice his finds were rare enough that the man wrote articles on them for a scientific journal and gave Hugh-ko credit as the discoverer. One weekend they traveled to Sado together to hunt fossil sea life in the island's sedimentary cliffs.

Also, he once took Hugh-ko and me to visit the fisheries research station in the Niigata port area. The biologists there were amazed at how knowledgeable Hugh-ko was, at age 11, about the sea life in the lab's tanks.

Another vignette of our life in Niigata: Some of the American missionaries there were fundamentalists and of course were raising their children in those beliefs. So, when Hugh-ko once took to the school for show-and-tell some of his fossil shark teeth, collected on a Chesapeake Bay beach a few years before, and explained that they were about 40 million years old, some of the children objected, saying that the Bible tells us the world is only about 4000 years old.

Another time, one of those boys was playing at our home on a Saturday afternoon when we decided to go downtown to see the movie "Shane." Naturally, we invited the boy to join us. First we needed his parents' permission; so we drove to his home. But, the parents were out; and the boy said he thought they would approve. So, off we went to the movie. A few days later, we got a carefully composed letter from the boy's father saying, in effect, we don't necessarily believe that all movies are the work of the Devil, but many of our parishioners so believe and we have to take care not to cause them to stumble …

Kimie and I were involved, after the fact, in two office romances while serving in Niigata. First, our librarian, Yoshiko Shirai, asked us to serve as go-betweens at her engagement ceremony to young chemical engineer Yoshiyuki Matsuo whom she had met at the ACC's English-language classes. Even though they had already met, fallen in love and decided to marry, Japanese social ritual called for the ceremony and required go-betweens. As they had met at the ACC, we were chosen. We gladly accepted the honor and carefully practiced the set phrases we would need to use.

Next, Fujita-san asked us to be stand-in parents for his wedding, since his father was deceased and his mother was far north in Sapporo and not well enough to travel. So, Kimie broke out her most formal kimono, and I rented a tux to wear at the wedding ceremony at a downtown wedding hall. Ever after, we stayed in close contact with both couples. Fujita's wife died in 1998; and during our trip to Japan in fall 1999 we visited her grave. We saw the Matsuos during several of our Japan visits, and exchanged e-mail with them. (Sadly, in 2003 Yoshiyuki died of pancreatic cancer.)

During our final year in Niigata, Hugh-ko and Kimie joined a woodblock print class. Together with lady friends of Kimie's, they became adept with the fine knives used to carve the blocks. Kimie also took classes in lost-wax leather dyeing (for coin purses, belts, etc.), tie-dyeing, beaded crocheting and other handicrafts. Her main interest, though, always was the socializing; and she always waved off any praise for her artistry.

In January 1963 Niigata had another very heavy snow: 30 inches from one storm. I was in Tokyo attending another Center Director meeting. From USIS-Tokyo's Japanese staff I heard that my area was catching it. I called Kimie that evening. She said it was bad enough that train service was suspended on the main rail line to Niigata.

The next morning, the resourceful Tokyo administrative staff arranged an alternate return route for me: up the east side of Japan, then a change of trains at Koriyama (where Kimie was in the station bombing in 1945) and west across the mountains, thus avoiding the line blocked by snow. Riding with me until I changed to the westbound train was Manning Hawthorne, ACC Director in Sendai.* We had visited Manning and Alice in Sendai.

Earlier when Manning's predecessor, Mark Peattie, was in Sendai, we had sent Hugh-ko there alone for a visit. The son of early *Readers Digest* editor Donald Culross Peattie, Mark resigned from the Foreign Service soon after to pursue an academic career.

As my train climbed to cross the mountains, the trackside snow became ever deeper. Just as we entered one tunnel, the engineer hit the brakes and began furiously blowing his whistle. The train ground to a halt. A conductor hurried through the car and descended to the tracks, joining other conductors flashing their lanterns and shouting to each other. A passenger facing me said there had been an accident. I opened my window, curious to see what was going on. At that moment the train

---

\* Manning was a great-grandson of Nathaniel Hawthorne. When so identified, he liked to add, "Also descended from a few horse thieves." We stayed good friends for over a decade, attended his daughter's wedding in Tokyo a few years later and exchanged Christmas cards until he died in the 1980's.

crew converged just below me, their flashlights focusing on a body steaming in the cold tunnel. It was a high school student, his head distorted from the train's impact. He apparently had been walking to school and took a shortcut through the snow-free tunnel. As the train continued toward Niigata, I reflected on how the tragedy would impact the student's family and schoolmates in that mountain village. Such incidents and images do not easily fade from one's memory.

In early spring 1963, USIS-Tokyo alerted us that we would have our first ambassadorial visit in many years. In 1961, Pres. Kennedy named Harvard professor Edwin Reischauer ambassador to Japan.* Most Japanese were as entranced by Kennedy's young dynamism as we were. With Kennedy in the White House and a renowned Harvard Asian scholar, born and raised in Japan (son of American missionaries and married to Haru, a daughter of the prominent Matsukata family) heading our Embassy, much heat went out of the anti-Americanism generated in the 1960 Security Treaty riots, to be replaced by warmer feelings toward the United States. (The Japanese generally had not heard of Ed Murrow, who was then Director of USIA, also a JFK appointee.)

So, now we at the Niigata ACC went into intensive planning mode, with frequent calls back and forth with Frank Tenny about what Reischauer wished to do on this visit.

An interesting note on how this bilingual scholar operated: Although fluent in Japanese, he always used an interpreter on official trips as insurance against any misunderstanding. Haru often accompanied him, too. Not as a language aide, though, as I will explain later.

Our 2½-day schedule for the ambassador had him making a speech at Niigata Nippo Hall, calling on the Governor and Mayor, lunching with two labor leaders, visiting a tulip farm for a lighter touch and fresh air,

---

* For more on Reischauer, see his My Life Between Japan and America, Harper & Row (1986). Haru told her story in Samurai and Silk. My copy is the Tuttle Company version, 1986.

and attending parties by the Governor and Mayor and a reception at our home. Also, doing a taped interview at a television studio.

Such a schedule requires detailed plans on logistics and staffing, with all political niceties and protocol fully worked out. A snag we ran into early was that the two labor leaders—from opposite political poles—refused to eat together; but the schedule only allowed for one lunch period with them. It turned out that Reischauer liked a light lunch and suggested just a lunch of Japanese noodles. So, we set up two back-to-back noodle lunches, one in our living room with the right-wing labor leader and the other in the dining room with the leftist leader. We had the noodles delivered from a nearby noodle shop, as Kimie's kitchen was tied up with preparing for that evening's dinner party.

The parties by the governor and mayor would be at the city's finest Japanese restaurants, with service and entertainment by some of Niigata's loveliest geisha, who were most interested in seeing the famous Haru Reischauer. All events went off beautifully and were fully enjoyed and appreciated by all. Kimie's planning of the dual luncheons and our home reception was great, as usual.

With the ambassadorial visit over and all our guests gone, Fujita, Fukui and I went out on the town to celebrate. To really kick back, Fujita-san suggested a downtown bar. As we settled in, the usual young bar hostesses joined us. Fujita began to weave a tale for them, claiming we were seamen from a foreign freighter and totally new to Niigata. After some 20 minutes, the manager happened to walk by. I had never seen him before; but he recognized me from media coverage of the Ambassador's visit. He bowed and addressed me as "Mr. Director," blowing sky high Fujita's tale to the hostesses.

An aside here on the subject of geisha. By now, most non-Japanese know that geisha are not prostitutes, but are trained from an early age to entertain at parties by offering witty conversation, drinks, singing and dancing. Their forte is inflating men's egos. Naturally, the profession may sometimes lead to affairs on the side.

Niigata geisha are reputedly Japan's most beautiful. In general, Niigata women are noted for their beauty, probably from the fine complexions they get from long stretches of sunless damp weather November through April. The area's women also had a reputation for "ruling the roost" at home. A local saying was that "In Niigata, willows and men do not flourish." Willows, because of much windy and snowy weather; the men, because their women dominated them.

In June 1963, I received orders for transfer to USIS-Tokyo. The time had come to wind down this Niigata tour and move on.

But first, a series of farewell parties for us. The governor's party for us was again at a Japanese restaurant, with geisha in attendance, etc. There, Kimie was attending only her second party where geisha were present (the first was the party for the Reischauers). An older geisha was assigned to Kimie, and they had a lively conversation about a geisha's life in the 1960s. "My" geisha was probably about 45 and still attractive. I decided to turn the tables on her: instead of letting her flatter me, which made me uncomfortable anyway, I concentrated on flattering her. That threw her "game" off, and she actually seemed to become smitten with me. As we left the party, she quietly asked if I could come back later that evening to see her. I had to beg off as diplomatically as I could!

Before transferring to Tokyo, we decided to sell "Hidari Jingoro"—our 1960 Datsun Bluebird. So, I contacted the head of the local Nissan dealership, whom I had met at Rotary luncheons. He promised to help. He soon found a buyer for us, a man from a small city in southern Niigata prefecture who really wanted an American car, but decided a left-handed Bluebird was more practical and a minor compromise. After driving the Bluebird and Carryall around the area for almost three years, we knew the attention a person can attract when, sitting in the front passenger seat (the driver's seat in a normal Japanese car), he throws his hands up or appears to be ignoring the road ahead. In our case, if Kimie was behind the wheel, the oncoming drivers' shock was even greater, as few Japanese women were driving in those days.

Our departure from Niigata was almost a mirror image of our arrival 33 months earlier. An even larger assembly of people—friends and dignitaries (and our two maids)—came to the train station to bid us goodbye, and the farewell bowing was deeper and more sincerely warm. Then we were off for Tokyo and points east.

# FIRST HOME LEAVE

## (SUMMER 1963)

The Foreign Service norm in the '60s was that an officer served overseas about seven years out of every ten, with the other three on "Washington assignment." One Foreign Service perk is home leave after each 2- or 3-year overseas tour. This is not mainly a vacation, but a chance for an officer and his family to re-connect with American life for a while before again going overseas. Without such breaks, they would tend to become expatriates in the truest sense, knowing their culture, society and family back home only second or third hand. Home leave helps to head off such alienation and to keep our diplomats better abreast of things American. Another rule was that an officer could travel "surface" just one way when taking home leave due to the extra time that surface travel requires compared to air travel; but his family could go surface both ways.

Now after three years in Niigata, we were off on our first home leave—25 days plus travel and consultation time in Washington, D.C. Through USIS-Tokyo I had arranged our travel and other necessary details.

In the 1960s, American President Lines (APL) still operated passenger liners across the Pacific: the "President Hoover" (oldest and smallest), "President Wilson" (which Kimie and Rits had taken in 1950), "President Cleveland" and "President Roosevelt," the newest. Our reservations were on the "Hoover," which, despite its small size, was one of the more stable because of its low center of gravity.

After a visit with Kimie's family, we had an early afternoon dockside sendoff by Kimie's siblings, Fujita-san from the Niigata ACC and Kimie's o-koto teacher. This was my first APL voyage, Kimie's second. To avoid the seasickness that had plagued her on her 1950 voyage, Kimie took Dramamine right away. Soon after we set sail, she was zonked out on her berth, not to revive until nearly dinner time, with Japan already out of sight below the western horizon.

This was Hugh-ko's first ocean voyage; and he had a ball, spending some time with other children in the play spaces provided and some time with us at the rail, watching the flying fish and occasional porpoises in the warm current flowing up from the tropics.

Another Foreign Service family on board was the Holland family. Harry was a consular officer in Tokyo, who had visited us twice in Niigata on consular business. E.g., a young Japanese woman had married a U.S. Air Force sergeant, but learned, after he suddenly died on Guam, that he had an American wife and children back in the USA. The woman and her son had returned to Niigata. Harry had visited Niigata to help the woman apply with the Air Force for child support. Harry's five children, aged about 15 to 3, also were thoroughly enjoying the sumptuous APL meals and the children's game room.

A nice part of trans-Pacific travel by APL liner was that the ships stopped in Honolulu for a day, as Kimie had in 1950. On our seventh day, the Hoover passed the most northerly Hawaiian island, Gardner Pinnacles, a volcanic core eroded down to perhaps a half square mile rock jutting some 250 feet out of the ocean. It is home to thousands of sea birds, including the sleek frigate bird. As the "Hoover" passed near the island, the bridge blew the ship's loud horn, raising thousands of alarmed birds from their roosts and nests.

At daybreak the next morning, Hugh-ko and I went on deck and found that the ship had just passed Kauai and slowed to about eight knots so as not to arrive in Honolulu ahead of schedule. In Honolulu, we explored the Waikiki area; but could not visit with Louise and her family because they now lived in Hilo on "the Big Island."

Five more days and we were approaching the Golden Gate. (No nerves this time about snagging the bridge. She had been on it many times and knew how high it was.) From Oakland we took a Southern Pacific train headed to Chicago. Going to the dining car the first evening, we met the Holland family returning from their meal. Harry looked pale, and said, "You should see the prices! We're going to have a family conference about our meals." His kids had ordered their food as if they were still freeloading on the "Hoover." (On "travel status" our allowance only partially covered expensive dining-car meals.)

Beyond Utah, the train climbed into Wyoming's high country, where we began spotting pronghorn antelope not far from the rail line. With four hours between trains in Chicago, we went to the aquarium where we were entranced by such rarities as a sawfish and large sharks. Then we caught the B&O's "Capitol Limited" into Washington, where I was debriefed at USIA.

For our return trip to Japan, the government would reimburse me based on the standard airfare; but Kimie and Hugh-ko's surface travel costs would be reimbursed at a set mileage rate. I should note that a major reason we traveled by surface was that Kimie always disliked flying. She tended toward acrophobia and always imagined worst-case scenarios when flying. As much as possible, we kept her on the ground (or large ships).

We settled into a D.C. hotel and contacted Rits and Bill, now joined by 9-month-old Sheila Marie Geoghegan, our first grandchild. I don't recall what we did besides visiting Rits and her family and Bill's family. We bought a used Studebaker for a cross-country drive, as we planned to see much more of the USA than we had during the 1950's, when our finances were tighter.

Also, I had two public missions to fulfill. Before I left Niigata, Mayor Tamaki of Tsubame had asked me to sound out the Mayor of Meriden, Connecticut, about affiliating with Tsubame as a sister city. In same the spirit that business rivals socialize together as Rotarians or Lions, he hoped to have friendly ties with Meriden, home of International Silversmiths, a firm sorely bruised by the competition from little

178

Tsubame. Also, Niigata Mayor Watanabe had asked me to make the same kind of approach to Long Beach.

So, after wistful goodbyes to our Rits and her family, we three headed north through Maryland, New Jersey and New York. We skirted New York City to save time and arrived in Meriden before lunch of the second day.

I had called ahead for an appointment with the mayor, who received me quite cordially. It turned out that he was not running for re-election that fall; but he promised to pass the sister-city proposal on to his successor. In Japan months later, we heard that Meriden's manufacturers had flatly turned thumbs down on the proposal.

Next, we drove northwest through Connecticut to Rifton, New York, where brother George and his family (7 children and counting) lived in a Hutterite Bruderhof (community).* We arrived in mid-evening, after bedtime for George's children. So we chatted briefly with George and Vonnie and then went to a guesthouse where they had arranged rooms for us. The next morning as we left for breakfast, five of their children were at the entrance silently waiting to greet us with the most beautiful smiles. We spent the entire day in the community. At that time, it still had members from the original group that had fled Nazi Germany in the 1930's. So, German was the second language even for many younger members. We had lunch with the community (perhaps 120 people) in the large dining hall and were shown the other facilities and gardens.

In contrast to the farms in Modesto and north Georgia where George and his family had lived before, Rifton's economic base was a woodworking shop that made playground equipment for direct and catalog sales. Most impressive was the close fraternal spirit shared by all—an entire community on the same spiritual wavelength. In the early afternoon we bade goodbye and set out again.

---

\* Hutterites are a religious sect organized into "intentional communities" for sharing worldly and spiritual resources. They are mainly in the eastern U.S., Canada and UK and number several thousand members.

Our next destination was Niagara Falls, so we drove west along the Erie Canal, through Buffalo to a motel near the falls. That evening we walked to an overlook for a preview of the falls. The next day we did our full-scale sightseeing, taking the elevator down behind the American Falls and riding the "Maid of the Mist" up the river to the roiling water just below the falls.

In summer 1963, the Interstate Highway system was still mostly on engineers' drawing boards. Driving was closer to the earth, so to speak, and more scenic, but also slower than today. So, we took a direct route from Niagara across Ontario to Windsor, crossed into Detroit and found a motel outside the city.

We had a small surprise there—"aging shock"?—when a couple next door knocked on our door that evening and asked if Hugh-ko (not yet 12) could baby-sit for their 5-year-old child. Earlier we had considered getting a babysitter for Hugh-ko!

The next day, we transited Michigan to Muskegon, where we caught the car ferry across Lake Michigan to Milwaukee. Amazing about that voyage was that, with a sharp wind blowing down the lake, the crossing was far rougher than our Pacific crossing had been. Waves were breaking over the ship's bow until we neared the Milwaukee side.

Our next stop was Madison, Wisconsin, to see Mother's brother, Uncle Rowland and his wife, Frances. We had a good visit with them and, before pushing on, heard their advice that we visit the Wisconsin Dells, close to our route westbound anyway. So, the next day we did the Dells, riding a tour boat on the Wisconsin River and enjoying its remarkable sandstone formations while the guide shared local lore with us. We then continued on across the Mississippi into Minnesota and found a motel for the night.

The next day, we stopped in White Earth to see a church built some 90 years earlier by my grandfather, Solomon Burleson, an Episcopal priest. In his buggy pulled by a pair of ponies, he rode a circuit of parishes on those frontier prairies in the 1860s, '70s and '80s. (His sons' biography of him says, "Fifty miles a Sunday over broad prairies, with two services and a Sunday school, was not an unusual record.") After crossing southern Minnesota, we entered South Dakota, drove through Sioux Falls where Uncle Hugh had served as the Episcopal bishop (1916-30) and went on to Springfield, where I was born.

On a bluff above the Missouri River, Springfield had but one main shopping street. At a gas stand I asked where the Indian girls' school was in the 1920s, and so got directions to the house where John, Mary, George and I were born. I took some photos and, lacking any memories of the place, drove on.

Through miles of cornfields, wheat, etc., we were astounded at the number of prairie chickens and pheasants flying across our course— almost as thick, it seemed, as the myriad flying insects we were used to encountering in farming areas. Checking into a motel in Chamberlain, also on the Missouri, we heard a report on the evening news that the number of pheasants (Chinese ringnecks raised and released for sport hunters) in the state was estimated at 6,000,000. We had seen 4-5 times more prairie chickens than pheasants. Does that mean the state then had a mind-boggling 25,000,000 to 30,000,000 prairie chickens?

After supper at a cafe near our motel, we walked to a large shop displaying an "Indian Souvenirs" sign. The inside was crammed with souvenirs; but I turned a number over and saw only "Made in Japan" labels on each one. Frustrated, I asked the sales lady, "Have you any souvenirs not made by Japanese Indians?"

"Not one," she answered. She did have on display a very interesting specimen taken from the Missouri River: a stuffed paddle fish, a very primitive-looking critter with a flattened 20-inch paddle in front, perhaps from the catfish family.

The following day we continued west, stopping occasionally at rock shops to buy arrow-heads or unusual stones. Then we entered the Badlands and made a roadside stop to briefly explore that wasteland and pick up a few fossils from the myriads scattered over that onetime ocean bed. That night we took a motel in Rapid City and walked through its Dinosaur Park. (Note: This is generally the route of today's Interstate 90.)

The next day at Mount Rushmore we had lunch at the cafeteria later to be the locale for the faked shooting scene in Hitchcock's movie "North by Northwest." I had buffalo steak. We spent nearly an hour taking in the great Borglum sculptures of the four presidents. This was, after all, an area where my family had spent summer vacations in the 1920's at the church's nearby Camp Kearney. Here too, Bishop Hugh Burleson had given the benediction when President Coolidge and other dignitaries dedicated the site as work started on the massive sculptures of our four presidents.

Next we drove north-by-northwest to Deadwood. Just outside of town, we saw a hand-lettered roadside sign, "Pan for gold. $3." That interested Hugh-ko, so we drove down a short dirt road to a creek bed, where a bearded prospector took Hugh-ko and, for a few dollars, showed him how to slosh the sandy soil in a gold pan. At the end, he put the few grains of gold that Hugh-ko found into a vial of water. In town, we went to a cemetery to see the graves of Doc Holliday and Calamity Jane, famed Old West characters.

Onward then into Wyoming, past the 900-foot Devils Tower glowing red in the sunset. (Locale for "Close Encounters of the 3rd Kind." Towns on the map, where I thought we might have dinner, turned out to be little more than tiny places with gas stations. So, I drove through to Gillette, arriving about 9:00 PM. Tired and hungry, we checked into a motel. Kimie insisted she desperately needed some sushi. In outback Wyoming in late evening! I went out and found a Chinese diner, where the chef was getting ready to hang up the "Closed" sign. I cajoled him into fixing three carryout fried rice dinners—no sushi. No "Rocky Mountain oysters" either!

Next day: over the Bighorn Mountains, down Ten Sleep Canyon (a 10-day journey in the "good ole days"). Then on to Cody by about 5 PM. We found a motel there, rested a bit and visited the Buffalo Bill Museum—a well-run, interesting institution.

Now a big day: up the North Fork of the Shoshone River into Yellowstone National Park. Just inside the park we saw a small hot spring at the roadside. No touristy signs, just a fat woodchuck warming himself beside the unspoiled little spring. We decided this was the perfect place for a snack and spent a pleasant half hour sharing the placid surroundings with the relaxed woodchuck and savoring our togetherness on this cross-country journey. In the Park proper, saw Old Faithful, the many other spectacular forms of volcanism here and the many bears begging food at the roadside like Bowery bums.

Our next destination was Sandpoint in northern Idaho to see Cousin Allan Burleson. So, we drove north from Yellowstone into "big sky" Montana and overnighted in a smaller town. On the second day we drove through Glacier National Park on The Highway to the Sun and spent the night just outside West Glacier. The following day we detoured to see Hungry Horse Dam, a most impressive high dam.

Then on to Sandpoint. We found Allan by checking at the post office, as we had only his P.O. box number. The postmaster insisted that I show my ID to prove that I really was a relative. Allan was living with his eldest brother, Edward, in a small rented house in town. He took us to lunch near Sandpoint and then, to extend the visit, rode with us to Spokane, which he often visited and where he had many friends. There he phoned one of those acquaintances and arranged for her to join us for an early dinner at the nicest hotel in town. She was "ninth-cousin Lena." Allan has always been a walking encyclopedia of Burleson family history and had actually established that this pleasant octogenarian lady was a ninth cousin.

Our last destination on our cross-country run was Port Townsend on Washington's Olympic Peninsula, where brother John now was pastor of a church, with Mother keeping house for him. Allan persuaded us first to detour 50 miles to see the Grand Coulee Dam. Driving into the sunset, we went up State Route 2, found the Grand Coulee turnoff and arrived there just after dark. We "did" the mile-wide dam the next morning, enjoying its sweeping grandeur, and then pushed on. Through the fields and past miles of fruit orchards in the Wenatchee

Valley, then over the Cascades at 4000-foot Stevens Pass to descend into the ever green Puget Sound area.

We caught a state auto ferry to Whidbey Island, drove up that long narrow island and rode another ferry across the Sound to Port Townsend—3,300 road miles from Washington, D.C., by the indirect route we had followed.

We had not seen John in over 10 years, nor Mother for about eight years. So, we had much catching up to do with both of them. John showed us around the picturesque Victorian-era town, which once had ambitions of becoming the state capital. He also took Hugh-ko and me for an afternoon of fishing off the town's eastern and northern shores. The fish were not biting; so Hugh-ko and I tried a bit more fishing from a short pier. Net result: I got an octopus on my line that quickly swam to a piling and would not be dislodged. I had to cut my line.

After two pleasant days with Mother and John, we had to move on. Next destination: Berkeley and points south. U.S. Highway 101 took us south to the capital, Olympia. We stopped briefly to tour a brewery and then continued south into Oregon.

In central Oregon we turned east to Crater Lake to spend an hour enjoying the beauty of 8000-foot Mount Mazama's silent crater with its limpid blue lake. Then down the Rogue River to US 101 again. We overnighted in Grants Pass and the next morning transited the Redwood Highway portion of 101 in northern California and reached Berkeley about dinnertime.

In Berkeley, we of course had warm visits with sister Mary and her family and with Kitty and her family. I also dropped by Cal to visit old friends at the East Asian Library where I had spent so much time in the '50s.

That was not the end of the line. I had not been footloose in southern California since 1945 and wanted to show my lady and Hugh-ko that part of California. And, I had to see the Long Beach mayor. So, after a week in Berkeley, we took the Studebaker back onto the road, driving down the coast to Long Beach.

At City Hall there, the mayor's secretary asked me wait to see the mayor's lady assistant. After about half an hour, that lady came out and coolly told me the mayor was busy; and in any case Long Beach was not interested in a link with Niigata. They had heard that Niigata was also negotiating with Khabarovsk in Siberia for a sister-city affiliation; and the city council would certainly not consider affiliating with a Japanese city that also had a communist sister city. That was that. No ifs, ands or "but, lady!"

So, on to San Diego. We saw the famous zoo there, drove by our 1935 home and visited the old Spanish Mission. I wanted to stay the night at the famous Hotel de Coronado, but Kimie saw the venerable structure as a fire trap, objected to the noise of planes flying overhead and insisted that instead we stay in a modern motel. We found one near La Jolla. Ever so strong willed and feisty, my girl! On the return leg we had a deadline for reaching San Francisco: Our flight reservations were set. So, Kimie refused a 7-mile side trip to see my former Vista home. Our only detour was a few miles off 101 to see Santa Barbara's Spanish Mission.

Back in Berkeley, Kitty's husband agreed to try to sell the Studebaker for us; and he kindly delivered us to the airport in San Francisco.

Our flight to Honolulu was jam-packed with Iowa firemen en route to a convention. They were having a ball and their noise gave Kimie a headache. By the end of the 5-hour flight she charged me with getting our onward flight to Tokyo (7 hours+) upgraded to first class.

But, first we took an inter-island flight to Hilo on Hawaii Island, where Louise, Charley and their four children now lived. After his time in Washington as administrative aide to one of Hawaii's appointed senators, Charley and the family yearned to return to Hawaii. Their chance came when Congress created a new economic development program for depressed areas. Charley's job now was trying to make U.S. Government loans for new businesses in Hilo. Despite the lush setting of wild fruits, orchids and palms on all sides, business was not lush there in the early '60s.

They met us at Hilo airport and took us to their rented home on a small peninsula jutting north from Hilo. The house sat on two acres of coconut palms with a long beach front. There, in the evening, we could see Hawaiians casting their throw nets for fish, and on the beach one could comb the sand for bits of olivene thrown off by the goddess Pelee's nearby volcanoes. Shades of Somerset Maugham, Joseph Conrad or James Michener!

The next day, while young Charley showed Hugh-ko his Hilo, Louise took us on a tour down the east coast, through a village that a few years earlier was overrun by molten lava and now stood empty—here and there a tricycle or blackened tree stumps embedded in the hardened lava. We stopped briefly at a "black sand" beach—fine lava granules steam-blasted from the lava flows when the fiery rock hit the sea. On another jaunt, we drove inland to Volcanoes National Park, where on every side we could see the evidence of recent eruptions. Many fascinating sights in the high country around Mauna Kea and Kilauea. All too soon, we had to fly back to Honolulu to overnight before our early morning flight to Tokyo.

At Honolulu International Airport about 7 AM the next morning, Kimie was uptight because I had not upgraded our tickets. But on board, we found just 8 other passengers on the whole plane—a DC-8. We could each stretch out on a full row of seats. And, with no passengers in first class, a stewardess from that section came back to economy to offer us food and drinks that would otherwise have gone unused in the forward cabin. A very comfortable and relaxed flight, in contrast to the one earlier from San Francisco.

So ended a very memorable first home leave. We had sailed 4,500 miles, ridden the rails 2,700 miles, driven 5,500 miles and then flew 5,000 miles back to Tokyo. We had visited all my siblings and their offspring, Mother, her brother and his wife, Allan and his brother. We had seen the area where my grandfather had served his parishes 80 and 90 years earlier. We had seen my birthplace, wide swaths of the West and the

Pacific coast, and parts of Hawaii. Time to get back to the work of making this great United States more understandable to the Japanese.

That fall in a Japanese newspaper I would see a memorable and symbolic photo: some of the first Japanese tourists able to afford a trip to Hawaii, learning about it first hand by walking on Waikiki Beach—in business suits and ties and black oxford shoes. Twenty years later, Americans would bemoan the Japanese buy-up of Waikiki property and worry that next they would buy the local golf courses and close them to non-Japanese. But, that's jumping ahead of our tale, isn't it.

# TOKYO YEARS--I

## (1963-66)

As we arrived in Tokyo in late summer 1963, several USIS officers who had been there 8-12 years were becoming short-timers. Such long service in one post was not common for State Department Foreign Service Officers, but had been countenanced by USIA since the core of our work, especially in Japan, was building personal relationships of trust and mutual understanding with "opinion molders" at the heart of the society so that America's message would get a fair hearing.

Whereas in Niigata my USIS title had been Branch Post Public Affairs officer (BPAO), I now was the Assistant Cultural Affairs Officer (ACAO), reporting to Cultural Affairs Officer (CAO) Walter Nichols, who reported to the Country Public Affairs Officer (CPAO)—the top USIS officer in Japan. Got all that?

That meant I would help the CAO plan and carry out a variety of cultural programs. Walt Nichols, like Branch Post supervisor Frank Tenny, was a "BIJ" (born in Japan) son of missionary parents. Unlike Frank, Walt had not studied Japanese language in high school or college. So, he read Japanese with difficulty and spoke a schoolboy form of the language, getting away with that through pure panache and personal charm.

We worked together for about 10 months, putting on lecture/discussion programs with visiting U.S. professors of American studies and specialists on defense and security affairs. The point of the latter two themes was to help Japan's policymakers and emerging "defense intellectuals" better understand U.S. defense policy and the domestic politics and geopolitical ideas that produced that policy. We sought non-ideological discussion of our bilateral security relationship with Japan.

After less than a year in that work, in mid-1964, I moved into a higher ranked position being vacated by one of the long-term USIS officers, Ivan Izenberg. The job: Research Officer, which much better utilized my background in Japanese studies. It later would also begin to "type-cast" me as a specialist and "policy wonk," rather than the generalist that Foreign Service personnel managers prefer.

In my Research Office, I had a staff of six Japanese, four of them professionals. These were outstanding people. Sen Nishiyama was always on standby to serve as the ambassador's interpreter. Less often so in the late '60s, when a State Department officer, Jim Wickel, came from Washington to do most of the interpreting for the ambassador. Sen was very much a colleague, rather than my subordinate. He was about 15 years older than I and a Nisei, born and raised in Utah. He had graduated from Cal Tech in the early '30s in electrical engineering. About then, his father died. Following Japanese custom, Sen and his mother took the ashes to Japan to be interred in a family tomb.

Due to the Great Depression and prevailing prejudices, Sen had been unable to find a decent job in the States. But, his Cal Tech E.E. degree drew keen interest in Japan, and he was offered a job in a telecommunications lab of the Japanese Government. To accept it he had to renounce his American citizenship. As he had dual citizenship, that was not complicated. About the same time, he met a Japanese lady to whom he was attracted and whom he soon married. So, his decision was not a tough one at the time.

After World War II, Sen became an important liaison and interpreter between Japanese telecommunications offices and Occupation offices. When the Occupation ended, the reopened American Embassy snapped him up, since a fully bilingual Japanese was rare. When I met him, Sen was probably the most proficient interpreter between Japanese and English in Japan. Later in life, he would be President of the Japan

Interpreters Assn. and a Vice President of the International Interpreters Assn. He also would author *Understanding and Misunderstanding* (in Japanese) recapping his experiences in cross-cultural communication, the first of several books he would write in that field.

Another of my staff professionals was Yumi Goto. The wife of a university professor, she had participated as a university student before the war in the first US-Japan student exchange and visited America under that program. Right after World War II she was an interpreter between Japanese railway officials and a U.S. army unit in Niigata. Later, back in Tokyo she was a translator at the Tokyo War Crimes Trials. When I met her, she had already authored books analyzing American humor from a sociological perspective. Her son later became a distinguished professor specializing in Southeast Asia.

Another author on the Research Office staff was Noboru Kaneko, who—on the side—was prolifically turning out humor books, some 10 titles by the late '60s. In our office, he monitored and reported on Japanese radio and TV commentary relating to issues in US-Japan relations.

The fourth professional was Kazushige Kaneko, "little Kaneko" because he was shorter than Noboru Kaneko. He was not little, however, in his dynamic energy and breadth of interests. His avocations were archaeology and comparative studies of Asian cultures. In the '60s, he frequently contributed articles to Japanese journals on these subject areas.

Our sterling secretary/administrative assistant, Miss Motoko Mizutani, and a typist, Miss Yanagisawa rounded out our administrative staff. The whole office was very congenial and close knit.

Our work entailed monitoring and analyzing Japanese views—public opinion and the elite attitudes—so as to keep USIS and the rest of the Embassy updated on how U.S. policies were being received. Since security ties had a major role in the relationship, we closely watched trends in attitudes. So, I began studying that subject myself and worked with other USIS offices doing programming in that area. We also did some surveys of public responses to USIS output—magazines, press releases, films etc.

Haru Reischauer remembered Kimie from her Niigata visit and now began having Kimie accompany her to various social events and meetings. For, as a girl, Haru had attended schools where the instruction was in English; and her family had mostly conversed in English at home. Kimie was more adept than she in catching nuances in Japanese and so became a key player on Haru's "support team" of Embassy wives.

Although assigned to Tokyo, we first lived in an upstairs apartment over the U.S. Consulate on the Yokohama waterfront, for the Embassy had too few apartments in Tokyo until another apartment building under construction was completed. We have fond memories of our truncated year in that elegant old building. It was convenient to the Navy PX and Commissary in south Yokohama and to Yokohama's Chinatown, where good shopping and fine eating could be had. Convenient also to Kimie's family.

And, Kimie knew the area. The waterfront had been a favorite strolling area during her girlhood. A few blocks north was South Pier where APL liners docked. The consulate was where in 1946 we met our Nisei friends, Roy Iwaki and Ken Kaneda, where in 1947 I had consulted with Consul Overton on dealing with the Army's refusal to let us marry and where, in 1950, Consul General Johnson had given Kimie and Ritsuko ID papers in lieu of passports. (In the 1970s, the property reverted to the City of Yokohama and the building was razed and replaced by a large museum.)

Two earth-shaking events occurred while we lived at the Consulate. We heard of JFK's assassination there; and Kimie was surprised one noon hour while she and Hugh-ko were near the fountain behind the Consulate, to see the water suddenly slopping back and forth, obviously from a real earth-shaker: the 1964 Niigata earthquake, which severely damaged parts of the city we had left just the year before.

With other diplomats living there, I commuted by train to Tokyo. And, Hugh-ko now entered junior high at St. Mary's, a Catholic boys' school in Tokyo and commuted with us as far as Shinagawa. This living arrangement would be temporary, as we knew from the outset. Suddenly our stay there became even shorter, for the State Department's Japanese Language School was moving from Tokyo to Yokohama; and its director was to have our apartment. So, we had but 10 months in the old consulate.

Now we had to find a rental in Tokyo until the new embassy apartment building was completed. The Embassy would pay up to $700/month of the rent, but nothing of a suitable size was available at that price in central Tokyo. Ultimately, we found a house in west Tokyo. Even there, we had to pay some $300 monthly out of pocket. During our move, we had our upright piano delivered to the home of Kimie's sister Sumie, whose daughter Kaori was becoming a serious piano student and would later teach piano.

Now Hugh-ko and I were commuting from west Tokyo (on the same train line I took in 1946 to go from the Signal Corps battalion to see Kimie). After some 9 or 10 months, the new apartments in the Embassy housing compound were completed. In those days we called it the "Mitsui Compound," for in 1952 the State Department had bought the site, a 10-minute walk to the Embassy, from the Mitsui, the old-line *zaibatsu* family from which UC's East Asian Library had bought its prized collection of books. On the 10-acre site, replacing a Mitsui family mansion damaged in wartime bombings, our government had built the apartment buildings, Harris House, Perry House and now Grew House.

In March 1964, we suddenly heard that Ambassador Reischauer had been stabbed. A deranged youth had vaulted the Embassy wall just as the ambassador was leaving for lunch and, stumbling, managed only to stab him in the leg. Reischauer was rushed to the Toranomon Hospital, two blocks away. For public relations reasons, he decided to stay there rather than go to a U.S. military hospital outside of Tokyo. We all took turns taking mail, messages, etc., to him and so got to know him personally better than we did through our official duties alone. (The PR turned sour when the ambassador got hepatitis from a blood transfusion there. The disease returned in his old age and ultimately killed him.)

Now we were offered our choice of an apartment in the new Grew House or in Harris House. We chose the older Harris house, where apartments were mellower and bilevel—bedrooms upstairs, living/dining area and kitchen downstairs. They had nice balconies with big sliding glass doors overlooking the former Mitsui gardens. We would live there for the next 4½ years, with a view of the Tokyo Tower and, from the flat roof, Mount Fuji when the weather was clear enough.

One Saturday in January 1965, Kimie and Hugh-ko went to Yokohama to shop and visit Sumie. Driving back about 8 PM, they were rear-ended on the highway by a large truck driven by a very drunk young driver. Kimie called me in great distress from a gas station at the accident scene. I immediately took a taxi for Yokohama. When I arrived there 40 minutes later, the Buick—new only six months earlier —was sitting on the roadway surrounded by police flares, its back smashed in. And, no sign of Kimie and Hugh-ko. A traffic officer at the scene said the occupants had been taken by police ambulance to a nearby hospital. Then I began to worry, for Kimie had said nothing about injuries. But the car looked wrecked enough for either of my precious ones to have been hurt badly.

At the hospital, though, I soon ran into Kimie and Hugh-ko walking down a hallway—neither of them visibly injured. Actually, Hugh-ko had been briefly knocked out by the impact. Fortunately, at Kimie's urging just a week earlier, I had had seat belts installed. (They were not yet mandatory.) And thereafter Kimie made sure that anyone riding in the car used a seat belt. Kimie had minor scalp cuts from rear-window glass that exploded through the car when the truck hit. Her less obvious injuries were strained arm and back muscles.

We had the wrecked Buick towed to the PX garage in Yokohama to be checked by our insurance company. The next day, friends drove us to Yokohama to see the car. Two GIs were standing there. One remarked, "Damn! Somebody must have been killed in that one!" We eased his mind by telling him that the Kimie and Hugh-ko, standing beside me, had been the car's occupants—wearing their seat belts.

There were later complications: the trucking company's appeal to me to help get their driver out of jail, the fact that the company had covered their insurance only with an IOU because they were so under-capitalized. In the end we got just the Buick's replacement cost. None of the costs of a temporary rental car. Nothing for pain and suffering, which continued over several years for Kimie.

In May 1965, we took a four-day vacation to Nikko. Hugh-ko was in a Boy Scout troop at his school and was to join the troop for a camp-out in upper Nikko a few days later. We rented a small suite at a lodge beside Lake Chuzenji and visited the shrines of lower Nikko, just as we had on our honeymoon in 1947. And, we boated and fished on the lake, landing a good catch of really great land-locked salmon.

One morning after breakfast, Hugh-ko and I decided to climb Mount Nantai, an extinct volcano rising straight up from the lake behind our lodge. Eyeing the mountain from lakeside, we guessed that it was 1500-1800 feet to the summit, maybe a three-hour climb and half that time to descend. So, we took Hugh-ko's Boy Scout canteen of water and two Tootsie Rolls with us and set off up the mountain's west slope. The first part was an easy walk in woods of broadleaf trees. Then we hit a steeper stretch where higher-elevation winds had felled many trees. We found ourselves trying to walk on slippery rotting logs to avoid the thick underbrush now growing there. Next we came to thickets of stubby conifers, which became ever more difficult to penetrate. By then it was nearly noon, and we were only about half way to the crater rim.

So, we crossed laterally to where rock slides had buried the conifers, assuming we could make good progress straight up the slides. Except that these were active slides. For every two steps forward we slipped back about one step, making the going very slow. Finally, about 4 PM we reached the top. From our climb of Mount Bandai three years earlier, we expected to find a refreshment stand at the top. We badly needed food and water, as the canteen was long since empty and the Tootsie Rolls gone. Sure enough, there on the far side of the crater we saw a small building and began hiking the crater rim toward it. An hour later, we stood in front of that concrete stand, crest fallen: It was empty, not yet open for the season. 5 PM and it soon would be dark.

Fortunately, a well-worn trail led down Nantai's south slope. We set out and made it to the town at the bottom in just two hours, hiking the last half hour in the dark. I found a phone and called Kimie to ease her concerns about us. And, we bought some food and drink before catching a taxi back to our lodge.

The next day, before driving back to Tokyo, we dropped Hugh-ko off at the Boy Scout camp. He would be bussed back with his Scout troop.

In 1965, the Japanese media began sharply criticizing America's growing involvement in Vietnam; and Washington's foreign affairs agencies asked USIS-Tokyo to begin regular reporting of Japanese reactions to that situation. That task landed on our little Research Office, and would remain a major chore of that staff for the next eight years. We began intensive daily monitoring of media commentary and close analyses of opinion surveys relevant to U.S. Vietnam policy. That filled many hours of my day until we left Tokyo in 1969. The spin-off benefit for me was that it forced me to closely hone my grasp of the language. I asked Sen and Goto-san to check my understanding of the nuances in the daily flood of commentary.

On the negative side, it meant much overtime, to the neglect of my family. The Embassy Political Section, the Ambassador and several Washington agencies were depending on our output, and sometimes called me directly or cabled requests for our assessment. They knew I could, for example, watch an 11:30 PM TV commentary or an early Sunday AM radio panel discussion and provide an accurate gist of it immediately.

In summer 1966 we took our second home leave. This time we could not book a ship from Yokohama. The Japanese had steadily become more affluent. Prime Minister Ikeda's income-doubling policy had achieved its goal well ahead of schedule so that the APL liners were all booked up. So, we flew to Honolulu and caught Matson's "Lurline."

Now Louise and her family were in Honolulu, and we could visit them before we boarded the ship. "Lurline" passengers were less of an international mix than those on the APL liners; and of course the voyage itself was shorter, ending in Long Beach. We fully enjoyed it anyway.

In Long Beach, we rented a car and drove to Hollywood for a 24-hour look-see. Within the first few hours, I was ticketed for failing to yield to a pedestrian in a crosswalk, i.e., for driving Tokyo style.

We visited the La Brea Tar Pits, Graumann's Chinese Theater and Griffith Planetarium and then drove east to Claremont. I wanted Kimie and Hugh-ko to see Webb School and something of the Sierra Madre range I had climbed as a high-schooler. Despite a brisk southwest wind, the L.A. smog was so thick that we could not see the mountains without driving up into them. At Webb School not much had changed, on the surface; and of course this was the summer vacation, so that few people were around.

We then went down to Pomona, where we would catch an eastbound Santa Fe train. Along the way, we saw lemons going to waste in a ditch beside an orchard and stopped to rescue a half dozen to use on our transcontinental journey.

After an overnight on the Santa Fe Superchief, we got off at Grand Canyon Junction and caught a shuttle bus to the Grand Canyon. We spent the day at that great site and, about 5:00PM, walked maybe 200 yards to the railhead where another Santa Fe train, with our baggage already on board, was waiting to take us on across the USA, through the "Four Corners" area and on to Chicago, where we caught the train to Washington, D.C.

Again, we visited with Bill, Rits, Sheila (now 4) and new brother Ray (age 3). Overall a bittersweet stopover because our time there was brief. This time we planned no extended road trip, but would take an indirect route to the West Coast. For, on the train between Chicago and D.C. Kimie was hit by sharp back pains. I took her to a doctor in D.C., who diagnosed muscle spasm, an after-effect of the accident, and gave her a painkiller to keep her fairly comfortable.

First we drove in a rented car to Chapel Hill, North Carolina, to visit first-cousin Mary Patterson, her husband Tom and Aunt Abby, still living at age 94 with Mary, her daughter. (Abby died the next year). We had a good 2-day visit and a tour of the historic UNC campus, where Tom was a professor of drama and Mary taught English lit.

From there we flew via St. Louis to Chicago. Waiting at the St. Louis airport for a storm to pass, I checked the phone book, and found a listing for Irwin Reif—our erstwhile commanding officer at the Film Exchange. I was tempted to call him and see if he recalled his secretary, "Ina-san," of 20 years before; but Kimie insisted that we not bother him. We next flew to O'Hare and caught a bus to Madison to visit again with Uncle Roland and his wife Frances.

From there we flew to Seattle to visit John and Mother, who was keeping house for him now in Renton, a Seattle suburb where John was pastor of the Methodist church. Or, I should say Mother (then 75) was attempting to keep house for him, as we noticed then the first signs of the Alzheimers disease that would soon force John to put her in a nursing home. E.g., while showing Hugh-ko and me the church facilities next door, she turned to me and asked who that boy was. The boy she had helped raise as a baby!

One afternoon, Hugh-ko and I went fishing on Lake Washington in a rented rowboat. Poor fishing, but we had an unexpected show. An ancient-looking bi-wing seaplane was practicing takeoffs and landings on the lake nearby. The next day's paper said it was a reproduction of Boeing's 1916 seaplane and was built for Boeing's 50th anniversary celebrations by some of the same mechanics who had built the originals.

Next, on to San Francisco to stay for about three weeks in Berkeley. I had asked sister Mary to find us rooms that we could use; and she located just what we wanted: a suite in the daylight basement of a private home. Hugh-ko spent much of his time with Mary's family and with Kitty's four children.

One morning early in our Berkeley sojourn, Kimie and I took a bus to visit friends on the U.C. campus. As we neared Sather Gate, we saw a crowd of people, mostly students, milling around. Placards advocating a spectrum of views were everywhere; and some were chanting slogans. It turned out that the California communist party's number-two man was on the bus with us and had come to address a Sather Gate rally that noon. The placards were pro, anti and everything in between.

Kimie and I passed through the crowd and, just in front of the Admin Building (where I had worked in the photo lab) we ran into an acquaintance. Standing there chatting with her, we noticed a dog nonchalantly standing in a fountain beside the Student Union. Curious about such odd behavior, we asked our friend about it. She explained that the dog had sat watching the whole time while the fountain was being built. When it was complete and filled with water, the dog simply stepped in, and stayed there for a considerable time each day. So, when the fountain was dedicated, it was named for that dog. Ah, Cal Berkeley! (That reminded me of a 1950's incident, when a U.C. frat house had enrolled its mascot dog as a student. The frat brothers took his exams, and eventually had him ready to graduate when somehow the university caught on and voided his diploma.)

Such was our introduction to U.C. Berkeley of the mid-'60s. Student activism was growing, but not yet big news.

One afternoon I visited my former faculty advisor, Bob Scalapino, at his home. We had stayed in contact over the 10 years since I left Berkeley. He had dropped by our Tokyo Embassy almost yearly, sometimes joining in USIS seminars. Also at Bob's that day was Prof. Marty Lipset, a noted sociologist, who had taught at Berkeley a few years earlier, but was then at Harvard. When the subject arose of the rising student activism, Lipset leaned back in his chair and, with tongue only halfway in cheek, said: "You know, Bob, what we have here is a gathering of social misfits. All through our history, the social misfits could keep moving west to get away from the settled and structured society they so disdained. So, they tended to collect here on the West Coast. The students now raising this fuss are 2nd- and 3rd-generation social misfits."

Side note: For the rest of my career, Bob Scalapino would show up *every* place I was assigned: He would joke that he was checking up on his former students; but in fact he (often with wife Dee) traveled extensively every year, especially to Asia. Usually, he could be persuaded to lecture for USIS during a visit or to star in a seminar on issues of the day. Over the years, he made himself perhaps America's most knowledgeable scholar of Asian politics and foreign policy. He often testified before Congress on Asian policy. Even now, retired and in his 80s, he continues to travel often and to lecture and write insightfully. (I visited his home again in March 2003 to pay my respects. Sadly, Dee died in 2005.)

In Berkeley, we took a rental car to Monterey, Carmel and Big Sur, which we had not seen in a dozen years. Also, Hugh-ko and I drove up into the Sierras for four days of camping and rock hunting—great quality time with my son, then almost 15.

In late August, I put Kimie and Hugh-ko on the APL liner, the "President Roosevelt," for their return to Japan. Then I flew out of San Francisco. In no hurry, I stopped in Juneau for some sightseeing, and took in such sights as the Red Dog Saloon and Mendenhall Glacier before hopping a Lockheed Tristar for Anchorage. En route to the next stop (Yakutat), the pilot came on the P.A. system and said, "Folks, you may have noticed we are flying below our usual altitude. That's because the cabin pressurizer isn't working. It's no big deal, and I'll be able to fix it at Yakutat. So, just relax and enjoy the close-in view."

I had indeed been enjoying the view: the spectacular mountains, glaciers and pristine waterways. At Yakutat, where most passengers got off to hunt or fish, I was surprised to see the pilot come walking down the aisle whistling and nonchalantly twirling a screw-driver. He went under the plane and apparently with that tool alone fixed the problem.

Beyond Yakutat, the pilot pointed out the Malaspina Glacier, "covering more area than the state of Rhode Island" as it spills out over the wide silt plain which it has created.

The small terminal building at the next stop was emblazoned "Cordova, Home of the Ice Worm" in large letters. A native Alaskan told me there really is a small worm that thrives in glacial ice. These days biologists would call that an "extremophile."

Then across stunning Prince William Sound and the rugged Chugach Mountains into Anchorage. As we neared Anchorage, I spotted Elmendorf AFB, where I had stopped for lunch 16 years earlier en route home from my first five years in Japan.

While in Berkeley, I had written to 2nd cousin Dr. Karl Bowman, then in Anchorage, that I would be there that weekend, but had had no reply. So I checked into a hotel and then scanned the phone book for his number. Soon I made the connection, and he and his wife insisted that I come and spend the weekend with them. Fine with me!

Karl was then director of the State Psychiatric Hospital—perhaps his fourth career. He had been a psychiatrist in Boston early in his career, and then at Bellevue Hospital in New York during World War II. In that capacity, he was contacted by *Time* magazine in 1940 when Rudolph Hess flew to Scotland from Nazi Germany with his oddball scheme for stopping World War II. *Time* wanted to know if Karl thought Hess was crazy. "I never diagnose a patient who is 4,000 miles away," was his laconic response.

In the late 1940s, Karl came to San Francisco to head the Psychiatric Section of the U.C. Medical Center; and then in the 1950's spent time in Indonesia when Berkeley had a USAID contract to help establish schools of psychiatry at major Asian universities. He retired for a few years after his first wife died, but then accepted the call from Alaska and went up there with his second wife. Tragically and ironically, in the early '70s he was struck down by Alzheimer's.

But, in 1966 he was sharp as a scalpel. That first afternoon, Karl and Betty took me on a drive down Turnagain Inlet. On the way back, a cold front doused us with rain for about 20 minutes. Then the skies cleared and we could see Mt. McKinley and Mt. Foraker 120 miles to the north. We had dinner at the Garden of Eatin', between the airport and the city on a round lake whose shore was ringed with float planes.

At the Bowman home that evening, we were watching TV when a neighbor came banging on the door, calling, "The lights are out! The lights are out!" The expression on my face must have made Karl think that I thought one of his patients had come visiting. Karl smiled and said, "Let's go see. He means the aurora borealis is lighting up the sky."

Sure enough, outside the northern lights were putting on a spectacular cosmic light show: great moving curtains of eerily colored light slowly and silently rippling in the heavens.

The next morning Karl took me on a tour of the hospital. I was walking down a corridor with him when one patient called out, "When were your born?" I must have looked perplexed again, for Karl took my arm and said, "Let's go in and visit with her." It turned out that the woman was an autistic savant. Give her a date, and in a few seconds she could tell you the day of the week for that date.

That afternoon, Karl and Betty took me to the airport for my final leg back to Tokyo to start a third 3-year tour.

# TOKYO YEARS--II (TURBULENCE)

## (1966-69)

About a year after Ambassador Reischauer arrived in to Tokyo in 1961, our CPAO (Country Public Affairs Officer) left for Washington and was replaced by Dr. Charles Fahs, a long-time Ford Foundation officer. A cultured gentleman, Fahs led the USIS staff with a fine hand. His wife, Jamie, was a well-liked, dynamic personality. Her voice was very low, and she liked to joke about people phoning their residence and, when she answered, assuming that they had Dr. Fahs on the line.

Now with Vietnam creating new tensions in US-Japan relations, Washington wanted a more media-oriented leader for USIS-Tokyo. So, Fahs was made cultural advisor to the ambassador; and Ed Nickel moved up from Deputy PAO to CPAO. Ed's background was in private-sector broadcasting and magazines. In the 1950's he had served twice in Tokyo in information positions. His deputy was now Clifton Forster, very much an East Asia hand, also with past Japan assignments. Clif and I would work well together over the next few decades and have remained in contact since retiring.

The intensifying Vietnam War meant a heavier reporting load on my office, allowing very little time for vacations or recreation and, regrettably, more sacrificing of my family's needs and interests.

That fall of 1966, I did take some weekends off, though. An Embassy political officer had close contacts with the "School Spirit Club" of Waseda University—a top private university. That led to a challenge from the Waseda students for Embassy officers to join them on a 100K hike (62½ miles). I agreed to join others accepting the challenge, despite the decade of off-and-on hip pain I had experienced since my fall at the Campus Theater.

So, shortly after I returned from home leave, five of us from the Embassy began training. Three weeks before the big walk, we did a 20-kilometer walk on a Sunday afternoon. The next Sunday, we did 35K. We rested the next weekend, and then the following Saturday took a train to a site on the Kanto Plain 100 kilometers northwest of Waseda, where some 200 Waseda students were assembling.

About 1:30 PM we set off, walking the shoulders of the asphalt roads at about 3½ miles per hour. We stopped once in mid-afternoon for about 15 minutes and then stopped at a roadside inn in the early evening for supper, perhaps for 45 minutes. Then full-speed ahead again into the fading light of evening.

At about 11:30 PM, roughly 50 kilometers from the start, we were led into a school gym to sleep on the bleachers, for two hours. Then we were off again, walking the dark roads between rice paddies and through towns. When we stopped for breakfast, again at a wayside inn, it was hard to tell how many of the original 200 were still charging ahead, as stragglers were strung out for miles behind us. All Americans were present; but one USIS officer, Eugene Windchy, had painful blisters caused by his heavy hiking boots. We urged him to quit, but he insisted he would keep going.

I was holding up okay, but my right knee was beginning to feel shaky from the strain of constantly being on the low side of the canted roads. About 1 PM we ended our forced march at the Waseda main gate—23½ hours after starting out and after about 20 hours of actual walking time.

Our blistered colleague, Windchy, arrived an hour later, hobbling badly. He was supposed to leave Japan for the USA the next day, but had to delay that by several days while his feet healed.

Besides the sense of accomplishment, for me an unexpected fringe benefit was that my arthritis-like hip pain was never again severe. I had walked it off!

About this time, Kimie joined a class of Japanese learning to create *Kamakura-bori*, the style of lacquered wood-carving developed in Kamakura. Every Saturday, she took the train to Ofuna north of Kamakura to the instructor's studio. There she and the class of about a dozen people painstakingly worked out patterns and designs, carved the wood and followed the instructor's guidance on applying multi-colored lacquers. Kimie started out making many smaller items, then carved wooden frames for hand mirrors and, advancing further, 12-14-inch wall plaques. Finally, in her third year, she spent a year of Saturday afternoons carving exquisite phoenixes on the legs and side panels of a large coffee table—a real masterpiece and now one of our family heirlooms.

In spring 1969, Embassy wives held an arts and crafts show in the party room atop Harris House; and we filled a table with Kimie's various productions and some that Hugh-ko made in his school art class. One officer viewing that array asked, "Hugh, why don't you just retire and become manager for your artistic family?"

In summer 1967, Kimie, Hugh-ko and I went for a weekend to Kujukurihama, a 40-mile hard-sand beach on the Pacific east of Tokyo. We spent an enjoyable first day swimming and watching fishing boats bring in their catch. The sand there was so firm that the boats could be winched out of the surf onto log rollers, and wholesalers' trucks could drive right up to the boats to purchase their catch.

On the morning of the second day, Kimie began suffering severe pain in her lower back. She had been getting *shiatsu* treatments for six months for the pain caused by the accident of almost a year and a half earlier. But, her pain now was extreme. I went to a pharmacy and got her some aspirin; then we packed up and left for Tokyo, cutting short our weekend. The next day, Kimie's pain returned, and I arranged through the Embassy nurse for her to see an elderly doctor at his nearby office.

He gave her a shot, but said he suspected a kidney stone and called for a thorough diagnosis at a U.S. military hospital.

We did that and the X-rays confirmed the old doctor's suspicions. Her muscle pain from the accident had, without our realizing it, been overtaken by pain from the kidney stone, and the shiatsu treatments had masked the cause. Hers was not one of the small grainy stones that people "pass," but a single stone the size of a lima bean. No passing allowed.

A few weeks later, I took Kimie to the Tachikawa Air Force Hospital. The operation took over three hours. Between her last X-ray and the operation, the stone moved to an almost inaccessible site. The Air Force surgeon could chip off but a small part of the stone. In the recovery room, the long ordeal sent her into shock; and only a sharp-eyed Japanese intern spotted the symptoms and called for emergency treatment. Ironically, before the operation Kimie had only reluctantly agreed to the intern's presence. Now he had saved her life! For the next seven years, Kimie would suffer repeated kidney and bladder infections due to the stone and yet keep her upbeat and cheerful approach to life, ever irrepressible.

We did have marital problems because of my overworking—a rollercoaster of good and bad weeks. Kimie had already concluded that the U.S. was in a no-win situation in Vietnam. I felt I had to "keep the faith" and defend U.S. policy. So, we argued about Vietnam. In later years she liked to say, "We fought like cats and dogs." Our relationship suffered.

In mid-'68 we had a distressed phone call from Rits. Her marriage had broken up. She needed our help. Equally as distressing for us: Her negative feelings toward Bill had spilled over also onto her little son Ray. She had consulted with a priest (She converted to Catholicism after marrying Bill, a Catholic.); and the priest suggested giving Ray up for adoption. Our initial impulse was to consider taking Ray in ourselves; but with Kimie's frequent kidney problems and the then unsteady relations between us, we were unable immediately to make such a decision. When we next heard from Rits, she had already arranged

Ray's adoption and now felt she had to get away from her situation in Maryland. She asked us to take her and Sheila in.

Within a week I had cleared that with the Embassy, and we sent her the airfare so that she and Sheila could come out to Tokyo. She and Sheila would spend the next 18 months with us, sharing the third bedroom in our apartment. Rits enrolled Sheila in a Catholic school, and soon found a job in the Merrill Lynch office close to the Embassy.

In 1966, Ambassador and Mrs. Reischauer had left Tokyo to return to Harvard. Our next ambassador was U. Alexis Johnson, a career diplomat who, like John Emmerson, had served under Ambassador Joseph Grew in the 1930s. I have earlier noted our contacts with him in 1947 and 1950, when he was consul general in Yokohama. Now he was one of State's most senior diplomats.

His wife, Pat, was a real trooper, a traditional Foreign Service spouse, maintaining high standards and insisting that other Embassy wives do the same. For instance, when the wife of a temporary officer from Commerce once came to a party at the Ambassador's residence wearing a very short white skirt and white leather boots, Mrs. Johnson quietly asked her to go and change into "something more appropriate." When the woman insisted that "people dress this way now in D.C.," Mrs. Johnson simply said, "Well, we don't dress that way here." Pat Johnson loved bowling; and Kimie, already on the embassy wives' bowling team, became her frequent companion on the bowling lanes as well as on her busy social calendar.

Rather suddenly in spring 1967, I took a trip around the world. USIA's head of research in Washington, Hewson Ryan, called a meeting of USIA research officers in Tel Aviv. USIA had posted regional research officers in Europe, Africa, India and Latin America, all except me sent by USIA Research in Washington. My job was created by and for USIS-Japan and not funded by USIA Research. Nevertheless, I was invited. Before I left Tokyo, I was asked to go on to Washington after Tel Aviv. As Washington is over half way around the globe beyond Tel Aviv, my ticket was written all the way around.

I stopped first in Hong Kong, where I was briefed by USIS and the Consulate on their programs. I next flew to Saigon, where I would spend the Easter weekend. I observed a press briefing at the famed "Saturday afternoon follies". A USIS cameraman there invited me to helicopter with him the next day to a field hospital run by Filipino doctors and nurses for Vietnamese civilians. I immediately accepted.

That flight was an eye-opener. The pilot flew high while we were over U.S. bases, but very low over VC areas, the reverse of what I would have expected; but he said that kept us safer from possible ground fire. The hospital we visited was depressing: one-story buildings with no panes or screens in the windows and only basic medical equipment. Ward after ward of wounded Vietnamese civilians, some of them children and not a few amputees. We also visited a nearby U.S. artillery base and witnessed the firing of a field gun: suppression and interdiction fire. The Filipina nurse accompanying us remarked wryly, "That may bring us more patients tomorrow."

I hopped next to Bangkok, spending part of a day at the USIS offices before catching my onward Pan Am flight. At Tehran I changed to a plane bound for Tel Aviv via Turkey and the Mediterranean to avoid overflying Arab lands hostile to Israel. At my stopover in Ankara's air terminal, I bumped into an American political science professor who had been a speaker at a USIS program in Tokyo a year earlier. "What brings you to Turkey? Are you with a tour group?" I asked in surprise.

"No. Came in an overland bus," he replied with a twinkle in his eye. "Got on in Pakistan two weeks ago and rode a series of buses through Afghanistan, Iran and Iraq—fascinating experience. But, now I'm sore and weary enough that I'm continuing by plane."

On my first evening in Tel Aviv, I accompanied a Jewish USIA research officer to a community center for a program on the state of Israel, gaining some insights on the spirit of that nation. On the Tel Aviv beach on a Sunday, I learned something about the Israeli physique.

Our meetings at the Embassy sparked good exchanges of views between the overseas research officers and USIA's research director. On a weekend afternoon we had a tour through Caesarea (with its Roman amphitheater facing the Mediterranean) to Nazareth, where we were shown Mary's Well and other sites from the ancient past. Driving back, we stopped at Mount Carmel for dinner. There our waiter pointed out the distant lights of Lebanon up the coast. The day gave me a clearer feel for the geography, political tensions and hard-scrabble life of that troubled part of our world.

From Tel Aviv, I flew to Paris for a 24-hour stopover. The first evening I visited a night club, and the next morning caught a cab to the Louvre. The driver took his fare, but failed to tell me that the Louvre was closed that day. So, I walked for hours, taking in Notre Dame Cathedral, the Seine and part of the Left Bank.

Then on to London for another one-day stopover, walking again to absorb some atmosphere. As I passed the U.S. Embassy on Grosvenor Square, I met some atmosphere face to face: a demonstration of maybe 200 teenagers, chanting, "DON'T DRAFT DAVY JONES! DON'T DRAFT DAVY JONES!" Until then, Davy Jones only had meaning to me in the phrase "Davy Jones' locker" (the bottom of the sea). Now I learned that the teenagers' Davy Jones was a member of the Monkees rock group and was living in the U.S., but faced being drafted for duty in Vietnam.

Next a Pan Am flight for New York. Over New York, a passing storm had piled up the air traffic. Finally we were diverted to Washington, my destination anyway. Some consultation there, and then on back to Tokyo, in time to hear news of the outbreak of the Seven-day War between Israel and the Arab states.

In 1968, a joint State/USIA inspection report on USIS-Japan noted that in the foreseeable future the Ryukyu Islands, including Okinawa, could be returned to Japanese control. USIS-Tokyo had little direct knowledge of the civilian information program that the Department of Defense (DOD) was running there. As I was then USIS-Tokyo's

Japan specialist, I was asked to go to Okinawa and collect information on the DOD program.

So, in May I flew down on a three-day fact-finding trip. The humid summer monsoon season was starting, when northwesterly winds from Siberia are replaced by southeasterly breezes blowing across warm tropical currents from the central Pacific. So, at Naha International Airport, I was amazed to see the concrete floors wet with condensed moisture. I was met by an Army sergeant working in the information program. Over the next several days I learned much about the DOD program—mainly press relations, English-teaching, scholarships to the U.S. for promising young Okinawans, etc. I also learned about the yearning for autonomy by Okinawans who did not consider themselves Japanese. For a millennium before the 1600s they had been an autonomous kingdom, trading with both China and Japan and developing a strong sense of cultural identity.

I have mentioned that from the early 1960s USIS had cultivated an emerging group of defense analysts and commentators. We provided them with articles, books, etc., and brought some top U.S. thinkers on defense matters to help them better understand U.S. views on collective security, deterrence and the Cold War. We also gave a few of them "leader grants" to visit the U.S. and delve more deeply into these matters at the Pentagon, major universities, think tanks, etc. After several years, Japan's political and government leaders recognized these men as experts who could advise them on security policy. In fact, one of them later became head of the Japanese equivalent of West Point.

Soon after I returned from Okinawa, Prime Minister Sato made a rare official visit there and declared, "The postwar period will not be over for Japan until Okinawa reverts to our control." That evoked a strong nationalistic response and put our government on notice that Okinawa's reversion had become a top priority. Japan's left-wing forces seized on that and began laying plans to foment a "1970 crisis" by making a political issue of Okinawa and the Security Treaty, which could be renewed in 1970. Frustrated in their efforts in 1960 to block renewal of the US-Japan Security Treaty, they hoped to stir up the public, already

209

in a negative mood over fears that our Vietnam involvement might draw Japan into war with Communist nations.

To make a long story short, the Japanese defense specialists now planned and held a conference on Okinawa, with token Japanese Government representation. In January 1969, they invited to Kyoto some top U.S. Asian experts, including Reischauer and Scalapino, key retired generals, admirals and active defense analysts. There, rather than a confrontation, they found they understood each other and could work out a framework for Okinawa's reversion. That became incorporated into formal US-Japan negotiations and was the basis for the final US-Japan agreement on Okinawa. No "1970 crisis" occurred.

In early 1969, DCM David Osborne placed me on a four-man team, including himself, to review U.S. Japan policy, defining key issues and suggesting how to deal with them effectively. We met several times; and Dave incorporated our input into a think-piece that he then sent to the State Department's policy planning staff. More and more the "policy wonk"!

About this time (1967-68) Embassy political and economic officers I had known in the early '60s came trickling back on new duty tours. I began to feel that I had "stayed too long at the party." CPAO Ed Nickel left to become CPAO in Saigon and was replaced by Ned Roberts, an old-line newsman who had been CPAO in Morocco.

Now new troubles were erupting in Tokyo, not from the labor unions and their political allies, but from radical students whom the leftwing parties did not control. This had brewed quietly over the years, starting in the early '60s with the plan to build a new Tokyo international airport at Narita in a rural area east of Tokyo. We read of helmeted left-wing students making common cause with conservative farmers averse to giving up their farmland. Perhaps incited by student radicalism in Europe and America, these students had joined forces with these farmers and claimed the new airport really was meant for the "U.S. imperialists'" strategic bombers. Now students began launching large demonstrations in downtown Tokyo and on their college campuses.

My 3rd-floor office in the Embassy Annex was a ringside window on this new political drama. The student demonstrators favored the boulevard below, as it ran past our Embassy and Japanese Government offices. I began calling it *demo dōri* (demonstration avenue). Usually, they followed the rules and were controlled by the riot police but not banned. Their placards lambasted U.S. imperialism while they chanted, "Yankee, go home" and the like.

The inner spirit, though, was not hostile to us individually. I had demonstrated this to Hugh-ko in 1963 when we were in Tokyo before boarding the "President Hoover." The three of us were walking toward the Embassy when students came parading down the street. When he heard their chants of "Yankee, go home," 11-year-old Hugh-ko grew incensed. "Why do they want us to go?" he complained. "Don't they know we're trying to be friends with Japan?"

"Hugh-ko, just watch," I said and turned and waved to the oncoming students, who responded by smiling and waving back. "See, they don't mean it for us personally. They just dislike the policies of our government and their own government."

Now, five to six years later the same tactics prevailed. In fact, some students were paid per-diem by big labor unions to join the demonstrations and enjoyed being involved in something bigger than their class work. Once, I was standing outside our building beside a young riot policeman watching the students go by. I sometimes did this to get a direct feel for how much heat there was in the demonstration. I remarked to the officer that the students seemed to be enjoying themselves. He answered, "Yes, if I were a few years younger I might be out there with them."

Just then some right-wing students came up with placards castigating the left-wingers and, right beside us, began an argument. Finally, the left-wing students broke off to rejoin the march, one of them yelling over his shoulder, "You're *anakuro!*" Puzzled, I asked the policeman what that meant. Surprised, he answered. "That is English!" Back in my office, Sen Nishiyama explained that it was their abbreviation of "anachronism."

The riot police had much new equipment for passive demonstration control: heavy trucks and buses built for blockading students from certain streets, trucks with turrets mounting water cannons, plastic shields and helmets for the police, all designed to control but not injure the demonstrators.

Late in 1968, student radicalism turned nastier, partly from intensifying rivalry among factions competing for student adherents. One weekend in late 1968, students laid siege to Japan's top university: the University of Tokyo—equivalent in Japan to Harvard, Yale and Columbia rolled into one. The spectacle of students trashing the buildings while holding the university and its president hostage ran live on national TV for hours that weekend, until the riot police finally moved in with tear gas, helicopters—their whole arsenal—and routed the students. One student was killed, as I recall, when he fell from a building. And of course was instantly treated as a martyr.

Public opinion began turning sharply against the radicals. Tolerated until then more as young pranksters than as a serious threat to public order, the students now began to be seen almost as felons bent on upsetting social harmony—a cardinal social sin to Japan's man-in-the street. In the early '70s, some students began throwing Molotov cocktails in crowded train stations, seriously burning bystanders and further antagonizing the public. The tiny "Japanese Red Army" emerged and made a big splash by hijacking a jetliner to North Korea. Another tiny faction horrified the nation when they holed up in a mountain chalet and lynched several of their own members. Student radicalism has never since enjoyed the tacit acceptance that prevailed before the Tokyo University incident.

Hugh-ko meanwhile was becoming an all-out teenager: playing drums, hanging out with other Embassy teenagers and beginning to date. But, Tokyo's smog situation was giving him trouble: lots of sinus infections and lost time from school. Now in high school at ASIJ (American School in Japan) some 15 miles out in west Tokyo, he was riding the bus 90 minutes each way. So, we were seeing less of him day and evening. He was attracted to the "psychedelic" decor of the late '60s, and had decorated his room with fluorescent designs, skillfully executed, but garish in our view.

In fall 1968, Tokyo American Cultural Center director Don Albright became involved with avant-garde Japanese musicians and film makers. That led to plans for a major cultural event: "Cross-talk Intermedia:" truly avant-garde music and art films, all to be staged in the huge basketball stadium from the '64 Tokyo Olympics. Hugh-ko was fascinated by what he saw emerging and got permission from us and his school to take time off to help with setting up the event. He knew where to buy many of the items that would be needed, like fluorescent paint, and he turned out to be a very useful helper.

Cross-talk Intermedia ran for two consecutive nights and drew near-capacity audiences. Kimie and I attended the first performance, and on the second night I took two senior Embassy officers whose curiosity had been piqued by the raves they had heard after the first night's show.

The staging was impressive. Sony had lent 36 huge hi-fi speakers, now arrayed in a circle around the top tier of seating, 40 feet above the stadium floor. Multiple projectors were set up on the playing floor and elsewhere in the huge gym. Some of the art films shown were projected not onto standard movie screens, but onto huge plastic balloons floating above the floor. Kimie and I were surprised to see that Hugh-ko had borrowed our canister vacuum cleaner to inflate the balloons.

The event was a great success, and we were happy to see Hugh-ko so enthused about the artistic endeavor. He had begun to seem bored with school, except for art class, where he excelled. That was partly because he had so many absences due to the sinus problem. And soon he had to have minor surgery to open up a badly infected sinus.

Finally, in the middle of his senior year we had to agree to his leaving school. He had fallen so far behind that he would not be graduating with his class. But, he also was eager to end his dependence on us. (Has that "syndrome" been observed before?) Somewhere he got the idea of enlisting in the merchant marine. We decided that a good dash of the world's harsh realities might be what he needed to mature further. So, from late 1968 he was off on an American tanker plying between the Persian Gulf, Vietnam, the Philippines and other Asian ports.

In summer 1969, we were due a Washington assignment, after three 3-year tours in Japan. And, new personnel policies discouraged such a one-country focus. The emphasis now was on developing generalists, whom State and USIA personnel offices could more easily move about the world. They were quite unimpressed by my argument that real advantages derive from having officers in Tokyo who knew Japan well and handled the language fluently. They countered with their "localitis" theory: that officers staying long in one country tend to identify too closely with the views of that country. In face-to-face discussions I countered, "When you know a country and its people well you can easily distinguish beauty marks from warts."

Actually, I was supposed to have a Washington assignment from 1968, but had a one-year extension at the behest of Deputy PAO Forster. Now I proceeded to book passage for Kimie, Rits, Sheila and me on the APL's "President Cleveland" in mid-July.

At our Harris House apartment we had a sayonara party with Kimie's family. Kimie cooked up a gourmet Chinese banquet for her siblings and parents. Her mother enjoyed that especially, remarking that she had paid for Kimie's Chinese cooking lessons out of her household allowance in the late '30s, and this was the first time she had a chance to taste the results. She was not disappointed.

The nagging question in our minds, though, was Hugh-ko. He insisted he wanted to stay longer on his ship. He had begun as a bus boy in the officers' mess and now had been promoted to work in the engine room, which he found interesting and satisfying.

Then, about 10 days before we were to sail from Yokohama, we received a telegram: "INJURED IN FALL ON SHIP. COMING HOME. HUGH." The cable address: Ras Tanura. I checked my maps and found that is an Arabian port on the Persian Gulf. To say the least, we were worried. How badly injured? How and when coming home? What airline? I immediately began checking. Our USIS admin office at first drew a blank, but then found that Hugh-ko was booked on an Air Arabia flight arriving in just a few days.

We went to Haneda airport to meet his plane, wondering if he would be coming off on a stretcher, with broken limbs or worse. The plane landed, but parked almost out of sight of the terminal's observation deck where we were waiting. Finally, a shuttle bus arrived just below us. A stream of passengers got off. No Hugh. Now we were sure he would be on a stretcher. Then, last of all, Hugh-ko hopped spryly off the bus, a guitar slung across his back. "Hi, Mom! Hi, Dad! I don't have a visa," he called out to us. He later explained that he had not had enough cash for a more detailed telegram.

The accident on his ship: He and an older Japanese man had fallen some 15 feet to the engine room floor while carrying a heavy pulley and chain down a steep steel stairway. The older man had a badly broken arm, but Hugh-ko was only knocked out. Both were hospitalized; but then the Arab port authorities got the idea that Hugh-ko had tried to kill his Japanese shipmate. They held a hearing, where they were forced to use their suspect (Hugh-ko) as the interpreter for the Japanese victim! They realized that wasn't quite right, and postponed the hearing until a Japanese consular officer could come and do the interpreting. The doubts were quickly cleared up.

The ensuing week was one of our busiest ever: Getting our son a temporary visa, applying through the Seamen's Club for his back pay, booking a third cabin for him on the "Cleveland" (one for Kimie and me, another for Rits and Sheila and now one for Hugh-ko) and completing our packing after nine years in Japan. We filled our authorized weight limit and then arranged for a trucking company to haul the rest to the "Cleveland" as hold baggage, leaving us with just our cabin luggage.

Then we were off for the Yokohama port—the five of us and our luggage in two Embassy sedans—a special favor from the USIS admin officer. Rits had not had a sea voyage since 1950, when she was seven; and for Sheila it was a first. As the "Cleveland" steamed down Tokyo Bay, we were listening to Armed Forces Radio's relay of NASA's broadcast of the launch of Apollo 11. The signal faded before we could hear whether the launch was successful.

Incidentally, earlier I had signed a memo giving Sen Nishiyama permission to serve as interpreter for the Japan Broadcasting Corporation (NHK) programs on our Apollo missions. Before long, Sen became a national celebrity for his skilled interpreting and hours on camera, and gained the nickname of "Voice of Apollo." That also opened the eyes of the Japanese public to the skills that interpreting demanded, and greatly raised the social standing of that profession.

Our voyage went smoothly; and the ship's news service informed us that Apollo 11 had launched flawlessly and gave us printed reports on the moonwalk.

In the mid-Pacific, the afternoon before Apollo's re-entry into the atmosphere, we passed through a large, widely scattered fleet of Russian "fishing boats"—all with large antennas pointed into space. That night, about 2 AM, some passengers went out on deck and saw the bright streak of the capsule's re-entry. In Honolulu the next day my girls spent a nice day shopping with Louise and her girls.

Our arrival in San Francisco was more complex than in the past. We had a mass of hold baggage and arranged with Railway Express to ship it to me in Washington. Rits had arranged through her Merrill Lynch boss in Tokyo to transfer to Merrill Lynch in Washington, D.C., and so would fly with Sheila from San Francisco. Kimie, Hugh-ko and I would take a Southern Pacific train across the country. So, we saw Rits and Sheila off and then checked into a Berkeley motel for the night before taking a train from Oakland.

That evening Hugh-ko dropped a bomb on us: He was not interested in living back east again and had arranged with some of his Embassy friends from a few years earlier to room with them in Washington state. Nothing we said would dissuade him from that.

The next morning we slowly awoke to the sound of chattering in Japanese outside our door! For a few moments we had the sleepy illusion that we were back in Japan, but soon realized we were in Berkeley and that the chatter was from Japanese maids. And recalled we had to get Hugh-ko onto a train for Seattle. This was hard on Kimie, to be suddenly bereft of both her children. She shed a few tears, which were rare for her.

Well, of course, we weathered that. We briefly saw Mary and Kitty's families, and then got ourselves onto a Southern Pacific train for Chicago.

The trip across the country was uneventful this time, and soon we were in a D.C. hotel and searching for a home. Just when we located a suitable apartment in Silver Spring MD, our hotel began a sale of much of its furniture. We bought an excellent set of solid-wood bureaus there. Still have it.

Our Silver Spring apartment was on the 9th floor of a 14-story building. After a few weeks, we realized that we were one of the few "goy" families among some 490 mainly Jewish families, many of them elderly retired couples or widows.

# WASHINGTON ASSIGNMENT

## (1969-73)

Back in USIA now, I was assigned to the TV-MoPix Division as policy officer for East Asia programs. That meant I would be offering policy guidance on TV programs and motion pictures for USIS posts in that area. Each of the five other areas—Europe, Soviet Bloc, Africa, Near & Middle East and Latin America—had a policy officer also. Sounds dry; but the day-to-day work was so varied that it was never dull. Some highlights --

One fall afternoon, a Chinese man from Taiwan TV was brought to me, as he spoke no English but knew some Japanese. He had with him reels of 16mm color movie film. From his broken Japanese, I made out that he had just finished a year learning TV production methods at an institute in Tokyo run by NHK for foreign media technicians. For his first solo project, he had come to the East Coast and hired a Chinese cameraman to film a program on the "Double-ten" National Day celebrations at the Republic of China's Consulate General in New York and at its embassy in Washington, D.C.*

But, his cameraman had never before filmed in color. So, I called our TV technicians, and they agreed to see what the man had. In the screening room's dim light I saw them staring in disbelief at the under-

---

* The Oct. 10 anniversary of Sun Yat-sen's revolution of 1911. Some years later, the Nixon/Kissinger "opening to China" downgraded our relations with Taiwan to a non-diplomatic level.

exposed footage and looking at each other meaningfully. At the end, they turned to me and asked, "What do you want us to do?"

"Can anything be done?" I asked. After discussing the options, they said the film could be transferred to 1-inch videotape, electronically enhanced, edited and then put back onto 16mm film. "So, can we do that for him? How long would it take?" I asked.

"When does he have to leave?" they asked in return. I checked with our Chinese friend and made out that he had to fly out the next day. Our technicians' faces fell. "Are you prepared to stay here with us tonight until the job is done?" they queried. I said I was game if they were. It was then almost quitting time. We all phoned home, and then went out for a quick meal before getting to work in the editing studio.

After 10 PM that night, we sent the Chinese gentleman off, happy as a lark with edited and light-corrected videotape and 16mm versions of his program. The next day one of the Mopix veterans came by my office to tell me that they had decided from now on to call me "the Yellow Peril." That began a great relationship between those pros and me.

In early December, the East Asia area office called a meeting between its Japan Desk Officer (the same Ivan Izenberg whom I had replaced in Tokyo in 1964) and several of us in TV-Mopix. The problem: Nixon had been in office some 10 months; and his Vice President, Spiro Agnew, was to make a January tour of East Asia. USIS posts in the area were complaining that their audiences knew nothing about our illustrious Veep and were demanding some kind of footage to introduce him via TV or direct screenings. The surprising upshot of the meeting: I was chosen to go to New York and work with USIA's Mopix office there to get film footage on Agnew. So, suddenly I was flying off to New York. On a Wednesday morning.

My visit started a bit shakily. A relative stranger to New York, I assumed that an address in the 1700s on Broadway would put it near 17th Street. So, I rode a bus from JFK Airport to a downtown terminal and then took the subway south to 17th and Broadway. Emerging into the upper air, I found the street numbers there way too low. So, I began walking north, and walking and *walking*. About 1½ hours and maybe four miles later, I arrived at the Mopix office, just a smidgeon wiser than I was earlier that morning.

I met with the office head and some of his veteran staffers. The plan that emerged: I would go alone to a commercial news film archive to seek footage on Agnew, order copies of that and then review the footage with the Mopix staff.

I spent some four hours that day checking indexes and scanning the available footage. The archive staff was very cooperative, but doubted that I would get enough to meet our need. I found that they had brief news clips of Agnew campaigning, playing golf, being sworn into office, etc. By the next afternoon (Thursday), the copied footage I had selected arrived at TV-Mopix's Broadway offices. After we screened it, the technician assisting me said it looked like enough to make up a short film introducing Spiro. But, it was supposed to be back at USIA-Washington by the following Monday. That meant we had to do the editing by the next day (Friday), so that it could be copied and air-shipped to Washington by Monday.

So, we worked *all night* Thursday. By about 7 AM Friday it was done. I had written a short script describing what the scenes were. The technician and I turned the edited film over to the production people coming into work that morning. He went home for the weekend, and I went to my hotel for a few hours of sleep before leaving that afternoon for Washington.

On Monday afternoon, the acting Mopix director, a senior civil servant with about 20 years on the job, came in to see the approximately eight-minute film. I read the script aloud as it ran. When the lights came back up, he sat there nodding his head. "Very impressive!" he said. "Very impressive, but we can't use it."

"What do you mean?" I asked in shock.

"You've got to understand. For seven, eight months we've been trying to get outside contractors to put together a film for us on Agnew. They tried, but all came back and said it can't be done: there's nothing on the man. That's what we've been telling Agnew's friends in Congress. Now you go up to New York and in three days produce a film on Spiro Agnew. That'll make us look bad on the Hill."

I knew this man was very close politically to congressional staffs, but I argued this was not really a film, just a "composite film clip." He insisted it actually was a film and ordered me to junk my script and have the Mopix technicians delete the continuities, so that it was nothing but disconnected film footage. I was very frustrated and told Izenberg what was happening; but we had to concede that the old pro knew the capital's political realities far better than we did.

When I went down to our Mopix lab later to get my butchered film, I took with me a poster I had bought in New York for the technicians: a stark black-and-white cartoon of New York after a nuclear holocaust. Amid of the ruins wandered a dazed man with a smashed TV set, looking for some place to plug it in. The technicians took one look and exclaimed, "Beware of Greeks bearing gifts!" After that they ceased calling me the "Yellow Peril."

Another memorable experience as TV-Mopix policy officer for East Asia was helping to set up the first satellited trans-Pacific panel discussion to East Asia on U.S. Asian policy. Working with Izenberg again, I helped arrange the studio and brief the guest discussants for this first-ever program. "Quarterback" for the U.S. was Ambassador Marshall Green, the State Department's top policy-maker for Asia. For the Asian side in Washington: Indonesian Ambassador Soedjatmoko, as cultured and urbane as any European intellectual. In places like Tokyo, Manila and Singapore, local foreign affairs specialists and journalists were poised to ask questions and comment.

While we were waiting in the studio for the satellite linkages to be tested and the volume level of the mikes checked, Green and Soedjatmoko exchanged chitchat. Green noted that in such discussions Western speakers sometimes tended to dominate the conversation and not give their Asian counterparts equal time.

Ambassador Soedjatmoko smiled and said diplomatically, "Yes, yours tends to be a much more verbal society than we have in Asia."

With a twinkle in his eye, Marshall Green picked up on that: "Of course, we have the same problem domestically. Social scientists say the average American male speaks 20,000 words a day, while the average American female speaks 30,000. My problem, dear Abby, is that when I get home in the evening, I have nearly used up my 20,000 words, but my dear wife is just starting on her 30,000!" Green was famous for his jokes.

Needless to say, the trans-Pacific dialogue went well, with almost no hitches. All agreed this format should be regularly used in trans-Pacific dialogs henceforth; but the expense meant it was not used often until newer technology emerged in the '80s and '90s.

Meanwhile Kimie was enjoying life back in the States. In Japan, she was in the spotlight as a diplomat's wife, a partner in a trans-Pacific marriage and someone bridging the two cultures and both languages. Many Japanese naturally expected her to conform to social customs that enmesh all Japanese in that close-knit society. Now, in our capital she could be just one more housewife, and take on those other roles only, for instance, in the activities of the Washington-Tokyo Women's Club or the Japan-America Society.

Before we left Tokyo, Kimie began having uterine bleeding. Not serious initially, by early 1970 it had become worrisome, and her gynecologist urged a radical hysterectomy. Seeing no alternative, we agreed. Afterward, Kimie said, "Now I feel like an it—not a real female any more." To me, this lady was always totally feminine and, even then at 51, youthfully girlish and utterly fascinating. So, I made sure that she knew every day thereafter that she had lost none of her appeal with me. In fact, taking her hormone pills from then on, she did become only more beautiful.

After I had been on the job some eight months in TV-Mopix, the conservative head of TV-Mopix persuaded equally conservative USIA

Director Frank Shakespeare* that he did not need policy officers second-guessing him. So, I was asked to move to USIA headquarters to become the Japan-Korea Desk officer. Once again I was succeeding Izenberg. That put me at the center of headquarters support for USIS operations in Japan and Korea, reporting to the Area Director for East Asia.

Immediately, I was asked to make an official trip to the area, especially for briefings at USIS-Korea. Two other missions were tacked onto my trip. The next CPAO for Tokyo, Alan Carter, was getting a quick (3-month) Japanese course at State's Foreign Service Institute and wanted me to stop over in Tokyo to look at operations there and give him my analysis of the USIS-Japan program. I volunteered to describe it to him then and there, having left the program less than a year before. He said he wanted a more up-to-date analysis. I did not argue further, as that would let me look in on Tokyo once more.

Second, I was asked to make a stop on Saipan. Since the end of World War II, first the Defense Department and now the Interior Department had administered the Pacific islands captured from the Japanese as the "Trust Territories of the Pacific Islands" (TTPI).** A process was soon to begin for holding plebiscites, voting by the island inhabitants to decide their future status. They would choose between independence, local autonomy with the U.S. handling their defense and foreign relations, or territorial status (like Puerto Rico).

Interior was asking USIA to assign an officer to Saipan (headquarters of the TTPI) to develop an information program to insure that the inhabitants understood their options. USIA needed to know what support the officer would have, such as housing, logistical support and schooling for any children. Since I was the next USIA officer

---

* A vignette on Shakespeare: In 1972, I had a group of Japanese correspondents meet with him. When one asked him what the main difference was between Democrats and Republicans, Jesuit-schooled Shakespeare said, "Well, for starters, we Republicans are a lot firmer on Communism. ... I guess that's about it."
** At Yalta, Roosevelt, Churchill and Stalin had renounced all territorial claims on Japanese-held areas. So, although we had captured these islands, we were but temporary trustees.

to be transiting the area, I was asked to go to Saipan and obtain that information.

Now USIA's travel office let me in on a little-known fact: With an itinerary that extensive, a traveler could kick in something like $50-100 and get his ticket written for around the world. I much preferred (and still prefer) the stretched-out days of west-bound flights over the truncated days and nights when one flies east. So, I was off on my second round-the-globe flight.

First leg: Washington to Los Angeles, where I stared in near-disbelief at my first Boeing 747 while waiting to board that gigantic plane. "That thing simply is too big to fly!" I said to myself. Another change of planes in Honolulu and onward to Guam. I arrived at about 6 AM, groggy from the flight and with nothing to do until my afternoon flight to Saipan.

Then, at my elbow came a cheery voice: "How would you like to be king for a day?" I turned and beheld a middle-aged American who turned out to be the owner of a small hotel there in Agana. I checked his price for an 8-hour stay, and found it reasonable. So I became "king for a day"—an ordinary guest in his very ordinary hotel, where he lived with his Guamanian wife, five kids and too few guests.

After a four-hour nap and lunch in a nearby restaurant, I went out for a walk on the beach. There I ran into a little Guamanian boy out with his goat. With no sign of shyness, he asked me to pull down the branches of a bush so that he could feed them to his goat. A little farther down the beach I saw a family out in the bay in thigh-deep water—parents, a boy and girl—fishing in a most surprising way. The mother and daughter held the ends of a long net in a semicircle. The father and son had a long rope stretched between them with flat 6-inch sticks tied onto it at intervals of about four feet. The father and son would charge through the water toward the net with the rope between them and the sticks churning up the water to drive fish into the net. They then hurriedly closed the net. They repeated this several times as I watched.

A few hours later, I was flying over the Northern Marianas to Saipan. A map helped me identify the islands passing below: Rota and Tinian, the latter being where the *Enola Gay* flew off to Hiroshima on August 6, 1945. Then we were circling Saipan. I could see the northern cliffs from which so many Japanese had leaped to their deaths a quarter century earlier to avoid the disgrace of capture by the attacking Americans.

On the ground, a young Micronesian bureaucrat greeted me. As he drove me to my hotel, I learned that he was one of dozens of young Pacific Islanders who had been educated in American universities and now formed the core of the TTPI administration: promising young men (and a few women) who were helping their home islands adjust to an era in which technology, telecommunications and air travel would mean their people would never again be as isolated from the world as they had been traditionally. For better or for worse.

That evening on the hotel veranda I had a vodka tonic while I watched the tropical sunset. On a coral reef about a quarter a mile offshore was what looked like a tank turret with its projecting cannon barrel, apparently a tragic remnant of the bitter battle of 1944. When I asked the waiter about it, he smiled and said, "Yes, everyone asks about that. When the U.S. forces were landing, that tank got stuck in the coral. So, it never saw action. The crew was court-martialed for getting stuck."

The next morning, as I was preparing to leave my room, a nubile young hotel maid knocked and asked if she could begin cleaning my room. Of course I agreed. Then she gave me a big smile and asked if I would do her a big favor. Leery, and with images from Hollywood movies rising in my mind, I asked what I could do. She took my arm and led me to a window. "You see that man out there?" A young man was watering the garden outside. "Would you please call him for me?" I shrugged and called to him. A minute later, I was going out the door as the young man came down the hall.

I spent the morning at the TTPI offices getting answers to most of the questions USIA had posed and learning what items were still vague enough to need further discussion with Interior. Then to Tokyo (via Okinawa) for an update on of USIS-Japan so that I could report to

Alan Carter. Next, to Korea, where I spent a week learning about that USIS program.

One thing that struck me about the Korean scene in 1970 was how much it resembled Japan of about 1950. Some dynamism, but also many problems that could need decades to overcome. Away from central Seoul, pony carts seemed to be a standard transportation mode for small traders and for farmers bringing produce in from the countryside. At the park atop Namsan hill (the site for Seoul's first TV towers) on a Sunday morning, I was told how USIS had rigged a large TV screen to show live coverage of the Apollo moon landing to Koreans visiting the park. There I also saw several *yangban*, country gentlemen in traditional costume, as if materialized there from the 17th century. A decade and a half later, they and the pony carts were scarcely ever seen.

Of course, a big difference between Korea then and Japan in 1950 was that U.S. forces were in Korea and on the DMZ (Demilitarized Zone) because they had come in to help accept the Japanese surrender in 1945, and because they had fought alongside ROK soldiers to help to drive out the North Koreans in 1950-53 and now were helping to brace South Korea against the threat of any renewed aggression.

From Seoul, I flew to Hong Kong to pick up Pan Am's round-the-world flight through Singapore to Bombay, where I took a rest stop in a British-era Hotel. My room overlooked Victoria Gate—a structure like Paris's Arche d' Triomphe, built for Queen Victoria's 19th-century visit. I paused in Bombay because my next hop was Bombay→Washington, D.C.

The next day, chasing the sun across 11 time zones, I flew Bombay-Tehran-Paris-London-New York-Washington, D.C., arriving in our capital about 5 PM. I met with Carter about 7-9 PM that evening, by which time, after a 35-hour day with maybe 90 minutes sleep on the plane, I was so punchy that I had to cut short my briefing.

That summer we had welcome news from Hugh-ko. He had begun feeling the pinch of not having a high school diploma. After spending time in Everett, Washington, and then North Hollywood, he understood that he needed to get on with his education. So, he came back to Maryland to spend the 1970-71 school year with us to complete his senior year in Silver Spring. We were delighted, of course. We had often worried about him since he had split for Everett two years before.

We moved upstairs from our 2-bedroom apartment to a 3-bedroom unit on the 13th floor where we had a fine view westward to Virginia's Blue Ridge Mountains. Hugh-ko curled his lip at the plain white walls of his room and set about repainting them pale lilac. Also, when he found no shirts that he liked in the stores, he borrowed Kimie's sewing machine, bought cloth of his own choice and proceeded to make his own shirts, with quite professional-looking results even though he had never sewed anything so complex before! Rits, meanwhile, was living with Sheila in a Virginia apartment.

In 1970, I again began translating for a U.S. Government translation service. All the jobs were from the Japanese media; and the translations went to Government agencies with an official interest in Japan. The subject matter was Japanese politics, economic and financial news. That helped me keep a polish on the language while I was away from Japan.

In fall '71, I took another assignment at USIA in a small unit of the Policy Office. Our job was to adapt a new system to help USIS posts to track and manage resources—a system derived from the "Program Planning and Budgeting System" (PPBS) that Robert McNamara had introduced in the Defense Department. USIA and other agencies were under White House orders to implement this; so we plowed ahead.

McNamara based the PPBS on his experience at Ford Motor Company. Cars, parts, output per hour, etc., can be tallied to measure operating efficiency. Much of what the Pentagon does or buys can be tallied, too. But, how applicable was PPBS to USIS programs aimed at improving images of America among foreign audiences, or explaining the U.S. system of government to people who have known only colonial rule? You can tally film showings and attendance and so measure program volume. But program effectiveness?

In 1957 when we management interns visited USIA's Mopix Division, we were told of one effort to measure the impact of a USIA documentary. After a test screening in rural Iran of a film on how our aid program had built a hydroelectric dam in the mountains, an Iranian farmer was asked what he liked about the movie. His answer: "The chicken." The USIS team remembered no chicken and so ran back through the film until, sure enough, in one scene a chicken crosses a road. The old farmer said he had never before seen such a fine chicken. Any message about American generosity or technical competence went right over his head. Such were our doubts as we tried to follow the Nixon-Kissinger directive on installing the PPBS.

That same spring, I had a unique experience: helping to interpret in the White House. A large delegation of Japanese cabinet officials, headed by Prime Minister Tanaka arrived to further advance US-Japan relations. They brought some interpreters with them, so that in talks between the Council of Economic Advisors and such officials as Japan's Economic Planning Agency head, trade minister and finance minister, I had a back-up role. We spent two days in the West Wing basement working over the key issues of that time.

We American interpreters were also asked to interpret at Nixon's state dinner for the visiting Japanese. Sounds glamorous, but listen up. The White House military aides told us to arrive at 5 PM for the dinner starting at 7:30. We had a half-hour briefing on our duties and then were held in a side room for two hours—standard military "hurry up and wait"—with nothing to eat or drink. At 7:30 PM we were led into the East Room and assigned chairs immediately behind the persons we would interpret for. I sat behind Director and Mrs. Kimura of the Economic Planning Agency. There I interpreted for the next 1½ hours, as the band played, the guests ate and brief speeches were given. At the end, we were thanked by the military aides and then dismissed. Four hours, no food or drink and then sent off into the night! Glamor?

In spring '72, we helped Hugh-ko buy a VW "bug" for his commute to Montgomery-Blair High School. Of course, he needed a driver's license, for which he and I went to the Maryland DMV. On the application form he came upon boxes marked "Race." Code 1—black,

Code 2—Caucasian, Code 3—Mongolian/Asian/Pacific area. As a half "Caucasian" and half "Mongolian," he puzzled over where to put his X. We went together to the DMV clerk. I explained that he was half Code 2 and half Code 3. "So, should he write in 2.5?" I asked. Gruffly, the clerk said, "Just check code 2." The inanity of our racial categories at that time!

June came and Hugh-ko graduated from high school. Now he told us he was returning to the Seattle area, specifically to Bellingham, where a lady friend majoring in education at Western Washington University had lined up a job for him: renovating bathrooms at her boarding house in lieu of rent. Again, we were puzzled: When and where had he learned such building and plumbing skills? Anyway, he loaded his few possessions into the VW and headed west.

We again were empty nesters and no longer needed a 3-bedroom apartment. Also we now received notice of a fairly stiff rent increase. That impelled us to go house hunting. We had lived in apartments for six years in Tokyo and now two years in Silver Spring. We yearned for the extra space of a real house. Before long we had located a very decent house in Chevy Chase on a short street that dead-ends in Rock Creek Park. By mid-September we had moved into the 3-bedroom two-story with a large back yard, a lovely weeping cherry in back and beautiful Yoshino cherry in front.

We borrowed against my life insurance to finance the down payment and found the mortgage payments manageable. It also helped that Kimie now decided to take a job as assistant accountant in a small company. The long-term benefit was that the job trained her in keeping accounts and balancing a checkbook. That made her better qualified than I to manage family finances. Ever after, she was the one who handled the checkbook and kept track of our bills. And, bless her frugal soul, she kept us generally debt free.

In those years, she also honed her skills as a superlative comparison shopper. A story behind that. Once, back in 1948, when Kimie and her mother were discussing food prices, I had butted in to ask if that was all they could talk about. In those days, I had barely realized what a rare gem Kimie was. So, I went on, "Can't we discuss something more serious? How about Shakespeare or something?" Well, it turned out that Kimie had read more Shakespeare than I—in Japanese translation. She would not speak to me for two days after my silly outburst. With inflation surging in Japan at that time, food prices were a "more serious" topic. In the following 52 years, I learned to value and appreciate her many talents, including a great capacity to keep in her head the current prices of major food items—and save us many dollars.

Kimie always loved seafood, especially crustaceans and shellfish. Now when we ate out, we sometimes went to one of the area's "raw bars" where one could feast on local oysters and clams, or to crab houses where tables were covered with brown paper or newspaper, and diners received an apron and a hammer for attacking the boiled crab. Peoples' eyes would pop when Kimie set aside the hammer and proceeded to break the crab shells with her dainty hands and crack the crab legs with her teeth. She would handily dispatch five or six crabs while I was working on one. I began calling that her "crab genocide."

I now (1971) was in the third year of my Washington assignment. Normally, such assignments ran three to four years before an officer was again sent overseas. So, I began dealing with Personnel on my next assignment.

# ONCE AGAIN AROUND THE WORLD

## (FALL 1971)

Now, an unexpected request from the Agency: that I go to Indonesia to join a three-person team to do a quick inspection of USIS-Indonesia. Retired senior USIS officer Jack Murphy, a Foreign Service secretary and I were to evaluate and report on the program.

Again there were add-ons to the trip. The PPBS which I had been working on was now ready to be introduced at USIS posts. CPAO Alan Carter in Tokyo was overhauling the USIS program there, cutting back and restructuring branch posts (calling them American Centers and their libraries, "Infomats,"). So, besides inspecting Indonesia, I was also to consult in Tokyo on how the Carter-designed USIS-Japan program would mesh with the PPBS. I was also to brief USIS-Bangkok, USIS-New Delhi and two West African posts on the PPBS. That meant my third round-the-world trip!

So, although we had been in our new house just 10 days and were still settling in, I said goodbye to Kimie and flew off. The itinerary: Washington→New York→Tokyo (via Fairbanks)→Hong Kong→Jakarta→Bangkok→New Delhi→Tehran→Athens→Kinshasa→Lagos→Dakar→ Miami→Washington.

Views from the plane window on New York-Fairbanks leg fascinated me as we flew over Canada's Northwest Territories—myriad lakes, the Mackenzie River—and Alaska's vast central wilderness.

In Tokyo, I found that Alan Carter had imported a cadre of young disciples, true believers all and dedicatedly overhauling the USIS program. Plans were in train to close the branch posts in Sendai, Niigata, Kobe and Hiroshima. Carter argued that rising fixed costs were rapidly eating into program funds and that improved transportation (e.g., Bullet trains) and communications now enabled USIS to program nationwide from fewer fixed facilities.

That was superficially logical from a manager's viewpoint, but ignored two vital factors: (1) the strong emphasis on personal relationships in Japanese culture, and (2) the need for American and Japanese staff on the scene locally to identify emerging leaders and "opinion elites." Intellectually sharp and always articulate, Carter held that such elites mostly work in Tokyo and major cities where we would still have American centers. (So, his assurance that USIS could still program in the cities losing ACCs rang hollow, for his logic already was writing them off.) He insisted that rising costs in Japan would in any case mean we could not continue to cultivate provincial elites. Perhaps so, but just then trade disputes were sharpening tensions in US-Japan relations. It seemed to me the wrong time to be shrinking our program.

From Tokyo through Hong Kong, to change planes there for the hop to Jakarta—and my first crossing of the equator. Approaching Indonesia's capital from the air, I saw the myriad islands of this archipelago, each larger one with its tall thunderhead, reminiscent of the tropical climate I had previously seen in the Pacific.

A USIS car picked me up at the airport. Jakarta's streets were filled with taxis (mostly older Japanese cars) and countless pedicabs, called *betjak*. Here and there new high-rise buildings stood among the one- and two-story buildings from the Dutch era and the humble homes of the Indonesian masses.

That evening I dined with the Jack Murphy, our team leader. Our team secretary would arrive the next day. Jack recapped the reason for the quick inspection: negative comments in an earlier State Department post inspection, and briefed me on the schedule and cast of characters.

USIS-Jakarta was headed by State Department FSO (career Foreign Service Officer) Marshall Brement, whom we met the next morning at a USIS staff meeting with most of his American staff. Brement had served earlier in Hong Kong and Taipei (after learning Chinese), in Moscow (after learning Russian) and in Singapore (where he could again use his Chinese). Few FSOs try to tackle two such "hard" languages. Brement also had French under his belt and had studied Indonesian before going to Jakarta. Highly intelligent and a hard-charger, he was quite gracious with us as inspectors.

Our schedule had us spending our first six days in Jakarta, then visiting the branch posts of Medan (northern Sumatra) and Surabaya (eastern Java).

The next evening (Monday) after dinner, Jack and I went to visit a young political officer whom Jack had known several years earlier. We knocked on his front door. Instantly we heard fierce barking and the impact of a large dog against the door. We stepped back in surprise, glad that the door was teak. The officer opened the door to greet us and apologize for the dog's ferocity. After we had been introduced, his German shepherd was friendly and well behaved. In fact, he soon brought from upstairs some of his squeaky rubber dollies—hand-me-downs from the couple's little girl. But, the officer's wife said that once when she was dressing to go out, her Indonesian maid brought a hanger for her dress, holding it out toward her. Just in time, the wife turned and saw the dog preparing to attack the maid, taking the hanger to be a weapon.

That week, we were invited to several dinners and luncheons. The American ambassador hosted one lunch party, with perhaps six Indonesian guests attending. I had a most interesting talk with Mochtar Lubis, a journalist whom former president Sukarno and the current president Suharto had jailed several times for being too outspoken. The man was a head taller than other Indonesians we had seen. I remembered that people in the north of Korea and China tended to be taller than those in the south. So, I asked, "Is there some part of Indonesia where the people are taller on the average than elsewhere in the islands?"

He replied, "No, not to my knowledge. My people are Bataks, from northern Sumatra; but some might say we have European blood."

"Oh!" I said in mild surprise.

"Yes, you see, about 150 years ago German missionaries came to bring Christianity to us, and my ancestors ate them." That with a straight face. Obviously, one of his stock jokes.*

At the same party I was amazed to hear two Indonesians talk of the previous year's visit by "our queen," the queen of the Netherlands. For, I knew that Indonesia had fought a bitter war of independence from Dutch rule. I surmised that upper class, educated Indonesians may not have fared too badly under the Dutch and so remained sentimentally pro-Dutch.

On a Friday, the secretary and I flew to Medan to see USIS operations there. Our route was through Singapore and gave me my first look at Singapore, the Malacca Strait and the swamps of eastern Sumatra (still a base for pirates who prey on shipping in the strait).

In Medan, the USIS BPAO gave us a quick tour of the USIS facilities, where a book discussion group was meeting. That evening we attended the BPAO's party for his local contacts. One guest was an American petroleum engineer who had spent some 20 years prospecting for oil in the islands. He described to me the conditions before World War II in the same swampy jungles we had over-flown that morning. They would barge their gear up rivers in the rainy season, build log roads into the jungle by felling trees crossways to their course, set up their drilling platforms on such logs and start drilling. In the dry season, the rivers receded, leaving their log roads and drilling platforms 10-20 feet above the muddy jungle floor. Today such areas are a major source of Indonesian crude.

---

* In 2005, an Indonesian lawyer from Medan verified these facts about Lubis, and told me that he had died several years before.

On Saturday morning, the BPAO and I had a long discussion on programs and ideas about reaching "target" audiences in the area; and I described the PPBS to him. Then he took me to a natural arboretum in the hills behind the city. As we arrived, rain began to fall. So, we saw only the central area with its cleared trails.

The rain lifted on our way back, and we stopped at a roadside fruit stand. The BPAO asked if I had ever tried durian. I had not even heard of it. He explained that many South-east Asian men dote on this exotic fruit and are said to love durian more than their wives. International airlines refuse to allow the fruit in plane cabins because of their intense odor. So, now my host bought one, had it sliced open right there, and we ate it—from *upwind*. To me the flavor was a combination of cheramoya and pineapple, but the odor was like garlic and very old eggs. So, best eaten when you have a head cold?

As we drove back, the BPAO related an experience he had on a weekend trip to Lake Toba in the mountains above Medan. The family took along their dog, a large golden retriever. When they arrived at the lake,* some tribesmen were lounging in front of the little store where the BPAO went to buy groceries. When he came out, he saw the men animatedly placing bets. One approached and asked how much he would take for his dog. Not for sale, of course. The man began haggling for an acceptable price. It turned out the man had bet the others that the retriever was large enough that—cooked up—he would feed the entire village! Cultural differences again.

Early Sunday morning, the Foreign Service secretary and I caught a plane for Jakarta. I had a window seat and, as usual, enjoyed studying the geography below and tracking our location with a map. About the time we crossed the equator again, the plane hit some turbulence and bounced slightly. I nudged the secretary, dozing in the next seat. "Did you feel that bump?" I asked her. "Yes. So?" she answered sleepily.

---

\* I recently read that the 20x40-mile lake sits in a huge caldera, the remnant of a titanic volcanic eruption some 70,000 years ago, far bigger than that of the famed Krakatoa south of Sumatra. Toba's ash, circling the globe in the stratosphere, altered climates for some years afterward.

"We just crossed the equator," I deadpanned. She came awake, giving me a dubious look.

During the next week, we saw more of Marshall Brement, the CPAO, and his family (wife and three children). More and more, he struck me as cold and calculating.

Near the end of the week, Jack Murphy sent me on a solo visit to USIS-Surabaya, in east Java. The BPAO there briefed me well on USIS programming there.

My hotel in Surabaya was a relic of the Dutch era, with mansard roofs and a mellow look. The plumbing in the room, too: The toilet had no seat and was flushed by a long chain hanging from a rusted tank high on the wall. The showerhead emitted maybe five thin diverging jets of lukewarm water. But, I was spending just one night there.

One noon hour, I visited an antique shop with many striking wood carvings: dance masks and *garuda*—the magical eagle of Indonesian legend and the logo of the national airline. I bought a stone Buddha head, which a museum curator back in Jakarta later told me was 20$^{th}$ century and carved for sale, not for religious use. At $80 it still was a bargain.

On the road to the airport at the end of my Surabaya visit, I was delighted to see some traditional Indonesian farm carts coming into the city with produce. They had huge 6-foot wheels (for navigating the rutted roads), were colorfully painted and pulled by two *large* Brahma bullocks festooned with bells. A picture for the *National Geographic!*

During our last few days in Jakarta, as we partied, ate out and worked on our final report, I developed heavy-duty diarrhea. An Embassy doctor gave me a broad-spectrum antibiotic to quell it.

Leaving Jakarta, I flew to Bangkok to brief USIS staff there on the PPBS we were putting together in USIA. Although it was designed to help them manage their resources, they tended to see it as bureaucratic interference with their real work, which they already knew how to do well. So, USIS crews in Bangkok (and elsewhere) were understandably unimpressed by the PPBS. Cross-cultural or intercultural communication is always difficult. Measuring the impact of U.S. Government information programs ...

Same reactions also in New Delhi, where I flew next. But, I made the trip personally worthwhile by taking a Sunday bus trip to Agra to see the Taj Mahal. (I'll later describe the Indian scene in discussing a longer stay there a decade later.)

Before leaving Bangkok, I had begun getting an itchy rash on my arms and legs. So, when I arrived in New Delhi and before going to Agra, I visited the Embassy's well-equipped clinic to consult with the American doctor there. He took one look, asked a few pointed questions and then called in his Indian intern. "Have you ever seen anything like this?" he asked the intern. The man had not. "It's a yeast bloom," the doctor said. "In Burma we had a man with a much worse case. It comes on when a broad-spectrum antibiotic wipes out intestinal bacteria that normally control yeast in your gut. The yeast cells then flourish and cause your body to react against them. You get this rash."

He gave me a topical ointment and reassured me that, since I had finished taking the antibiotic, my intestinal fauna and flora would soon be back in balance. To help that process, I quit eating or drinking anything that might contain active yeast. No beer in New Delhi's heat! And, no bakery products.

My onward route from New Delhi took me to Tehran, where I overnighted. That gave me a chance to follow my practice of taking long walks the first time I visit a city to get the feel for the atmosphere. Next I flew to Athens, where I would catch my flight into Africa.

I arrived in Athens before sunup, only to find that my downtown hotel room was not ready for me. The airline had made the reservation, the desk clerk claimed, without telling them I would arrive so early. My room would not be ready until midday. (SNAFU #1) So, despite travel fatigue, I went up to their rooftop café and ate a leisurely breakfast while watching the sunrise dye the Parthenon a kaleidoscope of pinks and orange. After finally getting into my room, I napped a little, had a late lunch and then strolled over to the offices of Air Congo, my next air carrier. "Oh, sir," I was told, "We must report a delay in your flight: It will not leave until late this afternoon." (SNAFU #2)

So, I would have extra time in Athens. I used that time to taxi to the Parthenon, where I strolled among groups of tourists and reflected on the theme "sic transit gloria" before returning to my hotel to check out. I then went again to the Air Congo office. There, chaos and confusion reigned as people milled about. The word was that the flight to Kinshasa would not leave until the next morning! (SNAFU #2-1) I asked the clerks there to contact my hotel and have my room saved for me.

First thing the next morning, I called Air Congo to ask for the new departure time for Kinshasa. "Yes, sir," came the cheery reply, "We expect the plane to leave before noon today." So, I decided to avoid more hotel charges by checking out and taxiing to the airport. At the Athens terminal, with no Air Congo check-in desk to be seen, I stopped by the Pan Am desk to inquire. "Oh sir, Air Congo shares a window with Air Atlantis," the helpful clerk informed me.

I went to the Air Atlantis window. "Sir, the information we have is that the plane will leave early this afternoon." (SNAFU #2-2) Three or four more hours to kill! I bought a long novel and sat down to wait. After about two hours, I looked up and saw that the Air Atlantis clerk was gone from his window, and still gone a half hour later. Then it struck me: Atlantis was a myth! I grew uneasy about my trip to Africa and went to the adjoining window to inquire. "Oh sir, he went home. There are no more flights for him to handle today." As I suspected, he was back in Atlantis! (SNAFU #2-3)

I called the downtown Air Congo office. "Sir, we are very sorry, but the new departure time for the plane is tomorrow morning." !!! ##!!! I asked them to cancel my reservation. My schedule would not accommodate that much delay. At the Pan Am desk again, I inquired about an onward flight to the U.S. They had nothing that day and asked me to make arrangements at their downtown office. So, by taxi again into Athens. At the Pan Am office, I stood in line behind a cranky

American complaining about the service, the food he had eaten and generally bad-mouthing Greece.

When it was my turn, I apologized to the Greek clerk for that American's bad manners. "If he knew his history, he would recall that when your ancestors were building the Parthenon, his and mine were probably still living in caves," I remarked. The clerk smiled, and proceeded to find me a cancelled seat on a flight leaving that evening for London.

Thus ended my trip into Africa, while sitting it out in Athens. Back in Washington, a USIA Africa hand explained that Air Congo had just two planes. Whenever the Congolese president's wife wished to go shopping in Europe, she simply commandeered a plane.

At home, I found that in my absence, intrepid Kimie had determinedly gone ahead and painted all inside walls of our new home and was totally exhausted. Of course I sidelined her and did the ceilings myself.

# CARLISLE PA

## (1972-73)

In early 1972, after 2½ years in Washington, for my next assignment I was offered a choice between an academic year at the Army War College in Carlisle PA or going to Jakarta as Cultural Affairs Officer (CAO). I did not relish the idea of working under CPAO Marshall Brement and so opted for the War College.

A year at the War College was meant to advance an officer's career and his chances for a promotion. I had been promoted the previous year (to the equivalent of a colonel or navy captain)—my first promotion in seven years due mainly to my career track having focused so much on Japan and policy positions rather than positions like CAO or IO (information officer). So, a year at the War College seemed my best choice. Looking back with 20/20 hindsight, I believe I would have done better taking the CAO job in Jakarta.

But, I have no regrets. We later found that the tropics would handicap Kimie's ongoing battle with her kidney stone and that my lady would fare poorly in hot humid climates. Her veins were small, keeping her natural cooling system from functioning properly in hot sultry weather.

Late in July 1972 we rented our Susanna Lane home to a Canadian Air Force officer attached to the Canadian Embassy and headed for Carlisle.

The Army War College (USAWC) occupies a site that once was the Carlisle Indian School, alma mater of such famed Native Americans as athlete Jim Thorpe. Government policy early in the 20th century was to absorb Native Americans into the mainstream and phase out protection of the tribes. The Indian School was a step in that process: making "good Americans" of the most promising Indian youth by schooling them in the ways of the white majority.

We saw evidence there that one consequence was to increase Indian kids' mortality rate through higher exposure to white diseases. For, tucked away in a corner of the campus was a cemetery for students who fell victim to our "civilized" diseases—headstone after headstone listing their name, tribe and year of death. Many had died in the 1918 flu epidemic. On a brighter note, we learned that residents of that area even today pass on legends of the Indian students' athleticism: how they would, for example, jog the 18 or 20 miles to Harrisburg for a track meet, win all the races and then jog back to Carlisle.

The post had an even earlier history. A relic of the Revolutionary War era was Hessian House, a smallish stone building that was a jail for Hessian (German) soldiers captured in our War for Independence. Also, the post was briefly occupied by elements of Lee's army just before the battle of Gettysburg.

Kimie and I were assigned a furnished apartment in Young Hall, a long building facing the athletic field ("Indian Field") where Kimie (now 53) and I sometimes jogged together. A good array of post facilities was available to us: a small PX, a commissary, an officers club where we could eat out when we wished, a well-stocked library, etc. I would be one of eight civilians (from State, CIA, Defense and a scattering of other government agencies) among over 200 lieutenant colonels and "bird" colonels.

Among my classmates were men who would later become famous during the first Gulf War, such as Norman Schwartzkopf ("Stormin' Norman"). The Diplomatic Advisor (and my faculty advisor) was Ambassador Herman Eilts, who would be our ambassador to Egypt during crucial Mideast negotiations led by Kissinger.

The first event at the college, even before classes began, focused on the Gettysburg battle. In an evening performance, two AWC staff officers took the stage in the auditorium to explain dramatically the Civil War situation and why each side saw the battle as so pivotal. One officer, dressed in Confederate gray, gave the South's perspective, while another in Union blue told how the North saw the situation. The next day, the entire class of 215 and any wives wishing to go (including Kimie) were bused 25 miles to Gettysburg to spend some 4-5 hours touring the Gettysburg area and grasping the battle situation on the scene. Memorable, impressive and of course depressing because of the huge waste of human life that had taken place there.

The War College year was not meant to teach us students how to make war, but rather to make us better understand the role of national defense in the whole framework of U.S. foreign policy and how it sought to keep the peace, especially with the Soviet bloc.

A fine aspect of the program was that the class was divided into about a dozen groups that studied and socialized together for two months at a time. We then were mixed into another group for two months more. That way, over the course of the academic year we became well acquainted with most of our classmates. Kimie enjoyed the many opportunities for socializing with the military wives, with whom she became very popular. No surprise there. She never ceased to grow and develop her talents.

For me another fascinating aspect was the trips. After Gettysburg, our next trip was to New York City for the entire class, wives included. We visited the UN, where we were briefed by then UN Ambassador George H.W. Bush and by UN officials. While the wives went to a museum, we men visited New York City Hall for briefings on city government and relations with other levels of government. We all attended a Broadway show. Those who wished to visited a Playboy Club. All in two days and a half.

A footnote on that trip: In Niigata in fall 1962, Kimie and I had collected several dozen paper nautilus shells, when these normally sub-tropical critters (of the squid family) apparently took a wrong turn and were swept into cold Japan Sea waters that paralyzed their swimming muscles and swept them up onto the Niigata beach. We had kept a box of these fragile shells (cousins of the sturdier and better known chambered nautilus) with our shell collection. Before going to New York, I phoned a seashell store there to ask whether these shells were of any interest. I was told that any in good shape were definitely needed. So, on the New York trip when we had a few hours free, Kimie and I went to the store. The proprietress was delighted and paid me $8 per shell. As we talked, she said her biggest problem was that Japanese buyers were scouring the world for good seashells and driving up prices. A trade problem you probably never saw covered in any newspaper.

For our next trip—students only this time—we could choose between one focusing on America's ICBM defenses and one to the Navy War College and Boston. I chose the ICBM trip. We flew by chartered plane from Harrisburg to Omaha, where we visited Strategic Air Command (SAC) headquarters and heard how SAC hoped to survive a nuclear attack, if one ever were launched. They admitted they could not survive a direct hydrogen bomb hit, but said they were hardening command centers elsewhere.

From Omaha we flew to Offut Air Base in South Dakota for briefings and then went by helicopter to some ICBM sites and down into the silos to talk with the crews manning them. Flying to and from the silos, we saw buffalo and pronghorn antelope. At one point our helicopter pilot swooped down to stampede about a dozen buffalo. What amazed me was that the antelope would not stampede. They stood stock still, depending on their natural camouflage for protection. Flying back, we passed over Mount Rushmore, impressive from the air, too. (If you ever meet a UFO pilot, recommend the view to him.)

For the final trip, in April 1973, we again had a choice: Panama or Canada. About 60% of us chose Panama. We again flew from Harrisburg, climbing up over the Three Mile Island nuclear power plant (to become infamous six years later) and headed down the East Coast, over Miami, followed a bearing west of Cuba to avoid that country's air space and then went into Panama City.

For the first day and a half we had briefings by the U.S. Embassy and various U.S. military commands. Near the middle of the second day we loaded into helicopters to fly the length of the Canal and visit the School of the Americas. En route, I was shooting photos when I dropped the lens cap of my camera, and watched in dismay as it fell some 1500 feet.

We spent about three hours at the school where Latin American officers were trained to provide security in their home countries. After lunch, we boarded the Panama Railway for the 25-mile trip back along the canal to Panama City, with a stop to observe ships moving through the Mira Flores Locks. I was interested to see that the electric "mules" towing ships through the lock were made by Mitsubishi, and that our guide at the locks was a young Hungarian who had fled his homeland during the 1956 uprising.

On our final day, we had a meeting with officers of Panama's government. President Noriega was supposed to attend but was tied up with more important business. At that time, the subject of the Canal's reversion to Panama's control was just beginning to heat up. So we probed the attitudes of the Panamanian officers on that. One of our classmates finally asked bluntly, 'But, really, why do you want control of the Canal Zone? Things seem to be working smoothly now."

A senior officer came to the microphone and answered, in English, "Because we have balls!" The War College officers roared, understanding instantly that it was a matter of nationalism and machismo.

Back at the War College, each of us was required to produce a research paper, either alone or with two or three other officers. I chose to write, on my own, a paper on a subject I knew something about: Japanese responses to the "Nixon doctrine"—his policy of "Vietnamizing" the war in southeast Asia and otherwise stressing Asians taking more responsibility for Asia's problems. The review committee liked my paper enough to include it among the few published by the War College that year.

In the paper, I discussed Japan's failure—up to that point—to ratify the Nuclear Non-Proliferation Treaty (NPT), which had become bogged down in inter-party politics in the Diet. State Department policy offices had concluded that Japan would not ratify. I knew that such an outcome would run too much counter to the Japanese public's anti-nuclear sentiment and so in my paper predicted NPT ratification in the next few years. A few years later, the National Diet proved me right.

Only about a three-hour drive from Washington, D.C., Carlisle was close enough that Rits was able to come up once or twice to visit, along with 11-year-old Sheila. So, we kept that family tie warm.

Notable events during our stay in Carlisle were the deaths of two Presidents—Truman in December '72 and LBJ less than a month later. On each occasion 21-gun salutes were fired across the athletic field adjacent to our apartment building, and a ceremony honoring each deceased president was held. An interesting exposure to military ritual.

Sadly, a death much closer to home also occurred that year: In February 1973, Mother finally succumbed to Alzheimer's. It was Mother's wish that, like her beloved husband, she be cremated and her ashes scattered on the Pacific. That was done at Fort Bragg within days of her death. Meanwhile, our three sisters notified us brothers of the date for a memorial service in Berkeley.

I flew from Carlisle, John from eastern Washington and George from Connecticut, where he and his family now lived in another Bruderhof community. John presided at the church service; and we all gathered afterward at Mary's home in south Berkeley to reminisce about our mother. It was there that we heard more sad news: Louise and Charley James were divorcing. Louise had already arranged to move to Fort Bragg, renting a small house from Kitty's former realtor, Larry Spring.

*Undaunted fisherman on Potomac - 1958*

*My little family in Silver Spring - 1960*

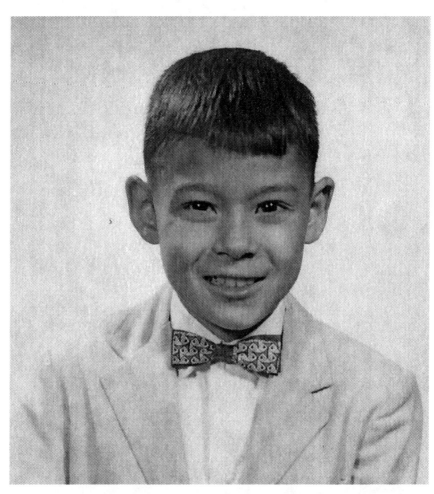

*Hugh-ko's first passport shot - 1960*

*With Kimie at Niigata ACC - 1961*

*At Niigata governor Tsukada's party - 1961*

*Me and Fujita in Niigata snow country - 1962*

*Giant kites in Shirone schoolyard - 1962*

*Reischauers arrive in Niigata - 1963*

*With Mother in Port Townsend WA - 1963*

*At Nikko - 1964*

*Kimie & Embassy ladies with Reischauers - 1964*

*Lady says, "No kissing in public!" - 1965*

*End of 100K walk at Waseda Univ. - 1966*

*Kimie's family at our Tokyo farewell - 1969*

*Kimie with War College wives - 1972*

*At War College - 1973*

*My passport photo - 1973*

*And her passport photo - 1973*

# PART III:
# MIDDLE AND
# LATER CAREER

# VIETNAM

## (1973-75)

With the academic year at the War College winding down, USIA Personnel contacted me about my next assignment. For several years, State and USIA had been requiring Foreign Service Officers to serve a 2-year tour in Vietnam. Families could not accompany them there, but instead lived in nearby locations—mainly Hong Kong, Manila and Bangkok—on "SMA" (separate-maintenance allowances) so that the husbands could visit them on weekends or on ordinary leave.

Now it was my turn for duty in Vietnam. Fortunately, in January '73 the Paris negotiations produced an armistice in that long tragic conflict. That meant that Kimie became one of the first Foreign Service wives to accompany her husband directly to South Vietnam. I was assigned as Policy/Research Officer for USIS-Saigon.

After stops en route in Seattle and Tokyo to see family and friends, we arrived in Saigon on July 14, 1973 (Bastille Day). Jose Armilla, whom I would supervise, met us at Tansonhut Airport. He took us directly to the house assigned to us, a two-story home of concrete and stucco originally built for French colonial administrators. In back were a courtyard, garage and quarters for two servant families. It was about a mile from the USIS offices and from the palace of the RVN President.

Armilla and his wife Ruth (both Filipino Americans) planned a trip the next day (Sunday) to the Mekong delta to buy antique Chinese pottery and invited us to join them. As it was a weekend and we had not yet met other USIS people, we welcomed the invitation.

So, just 24 hours in the country, we found ourselves riding in an embassy sedan into the delta area. The Armillas found some of the pottery they were seeking; and we bought field-ripe pineapples from a roadside vendor. A number of ARVN soldiers were patrolling a field nearby. After we left, Kimie said she had felt a very tense atmosphere there. About a week later, the press reported a clash with Viet Cong at that spot despite the ceasefire supposedly in effect.

USIS-Saigon was in between Country Public Affairs Officers. Bob Lincoln, who oversaw the transition to a peacetime USIS structure in Saigon, had left in May and his replacement was not due until some time in August. The replacement: none other than Brement—the CPAO in Jakarta I had avoided by going to the Army War College. The vagaries of fate!

Meanwhile, our acting PAO was Bryan Battey, the deputy PAO. Problem: his marriage had just broken up and his wife had returned to the U.S. Very shortly, he fell into a state of depression that required him to be "med-evaced"—evacuated for medical reasons. Field Program Officer Jim Culpepper then became acting PAO, in addition to his normal duties of overseeing our branch posts (Danang, Hue, Nha Trang, Can Tho and Dalat). He was to be gone for five days, traveling to India, where he had just served, to pick up his wife. During that time, I became acting PAO!

Brement arrived alone in early August. Alone, as we would soon hear, because during his home leave between his Jakarta and Saigon assignments he had parked his wife and children in New York, gone to the Caribbean, gotten a quickie divorce and returned to New York to tell them they were no longer his concern. After arriving in Saigon, he used an international phone hookup to marry a Singapore-based lady journalist, Pamela, whom he had known very well for the previous several years.

In September, Pam arrived. The first weekend after that, Brement flaunted his rank as minister-counselor by ordering up an Air America helicopter to fly him and his new bride from the roof of the Embassy to the beach resort of Cap Saint Jacques, 40 miles to the south, for a quick honeymoon.

After a few months, Brement ordered a staff shuffle. Several senior officers from the old JUSPAO days were leaving, and a normal USIS operation was in place. Jim Culpepper became deputy PAO. I was made Program Officer, responsible for supervising all aspects of the program except relations with the Vietnamese media, which remained the purview of the Information Officer.

Kimie, meanwhile, was making contacts in the diplomatic community, joining in such social activities as golfing near Tansonhut airport, joint shopping trips such as to the "pottery village" of Lai Thieu, a source not only of tableware, but also of such larger ceramic items as "buffies" or BUFEs—the GI acronym for "Big, Ugly F---ing Elephants." These actually were mainly created as plant stands for outdoor decorative plants. Other such stands took the form of oversized turtles and snails, some of which I still own.

Some American wives volunteered to help at orphanages in Saigon; and soon Kimie was persuaded to go, too. She came home crying and agitated. The poor condition of the babies and their clinging arms, desperately seeking affection, were more than she could take. Some years later, she had a similar reaction to much better cared for children at a Catholic orphanage in India, who clung to her legs. Her heart told her to give them love. Her Japanese hygiene ethic said, "I don't know what diseases they may have." And her practical sense told her that, with the responsibilities of a diplomat's wife, she could offer no basic solution to their problems. The emotional dissonance of those feelings distressed her.

We were not allowed to bring personal vehicles to Saigon. So, the Embassy and USIS had a liberal policy on assigning motor pool sedans to us officers. A car and driver were assigned to me; and when I was not using the car, Kimie could use it for shopping, etc.

When we arrived in Saigon, Kimie had declared she would not buy anything; but the naive charm of the big pottery creations and the psychology of group shopping soon eroded her resolve and we began acquiring a small collection of local products. A local art that appealed to her was the shell-inlay lacquer ware. With chicken-egg shell fragments and mother-of-pearl, Vietnamese craftsmen (often mere teenagers) created exquisite scenes and dramatic art works. We bought a large (2'x3') plaque of a tiger's head done in varicolored eggshell, with mother-of-pearl teeth and eyes and hung it on the stair landing below our bedroom suite. (Good for keeping evil spirits away at night.)

In fall 1973, a big event back Stateside: Hugh was marrying Patricia Ann Thomas, the lady for whom he had left us so abruptly after he graduated from high school in 1971. Kimie was suffering one of her recurrent bladder infections due to the kidney stone and so could not go. So, I would have to represent both of us at the wedding.

My long flight eastward helped me better appreciate the logic of great-circle route flights. I flew first to Manila—about 3 hours. Notable about the passengers on board: a number were escorting Vietnamese orphan babies to the US, thus earning free airfare. In the seat ahead of me was an Army chaplain with two baby boys. I don't think he slept a wink. Next, on to Guam—3 hours more. Then, in the dark night to Honolulu and Seattle. Of course, we had layovers of 1-2 hours at each stop, and I lost track of the time. John, then serving a parish in Seattle, met me at the airport; and I stayed in his home.

John officiated at the wedding and joined us all for the following reception at the marina club house, where Pat's parents, Harold and Helen Thomas, were members. A warm, delightful experience overall.

As I had to return to work, I aimed to see if jet lag could be canceled by quickly returning to one's point of origin. So, the day after the wedding, I flew to Tokyo, overnighted there and then flew to Saigon in an Air France 747. As we crossed the Vietnam coast, we ran into a major weather front, first scattered thunderheads which the pilot carefully dodged. Then north of Saigon, a solid bank of towering clouds. With

Gallic élan, the pilot revved the engine and punched into it. From my window seat, I watched in amazement as the forces in the huge thunderheads bounced us around like a feather and the 747's wings flapped like a desperate bird's. It was good to land on solid ground after some 15 minutes of that. Result of my jet-lag experiment: failure. A quick return to your point of origin only superimposes one jet lag onto another. It took me a week to feel normal again.

Came Christmas 1973 and my Kimie felt blue because we were so far from our children. We had the wedding photos and their Christmas cards, but none of our offspring to hug. Luckily, we were invited to spend Christmas with a younger USIS family, Dennis and Gretchen Donahue* and their three young children. Other friends also joined the party, and we whooped it up until mid-evening.

A kind of geographic shock while staying in Saigon was to be swimming and sunning at the Embassy pool on New Year's Day 1974 in the encompassing tropical warmth. No "dashing through the snow," just warm water lapping in the pool. And no jingle bells, just the din of car horns and motor scooters outside the Embassy compound.

In April or May '74, Kimie and I took a trip to Nha Trang on the southeast coast. I had to visit the USIS post there anyway to get acquainted with the BPAO and our program. That took much of the first day, with time out for an excellent seafood lunch at La Frigate restaurant (now relocated to Georgetown in Washington, D.C.). That was a Friday.

On Saturday morning the BPAO took us sightseeing in the city—past an ARVN checkpoint where two soldiers had caught and were skinning a 4-foot monitor lizard for their dinner, past the remains of a 600-year-old Cham temple (Hindu, from an era when south Indians spread their

---

* Gretchen died a few years later of an auto-immune disorder. Dennis later was CPAO in Singapore and after retirement was a Public Affairs Advisor to the US Pacific Command and to the East-West Center in Honolulu. In 2006 he became Exec. Director of the Japan America Society in Battle Creek, Michigan.

culture around Southeast Asia) and past a structure where 20 or so attacking VC were said to have been killed and sealed inside.

Then we took a short boat trip to an offshore island. We walked through a fishing village to the island's outer side facing the South China Sea. A small bay there had its shallow mouth closed off by a man-made rock barrier built loosely enough that the sea could filter through. On stilts in the bay stood a restaurant, connected to land by a floating boardwalk. There we had lunch, sitting at a table where we could look down into the clear water and see fish 15 or 20 feet down. Those fish, in fact, were the entree menu. You pointed out to the waiter the fish you wanted; and a diver would go down and spear it. By the time you had finished a glass of wine, you had your *fresh* seafood dinner!

Nha Trang was famous in South Vietnam as a source for delicious, tender and large (8-10-pound) spiny lobsters. Whenever someone was coming to Saigon from Nha Trang, people gave him lobster orders. On this trip we brought back to Saigon about six as accompanied luggage. Price: maybe ¼ that in the US.

That September, I also took a trip, without Kimie, to our USIS post in Dalat, a pleasant town in the low mountains of central South Vietnam. I flew there by Air America—an 8-passenger plane (the reason Kimie chose not to go). I was sitting just behind the pilot; and as we neared the Dalat airport, he turned and said, "Nose gear won't lock down. I'm gonna try and fix it." When I looked puzzled, he said, "Just tell the others, and watch." He then proceeded to do two or three sharp dives, snapping up tightly each time. Finally, he turned with a smile and said, "That last one got it!" The Dalat visit itself went quietly: I talked with the BPAO, attended an evening seminar and on the 2nd day visited an ARVN school for information specialists—classes on audiovisual equipment, creating pamphlets and psychological warfare.

As Chinese New Year (Tet in Vietnam) approached in January '74, Kimie and I took our first R&R leave, flying to Hong Kong for a four-day vacation. There we found everything closed down for the first few days of that holiday—everything but tourist excursions. So, we took a tour by catamaran to Macao, an hour southwest of Hong Kong to see the casinos of that Portuguese colony and such sights as the quake-ruined remains of a 17th century Japanese Christian church. The second day we took a tour of Hong Kong Island, from the floating villages of Aberdeen to the high hill where Jennifer Jones discovered that "Love is a Many Splendoured Thing." (Kimie and I had known that for over a quarter century.)

On the third morning, shops in the hotel arcade began reopening, so we strolled along to see what they were offering. At one jewelry shop, a ring mounting a large baroque opal caught Kimie's eye, opal being her birthstone. (I liked to tell her, over the years, that her birthstone was not the bland milky opal, but the fire opal—the best match with her personality.)

As we tried to guess its cost, the shop lady came out, grabbed our sleeves and hustled us inside. "Shanghaied in Hong Kong!?" I wondered. But, she sat us down, brought out tea and invited us to relax and discuss the ring. Well, to make a long story short, Chinese merchants believe that if they can make a sale to their first client of the year, they will have good business the whole year. So, although we kept saying we really did not want the opal ring, with its $800 price tag, the lady kept cajoling and cutting the price until, when we left, we had it for $350.

Besides the shopping, we also enjoyed riding Hong Kong's Star Ferry, a nickel ride across that very scenic harbor with its sampans, junks, naval ships, tankers and the "HMS Queen Mary," which is permanently docked there, just as her sister ship, the "Queen Elizabeth I," is a permanent attraction at Long Beach CA.

Two or three times while in Vietnam, we went by car to Cap Saint Jacques, the beach resort on the South China Sea about 1½ hours south of Saigon. It had decent hotels and plain restaurants but great seafood, especially the tiger prawns. The swimming was so-so.

In June 1974 Kimie and I took a recreational trip to Bangkok, only an hour's flight from Saigon. Like Hong Kong, Bangkok has great shopping, or did then. Kimie had learned from the wife of a USAID officer how to make artificial flowers Bangkok style, oversized with thin wire around the petal edges to help them hold their shape. So, one thing we picked up in Bangkok was Thai silk for Kimie's flower crafts.

Another goal of that trip: filling a request from Hugh-ko for a piece of elephant leather for the seat of an antique chair he had picked up at a shop where he sometimes worked for one of Pat's uncles. I located a Chinese shop that had many special leathers, mostly for jackets and fancy boots. I told the young man there that I needed a piece about 28" square for a chair seat. He showed me a few pieces and I selected the best. As he was about to wrap it, his elderly mother sitting in the back began firing queries to the young man and complaining (in Chinese). He explained, "She says this leather is too nice for a chair seat and I should not sell it to you." The lady only quieted down a bit after I explained that it was for a very expensive antique chair.

We took another trip to Bangkok in September, but during the flight Kimie began suffering severe kidney pain and some fever. So, on arrival we checked with the Embassy medical unit, which referred us to a U.S. Army clinic in the city. It began pouring, not cats and dogs but flying dragons and stampeding elephants as we caught a cab from our hotel. By the end of the 15-minute ride, the roadway was nearly flooded. As we waited to see a doctor, I saw that the school-yard next door was flooded about a foot deep. The problem is that Bangkok sits at the mouth of the Chao Phraya River, almost at sea level. So, rain runoff is sluggish. Later, I would see a Chinese merchant's mansion there built on land elevated by digging a moat around it and using the dredged earth to raise the house three or four feet.

The clinic's American doctor had X-rays taken, which showed that the stone Kimie had carried in her kidney for seven years now totally filled the kidney cavity. He gave us a referral to Thai kidney specialist, Dr. Thumanoon, whose clinic we visited that afternoon. That doctor gave Kimie an antibiotic and advised surgery ASAP. First, though, we had to return to Saigon to get our Embassy's authorization and medical travel orders and to wait for the antibiotics to ease her infection.

A week later we were back in Bangkok for Kimie's surgery. Dr. Thumanoon spoke fluent English, having trained in England and the

US; but Kimie worried about communicating with the Thai nurses in his operating room. The doctor assured her that his chief surgical nurse spoke English well and would be right there. He also promised to do his best to save the kidney, but would only know during surgery if that would be possible.

That night Kimie rested at Promitt Hospital while I stayed at a nearby hotel. The next day, Kimie was rolled into the OR for the surgery; but fought off the sedatives until she had confirmed that she could speak with the head nurse in English. While she was in surgery, I bought her a tank of tropical fish and potted orchids to brighten her recovery. The surgery went well; but she did lose the kidney. (The doctor showed us the offending stone—about the size of my thumb.)

After Kimie had recuperated five days at the hospital, the doctor advised a week of rest in a hotel there before she returned to Saigon. So, I moved Kimie into a room in our favorite Bangkok hotel (where its baby elephant mascot paraded through the lobby daily). I could not spend the entire recuperation time with her, as I had to be back to Saigon. She could now walk to the bathroom; and I arranged for her meals through room service.

Three nights after returning to Saigon, I had a late-night call from Kimie. In a terrified, shaky voice, she said that when she was in the bathroom a quantity of fluid had gushed from the incision in her back. I had her phone her Thai doctor, who sent a cab for her and moved her temporarily to a ward at his clinic. The next morning, I got travel orders and flew to Bangkok to join her. In turned out that she had a deep infection where her kidney had been. For the next several days, the doctor treated her. He then had her return to Saigon to be under the care of our Embassy doctors.

For the next few months, Kimie had to go each morning to the Embassy Medical Unit to have her incision drained and rinsed with a large syringe. She was also taking antibiotics. Despite all that, she resumed her social activities, but not golfing. The Embassy doctor said the stone may have grown rapidly in Saigon because she had not balanced her fluid intake against all her perspiring on the golf course.

Back at the office, CPAO Brement, with us for just over a year, got orders to be Political Counselor at our Moscow embassy. He was delighted, as he had served there previously. From that point on, he de-emphasized his USIS responsibilities to spend much time brushing up his Russian.

Brement had taken full advantage of his USIS position to amass a collection of our audio- and videotapes. In summer '74, he and a political appointee from USIA-Washington took an Air America plane to Cambodia's capital, ostensibly to consult with USIS officers, but mainly to shop for Buddhist statues and other antiques. They brought back a planeload, all transportation courtesy of the U.S. taxpayer. The man from Washington took what he could with him, but left the bulk of his purchases with Brement, who planned to leave Saigon by freighter so that he could ship his own Saigon and Phnom Penh purchases on that vessel. He asked that the USIA official's stuff be added to the household shipments of other departing USIS families. Most of it never got out of Saigon.

So, Brement's personality had not particularly endeared him to the USIS American staff. He gave little and took much. For instance, it was SOP that USIS officers took turns serving for a week as Duty Officer. That meant we were on call during off-duty hours when any emergency arose that needed immediate handling or when long-distance calls or urgent official telegrams came in. It also meant going to the Embassy each morning at about 7:30 to pick up incoming messages and take them to the CPAO to read before the Ambassador's morning staff meeting for section heads.

Whereas other CPAO's normally read such cables at the office at about 8:00, Brement insisted that we take them to his residence between his morning jog and breakfast. The first time I pulled that duty, his servant let me into the foyer of the CPAO residence. Brement called down that I should come up with the cable traffic—to his bedroom where, still sweating, he was preparing to shower and his wife Pam was still in bed. Not long afterward, Pam put a stop to USIS duty officers being thus invited into her bedroom.

Pam was generally well liked and genuinely appreciated the support other USIS couples gave her. One time, she was to hold a VIP dinner party and suddenly found that she did not have proper candles for the dinner table. Another USIS wife told her that Kimie Burleson made candles and might be able to help. While we were in Carlisle, Kimie had added that craft to her repertoire, using flat sheets of beeswax from a mail order catalog to quickly create single- or multi-colored candles of any length by rolling the wax straight or on the diagonal around the wicks. So, when Pam Brement called in desperation just a few hours before her party to ask about candles, she was stunned to hear Kimie calmly say she could make any length and color or color combination and have them at the residence within an hour. And, she did. Pam was effusively grateful.

We USIS Americans prepared a farewell party for Brement. Dennis Donahue, our talented publications officer, outdid himself in preparing for the party. The cover of his printed invitation to the party superimposed Brement's face on the Vietnamese monument at Tansonhut Airport with its inscription, "The noble sacrifices of the allied soldiers and airmen shall never be forgotten." Having witnessed how shamelessly Brement had exploited his position, we all got the irony immediately. Dennis also had the famous nude centerfold of Burt Reynolds blown up to about four feet and replaced Burt's head with Brement's—our farewell gift to him. He loved it!

Perhaps six weeks after the Brements left, we greeted our next CPAO—none other than Alan Carter from Tokyo. The day after his arrival, Carter told us that he and his wife had split up and we should not be surprised if he found other female companionship while in Saigon. In short order, he had a young USIS officer (loaned to us from the military and very knowledgeable about Vietnamese affairs) introduce him to a very fancy looking Vietnamese woman.

Alan also soon announced that he would reorganize the staff top to bottom and introduce the same "streamlining" of facilities and programs that he had implemented in Japan. No matter that the two situations were totally dissimilar. Now, too, we would have a PPBS supplement called the ARS (audience records system) for tracking and tabulating

USIS programs so that the post could better control and allocate its resources. That in Saigon of September 1974!

At his 2nd or 3rd staff meeting, Carter asked us to help him prioritize programs. We drew up a list of all programs, publications and activities. He then asked us to numerically rate their relative importance. That done, he compiled our ratings and averaged them out. Since we each tended to have slightly different ideas on the relative importance of each item on the list, averaging them made them tend to cluster near the middle of his 10-point scale. Carter could not understand why and became very frustrated, almost angry, asking us to be more honest in our judgments. He seemed unable to understand when I pointed out that it was the averaging that tended to yield the clustering.

In the reorganization, Carter moved me back into the Research Officer position and added my Program Officer function to the Deputy PAO's duties. As I was already deep into the planning of a major cultural program, he left me in charge of that, the Saigon visit of the Martha Graham Dance Company.

USIA had contracted for the troupe to make a seven-nation tour of East Asia in fall 1974. I was asked to locate possible theater stages in the city for two performances. As "point man," I went with two local employees to visit theaters around Saigon. One in the Chinese section had a huge stage and 2000 seats; and I thought that would be it. One in central Saigon was scruffy and had a medium-size stage. A caretaker and his family were living behind the backdrop, permeating the theater with food odors. Yet, when the Graham troupe's advance man came, he chose that theater. We had to pay half the rental up front so that they would have enough capital to refurbish the theater.

My committee of Vietnamese staffers worked through the incredibly detailed preparations: creating banners, renting floodlights, arranging for volunteer ushers, VIP guest lists, ticket printing/sales, hotel arrangements and all other logistics, plus planning ancillary activities for the dancers during their two-day stay. That included a DCM's reception and a master class for ballet students at Circl Sportif (a local athletic club).

274

Just days before their arrival, we were told that Martha Graham herself would not come to Saigon. We had received cables describing the troupe's first stop, Manila, where President Ferdinand and Imelda Marcos had held a palace reception for the entire company. And their second stop, Tokyo, where high government officials had also feted them, So, we hoped merely to execute our plan without flaws or incident.

We used USIS's sedans to bring the troupe from the airport to their hotel. I had checked the rooms with the hotel staff and approved their condition. So, I was shocked when, minutes later, the troupe's manager came storming down, shouting, "This is the filthiest hotel I've ever seen; we're not going to stay here!" It turned out that a large Asian cockroach had hailed him as he unpacked. The French plumbing did not include water traps, and that allowed the ugly beast to come up through the washstand. The hotel manager and I arranged for him to get a different room and persuaded him that the cockroach's presence was a fluke.

The Company had a great session the next day with the young Vietnamese ballet students at Circle Sportif and left enthused with the experience.

Before the Company went to rehearse and check out the theater and lighting, I walked through the dressing rooms and rest rooms spraying "Spring Flowers" deodorant around to kill any lingering odors. The matinee performance by the dancers played to a full house of mostly younger Vietnamese and some U.S. Embassy staff people. The evening show was a greater success. The theater front and oversized banners we had ordered were lit by floodlights and gave the appearance of a Broadway opening. Vietnamese VIPs arrived in military dress uniforms and tuxedos. The dance numbers were enthusiastically received. A total success overall.

Bidding us farewell at lunch near the airport the next day, Company members said, "We thought Manila and Tokyo were the high points of this tour and expected Saigon to be the low point. But, this stop has been the best—the one we enjoyed most and will remember the longest." Reward enough!

For, I certainly got no reward from Carter. When he wrote up my performance rating for the year, he made no mention of my work as Program Officer or with the Graham troupe and gave me a very so-so rating. When I pointed out the omission, he said he had not observed my work as Program Officer (admittedly, mostly performed before he came), and anyway he was required to rate my work as Research Officer since that was what he had mostly seen. I exercised my right to add comments on the rating, pointing out how I was being short-changed.

Portents of a darker future for South Vietnam began to appear in the second half of 1974. In August '74, Congress reflected America's growing antiwar sentiment by banning any more military aid to Vietnam. The South Vietnamese leadership may have thought the Pentagon would find a way around that, for they did not react noticeably at first.

About that time, our Vietnamese maid asked us for time off so that she could help her brother campaign in a local election. She explained that if he were not elected he would be drafted into the ARVN. She admitted he was only running to avoid the draft. That made me realize anew how little real patriotism ordinary South Vietnamese felt for their country.

In mid-October, Viet Cong raiders hit a major fuel storage depot down the Saigon River, setting it ablaze. The heavy pall of gray-black smoke rose on the horizon for almost a week, making us feel that the armistice also was in danger of going up in smoke.

One evening late that month, Kimie and I and some other USIS Americans were heading for a program at the Vietnamese-American Cultural Center. Crossing a street, we saw a motor scooter speeding toward us. Veering and trying to stop, it struck Kimie and knocked her down. She was dazed and had a scraped hand and bruised arm. I rushed her to a nearby hospital. An American doctor there bandaged her and then wanted to check her pulse and blood pressure. When he reached into his desk for his stethoscope, it was missing. He swore and said such equipment was regularly stolen. We had similar experiences with our household help. Food items were at risk; and we tried to halt the stealing by giving the cook and maid monthly rations of some staples.

One day we heard that USIS film officer Kurt Wenzel was letting his cook go, even though she was known to be a superb chef for Vietnamese and French cuisine. When I asked Kurt about her, he spoke highly of her cooking, but added, "But, she's expensive." It turned out that he meant she regularly took from her employer's kitchen enough to feed her family and her brother's family—maybe seven people all told. We hired her and greatly enjoyed her cooking, but found that Kimie's monthly ration system did not break her food-filching habit and so let her go after about four months.

I began to see this as the mentality of formerly colonized people. A foreign nation had seized their country. So, ordinary people felt no compunction about trying to get ahead by stealing from the alien rulers. Vietnamese were mainly interested in their family's survival and did not distinguish between the former imperial power and us Americans. We later found this true also of some of our servants in Korea, which had been a Japanese colony.

Five days after Kimie was injured, we had an outing on the Saigon River. The Embassy owned a 40-foot power cruiser that Embassy staffers could rent for a spin on the river. So, about 12 of us in USIS took it out to celebrate our admin officer's birthday. We ordered up a big batch of spiced crab to supplement our snacks and drinks from the commissary. En route up river, we passed Vietnam's President on a similar excursion, except that he was water-skiing. Her arm still bandaged, Kimie had a great time.

In December '74 Kimie and I took our second R&R leave, this time to Japan, as we had informal word from USIA Personnel that our next post was unlikely to be in East Asia. We flew "space available" on Air Force cargo planes. First, a C-130 from Saigon to Clark Air Base, north of Manila. At Clark we had comfortable quarters in a guesthouse on base ($25/day) while awaiting a flight to Japan. Our wait stretched to four days, which we enjoyed by exploring the nearby town, taking craft classes on base, seeing movies and otherwise killing time. Mount Pinatubo, over the horizon, was not yet even smoking.

Finally, we caught a chartered 727 flight via Okinawa to Yokota Air Base (west of Tokyo). While waiting for our baggage at Yokota, I noticed that a modern baggage carousel was under construction there. Striking up a conversation with the American supervisor, I gestured toward a Japanese crew working there and asked if communicating with them was a problem. "No, no trouble. They speak enough English. My only trouble is getting them to take breaks. I swear, I've put these carousels in at bases all over the world, and I've never seen people who work as hard as these guys!"

Kimie and I spent four days with her family in Yokohama. We had intended to see a few friends in Tokyo also; but Kimie's kidney incision, which had been closed for about two months, began swelling and she had a slight fever. I called the Embassy in Tokyo and got an okay for her to see a doctor at the Yokosuka Naval Base, 25 miles south.

The doctor there lanced her incision, drained a lot of fluid, gave her an antibiotic and wrote a recommendation that Kimie have an operation to clear up the deep infection. My always upbeat trooper took it all in stride, but certainly did not relish the idea of a third operation, which would "triple track" her scars from the Tachikawa and Bangkok operations.

While in Yokohama, Kimie packed into her suitcase six silk kimonos that sister Sumie had been holding for her, so that when we left Saigon they would go with us.

Then back to Yokota. This time, no delay in catching a plane—a huge C-5. Walking up its ramp into the huge cargo bay, we were awed then to see that we had to climb a kind of ladder some 12 feet to the passenger cabin. Back at Clark, we overnighted again before taking another cargo plane to Saigon, arriving in time for our second Christmas in Saigon.

In early January 1975 a conjunctivitis epidemic was plaguing the Embassy staff; and on a Thursday evening my left eye began bothering me. At Kimie's urging, I went the next morning to the Embassy Medical Unit and saw the #2 doctor there. I got close enough that he could see my red eye, and he wrote me a prescription for the usual medication.

Over the weekend, my eye grew worse and more painful. Kimie looked at it closely and grew alarmed. "I don't think that's the same thing!" she declared and insisted that I go in on Monday morning to see the doctor again. This time I saw the top doctor (who would later head State's entire worldwide medical program). He agreed with Kimie and sent me immediately to see a US-trained Vietnamese ophthalmologist, Dr. Cuu, whose clinic was within walking distance of our house. Dr. Cuu quickly sidelined me, for it was uveitis—inflammation of the iris—threatening my sight in that eye. For three weeks, I had to stay home and take eye drops in semi-darkened rooms because of light sensitivity. When it was finally cured, damage to the iris had made that eye permanently sensitive to strong light.

By late February, further treatment in Saigon had stabilized the infection in Kimie's back enough that she could have the needed surgery, this time at Clark Air Base Hospital. We again flew there by Air Force transport. I stayed with her several days for her check-in and surgery. Then I had to return to Saigon while Kimie recuperated. The day I left, I was walking Kimie in the ward hallway when we saw that Kimie's surgeon was now a patient there: he, too, had had kidney surgery!

Over the next week, Kimie and I communicated by phone and APO mail. Because now, in early March, we had a disturbing situation in Vietnam. In January, North Vietnamese were active in the mountains of central Vietnam, marking what would later be seen as the end of the shaky truce and the beginning of the end. We know now that Hanoi had accurately read the import of Congress's cutting off military aid to the south. Its forces increasingly probed in the highlands. The tension became palpable even in normally relaxed Saigon. Then a highland capital suddenly fell, and the ARVN fled to the coast in a disorderly rout.

The Embassy security office ordered all sections to draw up lists of Vietnamese who might be most vulnerable if the south fell to the communists. We duly turned in those lists. I later heard they were discarded when Ambassador Graham Martin objected to any action giving the appearance of our abandoning our RVN allies. As the end neared, Washington insisted that new lists be drawn up, but by then few American officers remained in Saigon to do so. That contributed directly to the final chaos seen on TV around the world.

In this same time frame, the tragic crash occurred of a C-5 carrying Vietnamese orphans to the US. Most of the children, riding in the cargo bay, were killed together with the adults escorting them. One of these was an acquaintance of ours.

By late March, USIA had issued blanket travel orders for us Americans in Vietnam so that we could leave whenever the CPAO and the Embassy saw fit. We pulled in our BPAO's from the branch posts; and they began leaving. They had harrowing tales to tell about the dangers they experienced in leaving, from Da Nang, Dalat and Can Tho especially.

Now Kimie told me by phone that the doctors at Clark were ready to let her go, to any place except Saigon. I had just received orders for assignment to Tokyo: Saigon's imminent fall had nullified the earlier info on my next assignment. So, I insisted to the Clark medics that the situation was stable enough for Kimie to come and help supervise the packing of our household effects. I knew she would want to manage that. In fact, a late March letter from her said, "Hey, the news in the paper on RVN is very bad. I hope it'll hold up until I get there to pack the things." So, about April 1, Clark AFB put her on a hospital plane bound for Saigon. Fine, except that the plane first went around to five U.S. air bases in Thailand. It was late afternoon before she deplaned at Tansonhut.

I had begun the packing, and now we had packers from Embassy General Services. Kimie, in her usual manner, was running on nerves and would not ease up. We packed many things into wooden crates and mailed them out through the APO at Tansonhut, where long lines of Americans with similar packages were snaking through the hallways.

Among the things I mailed to ourselves in Tokyo was our leftover liquor. I knew we could not mail liquor into the U.S., but thought that it would be OK between overseas APOs.

On April 6, I was in my office when we began hearing a low-flying aircraft and explosions. I went outside to see what was happening, and saw a US-made fighter pulling out of a dive. Immediately, another explosion and a plume of smoke rose over the treetops. I went to phone Kimie, but could not get an open line. Then we heard that a South Vietnamese Air Force plane had bombed the presidential palace just half a mile from our office. We thought maybe the VC had captured it and staged the attack.

As it was now noon, I had my driver take me home for lunch. I found Kimie agitated, but in control. Our cook and maid thought the noise, a mile from our house, was construction blasting; but Kimie, my veteran of Pacific War bombings, knew what it was and made them take sofa cushions and hide under tables. After we heard on Armed Forces Radio that a disaffected South Vietnamese pilot had done the bombings, Kimie said, "I don't care who did it, I'm leaving!" She was right, of course. So, that afternoon at the office I had our administrative staff begin arranging to get Kimie out.

Until December, our next-door neighbors had been Mark and Annie Carr. He was the Bank of America representative in Saigon, but now was assigned to Singapore. So, I arranged for Kimie to fly to Singapore and there contact Annie Carr for tips on what she could do until I arrived. On April 8 I put Kimie on a Singapore Air flight. It taxied up to the terminal and lowered its rear boarding ramp without ever cutting its engines, picking up Kimie and one other passenger. Kimie told me later that the plane began taxiing back to the runway even before she got to her seat. Such was the pilot's concern about possible communist mortar fire—three weeks before Saigon fell.

On about April 10, Embassy General Services picked up our packed shipment and took it to the Embassy warehouse. That night, still in our house, I was doing some cleanup when suddenly there was a muffled boom like distant thunder. Then a shock wave shook the house and knocked down the trap door to the attic crawl space. Communist raiders, we later heard, had blown up an ammo depot 20 miles away in Bien Hoa.

The next morning, our maid was cleaning out the kitchen. I had told her she could have any of the remaining food stores. That was considerable, as Kimie had stocked up for parties. Sniffling, the maid said, "This is the last good food my children will ever have!" I felt so helpless, with no reassuring words for her.

I should have mentioned that earlier we had accepted a Siamese cat, Sammy (Samantha), from a New Zealand diplomat and his wife who were going home. They could not take the cat with them because New Zealand laws would require them to send the cat to Britain for six months' quarantine before they could fly it to New Zealand. Now we persuaded Hugh-ko to take the cat. But first, to send the cat out of Vietnam, I had to get her vaccinated by a vet near the airport. I spent three hours in line in the tropical sun to get the cat inoculated. Then I had to arrange for her shipment. Pan Am would only take pets in cages of a certain size (and expense). I found that Flying Tigers was less expensive. (Aren't you glad I capitalized that name?) And at a market I found a large wicker basket. The day that I, too, was leaving, I tricked Sammy into the basket and delivered her to Flying Tigers, to me a most appropriate carrier for a Siamese.

So, I flew to Singapore, with eight pieces of luggage. There I found that Annie Carr had not only given Kimie pointers, but had taken her under her caring wing and kept her busy with social activities pending my arrival. Now, the Carrs took us to Singapore's botanical park and to a theme park then being developed on Santoso Island south of Singapore. On the long ride over by an elevated tram, we could see a large cargo ship bow down in the channel. Mark Carr said it was rammed during the night and was sinking. Sure enough, on our return trip we could see the vessel now nose down, ready to go under.

From Singapore, our next stop was Rome. With Kimie's three bags and my eight, we were heavily laden. At Rome's airport we counted the suitcases and found one was missing. It finally showed up from a back room after we pressed Pan Am's agents for about an hour.

In Rome we took a standard bus tour and then went back on our own that afternoon to see more of the Vatican. The next day, we were off to Zurich; but at the airport a baggage-handler strike was on, with a jam of tourists trying to check in. I assumed the connecting flights would be delayed as this jam-up filtered through. Not so. In Italy, assume nothing. About 10 minutes before our Swissair flight was to depart, a Swissair rep located us, got us pushed through and herded us at a trot to our plane, which had already left the gate and had to lower a ramp for us to board.

After overnighting in Zurich, we caught a train for Geneva—a beautiful trip through that picture-postcard country. In Geneva we checked into our hotel, and that evening had dinner with friends from our Tokyo days, Bob and Setsuko Pfeiffer. They had been our next-door neighbors in Harris House when he was assistant labor attaché. Now he was on the US delegation to the International Labor Organization. (After Bob died prematurely of a heart attack in the early 1980s, Setsuko would spend many years teaching Japanese at State's Foreign Service Institute.)

The next morning Kimie and I walked to the lake to enjoy the view, spending a few hours there. Returning to our hotel, we found our things gone and someone else's luggage in our room. Shocked, we went down to the desk to ask what was going on. "Oh, but you are leaving today," a desk clerk explained, "and we needed your room." I was flabbergasted and pointed out that we had paid for a whole day, not just overnight. But, our things were already locked in a closet and the person with the key was out to lunch—a case, I suppose, of "possession is 90% of the law." We had to settle for spending the next several hours in the lobby and using the lobby restrooms. But, really!

From Geneva, we flew to London and on to Washington, D.C. There I reported to USIA, was debriefed and began checking on other friends from Saigon. On TV we saw scenes of the chaotic final evacuation as

Saigon fell.* We also visited with Rits and Sheila and stopped by our Chevy Chase home to visit with our renters.

Too soon, we had to move on. Our trek through Europe had used part of the time we would have spent on home leave. So, we had a relatively short stay in Berkeley with the family there before flying to Seattle to visit with Hugh and Pat. They took us to Mount Rainier, driving the circular tour around that great mountain's lower slopes and up to the inn at Paradise. We also became better acquainted with Pat's family. Then on to Tokyo.

---

* We had our physical exams at State before proceeding to Tokyo. The doctor who checked my eyes was able to tell me that my Vietnamese ophthalmologist, Dr. Cuu, was evacuated and in the D.C. area.

# AGAIN TOKYO

## (1975-78)

Just as we had found Japan, especially Tokyo, very changed when we returned in 1960, things again were quite different in July 1975 compared to six years earlier, when we had last served there. Simply put, the Japanese were upgrading their infrastructure in stages, first from the late 1950s through 1964 for the Olympics, then again in the early 1970's, each time raising the quality and making all safer and cleaner. And more expensive. Things such as antiques, handicrafts and the like that were cheap by our standards in the '40s, '50s and '60s were no longer so by the mid-70s. In part because many Japanese now had the leisure to appreciate, and wherewithal to afford, these things. Demand was up; so prices were up. In part, too, because the yen was now 200-something per US dollar, down from its long-time ¥360 rate. Now the only real bargains I could find in Japan were books, new and used.

Also, the society's value system had changed incrementally, in step with such physical changes. Age-old austerities were being cast aside; relative affluence was more expected. A younger generation that had not known war and had only dim memories of early postwar privations was entering the work force. Urbanization had proceeded apace, with a much smaller part of the population living on farms. Now, new issues—mainly economic—preoccupied the media and public discussion.

One afternoon I met at a Tokyo coffee shop with one of my former students from Niigata University's Humanities Faculty. He had been the most outspoken and freest to criticize U.S. policy. Now he was an employee of a very big company, Mitsubishi Real Estate. Of course he was glad we had pulled out of Vietnam and so felt mellower about America. But, he insisted, "I still don't like big powers."

"Well," I replied, "but it looks as though Japan is on track to become a major power soon. What then?"

"I guess then I might not like Japan either," he replied with a smile. I believe what he had in mind was major military power; and I would guess that he likes Japan today, as Japan has been very circumspect about boosting its military power.

Now I was back working with some of the same Japanese staff that I had in the late 1960s: Mizutani-san, my ever-competent secretary; Yumi Goto and Miss Yanagisawa. Sen Nishiyama had retired in the early '70s to help Sony President Morita with his overseas relations. Both Kanekos had retired as well. "Big" Kaneko now could focus on his writing, while "little" Kaneko was now avidly pursuing what had always been his prime interest: Asian cultural anthropology. Three new people had come in, mainly to run the DRS and other computerized records.

A cable in my "In" box when I arrived tersely noted the receipt in Hong Kong of 300 lbs. "HHE of Hugh L. Burleson." I knew we had packed closer to 3000 pounds of household effects and so quickly wired Hong Kong to request immediate onward shipment, and clarification of the amount. I was hoping against hope that "300 lbs" was a typo. That began a tortuous series of communications, which boiled down to this: Our main shipment never left the Embassy warehouse in Saigon.* Other officers' shipments packed up later and set down near the front of the warehouse went onto the "SS Mayaguez," the last ship to sail before the communists moved in. (After leaving Saigon, that ship was hijacked by Khmer Rouge raiders in a Cambodian port, but freed safely a few days later when U.S. Marines attacked the hijackers.)

---

\* On a TV program 30 years later, I heard that the whole Embassy warehouse was burned.

Some faithful souls had picked up "loose pack" items, including our 300 pounds, from the warehouse and got them onto a cargo plane to Hong Kong. We were very grateful that the 300 lbs included a lacquered coffee table that Kimie had spent some 200 hours carving in her weekly *Kamakura-bori* lacquering class in the late '60s. The other items were ceramic "buffies" and the like, which now adorn our rear patio and front porch.

In October 1975, the State Department issued instructions on filing claims for HHE lost in the fall of Saigon. Kimie and I labored for weeks diligently following those instructions: listing the lost items, purchase dates and prices, estimated value at time of loss and estimated replacement cost. Our claim totaled over $14,000. In the end, State allowed only $4,000 against that claim. We tried to contest that, to no avail. When I included in my 1975 Tax return a loss for the difference, dear old IRS disallowed it, saying it had to assume State's award against our claim was fair. Truly adding insult to injury.

What hurt most was not the monetary loss, but losing treasured items. They included Kimie's precious silk kimonos that we had picked up from Sumie and which alone would have cost at least $4,000 to replace, a portfolio of 30 Japanese woodblock prints collected over the preceding 28 years and taken to Saigon for framing, plus many other items from our years together. The wartime trauma of having all her possessions incinerated in the bombings had healed for Kimie; but this new loss brought her renewed trauma. For years afterward, she would sometimes pop out with "Say, where is (such and such item)?" and then recall that it was among the things we lost in Saigon. For a while, she vowed never again to buy any permanent possessions; but her aesthetic bent was strong. The things lost were an expression of her personality and her interests—who she was. So, after some months she slowly began acquiring new objects and *objets*.

Another message awaiting me when I arrived in Tokyo was from the local APO, noting that I had mailed liquor through the APO system in violation of the rules, and that it had to be disposed of. Apparently I was betrayed by a bottle that broke in one of the crates I mailed from Saigon. I sent back a memo admitting that I honestly had not realized liquor may not be sent between overseas APOs. I maintained—again honestly—that I thought it better to have shipped it to our Japan APO than to let it fall into communist hands in Saigon. I expressed the hope, tongue in cheek, that the disposal of that liquor had thoroughly disinfected the APO's pipes. I heard nothing further about my transgression.

During my next three years of working in Tokyo—my 15th through 17th years in Japan—I would be seen as USIS's resident Japan expert. But, since the Foreign Service favored generalists, not specialists, I would retort wryly that I was a Japan "over-specialist," not an expert. True, for after so many years of interacting with all sorts of Japanese (intensively so with my Kimie), on-the-job study and analysis of Japanese views of and reactions to the outside world—how their values led them to deal with change, with foreigners and with each other, I had a good general feel for what made them tick.

At one of Ambassador James Hodgson's staff meetings soon after I had arrived, he was reviewing the state of US-Japan relations and noted what "smooth sailing" we were having. The Okinawa matter was now quiet. No Vietnam War to sour the public's feelings toward us. No major issues or problems. So it seemed. A few months later the "Lockheed scandal" broke: Japanese politicians, including Prime Minister Tanaka, had taken huge bribes from Lockheed to push Japan's purchase of Lockheed fighters. Much sound and fury ensued that eventually drove Tanaka from politics and caused the US to enact tough legislation making it illegal for any U.S. firm to "oil" its transactions abroad with payoffs, bribes or "commissions."

For Kimie (now 56) and me (48) those were good years, too. Smooth sailing in our personal relationship. Kimie's kidney problem was behind her, and she would remain generally in sparkling good health for another two decades.

I shall never forget an occasion when we were attending a party at Deputy PAO Bob Kays' home, Japanese and American guests filling the house and rear garden. I was outside when suddenly I heard Kimie break into laughter in the house. Her high delighted laugh rang out like tinkling

Christmas bells. I went in to investigate. Turned out she had been passing around a tray of snacks. When she came to CPAO Bill Miller, she said to him in jest, "If I were a geisha, I'd get good pay for this." Humoring her, he reached in his pocket and put a coin on the tray. That sparked her beautiful laughter. The lady had a fine sense of humor.

During 1975-78, Kimie studied pottery-making at a kiln in north Kamakura, riding trains there once a week. She was joined by another USIS wife, Margaret Kendall—the wife of Harry Kendall, who was supervising our six remaining cultural centers. We still treasure the pieces that Kimie made at that kiln.

Her interest in pottery also led to our joining an Embassy group tour to Mashiko, a town about 60 miles northeast of Tokyo noted for its folk-art pottery. Some of the ceramic items we now have (or gave to Hugh-ko and Rits) are from our two trips there. During the group tour, we had the honor to meet famed potter HAMADA Shoji, one of Japan's officially designated "living national treasures." His folk craft style won world recognition after he was "discovered" by famed British potter Bernard Leach. Our group spent about an hour with Hamada at his home as he showed us part of his ceramic collection and his own work. About a year later he died, in his 80's.

I had one medical problem at this time: varicose veins in my right leg, partly hereditary and perhaps aggravated by five years of hauling UC's East Asian Library books up four flights of stairs in Boalt Hall. By the mid-70s, the veins were becoming uncomfortable with prickly pains. So, I arranged to get "vein stripping" surgery to correct that. It is good that one gets general anesthesia for the procedure, as it must be a bloody mess. The surgeon starts near the ankle with an incision where he cuts loose the veins to be removed, and then goes on up the leg removing the bad veins through a series of incisions, all the way to the groin area.

That was done for me at the Army hospital in Zama, near where I got my discharge 30 years earlier almost to the day. Of course Kimie came to visit. While she was there, the uppermost incision began seeping and I had to call a nurse for a patch. When I returned to work a week later, the USIS admin officer told me he had asked Kimie how I was doing. He reported that she said, "Oh, he is fine, but he's breeding." The old "R" and "L" bugaboo, again.*

While I was away from USIS-Japan 1969-75, my old job as Research Officer had been redefined, broadened and upgraded. Now, as Policy & Research Officer, I was responsible, for example, for drafting the annual Country Plan, which defined the public affairs situation and any problems facing our efforts to make America and its policies understood. That draft guided the cultural and information sections and the CPAO in writing up their action plan for the following year. That, in turn, was cleared with the embassy and USIA in Washington.

Data on programs were accumulated in the ARS (audience records system), which I now managed. My predecessor had begun moving the ARS onto computers. As personal computers did not yet exist, we had an outside company input the data. I spent much time in 1976 nailing down a contractor and supervising the computerizing of our records.

In May 1977, we joined a tour to Korea organized by the U.S. Forces, with several days in Seoul and a trip to the DMZ. It was mostly a shopping tour. And, that summer we joined some Embassy Americans and Japanese staff on a weekend bus tour around Mt. Fuji—very scenic and just plain fun. We saw Shiraito ("white thread") Falls—hundreds of fine streams falling from under an old lava flow. We also visited a winery in the mountains north of Fuji and a picturesque rocky gorge; and we had stunning views of Fuji at sunset, with the mountain mirrored in Lake Kawaguchi as our bus started back toward Tokyo. A month later, Kimie and I re-visited Nikko to mark our 30th anniversary and had our photo taken again at the Yomei Gate as we had on our '47 honeymoon and in 1964.

---

\* With such modern methods as electronic voiceprints, etc., linguists have shown that the Japanese R actually falls precisely between our English R and L. So, when a Japanese tries to pronounce our L, we hear it as an R. When we pronounce either an L or R, the Japanese hear no difference.

On December 17, 1977, Kimie's father, Kojiro Yamada, died at age 83. Six or eight months earlier he had fallen and broken a leg. He recovered from that and was walking again, but was much less active and noticeably weaker. One Saturday morning, Kimie went down to Yokohama to visit Sumie, at whose home their father was then resting. About mid-afternoon I had a call from Kimie. She said her father seemed much weaker and I had better come down, too.

When I arrived and saw him, I was shocked at the sunken appearance of his face. Perhaps an hour later, just after Sumie gave him a sip of water, he suddenly gasped and was gone. In the succeeding weeks, I learned much about Japanese funeral rites and the social and religious codes involved.

But, a few days after that loss, we joined another Armed Forces tour on which we were already booked, this time to Taiwan and the Philippines. We spent three days in Taipei, shopping and taking a guided tour to nearby mountains where an aboriginal tribe* lives and performs traditional dances for tourists.

Some of us also visited a porcelain factory outside Taipei. Most interesting was watching young artists painting designs on finished porcelain objects. Kimie and I were intrigued to see butterflies being painted skillfully onto a large platter, but wondered whether the paint would hold up with use. I asked a supervisor if the platter could also be made with the butterflies under the glaze instead of on top. He said that would require more expensive paint in order to hold its color when the glaze was fired. He said the platter we were looking at would cost US$45. "So, how much would it cost with the butterflies under the glaze?" I asked.

"Oh, very expensive!" he answered. I persisted and he finally came back with a price of $65! We placed the order right there and six weeks later received the platter from Taipei by international mail.

---

\* Their ancestors had migrated in prehistoric times up the island chain from Southeast Asia. These tribes in Taiwan therefore are not Chinese.

We also visited Taipei's national museum, where the many stunning treasures that Chiang Kai-shek's Nationalists brought from the mainland were on display. In the museum gift shop we found other treasures: mounted scroll paintings on silk that art students had copied exactly from ancient originals in the museum, but priced at $15-20! Perfect for gifts.

Then on to Manila, to a fine hotel on the waterfront of Manila Bay. On our first evening, a college girls' choir gave a concert of Christmas music in the hotel atrium, a beautiful introduction to the Philippines. Over the next few days, we toured Manila's Intramuros section and Corregidor, which we reached by a fast surface-effects boat. The Corregidor fort where American forces made their final stand 1942 was still there. We saw the tunnel that was their refuge and hospital during the siege, as well as the huge 20-inch mortars that had lobbed shells across to Bataan after our units there had surrendered and been led off on the cruel death march.

A USIS couple we were close to in Tokyo in the 1960's was the Goshos— Hank and Jeanne. Kimie and Jeanne did a lot of golfing together on U.S. Forces' courses. And, Hank and I sometimes played poker together. Hank was a savvy player; but one memorable evening I won twice in a showdown when he was holding a high pair and I beat him each time with three deuces. Once more that evening it came down to him and me. He said, "I swear, Hugh, if you're holding trip twos again. I'll …" I was, and won again. He had a great sense of humor, and we remained close friends for decades after that, until cancer felled him. His ashes are interred near SeaTac Airport, as he was born in Seattle.*

In the later '70s, after Hank retired, his son Merrill (a NOAA a marine mammal specialist) was attached to the Embassy, but without diplomatic status. Working for the International Whaling Commission, his job was to visit Japan's whaling ports, identify the whales being landed and report the data to the Commission. We were able to help him and his

---

\* Hank's World War II career, including duty with Merrill's Marauders in Burma, where a Japanese mortar round destroyed one of his kidneys, is described in Yankee Samurai (Pettigrew Enterprises, Detroit, 1979).

family buy commissary items, especially for their new baby, until his status was regularized and he and his wife could also use the PX and commissary.

We were involved in an odd little incident in spring 1978. For years the Soviet KGB had had East Germany periodically issue a little black book, *Who's Who in the CIA*. They applied their own standards in trying to guess which Americans might be CIA agents using the Foreign Service as cover: Anyone who spoke a difficult language, anyone who spent an unusual amount of time in one country, etc. Whether they were correct or not did not matter; its purpose was disinformation to harass our foreign affairs agencies. With my language and Japan focus, I naturally was listed. That spring, a new edition went out to Japan's major national dailies. Somehow, the usually responsible daily *Mainichi Shinbun* chose to list on a front page the names of officers in this bogus "guide" who currently were serving in Tokyo—with addresses and phone numbers. It may have been merely a slow news day, or possibly money changed hands. We cannot know.

A short time later, I received a post card from a man in northern Japan who wrote that I should be ashamed and warned me to get out of the CIA post haste. I gave this to Embassy security, which passed it to Japan's National Police Agency (roughly equivalent to our FBI) for follow-up. The whole matter led Kimie to imagine another of her worst-case scenarios. She was skittish for weeks.

Late one evening, our doorbell rang. I went to answer; but Kimie feared it might be connected to the threatening post card, even though the housing compound had security guards. She tried to keep me from answering the door. I went anyway. It was a USIS officer from the next building. When I turned to reassure Kimie, there stood my samurai guardian watching from a bedroom doorway—holding a baseball bat! Once she had been trained to use the short sword, but in her youth she had wielded baseball bats, too!

The officer did have disturbing news: the ambassador's interpreter, Jim Wickel, had just died of heart failure in the next building. Kimie was needed to help console his Japanese wife. So, we both went.

In late spring 1978, our Washington personnel office began calling me about my next assignment, noting that for proper career development I must go to another geographic area. CPAO Clif Forster urged me to make an effort to get my tour in Tokyo extended, as we had done in 1968. But, Washington was not buying our argument this time.

The personnel officer in Washington working my case began calling at early hours—4 and 5AM. Once he called at 3AM, explaining "I want to get off early today and need to talk with you before then." I think he never understood he was reaching me in Tokyo at such ungodly hours. Or maybe …

The gist of his calls was that no extension of my Tokyo tour would be granted. I had two choices. One: CPAO in Chad, which would require my first learning French. Chad was then slipping into civil war, fomented by Libya. I could not see Kimie taking well to life in a Francophone nation in the Sahara. My other choice: Deputy Branch Public Affairs Officer in Madras, south India. No language training needed, as English is the common language in India. Tropical, but clearly the better choice. The one drawback: they needed me ASAP, meaning a transfer to Madras without home leave. We accepted that.

When I went to the consular section of the Indian Embassy in Tokyo for our visas, the visa officer there scanned my application. "So, you are going to Madras! Have they told you about Madras?" he asked politely.

"Not really. I just know generally where it is."

"I am from Madras," he said with the rolling "r" and gently lilting tone I would soon be hearing. "You know, we say in Madras that we have the hot season, the hotter season and the hottest season," he chuckled.

"Ah, well," I answered, "Perhaps it's no worse than Saigon." Of course, I was recalling the health problem Kimie had in Saigon.

So, we packed up, shipped our effects and our '76 Buick. Madras is 1100 miles south of New Delhi, where the Embassy has a commissary;

and we would have to foot the costs of shipping any purchases from there while we served in Madras.

# MADRAS & SOUTH INDIA

## (1978~1979)

Although the Foreign Service called ours a direct transfer, we would go first to Washington, D.C., for briefings. We stopped over in Seattle to see Hugh and Pat, then pregnant with their first child. Then on to "the other Washington." After the briefings, we had time enough to see Rits and Sheila and a few friends and then flew by Pan Am via London to Frankfurt.

As we were arriving on a weekend, I had arranged for a travel break there to lessen the jet lag from the 11-hour time difference between D.C. and India. I had booked a tour by bus down the Main River, past its many castles to the great castle at Heidelberg, where we spent several hours walking through the castle and its grounds and enjoying the panorama. Then to a nearby winery for dinner. On Sunday we flew on to New Delhi.

At New Delhi International Airport about 12:30 AM, a bleary-eyed younger USIS officer met us and helped us through the slow, slightly chaotic "airport formalities." Meanwhile, Kimie changed some of our dollars into rupees, but got nothing smaller than 10-rupee notes. So, when we exited the terminal and were mobbed by baggage porters, we could only hand out 10 rupees each—10 to 20 times the normal tip. Tired and hot, we really did not care and were glad to have the young officer get us to our downtown Delhi hotel.

Up bright and early the next morning, we went to the hotel's exotic mogul-decor dining room for breakfast. The menu offered an array of Western and Indian cuisines. While we were studying that, out of the corner of my eye I saw movement on the molding atop the opposite wall—a small rat casually trotting along as if on its morning commute. To avoid spoiling her appetite, I said nothing to Kimie; but a few minutes later, we both saw the same rodent leap onto the lower tray of a nearby tea wagon. Kimie had trouble downing the breakfast she had just ordered.

In our room, getting ready to leave for the USIS offices, I saw a mouse dart from our closet to the bathroom. I went in, cornered it, whopped it with a hotel slipper, flipped it into the toilet and flushed. "What was that?!" Kimie called out. I had to confess to the murder. Luckily, we were staying only one night; but for Kimie it was a sobering introduction to Mother India.

After a half day of Embassy and USIS briefings and the customary meeting with the ambassador, I was ready to get underway to Madras. We took an early afternoon Air India flight south, with an intermediate stop in Hyderabad. We found the onboard meal unique: plain yogurt, sweet milky tea, curry rice and the like. Arriving in Madras, we were met at the airport by Mack Fry, the BPAO, and his wife Pat. We learned they both were from the Missouri Ozarks. Mack had had a 20-year Navy career, the last part as a PIO (public information officer), mainly in the Mediterranean and Atlantic.

Riding from the airport into Madras that Friday, we saw the city as a sprawling conglomeration of villages and towns. Few large or tall buildings. Many buses and a uniquely Indian mix of transport modes: trucks of all sizes, taxis and private sedans, motor scooters, bicycles, pony carts, bicycles, wandering cows and water buffalo and many pedestrians, some barefoot. Tropical Vietnam+. Temperature: in the low 90s.

Mack and Pat took us to a hotel, because the house assigned to us was getting some final refurbishing, and the "courtesy kit" of household items for our use until we received our shipment had not yet been delivered. Mack invited us to a reception the next evening. Also, he warned us not to use hotel water for drinking or even for brushing our teeth. How to brush our teeth then? Order soda water. That turned out to be an adventure, for when you add soda water to a mouthful of brushings it foams up geysers!

The next day, a sedan picked us up with our luggage and took us to our house near the Madras River, one of three yellow stucco 2-story consular residences in a row outside of the Madras Club. A fourth, larger residence lay behind, the Consul General's house. As we neared our house, we noticed a sign for the "Madras Boat Club" close by. Rowboats to rent on the river, perhaps? We would check into that later.

The gate to our house was opened by a small dark man whom our driver explained was our *chokidar* (guard) cum gardener. The driver told the man that we would be going to a party that evening and he should tell the maid that she need not prepare us an evening meal. At each instruction, the man shook his head in a weaving motion as if disagreeing. What an unpleasant fellow, we thought. But, the driver turned and said he understood and would tell the maid. The sideways head bobbing, we learned, was south Indian body language for affirmation.

The Frys had arranged for my predecessor's maid to work for us. So, almost as soon as we were unloaded, Kimie and the maid went out to buy essentials that would make us self sufficient in our new quarters. The house had two bedrooms upstairs, and downstairs a large living room, dining room, study/library/card room, ample kitchen and a pantry closet—about 3,000 square feet of living space.

That afternoon, we walked next door to the Madras Club to introduce ourselves and sign up for membership. The club was a British Raj institution that long ago sported signs reading "No Indians or dogs allowed." Now Indians ran it for a mixed membership of upper crust Indians and foreigners. We found that the club served meals. We'd be able to "eat out" by walking 50 yards from our front door! It also showed movies twice a week, had a pool room, tennis court and a well-kept lawn running down to the Madras River.

That evening, the Frys' driver came to take us to the reception. There we met the rest of the USIS Americans, some consular officers, Madrasi professors and business people. The entertaining style was relaxed but sumptuous. Mack explained that much of the western food came from a mail order service in Singapore that shipped fairly promptly. Just a few things were from the Embassy commissary in New Delhi.

Sunday morning, we walked a few hundred yards down the road to satisfy our curiosity about the Madras Boat Club. Entering, we walked between rows of mimosa and casuarina trees and soon saw that the boats were not rowboats but racing sculls, a sport bequeathed to the subcontinent by the British along with cricket, soccer and tennis.

We were about to turn around and leave when some Indian gentlemen drinking beer under the trees hailed us. When we identified ourselves as newcomers to the U.S. consulate, they greeted us enthusiastically and insisted that we join them for a beer. We tried to decline, saying that our maid was preparing our lunch. They would not let us say no and had one of the club's waiters phone our maid to tell her we were eating out, for one of the men now invited us to lunch at his home a few blocks away. He turned out to have quite a mansion, well equipped with modern electrical items and even a fancy stereo set-up. He owned one of Madras's best appliance stores.

The lunch was south Indian style: a buffet of plain yogurt, *dahl* (ground beans) and various veggies and nuts, plus a kind of wheat chip. No eating utensils. Instead you had to mix and pick it all up with your fingers. I tried to scoop up the yogurt and dahl with the wheat chips, but they tended to break and leave me awkwardly trying otherwise to fish up the food. South Indians are generally quite dark skinned, and Kimie found it disconcerting to see so much yellowish dahl and white yogurt all over our hosts' dark fingers. I guess we flunked Tamil Culture 101 that day.

Before we left that day, our host also invited us to the christening of a grandchild the next day. We had to beg off, as it would be my first day at work and Kimie was to go shopping with Pat Fry. I know we missed many nuances of Tamil hospitality, being so new. We later learned that the Indian hunger for an American visa often led them to work hard to build ties with US diplomats—not saying, though, that was our hosts' motivation that day.

USIS and the Consulate General in Madras provided services for India's four southern states: Tamil Nadu (capital, Madras), Andra Pradesh (capital, Hyderabad), Karnataka (capital, Bangalore) and Kerala (capital: Mangalore)—a huge area of nearly 200 million people. The staff: eight American consular officers and a secretary, four USIS officers plus some 45 Indian employees in total. The consulate is a two-story building on a walled two-acre compound in a city of about one million people.

USIS did cultural and information programming intensively in Madras, of course, but also periodically sent program teams out to the other states and major cities of the region, with our Indian staff working constantly to cultivate ties with key officials, academicians and cultural figures in the area.

Each week, the Consulate received a feature film that USIS screened for the foreign community in the consulate theater. Indians were not supposed to attend, not for discriminatory reasons but because some of the films were theoretically in Indian theaters; and we were not to compete with that system. If the foreigners brought Indian friends with them, we had to assume they were office staff or "family members."

One time we had a James Bond film, the one in which Bond romances a Soviet girl spy. As I entered the theater, I found myself walking beside the burly Russian consul general, who usually avoided such vehicles of capitalist amorality. I greeted him cordially. He smiled and (as if to justify his presence) said in a booming voice, "I hear this movie is about detente!" Of course, at that time détente was a keynote in US-Soviet relations.

After we had been in Madras a month, our household effects arrived and were delivered to our home, the big cartons filling the dining room and part of the living room. Before we knew the delivery date, we had scheduled our first in-home reception. Now we had three days to get the boxes out of the way. I worked all possible hours opening boxes and helping put things away. In the process, I strained my right foot and ultimately had to see a British-trained Indian doctor about it. He gave me an ace bandage to wrap the foot, and a painkiller. For 10 days I noticed no improvement as I hobbled around on the job.

Then, Fry picked me to head a program team (myself and three Indian employees, one of them an audio-visual specialist for our portable audio and movie systems) to put on programs in Hyderabad for a weekend. We arrived in that city by plane in mid-morning and checked into our hotel. I was still limping. My senior aide, R.T. Murthy, asked, "Would you like me to help you with that foot before we do the first program this afternoon?" I asked what he had in mind. "My grandfather was an expert in ayurvedic medicine and taught me many of the techniques. I think I could ease your pain."

"Using medication?" I asked, privately dubious and wary. I knew nothing about this traditional Indian medicine.

"No, with a kind of massage," Murthy said.

"Well, what I have been doing for it has not helped. I'd be glad to try anything for relief," I said.

"First, take off that ace bandage. It is only interfering with your blood circulation and delaying healing," Murthy said. He had me lie back on the hotel bed and began massaging my lower *left* arm as if trying to squeeze the blood out the end of my fingers while I remained totally relaxed. Mind you, this was to treat my *right* foot.

After about 15 minutes, he said, "All right, now try standing." I did and was surprised to find that most of the pain was gone. He repeated the treatment twice more during the next 30 hours. By the time we left Hyderabad I was pain free.

My Indian colleagues were returning directly to Madras, but I had been called to New Delhi to consult with the new CPAO, Jay Gildner. I first flew to Bombay, where a baggage handler strike was on. I had to stand in the crowded terminal on a concrete floor for over two hours before my baggage was put onto my New Delhi flight. That made the pain in my foot begin to return. By the time I returned to Madras two days later, I was limping again. But, Murthy gave me a few more treatments, and I was cured.

In New Delhi, Gildner questioned me about what I knew about the Data & Records System (DRS, successor to the ARS), which Washington had ordered him to implement for all of USIS-India—the largest USIS operation anywhere. I had just installed it in Tokyo. So, I could offer some insights.

Kimie and I discovered an interesting situation in Tamil Nadu: it was a dry state. So, for instance, when the governor gave a reception for the diplomatic corps (12 or 13 foreign consulates in Madras) and ranking local Indians, the beverages were tea, juice, soda, etc. We diplomats could drink alcohol at home or at our own parties. Then, how about the Boat Club beer drinkers we met on our third day in Madras? There was a loophole. If an Indian could persuade a doctor to certify that he needed alcohol, e.g., for insomnia or "nervous disposition," he could get an official permit to buy and consume liquor.

A more pleasant surprise: In India, Kimie's birthday was a national holiday, because it was also Mahatma Gandhi's birthday.

My next program trip was to Bangalore. The program: a concert by the Stradivarius String Quartet and a USIS reception for them. Of course, the musicians were not carrying Stradivari instruments around India.

Again, my Indian team and I made the advance contacts, arranged for the concert in a ballroom of our hotel and then flew to Bangalore to meet the quartet members arriving from Calcutta. Their plane was delayed by weather and a dispute over cultural values. Throughout the tour, the cellist booked a separate seat for his cello so as to keep the instrument with him at all times. The flight from Calcutta was overbooked, and the airline had tried to bump the cello into the baggage hold. The cellist ultimately had to call our consulate in Calcutta to prevail against that. We had a good audience in Bangalore and a well-attended reception and then flew to Madras, where the concert was also a success.

By fall 1978, I had learned more local lore. An intriguing legend in Madras involved St. Thomas the Apostle ("doubting Thomas"). Between Madras and its airport stood St. Thomas Mount—about 250 feet high. Atop it was a small Christian church and an orphanage run by Indian Catholic nuns. The legend held that when the disciples took up their evangelical missions, Thomas the Apostle was assigned to India.

To us that may sound preposterous, because the history we learn tells us the Mediterranean world had no contact with the Orient until the time of Marco Polo and later Portuguese and Spanish explorations. For, the rise of Islam during the "Dark Ages" cut Europe off from the Orient and created a gap in the West's knowledge of the East. But, we now know that from early Roman times, there was overland commerce across Asia to China and India via the Silk Road, and also trade by sea. In Bangalore's museum I was surprised to see Roman coins from the 2nd and 3rd centuries AD, but was told that India actively traded with Rome in those times. Also, far down the west coast of India, in Cochin, was a Jewish synagogue whose history reportedly traced back to about the 4th century.

In the 16th and 17th centuries when Portuguese explorers began sailing into India's west coast ports, they reportedly found Christian parishes whose members claimed their church had been founded by St. Thomas in the 1st century AD. In Madras the Portuguese were told that St. Thomas had died there, at the summit of the hill now bearing his name. The legend says that Thomas, proselytizing in Madras, made many converts. But, when he sought to convert the daughter of a leading Brahmin priest, that sparked real anger and an assassination squad was sent after him. Thomas is said to have fled first to Little Mount, in the south part of today's Madras. There he hid in a cave. Today, a Christian church stands over the site, and one can go down stairs behind the altar into the basement and see a natural cave, which is blessed with an unfailing spring flowing from the bedrock. In one rock wall is a hand-shaped depression, said to have been made by Thomas while in impassioned prayer. When the assassins flushed him out, he fled to the larger mount, but was caught there. The legend says a spear thrust to his side killed him.

The Portuguese following up on the legend reportedly dug where the locals said Thomas was buried. Turning over a plain stone marker on St. Thomas Mount, they found its under side incised with a cross. That stone is now in the nearby church and treated as a precious relic. In the grave they found bones and a spear point. A cross now marks that site. And, in the Catholic cathedral in Madras, they will show you a finger bone of St. Thomas, if you ask. The rest of the bones went long ago to the Vatican.

We know that great and fervent faith can help lend credence to, and even embellish, many seemingly far-fetched stories, miracles, etc. But, in Madras serious and cultured Brahmins and Muslims have no doubt that the legend is true.

Besides the Madras Club, the Cricket Club and other less distinguished structures from the British era, we visited the Madras museum, where in the adjoining church's graveyard one may see the graves of British soldiers and civil servants. Many of their markers state that death was due to "heat prostration." In the museum are some of the uniforms they wore: heavy wool cloth with high collars better suited to the Scottish highlands than to Madras's torrid heat. No wonder so many died from the heat!

Kimie and I had arrived in Madras's "hotter" season. In mid-January we experienced the merely "hot" season, when early morning temperatures fell as low as 68°F and our Indian servants arrived wearing sweaters and shivering. By mid-afternoon the temperature would climb to about 85°. In March the "hottest" season began—morning temperatures in the mid-80s and mid-afternoons as warm as 110°, with humidity above 75%. We were dumfounded, in those conditions, sometimes to see poorer Indians walking barefoot on asphalt roads partly melted by the heat.

In April 1979, we were able to take our deferred home leave. We now learned an oddity of U.S. diplomatic service in India. Decades earlier, the U.S. had sent millions of tons of wheat at a time when India could not adequately feed its people. India paid us in non-convertible rupees. In the 1980s, the U.S. Treasury still had a heap of those rupees and constantly sought ways to unload them. One way was to pay Air India in rupees when we traveled within India. Another way: Cunard Lines periodically sailed the QEII ("Queen Elizabeth II") around the world, with a stop in Bombay and could use rupees to pay port charges and fueling costs. So, our home leave itinerary included a leg on the QEII from Southampton to New York, minimum first class rate.

We took Pan Am from Delhi through Bahrain and Frankfurt to London. On that flight we caught a glimmering of Pan Am's coming decline. Kimie met a European lady exiting a rest room. She warned Kimie that it was out of paper. Kimie always carried an emergency supply in her handbag, so that it was no problem for her. But, when she told a stewardess about it, her response was, "Well, just wait until the next station."

In London, we took a tour to Windsor Castle, Eton and Oxford and another to Stonehenge (where Kimie found a £10 note blowing across the grass) and Winchester Cathedral. We arrived at the cathedral on April 12, Maundy Thursday that year. I remember because we were allowed only to tour the cathedral's exterior. The Queen was to visit the next day, Good Friday, and rehearsals were going on inside. As we walked around the old building, a group of little choirboys came out for a break, and some of our tour group began asking them to pose for photos. Finally, one little boy piped up, "But we're not public!"

We also "cased" Kew Gardens and Westminster Abbey. Then, by train to Southampton to board the magnificent QEII. The captain was on deck to greet each of us as we boarded; and a photographer shot each such "historic" moment.

On our trans-Pacific APL voyages in the 1960s, we learned you can avoid fattening up on sea voyages by sticking to proteins and salads, skimping on carbohydrates and power-walking the decks a couple of times a day. Kimie found the QEII cuisine less flavorful than on the APL liners and so asked for Tabasco Sauce during our first meal. The steward brought her a new 2-oz. bottle and returned the same bottle to her at each meal thereafter. By the end of the 4½-day voyage she had used it all!

We enjoyed the movies and other entertainment on board, but found the north Atlantic less interesting than the Pacific. No flying fish, whales or porpoises in sight. The color of the water, more gray than blue. So, we focused on enjoying what the ship itself had to offer.

Departing from Southampton, the QEII crosses the Channel to pick up passengers at Cherbourg, where one can still see fortifications the Germans built to fend off any Allied invasion. Then the ship heads west. The evening of the fourth day, passengers must put their large luggage outside their cabins for early-morning pickup. That speeds up the disembarkation in New York, but also makes the voyage seem even shorter.

We went up on deck for the QEII's dawn arrival in New York harbor, sailing under the Verrazano Narrows Bridge and past the Statue of Liberty as the rising sun did a light show on the skyscrapers. As we watched, we heard that the tugboats were on strike so that the QEII would have to dock itself! And how does such a huge liner accomplish that feat?

First it went upriver just past its dock and then let the current slowly swing it 90°, bow in, and bring it in line with the dock. An officer with a walkie-talkie on the flying bridge kept the main bridge constantly informed of their position. At just the right moment, slight power was applied and the ship slid smoothly into the dock. We passengers on deck all applauded this demonstration of British seamanship.

Disembarking, we heard the crew talking about an upcoming cruise to Latin America. We checked into our hotel, and later that morning went down to lower Manhattan to tour the World Trade Center. From the observation deck overlooking the city we were surprised to see the QEII already heading down river for its cruise southward.

Our home-leave address now: Chevy Chase, Maryland. So, after a day and a half in New York, we rode the Metroliner to D.C. We took an Arlington motel room and began visiting around. First, to see Rits and Sheila, of course. In fact, we were able to catch Sheila's high school graduation. Our first grandchild a high-school graduate!! We also visited some Burleson cousins.

We accepted an invitation to visit David and Dorothy Robins Mowry on Maryland's east shore. Dorothy was the dynamic women's affairs officer brought to Tokyo by Charles Fahs back in the '60s; she stayed until the mid-1970's, when she resigned to write a book, *Political Women in Japan*. David Mowry was an attaché from the Commerce Department, which always has several representatives in an Embassy as large as that in Tokyo. They had married in Tokyo and now were retired and living in their beautiful new home in St. Michaels on the east shore of the Chesapeake Bay.

The town's early history is recalled in its epigraph: "The town that fooled the British." So called because when the British fleet sailed up the Chesapeake on the attack during the War of 1812, the townspeople put lanterns on tall poles or in trees. So, when the British attempted a night shelling of the town, all their shots went beyond the town.

Dorothy and David were on a small arm of Chesapeake Bay and had their own boat dock. Their boat was off being refurbished; but we went down to see their dock anyway. Kimie immediately spotted crabs on the pilings, the delicious Chesapeake blue points. Recalling our Patuxent crabbing days two decades earlier, she excitedly asked if we could net some. The Mowrys took us back to their garage to fetch several wire nets on poles. In about half an hour back on the dock we got maybe 14-15 crabs. We boiled them up in the Mowry kitchen and later ate some with Rits. (Sheila was partying at the home of a classmate.)

Kimie and I also took our periodic physicals at the State Department Medical Division and passed nicely—except, Kimie's blood pressure was too high. We thought that was because she did not particularly care for the tropical assignment. Spotting her high blood pressure, the examining doctor said, "Well, young lady, we may not be able to clear you for duty again in Madras." He asked her to see the USIA nurse daily for a week to have her blood pressure re-checked.

My "young lady" (a few months shy of 60, but looking 20 years younger) was delighted with the idea of not having to continue in Madras. So, her blood pressure promptly returned to normal and stayed normal for the rest of the week. Reviewing those findings, State Medical cleared her again for Madras! A real-life Catch-22.

With all of my father's siblings gone from this life, the sole survivors from my parents' generation were Uncle Rowland and his wife Frances. So, after about eight days in the D.C. area, we flew to Madison to see them again on an overnight visit. Rowland had been in declining health, but seemed to have recovered some strength, so that we had a good visit with him and Frances.

From there we flew to the Bay area. Sister Mary was now remarried and living for the summer in Santa Rosa with new husband Harry Zollinger. Hugh-ko, Pat and baby Saijo came down; and Rits and Sheila also joined us there, as did Louise and Larry Spring —now married—and Kitty & Boyd Weeks and two of their children, so that we had a not so mini reunion.

Next stop: Seattle, where we spent more of our home leave with Hugh-ko and family, staying at a nearby motel. Of course, we did some sightseeing and gained a better feel for the Seattle area. Hugh-ko was then working for Bayliner Boats, using fiberglass and other newer materials.

I also met there with Barrie Austin, a Yorkshire man, then a Boeing sales agent and board member of the World Affairs Council, to learn how the Council operated. From Barrie I heard they badly needed an executive director but could not pay a salary.

Before resuming our trek back to India, I called Clif Forster, then CPAO in Tokyo, to ask if he knew of any empty Embassy apartments in Tokyo where we could stay for several days. His response was unexpected: He and Nancy would be out of town, and we were welcome to stay in their home—the CPAO's residence!

We next flew to Juneau, which Kimie had never seen, and took a room in a hotel right on the Inland Passage. We had a scrumptious salmon dinner in front of a picture window overlooking the water. Twice we saw eagles soaring past. It being June, we later found ourselves trying to get to sleep at 11 PM with the evening sky still fairly bright.

The next morning, we hired a woman cabby to take us sightseeing, around Juneau and then up to the Mendenhall Glacier. In that beautiful clear morning, we reveled in the wonderful scenery and fresh air and then flew on to Anchorage to catch our flight to Tokyo. While we waited in the Anchorage terminal for our flight, a JAL flight came in. We had been wandering through the gift shop looking at the attractive local crafts, scrimshaw, etc. The quiet of the shop now was broken as dozens of Japanese flooded in. The cash registers rang constantly as they scooped up souvenirs for friends back in Japan. (File that scene in your memory: I'll be referring to it a decade later.)

Arriving over Japan, we could see the top of Fuji piercing a thick layer of clouds. Then our plane punched down into that pea soup. June rains were trapping the Tokyo smog under their cloud blanket. Kimie and I looked at each other and sighed, recalling Alaska's glorious clear air that morning.

Staying in the Forster home, we were quite spoiled. They had left their maid on duty to get breakfast for us and otherwise tend to our housekeeping needs. So, we could freely travel to Yokohama to see Kimie's family, visit friends in Tokyo, shop and mail our purchases through the APO to ourselves c/o the New Delhi Embassy. A pleasant close to our leave.

Except— After about five days there, we got a message from Louise in Fort Bragg: Uncle Rowland had died. We later heard that Louise flew to Madison to help Frances sell and close down her home of many decades, and then arranged for Frances to live with her and Larry in Fort Bragg.

309

Meanwhile, we continued west and south. We flew from the new Narita airport to Hong Kong. With reservations in the Peninsula Hotel, we were met at the airport by one of the hotel's fleet of Rolls Royce courtesy sedans. Which calls to mind an amusing tale a younger African-American USIS officer, Ted Ashford, once told me. During his first overseas assignment in Manila as a junior officer, Ted and his fiancée got married by long-distance phone and met for a honeymoon in Hong Kong, with a booking at the Peninsula. He had not known of the Peninsula's Rolls Royce shuttles. So, when they got into the one picking them up at the airport, Ted played "cool." He looked about and casually asked the driver, "Where's the bar?"

We again enjoyed riding the Star Ferry across the harbor, now a 6-cent fare. Inflation, you know. We limited our shopping this time, because our next stop was Bangkok.

We stayed in Bangkok long enough for just a bit of shopping and relaxed sightseeing. Our friends the Kendalls had transferred there from Tokyo and took us out for dinner—on a large boat that sailed up the Chao Phraya River and back again while we ate. A delightful treat. On the final day, I contacted Air India about our reservations into Madras. The Bangkok office said we would have to confirm in Kuala Lumpur. Not real reassuring.

In KL we would have four hours before our Air India flight left, and I hoped we could take a quick trip into the city, which we had never seen. So, at the KL terminal I quickly sought the Air India agent. Every airline person I asked was vague: "I saw him about an hour ago." Or, "He's often out of his office." Ultimately, the man showed up about 40 minutes before the flight and casually assured me there would be no problem about our reservations. That late, a jaunt into the city was out of the question.

Back to Madras and back into the saddle. Right away, Mack Fry sent me to Bangalore to do another program, a quite interesting one. First though, three relevant facts/situations.

India's caste system was legally banned long ago, but persists with vigor in a host of social practices. To counter the worst discriminatory impacts, the government applies affirmative action with disadvantaged castes when filling government jobs. That causes resentment and tension just as it has in the United States. So, in the '60s and '70s, Indian jurists and lawyers were closely watching the course of our affirmative action policies.

Second, the Bakke case was then before the U.S. Supreme Court—the suit by UC-Davis student Bakke charging the university with reverse discrimination for using racial quotas to deny him entry to its medical school.

Third, Bangalore, a pleasant city in the mountains where the British once retreated for rest and relaxation during the "hottest" season, had a leftist government in 1979. Communists and socialists predominated in such professions as law. So, USIS programs had been fairly unsuccessful in reaching important opinion leaders in that field in Karnataka.

Now we had subject matter, the Bakke case, which interested them. So, we put together packets of printed materials on affirmative action, a PBS video on the Bakke case and relevant books. Our Indian staff used letters and phone calls to persuade the chief justice of the Karnataka superior court to invite key jurists and lawyers to a USIS program in Bangalore. Two Indian staff members flew ahead to make the final arrangements and deliver the materials and books to the participants.

I took a train instead, so as to get a close-up look at the countryside during the climb into the hills. I struck up a conversation with my seatmate, an educated man. He turned out to be an officer of the Indian Tobacco Commission. He mentioned the huge paperwork load they had, and I said that we had installed an office computer to handle our record keeping.

His interest perked up, and he told me a tale then typical of Indian bureaucracy. His office had submitted a proposal to New Delhi to install a computer system, justifying it as labor saving. The sniffy reply from the capital: India has abundant labor and needs no labor-saving devices. His office then re-worked the proposal, this time justifying it as "time saving." Now it was approved. After all, no one can stretch a day beyond 24 hours!

Another point of interest for me on that trip was a granite hill that we passed. All over its bald slopes people were chipping away at the rock with *hand tools* and carrying away the stone for buildings, landscaping, etc. I now saw that a unique item I had observed in the Madras area came from here: *granite* fence posts. Termites were so active in the area that wooden fence posts would quickly disappear. So, with great patience and skill these stone chippers used chisels and wedges to break away (not saw) from the granite mountainside fence posts five to six feet long with a cross section about 4 inches square. Totally termite proof, naturally. These were then strung with barbed wire!

Our program, at Bangalore's Indian Institute of Management, went very well. We had chipped through the resistance of some 24 senior judges, lawyers and educators who attended and engaged in lively discussions. They warmly appreciated the books and printed materials we had brought. Best of all, on the day before the program we learned that our Supreme Court had upheld U.C.'s affirmative action policy, turning back Bakke's suit. So, we also had timeliness. The Indians saw the ruling as confirming the correctness of India's policy toward its underprivileged castes.

At the luncheon afterward, one of the Institute faculty members gave me another illuminating insight into India's bureaucracy as of 1979. He said that his salary and that of the other faculty members had been set in the 19th century by the British *and had not risen one rupee since*! The only way he could hold his prestigious job was by drawing on inherited family assets.

Of course, things must have changed by now, for Bangalore is now flooded with high-tech enterprise and has become India's first "silicon valley." But, 20 years ago resistance to change was apparent, especially in south Indian culture. Our contacts there liked to boast that theirs was the true Indian culture, whereas north India, repeatedly invaded and ruled by alien peoples over the centuries (Alexander's Greeks, Afghans, Persians, Moslems, the British), had become a hybrid culture.

That contributed to local resistance against the imposition of north Indian culture and language. Our most senior employee in Madras, S. Krishnan ("Krish"), once complained that in New Delhi cab drivers tried to make him speak Hindi. Krishnan much preferred to speak English, which he handled masterfully.

Krishnan's daughter was married while we were in Madras. That was the first wedding we attended in India and the only Brahmin wedding we would witness. It was fairly low key, but with elaborate ritual and costume. A unique feature: at one point in the ceremony the bridegroom pretends to get cold feet and exits the wedding hall. The bride's father must go after him and bring him back. But, Krish, a bit slow to react, took some five minutes to bring back the now "reconciled" groom. Everyone was chuckling.

From Krish we also learned of the loophole in Tamil Nadu's prohibition law, which I mentioned earlier. He was a loophole beneficiary. So, when we went out with Krish for a "lubricated" lunch, he would show his permit and drink liberally. Sometimes we had luncheons for our Indian contacts at our house and invited Krishnan as well. Kimie learned to have his "medicine"—Johnny Walker black label—available in quantity.

In summer 1979, CPAO Jay Gildner asked me to apply for the #3 position (Policy Officer) in New Delhi. He wanted me to help computerize the DRS—Data & Record System—as I had in Tokyo. I agreed, of course. It would mean a better climate for Kimie. Washington confirmed me for the job; but New Delhi gave me a few months to wrap up in Madras, as BPAO Mack Fry was scheduled for leave in the U.S.

Before he left, I took my most extensive program trip: to southwest India's Kerala state, described in a 1988 *National Geographic* as "one of the most densely populated rural areas in the world." Dominated at many levels of government by communists, this area was a tougher "sell" than other parts of south India. First we—Krishnan, an A/V

313

technician and I—flew to Trivandrum, almost at the southern tip of India, checking into a pleasant, airy hotel on a palm-lined shoreline. Our first morning we breakfasted with the president of Trivandrum University. Then with some of the professors we held a video and discussion program. That was Saturday morning.

That afternoon we drove south by car for sightseeing. First to a 300-year-old teak castle near Neyyatinkara. The exquisite woodworking skills of its builders made it well worth seeing. I also was attracted to the view out one window, a tree full of "flying foxes," huge fruit bats with wingspans up to 30 inches. Then we drove south through Nagercoil to Cape Comorin, the absolute southern tip of India and watched the sun set there.

The cape carries religious significance for some Indians, who call it "the cape of the three seas," for to the west is the Arabian Sea, to the south the Indian Ocean and to the east the Bay of Bengal (if you ignore a slight intervening obstacle—the island nation of Sri Lanka). I also found seashells for sale at beach stalls there and bought a few.

I spent Sunday relaxing at our Trivandrum hotel and on the beach. I was intrigued by the "mud hoppers" there, fish 4-6 inches long that seemed just as content out of water as in it. They would flip themselves up onto wet rocks, crawl about on their front fins, quarrel over favored spots and flip back into the water after up to ten minutes in the open air.

On Monday, we made courtesy calls on local officials and then caught the train that would take us up the coast about 2½ hours to Ernakulam-Cochin. Settling into our train seats, I broke out some of my snack items to share with Krishnan, who was telling me the local lore and what we could expect in Cochin. After a while, I glanced at my plastic bag of snacks on the window frame and was amazed to see that ants had invaded it, riding the rails and cadging our food! I had seen amazing survival skills in India, but hobo *ants*!

In Ernakulam, we spent the afternoon showing films and holding discussions. Kerala society once was matriarchic and, in some areas, polyandrous (one woman: plural husbands). Family names were matrilineal (mom's last name, not dad's). So, I was prepared when some of our best interlocutors proved to be the lady professors.

One lady gave me some other interesting local lore. The ubiquitous coconut tree in Keralese is called the "mother tree" because so much of the people's livelihood has long depended on the tree. The fruit itself, of course, is an important food source, and its semi-dried meat (copra), a source of oil. The fiber (coir) and fronds of the tree were used to build homes and shelters. Trunks could be hollowed and made into canoes for fishing. Etc.

At Ernakulam, we had rooms in a hotel on an island in the bay and reached it by small boat after the afternoon's programs were finished. The hotel had a large dining hall, where we had late afternoon tea. But, Krish had arranged for us to have dinner in Cochin, at the tip of the southern peninsula that helps enclose the bay.

Cochin was the original port city and had long been the home of a Jewish colony, as I noted above, dating from the 4th century A.D. After Israel was formed in 1947, members of the colony began emigrating to Israel. By 1980, few families remained. Krishnan had contacted one of these about our visit. They knew Krish well and invited us to dinner.

We took a boat across the bay to Cochin and then a cab to an old Christian church the British had used. A fascinating feature there: holes through the church walls for ropes. Indian men once were hired to squat outside ("Couldn't have the beggars inside, you know.") and pull on the ropes to swing overhead baffles that moved the humid tropical air over the British during services. On the nearby shore, we saw men fishing with nets strung on long bamboo and sapling poles. With ropes and pulleys, they raised or lowered the nets—a fishing method they learned from the Chinese long ago.

Next, our taxi took us to the Jewish synagogue, where our host let us in. The structure dated back to about the 17th century. Earlier synagogues there were done in by storms, fire or termites. The floor and lower walls were covered with beautiful blue and white porcelain tiles from Ming dynasty China. Our host took us to his home, where his wife had been preparing dinner. I felt honored to be included.

Later, back at our hotel I had a problem with the wild life. My bathroom had latticed windows and no screens; and a horde of mosquitoes had squatters' rights. They seemed addicted to fresh meat—me. I found that my only defense was to lather up quickly so that any attackers would commit suicide in the soap. Still, by the time I crawled under the mosquito netting draped over my bed, I probably had eight or ten wounds from that battle.

The next morning, I went out early with my camera and was rewarded by some gorgeous tropical dawn scenery. That day, we again did a round of programs and official calls—renewing USIS ties in the area. Then back by plane to Madras.

Before the Frys left on their vacation, we had another musical presentation for our Madrasi public: a lady pianist. In my absence, Mack had set up the programs: an invitation-only event at the consul general's residence and a ticketed concert at the Madras Club. The first concert was *al fresco* on the flagstone veranda of the consul general's home, with a humid breeze blowing off the nearby Madras River.

Problems developed. During the first few numbers, we began hearing extraneous squeaks from the piano. The moisture, it turned out, was making one pedal squeak. During the next number, I slipped away to our house, just in front of the consul general's property and came back with some WD-40. That squelched the unwanted accompaniment.

Another problem: humidity from the river also was condensing on the ivories. At every break, the pianist had to wipe off the keys with a towel from the consul general's kitchen. Finally, even though mosquito coils were smoldering on the perimeter around the seats, people still had to swat at small flying gatecrashers.

When Mack Fry left, I was in charge and so tied down in Madras. That meant our two junior officers, David Noziglia and Bill Dawson, could go out on more program trips.

In Madras, Kimie and I made friends with local artist colony members, the Vasudevs especially. The colony adjoined the beach north of the city center. That summer of 1979 they invited noted ceramist, Mansimran Singh of Delhi Blue Art Pottery, to teach a class at the colony. Kimie and other mostly foreign residents signed up for the three-day class.

On the third day, they built a kiln of mud brick and sand. Class members then loaded their products in the kiln and went off to dinner. We went back in mid-evening to check on things. The kiln was smoking lustily, which Kimie told me was a bad sign. From her north Kamakura experience a few years earlier, she knew that a kiln, once fired up, should be too hot to smoke.

The next morning when she went back, the Vasudevs and others were trying to re-build the kiln. New Delhi ceramist Singh was gone in the night. The whole project turned out a bust, for the clay products in the kiln never got hot enough to become ceramic.

Speaking of the Madras beach, we learned that "catamaran" is a Tamil word, not for the sleek, fast double-hulled sailing craft we know in the West, but for simple double bamboo rafts mounting a sail. They were still common on the Madras beach at that time. Dirt-poor fishermen there built their own catamarans, as they have for millennia, and sailed them out, sometimes several miles, in pursuit of fish schools.

We spent very little time on Madras's beaches otherwise. Many *dalit* (untouchables) lived in clusters of sorry hovels near the beach, with at best one source of water per village. And no toilet facilities, so that the nearby beach served that purpose.*

That was a problem near our neighborhood, too, where clusters of the meanest sort of housing also were seen. The residents simply used open spaces, roadsides, etc., as toilets.

---

\* In the tsunami disaster of December 2004, most victims in that area were untouchables and fishermen.

In November 1978, we had a week of very heavy rain. Before that started, we spent a weekend about 20 miles down the coast at a hotel in an area once (a few hundred years ago) a Dutch East India Company settlement. On Sunday mid-morning I noticed heavy dark clouds approaching from the south. So, we left early. Even so, the rains hit just as we were re-entering Madras. By the time we got to our house, we were in a real downpour.

In one day, 12 inches fell and our yard was partly flooded. The Madras River nearby is tidal, so that when high tide met the flooding rivers, many low areas flooded—especially *dalit* villages. Their homes were unbaked mud brick and tended to dissolve and wash away. The servants of James Todd,* a consular officer living two doors away, reported after the flood that their homes were destroyed. Our servants, too, had damage. The American wives, including Kimie, consulted and offered to pay for rebuilding. When they asked what that would cost, the servants said 100 rupees—less than 10 dollars. The American wives knew that meant building the same kind of flimsy structure, and offered to give them enough to rebuild in concrete block—about $70 dollars per house. The servants declined that offer. No one in the village had such a house. So they could not build like that. Nor did they know any other place where they could build.

Not far from our home was the residence of the Japanese consul general. We had met him and his wife at a diplomatic function shortly after arriving and had sometimes socialized with them and other Japanese staffers. So, we were invited to their 1979 New Year party with its rich spread of traditional New Year foods flown in from Japan. Kimie sometimes visited their home to play bridge or mah jongg. Before long, she learned that the consul general's wife was an insomniac, so that her mah jongg parties might run all night.

---

\* Jim Todd (1921-2003) was one of the first Afro-Americans in the Foreign Service (hired in 1945), and declined most of his home leaves because of bias he and his family would face. He said that during his first home leave—after duty in Cairo—they drove to his home in North Carolina and on to Florida. Faking an Arab accent, he passed as Egyptian and so avoided the worst aspects of Jim Crow treatment.

We pitied the junior Japanese officers, who might be called at any time of day or night to fill out a bridge or mah jongg table, and then were expected at work in the morning.

Still hurt by having lost our household effects in Saigon four years earlier, Kimie had arrived in Madras vowing again not to buy any permanent items. She stuck by that for about two months. Then one Saturday Mrs. Todd sent a Moslem carpet vender to our house with a load of wool oriental carpets up to 6'x 9' in size. We ended up buying three then and two more later. Also, we discovered a shop in downtown Madras that offered fine carvings in teak, rosewood and other south Indian hardwoods. Kimie's resistance melted away.

In early September 1979, Mack Fry returned. He and Pat had left together, to stay first with relatives in the Missouri Ozarks. But, now Mack told me he had gone on alone to the east coast to stay at a singles' resort. He said, "Hugh, I had an incredible time! I did things there I'd never before dreamed of doing—never even knew were done. And, I *loved* it!"

During the final few weeks before Kimie and I left for New Delhi, Mack seemed to be in another world, even alienated from his past personality. Then Kimie and I packed up and left for New Delhi. The Frys apparently broke up during his next home leave, from USIS Stockholm. I later heard that he had created situations there that led to his leaving USIA altogether.

# NEW DELHI
## (1980-1981)

Arriving in New Delhi, we were temporarily assigned to the Deputy PAO's quarters, a rambling older two-story house close to the Embassy, but a couple of miles from USIS. The next DPAO, Bob McLaughlin, was due in from Vienna after home leave. So, I was also acting deputy PAO and, when CPAO Gildner was away on vacation, I was acting CPAO at this largest USIS post!

There is a tale from U.S. history that when Teddy Roosevelt was Assistant Navy Secretary in the 1890's, a time of rising tensions with Spain, the Navy Secretary was out of town one weekend. Incensed by some Spanish action, TR fired off a cable ordering the U.S. Navy flotilla in Hong Kong to steam to Manila Bay for possible action against the Spanish. His order was countermanded the next Monday when the Secretary returned. Ever since, when an officer is to be acting in a higher position, he may jokingly promise "not to send the fleet to Manila Bay." I.e., when in an acting capacity, one does not take bold initiatives. So, I didn't, but reviewed and signed off on many telegraphic messages.

The climate in New Delhi is very different from that of Madras, being 1100 miles farther north, but on the same latitude as Key West. New Delhi's climate is far drier, with the Rajasthan Desert just a short distance to the west. In fact, November through February the weather was much like late spring in southern California. By March, hot weather sets in and desiccates the landscape until monsoon rains come in June and July. Our first (and only major) dust storm hit that April, when hot winds over the desert kicked up huge clouds of dust. In New Delhi we had no surface wind, just massive clouds of dust rolling in over the city, reducing visibility to about 100 feet and blocking out the sun.

As capital of "Mother India," Delhi hosts many foreign embassies. Those of Commonwealth nations are called "high commissions". An array of government buildings, mostly from the British era, also marks New Delhi. So, diplomatic life there was like what we had seen in Tokyo—much socializing and partying within the diplomatic community.

Let me make clear that, while some pundits love to caricature "diplomatic parties" as fluffy frivolity by "the striped-pants set," for on-the-job diplomats they are work, often involving substantive diplomacy. Attending may be mandatory, and you have to stay alert and ready to assist a senior officer at any time. Such as, "Hugh, the PAO needs to talk to the Information Minister. Could you please intervene with that chatty woman talking to him and get her to talk instead with some of the embassy wives." To be sure I was on my toes, I learned to take a single vodka tonic at the outset of a party and then switch to tonic water only. No one knew but the bar tender.

A party might begin as strictly social. Then, after the non-substantive people had left, we could focus more on people who might help advance USIS efforts to get better treatment for the U.S. in the Indian media or whose views we needed on our cultural programs. And, the striped pants image is about a century out of date.

Just after I arrived, we presented the Orpheus Chamber Ensemble and, a year later, the Pilobolus Dance Company. For, India was very much a Cold War battleground, and we sought more respect for American culture. Not long after India gained its independence, Secretary of State Dulles—constantly censuring India's proclaimed neutrality in the Cold War—had soured US-India ties. The Soviet Union quickly moved to persuade India that its Gandhian ethic and pacifism best accorded with communist peace themes. We had to work hard to get much of a hearing for US policies. So, until the late 1980's, India was much friendlier with Moscow than with us. The Russians were major arms suppliers to India and strongly supported India's far left parties, and often got the Indian media to carry disinformation about the U.S. and its policies.

Whereas Madras traffic had been "interesting"—seldom jammed, but an amazing mix of transportation modes—New Delhi, had maybe four times more traffic. Added to the traffic "stew" were camel carts, many wandering Brahma cows (in lieu of water buffalos) and far more pedestrians. Some behaved as though whatever befell them on the roads was not their responsibility, but simply their karma.

Many Delhi streets are wide boulevards and give a spacious feel to the city. In 1980-81 some were lined with slapped-together shanties of people who came in from their villages to escape abysmal poverty or to get off-season work. One result was that, as you looked across the city's expanses in early morning, the air close to the ground was thick with smoke from villager cooking fires, fueled mostly by dried cow dung. As the sun created convection currents, the smoke gradually dispersed but still left an overall brown haze and distinctive odor hanging over the city, only gradually to be replaced by exhaust fumes.

Kimie and I were constantly amazed by India's extreme contrasts. Hellish poverty and suffering for the weakest segments of the society versus great wealth in the upper classes, who assumed a natural right to enjoy their karma without regard for the illiterate masses. Of course, India had been that way for millennia—a span of time that enables a society to build up many rock-solid customs and beliefs.

We saw people with grossly deformed limbs crawling about and begging, and even heard that some were slaves of other people who had deliberately crippled them so that they could earn more from begging. In Madras Kimie was distressed in Madras's markets when approached by bandaged lepers begging for *baksheesh*. Until she was told they were let out of the leprosarium one day a week to beg. At the same time, India has many wonderful people, as cultured, urbane and thoughtful as any in the West. Yet, their cultural history had led them to a unique value system often quite different from ours.

Hindu values tend to make Indians vegetarian, to avoid taking life. At one party we gave for Indian acquaintances, I came upon two Brahmins debating whether eggs could be consumed. They finally agreed that if an egg were unfertilized, it would never develop into a living animal and so may be eaten. Perhaps most extreme are the Jains. I met one on the staff of USIS Bombay who, over a vegetarian lunch, told me that (1) they did not use garlic as they understood that it kills intestinal microbes, and (2) that they do not drive cars lest they run over and kill some living thing.

After we had lived in the DPAO house for two months, DPAO Bob McLaughlin arrived. He was expected to take a newly leased house beyond embassy row; but after he and his wife had seen both houses, they chose the former DPAO house where we were then living. We were not unhappy about that, even though it meant moving again. The alternative house, rented by Embassy General Services, was a large home in Shanti Niketan ("peaceful neighborhood") two miles from the US Embassy and had large rooms for official entertaining. It stood on a half acre with trees, a lawn and flowering plants. The garage in the back had 3 servants' rooms above it. Quite pleasant.

We hired two men as house servants, one of them our Madras "house boy." Because of all the embassy furnishings in the house, the Embassy paid the salary of our *chokidar* (night guard), but we tipped him each month to assure loyal service (i.e., not sleeping at night). We made the mistake of supplying him with a wicker chair so that he need not stand through the night; but the chair was too comfortable: He did sometimes did sleep on duty.

Shanti Niketan residents all kicked in to hire a man to patrol the neighborhood each night, not to prevent crime but to assure that all *chokidars* were awake! We often heard him blowing his whistle as he made his rounds.

The whole time we were in India, we felt we were playing Russian roulette with our health, as food or drink so often might be polluted. As in Madras, we could not drink the New Delhi tap water. The Embassy routinely furnished each officer's home with a 10-gallon crock with a porous ceramic filter in the top; but one did not simply pour tap water into it. First you boiled the water for 20 minutes in a large teakettle, because some protozoans in the water encyst at one stage of their life cycle and can survive shorter periods of boiling. After the water cooled, you poured it through the filter. Then it was safe to drink.

Our servants tended to see this as an odd custom, maybe even a mere superstition. If not watched, they would take short cuts—boiling the water for less time or skipping it entirely. Then we had to re-sterilize the whole crock. Soon enough, Kimie gave them religion about this, but often supervised the process.

Fruits and vegetables were a problem if they were to be eaten raw. To prepare them we had to: (1) Wash outdoors to remove visible dirt, (2) wash in kitchen in detergent, (3) rinse off detergent, (4) rinse in bleach diluted with purified water, (5) rinse off bleach with purified water. That tended to deter us from making green salads. We tried raising lettuce, onions and radishes in a garden outside our kitchen, but soon found that birds were reaping our crops. I got a bird net from the States; but birds sometimes got under it. It seems that *all* living things in India have special survival skills.

Kimie had taken up golfing in the late 1950's while we lived near D.C., and also played in Tokyo and Saigon. She continued with it in India. One golf course west of the city was open to embassy golfers just for the green fee. I played there with Kimie a few times.

Another course, south of the city center, was only for members of the India International Center; and therein lies a tale. I applied for membership, as that would also entitle us to attend the Center's cultural and academic programs. For some time the Center did not respond. Meanwhile, Kimie made good friends with a British couple, John and Vera Stanley, already members of the Center. Vera heard from Kimie of this delay and soon got our application pushed through. One day a few months later, Kimie had just finished a round of golf there when one of the office staff called her inside for a talk. To make a long story short, about a year earlier an Embassy officer, also a Burleson and with a Korean wife, had been a member and apparently left Delhi without settling his bill. So, the club assumed we were that couple, back for seconds. End of digression.

Now USIS-India was chosen by USIA-Washington to be the first post to put its DRS (Data & Record System) onto an in-house Wang computer system. Our DRS was on computers at an Indian computer service company. My staff included five Indian staffers under Ashok Ambekar maintaining our DRS.

In early 1980, USIA sent a computer expert to sell us, especially CPAO Gildner, on the advantages of this change. We would get a Wang minicomputer and do our own data processing. In March, I was asked to go to Washington for training on the software. So, off I went by Pan Am to Washington. I spent a week at USIA headquarters learning what the minicomputer could do. Then right back to India.

That summer we began building a special computer room for our Wang system. What an experience! Our contractor had never built a computer room, but had detailed plans from Washington for the raised floor and other requirements. His workers had only hand tools, except for one electric drill, which lacked the chuck key needed to change bits. So, they would stick an old Philips screwdriver into the chuck hole and hammer on it to loosen or tighten the chuck. When the whole job was finished, we had a computer room as modern as any, with beautiful teak paneling.

That fall the computer system arrived, along with a USIA technician to install the software and test it out. As power failures and voltage surges and drops were frequent, we also had a UPS—uninterruptible power system, basically a backup battery and switching system to protect the computer.

Next (May '80), Ashok and I were asked to go to Washington for more DRS training, plus some side trips—first to Wang headquarters north of Boston for briefings and, after our training in Washington, a visit to "Silicon valley." So, I was off on still another round-the-world trip—my fourth? It began badly, with our Pan Am flight arriving 10 hours late. The scrambled schedule also messed up the flight provisioning—no food for the first 9 hours, until we complained at Frankfurt. Alas, Pan Am! We knew you in better times.

We overnighted in London and arrived in New York on a Saturday. That gave us the weekend to overcome jet lag. I rented a car at JFK (Coincidentally, the license plate bore the letters DRS!) and drove first to Norfolk, Connecticut, for an overnight visit with brother George and his family at their Bruderhof community. Ashok was fascinated with their life style, as it reminded him of India's ashrams.

On Sunday we drove to Boston for sightseeing. Regrettably, the historic district was closed to be refurbished for the next week's "Tall Ships Festival"; but we took in Fanueil Hall, Old Ironsides, the site of the Boston Tea Party and Bunker Hill. Driving through Cambridge, I had to stop for a snapshot when I spotted "Kimie's Tavern" on one street. We took a motel close to Wang headquarters, spent the next day learning about Wang technology, then drove to Boston, turned in the rental car and flew to Washington.

There, several days of briefings, hands-on time with the computers and sessions with DRS system specialists. Then we flew to San Francisco and drove to Silicon Valley, where we overnighted with a cousin of Ashok, a software product manager at Intel, who gave us a tour of a plant where chips were produced.

Now Ashok and I parted ways. He was returning via Atlanta, where he had another cousin. I would make Seattle my next stopover: to see Hugh, Pat and our 17-month-old grandson, Saijo.

En route to Seattle, my plane flew close by Mount St. Helens, which had erupted three weeks earlier. We could not see the crater because of smoke and fumes, but could see the wide area of devastation and gray ash as far as Mount Adams to the east. Something I learned later relevant to the eruption: For years, Yakima Community College's art department had been buying volcanic ash from the Mt. Vesuvius area of Italy for use by ceramics students. Now, several dozen miles east of Mount St. Helens, the campus was buried under many inches and tons of ash. Cancel that last order!

Hugh and Pat, then living south of SeaTac Airport, planned to buy a new car that weekend. So, I went with them, happily watching over 17-month-old Saijo while they chose a Chevy Citation. While waiting, we heard a light plane nearby. Saijo exclaimed, "Hey-copta, hey-copta!" I tried to explain that it was an airplane, but—living under the flight path of jet airliners—he knew airplanes don't make that kind of noise and so insisted it must be a helicopter, until the plane came in view and we learned something about light planes that are not jets. Saijo's verbal precocity would be noted again later. Like, about a year later his mom recorded his fair rendering of "Take me out to the ballgame."

From Seattle, I headed west, with a stop in Hawaii to see Charley James and his family, now including his new wife. Then a flight to Osaka, where I stayed with the Goshos and visited Expo 80 before going on to New Delhi. As I walked through the terminal in New Delhi, again in the wee hours of the morning, I noted a group of young American women sporting t-shirts emblazoned, "A Woman's Place is Atop Annapurna." We later heard that they had made it to the top, but one member was killed on the climb.

After our computer system had been tested out, CPAO Gildner and I held a special staff meeting for the American and top Indian staff. I had Ambekar and his computer whizzes attend. My aim was to allay any computer phobia (then endemic worldwide) by showing that computers can be as user-friendly as any copy machine or electric typewriter, but far more capable. So, I introduced Ambekar and, turning to his two computer men, said, "And these are R2D2 and 3CPIO." That brought down the house and lightened the mood. We led a tour of the computer room, had a hands-on word processing session and showed some printouts the computer could produce. Soon, many staff members, Indian and American, were busily using the workstations. In the following months, I visited Bombay and Calcutta to help USIS staffs with their DRS.

That same year, Kimie and I joined a small Embassy group on a weekend trip into the Himalayan foothills to Simla, once an important British "hill station." We drove via the Grand Trunk Highway. A grand name, but what we would call an old-style 3-lane highway, with the center lane for passing. It was frustrating when big trucks would hog that center lane for miles, allowing no one else to pass in either direction. A couple of times we saw old dust-covered wrecks in that center lane or on the shoulder. Removing them? Someone else's karma.

On the wheat-growing lowlands of India's Punjab state, we also had camel carts crossing the highway, farm tractors sharing the road at 15mph and of course the wandering cows, though fewer than in New Delhi.

By early afternoon, the road began climbing, with frequent peek-a-boo views of the higher Himalayas, until we reached Simla at over 7,000 feet (still "foothills" to the mighty range), far above the warm-to-hot lowlands. This was where the British viceroys had spent five months of every year during the long rule of the British Raj. This also was where Lord Mountbatten and Pandit Nehru developed the plan for India's release from British rule.

Our reservations were in a hotel that was once a maharajah's hunting lodge. It had many original furnishings, including old weapons and mounted animal heads on the walls. There were perhaps 15 guest rooms. Those were chilly at night, but we found that bed warmers were a standard service: the servants put covered metal pans of hot water between the sheets in the middle evening so that we did not have to climb into cold beds. During the day we patrolled the many shops in town, and found a few things worth buying.

Our group made a late start for the return trip, so that we ended up driving most of the Grand Trunk Highway at night, my hairiest driving experience ever. We would meet trucks coming along without headlights; and the dust-covered wrecks still on the highway were hard to see until you were right upon them. But, we made it safely home.

In spring 1981, Kimie and two other Embassy ladies took a four-day trip by Embassy sedan (rented, with Indian driver) west into Rajasthan through Jaipur and Jodhpur as far as Pushkar's camel market, where they sampled milk fresh and warm from a camel. In Jaipur they had reservations in a sumptuous maharajah's palace in the middle of a lake, reachable only by boat. When they arrived, they were told their room was still occupied; but they kicked up enough of a fuss that they were given a suite that once was the maharani's—far superior to what they had reserved. Kimie returned with a better understanding of India's breadth and variety.

Our most memorable trip was to Agra and vicinity with John and Vera Stanley. Vera grew up in India, the daughter of a British Army officer, and sometimes betrayed the attitudes of an unreconstructed colonialist. She could wax very heated about how Indians were "ruining" what the British had put in place. We sometimes could scarcely conceal our mirth over her spirited criticisms. I think she was the one who told us the tale (perhaps true) that during a 19th Century campaign against an obstinate maharajah, the British forces were closing in on the palace and the mogul's staff all fled. The maharajah was captured still sitting on his bed because his staff had failed to turn his slippers so that he could easily step into them.

We drove to Agra, about 100 miles south of Delhi, in the Stanleys' car (not a Rolls Royce, although he was the agent in India for Rolls Royce Aircraft Engines). As we arrived close to sundown, the late afternoon sunlight striking the Taj Mahal was dyeing it pinkish orange—a magical scene. Regrettably, no flying carpets were in sight.

After checking in, we walked through the park-like garden and then had dinner. Coming back through the lobby, we saw an elephant and camel out front and were told that for 10 rupees we could be photographed sitting astride those beasts. Off to the side sat a snake charmer, who for a few rupees would put his cobra through its act. (In Shanti Niketan we often had door-to-door snake charmers ringing our gate bell and offering a show.)

The next morning, we went first to the Taj, now appearing quite different in the morning sun. We toured the building and grounds and heard the story and romance behind the broken-hearted Shah Jahan's magnificent tomb/edifice for his wife. Then we went to the Red Fort, a few miles upriver. Shah Jahan's son built this huge complex of the local rust-red sandstone. The final irony to Shah Jahan's story is that his rebellious son imprisoned him there in the Red Fort, with a window in his room from which he could gaze at the Taj in his final sad years.

329

From the Red Fort we next drove perhaps 15 miles west to the eerie city of Fahtipur Sikri. Mogul ruler Akbar had built this splendid palace and city with exquisitely carved marble structures and water systems to feed fountains and pools. Soon after, though, it was abandoned due to a failed water supply. There it sits today, empty except for tourists like us who traipse through to marvel at the magnificent construction that ended up signifying extravagance and past glory. (Faulty environmental impact study?)

Then back to our hotel for a second night. That evening after dinner we strolled through the hotel's shops. In a carpet shop (no flying ones) Kimie and I spotted a stunning all-silk carpet woven with a dynamic scene of mogul warriors hunting on horseback against a deep crimson background. As we admired it, the shopkeeper began urging us to buy it—"Only $4500! And it took two years to weave." We made him understand we were uninterested at that price. The price began coming down: $4000, $3600, $3300. Soon he was quoting $2700, paid even by our personal check. We still walked away from it, but often thought afterward that we should have taken it at that last price. It was *beautiful* and unique.

The next day we headed north from Agra, but not for Delhi and home. First we would stop at the Bharatpur wildlife sanctuary northwest of Agra. This is an extensive marshy area where a wide variety of bird life from central Asia and Siberia winter over; and of course the birds attract some predators, and tourists. We spent some hours admiring the scene, its many waterfowl, wild peacocks, several species of kingfisher, etc. And we had lunch there before returning to Delhi.

Some local color from New Delhi. Some Americans in the embassy liked to explore the more exotic aspects of the culture. Some quite normally sampled the culture, such as by taking courses on Indian art at the National Museum, as Kimie did. Others did so with shopping binges that let them decorate their homes in a semi-mogul style.

Before we came up from Madras, tales of the long-gone, lavish mogul life style inspired a senior embassy officer throwing a party at his home to have his arriving guests greeted by a pair of live elephants (rented) standing on either side of his driveway. After partying and drinking inside, the guests walked out between the elephants again, now turned around to face the departing revelers as *pink* elephants–spray-dyed pink only on that one side.

USIS audio-visual officer Jim Magee and his wife Ann took it upon themselves to make such partying a tradition. It was a second marriage for both, and Jim went that "extra mile" to keep romance alive with his "girl from Epanema" (where Ann actually lived with her American parents when Jim met her). Jim and Ann had a 3-story townhouse with a roof terrace on which they had a tandoori clay oven installed for rooftop barbecue parties.

On their wedding anniversary each of the two years we were there, they invited us and other friends to celebrate with them. The climax came when Jim would bring Ann her anniversary gift, a ceremony that all of us witnessed standing in the front of the house. The first year, as we waited we heard Indian musicians coming, playing a lively raga. Behind them, Jim rode up on an elephant in colorful regalia. The elephant stopped before us and knelt to let Jim get off to present his gift to Ann. The second year, same scene, but this time with an Indian bagpipe band and Jim riding up behind the band on a white horse to offer his present. Jim, incidentally, appeared in the movie "Gandhi" as an extra—one of the British officers in the court martial scene after the appalling Amritsar massacre.

Speaking of white horses. One day I was at work in my office when one of our Indian employees, Joginder Singh, came in. Approaching my desk, he deadpanned, "Have you ever been to a sick wedding?" That was a time when we were first speaking of "sick" jokes, etc. But, I caught his double meaning, for I had been in north India long enough to know that Indians named Singh and wearing turbans are Sikhs.* For the humor of it, he had mispronounced Sikh (properly pronounced

---

\* Sikhism is to Hinduism what Protestantism is to Catholicism, and religious intolerance flourishes in India. Many Indians freely voiced prejudice against Sikhs. Some warned, "Don't ever take a Sikh taxi at midday. You know, their brains get all hot under those turbans and that makes them drive crazy."

"seek"). Wary of offending his religion, I smiled and said, "No. Neither to a Sikh one nor to a sick one."

Anyway, he was inviting me to his daughter's wedding, which would take place within walking distance of our Shanti Niketan home. It turned out to span the entire weekend. A tent pavilion was erected next to the Singh home for the main ceremonies; and a larger one was put up across the street to provide sumptuous snacks to all guests. "All guests" meant the entire neighborhood, as well as those of us invited from the Embassy. Jay Gildner was there for the main ceremonies with his 8mm movie camera.

The highlight came when the groom, wearing an elaborate traditional Sikh outfit, rode up on a resplendent white horse to claim his bride. An interesting contrast to the Brahmin wedding we had seen in Madras.

Two months before we were to leave India in the summer of 1981, Kimie and I both came down with dysentery, despite all our precautions. Fortunately, it was not amoebic, which can cause lasting damage to one's intestinal tract. And, we were not alone in succumbing.

A few months earlier, a young officer, Gil Sherman, had contracted it. The situation was ironic for its cultural implications. He had been in India almost three years without catching dysentery. But, one day he was driving home in 100° heat when he got a flat tire. Pulling over at a traffic circle where an Indian policeman was directing traffic, he began the sweaty chore of switching to his spare tire. Before long, the policeman came over and offered him water. Gil knew it probably would make him sick; but felt he could not refuse the kind gesture. He accepted the water and, sure as shootin', soon was sick.

We may have caught our "bug" at a Delhi hotel restaurant, but could not know for sure. We got prompt treatment at the Embassy clinic and were soon cured. Fortunately, because our time to move on again was rapidly approaching.

About then, the Foreign Service instituted an "open assignments" system: Each personnel office sent out lists of positions soon coming open. An officer whose tour of duty was nearly over could bid for any jobs that interested him. A new option being offered was a "Pearson assignment" (initiated by Senator Pearson), positions with local governments or non-profit groups in the U.S. The officer stayed on USIA's payroll but spent a year or two with the organization, which benefited by getting an officer for nothing, while the officer and his agency benefited from his immersion in the U.S. public affairs scene.

During my last stopover in Seattle, I had learned that the Seattle World Affairs Council (WAC) was at a nadir, having just lost (through death) a key member who had essentially been running the Council. So, when I saw the announcement about Pearson assignments, I wrote to the Seattle WAC to see if they would like to a bid for a Pearson officer. Of course, they did and, in their request to USIA, mentioned me as a candidate. Meanwhile, I applied to USIA Personnel for that position. So, *mirabile dictu*, it came to pass in spring 1981 that I was chosen as Executive Director of the Seattle WAC on a Pearson assignment.

We again arranged to cross the Atlantic on the QEII, but with different stops en route. We flew first to Cairo, where we had friends from the late 1950s in Washington, Tom and Dee Thommasen. He was in a U.S. Navy medical research unit there; and they had a spacious rental house in Cairo's suburbs with room enough for us. During our four days there, Tom and Dee took us to see the pyramids at Giza and older pyramids farther south. We also attended the stunning nighttime light show at the Sphinx, where the Sphinx itself appears to relate its own history and that of the pyramids, while floodlights and spotlights alternately illuminate sphinx and the scene being described. Awe inspiring! We also visited a major mosque, ate at restaurants with modest prices but great atmosphere and did some light-duty shopping. Then Tom and Dee took us to the airport.

Our plane was about to leave when suddenly the P.A. system told us there had been a bomb threat and we must return to the terminal and unload and identify our luggage. We finally took off about 1½ hours late. We were nervous about the delay, because we had to connect with a London-bound flight in Athens. So, Kimie was in no mood to appreciate the view when we overflew Crete and some of the Aegean islands.

After we had secured our baggage at the Athens terminal, we still had—according to the schedule—30 minutes until our London flight's departure, so I casually asked directions to the gate. "Oh, that leaves from the other terminal," we were told. That turned out to be several miles away. Hurriedly hailing a cab outside, we explained our predicament to the driver. "Oh, then you are lucky!" the cabbie exclaimed jovially. "I drove in the Italian Grand Prix!" And he proceeded to speed off like a race driver. White-knuckle time for us, but, we arrived safely and made our flight.

In London, we had lunch with Vera Stanley. She and John had just retired to "the midlands" to live in a 17th century cottage they had bought. She came all the way in to London to see us. We also toured Warwick Castle, lunched at a 16th-century restaurant and "did" Stratford-on-Avon. Then again, we were off to Southampton and our beautiful ship.

# SEATTLE

## (1981-1982)

In Washington, D.C., the usual briefings, debriefings and physical exams (both of us passing handily this time). The personnel officer who helped set up my Pearson assignment arranged for me to visit several cities with notably strong World Affairs Councils so that I could learn how they operated and mobilized community support.

Of course, we visited Rits; but Sheila now was at the University of Puget Sound in Tacoma WA. We would see her on the other side of the US. And, we bought a car, as we planned to drive across the country again.

Our first stop on the road: Pittsburgh, where I was to meet Al Capone (Alberta Capone, that is, but familiarly called Al), executive director of the World Affairs Council there. While Kimie waited, she briefed me on how that Council recruited, trained and extensively used volunteers for its foreign visitor program and other activities. After overnighting just beyond Pittsburgh, we drove on to Cleveland, where I heard that their Council's very different setup, with much less reliance on volunteers, operated with a sizeable endowment from donations by wealthy citizens and so could keep a paid staff.

Our next destination was San Francisco. By then (1981) much of the Interstate Highway system was in place. So, we sailed along I-80 through the Midwest. We hit one stretch—maybe 10 miles—still under construction in Nebraska, where flying gravel from a truck chipped our brand new! windshield. In Wyoming, I started a detour to see the Grand Tetons and Jackson Hole, but Kimie *strongly* objected, even though we had no set schedule to meet. So, we continued into Utah, stopping beside the Great Salt Lake for lunch and a walk on the beach white with salt. On to overnight in Winnemucca, Nevada, where we began seeing the gambling & night life of that otherwise dry state. We stopped in Reno during the lunch hour for a quickie. No, not a divorce: I was not *that* upset at not seeing the Grand Tetons! A quickie go at the one-armed bandits, winning enough to pay for our lunch before heading up into the Sierras. We stopped to rest beside Lake Tahoe and then went on to San Francisco.

There I had good briefings at the World Affairs Council and Japan-America Society offices. We stayed with Mary and her husband Harry in their Berkeley home. Harry was working in the state government, inspecting public housing projects. Mary was pursuing her career as a student counselor in the Berkeley schools. Some years earlier she had divorced Al Lewis over his disapproval of her launching a new career after their children were grown. Mary had returned to Cal for an M.A. to prepare for a career as a counselor.

From the Bay Area we drove north to Fort Bragg to see eldest sister Louise & Larry Spring, now married and sharing their home with Aunt Frances. We also visited Kitty and Boyd, who lived on the coast north of town. Their acreage included "fossil" sand dunes (long stabilized by trees and vegetation) and some pastureland for Kitty's animals, which included a dozen chinchillas and a rescued wild burro!

One spin-off of that visit: Aunt Frances insisted that we take with us Rowland's 1962 Chrysler, which she had been storing with Larry Spring for me. She also gave us four antique living room chairs from their Madison home. So, for our trip to Seattle (700 miles), Kimie would drive the Cutlass and I, the Chrysler.

We took Highway 101 north to enjoy the scenic Redwood Highway. Driving among those great trees is an otherworldly experience. Then, on through Oregon and into Seattle.

For four weeks, we lived in a motel near the Seattle Center (the '62 Worlds Fair site), while I got started at the World Affairs Council. And we house hunted, working with a WAC member, a realtor who showed us homes in north Seattle. Ultimately we found a comfortable home on south Bellevue's Somerset Hill with a great view of Lake Washington, the Seattle skyline and the snowy Olympics on the horizon.

I found things at the World Affairs Council fairly flat. The office was a suite of two rooms in the mid-30's-style Mayflower Park Hotel. The Council had a 50ish widow, Martha, on salary as secretary/office manager. A hard worker, she was indispensable, for she knew all the details of the organization. The board made up about a third of the membership. The budget, not counting Martha's salary, was about $10,000. Much rebuilding was needed.

One function of USIS posts is the "foreign leaders" program—spotting up-and-coming leaders abroad who might benefit our bilateral relations by being sent on study tours to the U.S. In many American cities, the local World Affairs Council receives and handles such "international visitors," the term used within the United States. That was (and is) the case in Seattle. During 1981-82, we had perhaps eight or ten such visitors. One, a Chinese economist, was a guest at our home for Thanksgiving '81. We also had Hugh, Pat and 2½-year-old Saijo over for that big dinner. Dr. Yang greatly enjoyed the home hospitality; and we exchanged Christmas cards for the next 15 years. During those years, as US-China relations warmed up, Dr. Yang spent 2-3 years studying in the U.S. and then served on the faculty of an important Shanghai economic research institute.

The focus of my efforts with the Council was building membership and raising funds so that the Council could do broader programming. We managed to increase membership by one third. Fund-raising was not so easy. That was the "Reagan recession" year; and such donors as Boeing and Weyerhaeuser insisted they must focus on giving for "human needs" (welfare for the poor, etc.). So, we managed only a modest increase in WAC funds.

We had some notable programming successes. That year we initiated the Consular Corps Reception as a major social event that continues even now as an annual highlight of WAC programs. I also persuaded the Battelle Research Institute to co-sponsor with us a seminar on world hunger—3rd-world food shortages—a two-day event that attracted good media publicity and drew about 100 attendees, including Seattle's Mayor. One feature was a luncheon in which attendees drawing short straws received a 3rd-world lunch. Some of the short-straw people found their 3rd-world lunch unsatisfying enough that they tried to bargain with the long-straw people for a share of their food—symbolizing the need for foreign aid.

Otherwise, our programs were mostly individual speakers, for which we could attract smaller audiences of 20-30.

For me, the work was like a reverse USIS Cultural Center program, as we were bringing mostly foreign speakers and visitors to our mostly American audiences. Martha was very good at contacting people, tracking schedules, etc. About half a dozen board members provided solid help. But, we sorely needed more money and staff.

While in Seattle, Kimie and I joined the Japan-America Society and the Bellevue Sister City Association, which was affiliated with Yao, a part of Osaka. Also, Kimie was happily involved in social activities again. We had welcome visits from granddaughter Sheila, then a college junior. Of course we saw Hugh and his family a number of times. Pat gave birth to a second son, Kai, in January '82. Good timing!

A real treat was a visit by Kimie's sisters Hiroko and Sumie and Sumie's younger daughter Kaori, by then a busy piano teacher. We did some local sightseeing with them. Then I took them on a tour around the Olympic Peninsula. Kimie stayed home so that the car would not be overcrowded. I promised to take her another time. For my readers who have not done that peninsula circuit, some details.

From Bellevue, we drove north of Seattle and rode a ferry to Whidbey Island and drove up that island to the next ferry landing, which took us to Port Townsend, with the scenic northern Olympics in the background.

There at a quiet park beside the Sound we enjoyed the great picnic lunch Kimie had packed. From there we drove west through miles of fir forests on Highway 101 to Port Angeles. Then up into the mountains of Olympic National Park, climbing 5000 feet to Hurricane Ridge. From its alpine meadows we had stunning views of the inner Olympics, including 9000-foot Mt Olympus. Here and there were wild deer, very relaxed with tourists. And, a short hike up a gentle slope brought us to a ridge where we had a panoramic view of Vancouver Island, the San Juans and distant Vancouver in British Columbia. A sea haze prevented us from seeing all the way to the Pacific about 50 miles farther west. The ladies were thrilled to find a pristine summer snow bank there and happily sampled its pure snow.

We went back down the mountain to 101 and drove about 25 miles to Crescent Lake, where I had reserved an A-frame cabin at a resort on the lake's north shore—very quiet and restful. We ate dinner at the resort's restaurant, but breakfasted the next morning in our cabin on food we had brought with us. Then southwest through more miles of timber country, skirting the northwest corner of the Olympics. Then we turned off Highway 101 to drive some 18 miles into the Hoh Rain Forest, a magical spot where an average annual rainfall of 180-200 inches sustains a wonderland of greenery and moss-garlanded trees—amazing flora and fauna. This is the home base of the banana slug—yellow-green, up to eight inches long, most healthy looking and unconcerned about tourists.

We continued south on 101, with striking ocean views along the way. North of the Quinault Tribal Reservation, we stopped to walk on an unspoiled beach lined with evergreens. No other humans were in sight even though this was August. It must have seemed like the edge of the world to our visitors from crowded Japan! We stopped for lunch at the Quinault Lodge, a large, mellow early 20th century place with atmosphere and reasonable prices. It now is listed among the historic lodges of the West.

Finally, we rounded the southwest corner of the Olympics and headed east to Olympia, the state capital and then northeast through Tacoma. We stopped for a short visit with Hugh-ko and family and then returned to Bellevue, arriving home before dinnertime. A most recommendable two-day trip!

The original understanding with USIA was that my WAC assignment was one year, renewable for a second year if all parties agreed. But, USIA had a new director, Charles Wick, a Hollywood pal of Reagan, who had strong ideas of his own on many things. In June '82 he discovered the Pearson assignments and didn't like them. "The private sector is supposed to give, not receive!" he opined and vetoed any renewals. So, I had to inform the WAC directors that I must go back to Washington D.C. when my year was up. I was 55 years old and not eligible for a pension for another five years. Nor was the WAC yet in any position to offer me a salary.

On the Open Assignments list of positions opening up in Washington, I saw and applied for a policy position: countering Soviet disinformation activity. Our experiences in India, where its ties with the USSR gave the Soviets free rein in spreading disinformation, made that position appeal to me. By July, I was confirmed for the job.

We gave our Chevy Chase tenants three-months' notice of our return to our Susanna Lane home. And, we managed to sell our Bellevue home quickly. We packed out by late August, had our things sent to Maryland and stayed in a motel for our final few weeks.

We decided to drive across the continent, but this time via the Trans-Canada Highway to avoid late summer heat farther south and to see more of North America.

So, about mid-September, we drove up Interstate 5, then turned east through the North Cascades. We had a picnic lunch beside a glacier-fed river, and in the early afternoon made an ice-cream stop in Winthrop, once a very ordinary town just east of the Cascades, but now re-created as an Old West town, complete with plank sidewalks and unpainted buildings. Next, onward into the Okanogan Valley, which runs from north central Washington into Canada.

Ten miles from the border, we bought some snacks, including half a dozen apples. A mistake. At the border the Canadian Customs agent told us we must discard the apples to prevent the spread of apple maggots. Not so fast, said I to myself, and stood there and ate three of the apples (no maggots!) before chucking the rest into a covered bin.

We stayed that night in a motel beside Osoyoos Lake just over the border in Canada. A beautiful spot where we had the local trout for dinner and then walked beside the lake. I later learned that, too, was a mistake: The lake is known, by local tourist agencies, as the home of a water monster like Loch Ness's "Nessie." Close shave!

The next day, we turned east on the Trans-Canada Highway. Before leaving Seattle, we arranged with Allan Burleson to meet at a nature preserve just north of Idaho's panhandle, where he lives. We arrived about mid-day and found Allan waiting. We quickly looked over the nature preserve in marshy land beside the Kootenay River. Then in separate cars we drove to Cranbrook, where we had a late lunch and said farewell to Allan. Immediately east of Cranbrook, we turned off the Trans-Can onto Highway 93, running north toward the headwaters of the Columbia River. We overnighted at Radium Hot Springs just west of the Canadian Rockies' main massif.

The next day (our third on the road), we transited the narrow Vermillion Pass (5000 feet), then down again and on north to Lake Louise for lunch and the magnificent view of the lake with 3000-foot rock cliffs as its backdrop. Then south for a brief stop in Banff. Now we left the Rockies behind and drove through Calgary, stopping at a motel east of that city.

Now we would begin our long trek across Canada's prairie states. At Medicine Hat near the Alberta-Saskatchewan border, we again picked up the Trans-Canada and on Day 4 went into south central Saskatchewan. The land was relatively flat and featureless, but pocked with many ponds and small lakes, each with its resident ducks and other water birds. We also saw some small groups of pronghorn antelope. So, the area is somewhat more attractive than our prairie states.

On Day 5 we passed through Moose Jaw and Regina and stayed at a motel in central Manitoba. On Day 6 we transited Winnipeg and reached Kenora in time for a relaxing lunch at Canada's end of beautiful Lake of the Woods, which extends into Minnesota. Now we were in Ontario and, quite suddenly, among innumerable scenic lakes of all sizes.

On the 7th day, we briefly visited Kakabeka Falls, a fascinating cataract over ancient shale rock. By noon we were in Thunder Bay on Lake Superior (Hiawatha's Gitchigumee), had lunch and then drove all afternoon along Superior's north shore before taking a motel beside a large peaceful lake. After dinner at a nearby restaurant, we sat on our room's veranda among maples in glorious yellows, reds and oranges and listened to the eerie calls of the loons while sipping some local wine.

Day 8 took us along Lake Huron's north shore to Sudbury, where we turned south to Toronto and finally Niagara Falls—on the Canadian side. What struck us during that day's drive was that, whereas over the previous 2000-odd miles the traffic had been quite light, from Sudbury south we were in fairly heavy traffic—an indicator of how concentrated Canada's population is in its southeastern quadrant.

After checking into a motel, we strolled over to the falls for an evening meal. A misty rain had begun falling, so that we could hear the falls but not see them. At a restaurant beside the falls, we sat down for dinner. While we were eating, the mist suddenly lifted; and we faced a magical scene: those awesome falls, illuminated by colored floodlights.

We took time on Day 9 to see the falls again in daylight, rode a high Ferris wheel, which gave us a panoramic area view, and spent another night resting up from our long cross-Canada trip. On Day 10 we crossed into the U.S., bypassed Buffalo and drove into the Genesee River Valley, to see Letchworth State Park, named after one of Mother's cousins and so of personal interest for us. We then drove southeast down the Cohocton and Tioga valleys to Corning, where at day's end we toured the Corning Glass Museum. A worthwhile stop.

On Day 11 we continued east to Interstate 81 running south across Pennsylvania. We skipped a chance to revisit Carlisle and the War

College, as our target was Rits's home in Virginia's Shenandoah Valley, west of Washington, D.C., between the Blue Ridge and Allegheny mountains. Rits and her beau had purchased a Victorian-era country home there a few years earlier and furnished it with furniture of that period. From there they both commuted daily some 70 miles each way into the D.C. area. We arrived on a late September afternoon and had a good visit before continuing the next day into the D.C.

Finally back in Chevy Chase, we spent a few days in a motel again while awaiting the delivery of our household effects. Then we were back in our house.

# 2ND WASHINGTON ASSIGNMENT

## (1982-85)

We enjoyed being back on Susanna Lane and getting re-acquainted with neighbors still there after our 10-year absence (at the War College, Saigon, Tokyo, Madras, New Delhi and Seattle). I found many repairs and much maintenance needed on the house, such as replacing the old windows with dual-pane insulated windows.

Also, the back yard had become a jungle: seven tall mountain cherries, beneath them a thicket of forsythia bushes, a large black beech, and along the back property line a partly hidden and overgrown holly hedge. So, I bought a ladder, pruning shears, chain saw, handsaws, etc., and, weather permitting, began radically pruning the excess growth, taking down four of the mountain cherries. That gave us a near constant supply of firewood for the living room and family room fireplaces for the next two years.

Kimie, meanwhile, supplemented our furnishings to make the house into a home reflecting her fine decorating sense, something she could not do overseas in government quarters. I now became more fully aware of her creative genius and good taste as a homemaker. Of course, we also had some of her creations—the carved lacquer coffee table (flown out of Saigon), wall plaques, artificial flowers, etc.—to add to the furnishings we had in storage. And, we replaced an older dining set and some living room furniture. So, yard work and helping Kimie equip the house filled quite a bit of my free time during our first year back in Chevy Chase.

At the office I took on my job with zest.   It was a new position: Disinformation Response Officer in the Policy Office of USIA, headed by James Thurber III (yes, a grandson of the humorist).   A bit of explanation.

Besides the military and diplomatic US-Soviet competition during the cold war, Soviet KGB officers were busy everywhere with "active measures"—every conceivable form of trickery to deceive other nations about the nature of American society, government and policy. The US government called this "disinformation." It might be something as simple as getting a foreign journalist or newspaper, by persuasion or bribery, to run an anti-US article loaded with distortions or falsehoods about the U.S., as I had seen so often in India.  In that sense, it was not mere propaganda or simply presenting a particular viewpoint based on accepted facts.   Often their aim was to have reputable news agencies pick up a planted story so that it would become accepted as "common knowledge." Agence France Presse (AFP) was often an outlet for such KGB schemes.

Our foreign affairs agencies, including USIA, had long assumed that the free flow of information would adequately relay the truth and keep such phony stories from wide acceptance—at least in the Free World.   But, the KGB was getting better at its nefarious work. Newly independent nations (former colonies) often had inexperienced, underpaid journalists; and our Vietnam failures made many people alike distrust our government and tend to believe nasty things about us. So, we now had to forgo complacency and directly confront and expose the stream of disinformation flowing from the KGB and its friends.

Under State Department leadership, several agencies, including CIA, FBI and USIA were just then (fall 1982) creating an inter-agency working group to develop effective ways to blunt the impact of Soviet "active measures."   I was USIA's man in the group and attended biweekly meetings at State to work out strategy and tactics. Early on, we agreed that truth was our sharpest weapon for foiling the Soviet thrusts. So, I began issuing guidances to help our posts spot Soviet-inspired disinformation and work on getting the facts out.   Daily I scanned Moscow's output and summarized for our posts its ever-shifting themes so that they would recognize the Soviet "line" if it showed up in the local media.

The FBI's role was to provide the group information on "active measures" discovered in the U.S. For instance, post cards suddenly began showing up around the U.S., purportedly from Ku Klux Klan groups, associating our government with a nasty racist line on the upcoming 1984 Olympics. We could guess that the purpose was to get Africans and other "colored" races to boycott the LA games, just as Western nations had boycotted Moscow's games. Within days, the FBI gave us proof that the post cards were from no KKK group, but had been mailed from post boxes near Washington, D.C., probably by KGB men at the Soviet Embassy. We wired that to our overseas posts.

About this time, the Soviets shot down a Korean airliner off the Kamchatka Peninsula, and immediately began issuing a flurry of cover-up stories. We had many meetings on dealing with that. Ultimately, because the International Civil Aviation Organization (ICAO) did not wish to hammer the USSR about this, our team issued no formal report on the incident. But USIA allowed me to publish a chronology, "The Shootdown of KAL 007: Moscow's Charges and the Record"—the only document our government ever put out on it.

CIA's input on other cases helped expose phony KGB stories by drawing on its sources worldwide. With such facts, we could quickly shine a bright light of truth on these "active measures," helping to discredit those and much of the Soviet propaganda effort. I like to think that we helped force Gorbachev to adopt his *glasnost* (openness) policy that some five years later led to the Soviet "humpty dumpty" falling with a great cracking sound.

In November 1982, I had one more great multi-country trip. The inter-agency group, led by State's Dennis Kux, needed closer coordination with officials in Europe dealing with the same problem. So, we set off on a round of visits to European capitals: Brussels (to meet with NATO and Belgian officials), Bonn, Oslo, Stockholm and Copenhagen. Part of the group also visited London, while I went alone to brief officials in Ankara. These visits generally achieved their purpose.

I enjoyed the fringe benefit of seeing parts of Europe I had not previously visited, getting a feel for NATO headquarters, taking in Bonn's atmosphere and a Beethoven concert in the composer's home town, exploring Old Stockholm (and finding a *sushi* restaurant there!) and sampling the flavor of Turkey in Ankara. It was a unique 11 days.

Back on Susanna Lane, in spring 1983 I rented a garden plot at the end of our street to raise veggies that are best home grown. I had best luck with okra and Chinese long beans over the next two years. Later I would take okra and long-bean seeds from that plot to my next overseas post, where they also did well.

One rainy evening that spring I had an eerie experience. In a downstairs bathroom I heard frogs croaking outside the window, a below-grade window in a window well facing the back yard. I had a plastic cover over it to keep out rain, so I was puzzled. I cranked open the window and, with a flashlight, spotted two frogs eyeing me as they sat comfortably in the window well in a pool of water that was threatening to overflow into the bathroom.

Over the next few days, I tried caulking the corrugated steel well, but soon found it was too rusted out to hold. Over the next week, I had to excavate the whole window well, dig a 5-foot deep trench 25 feet long around the back of the house and install a french drain to relieve the water pressure on the window well. Good exercise for a 56-year-old. I put in a new steel well shield, double-coated it with tar and poured 4 inches of concrete around that to prevent a recurrence. Totally spoiled the romantic dreams of some frogs, I'm afraid.

In June '83, Hugh-ko and his family came for a visit, a first ever trip to the East for Pat and the two boys. A precious memory: As we exited National Airport's terminal with them, 17-month-old Kai exclaimed. "Hot!" He had never before experienced the heat and humidity common in Middle Atlantic summers.

We did some extensive sightseeing with them in the Washngton D.C. area and even to Williamsburg Virginia. Overnighting in Williamsburg, Hugh-ko and Pat went out for an evening in the reconstructed colonial capital while I stayed with the two boys and introduced them to fireflies around our motel.

That summer, Sheila, newly graduated from the University of Puget Sound, came as a most welcome occupant of our guest room while she worked as a State Department intern. After that, she took other temporary jobs while seeking work that would point toward a career. In the fall, daughter-in-law Pat's parents came for a week of sightseeing. We took them to some of the same places we had taken Hugh-ko & Co. but added other historic sites. Harold Thomas was near the end of a long career in education.

Kimie meanwhile was busy with Washington-Tokyo Womens Club activities: bridge, golf, bowling, matinee concerts at the Kennedy Center, etc. I was again doing translations for the government, as I had in 1957-60 and 1969-73. Yard and house work and tending my veggie patch gave me good exercise.

I also had the interesting experience of helping at the 1983 Economic Summit in Williamsburg. USIA officers were sent to help foreign newsmen cover the Summit. Frank Baba, a Nisei we had known since 1958 and who served with us in Tokyo, instructed me on interfacing between the White House staff and the Japanese press corps —50 to 60 strong. The fringe benefits: free meals, a VIP tour of the colonial-era buildings and a summit-end personal thank-you to the support staff from President Reagan. Also, a thank-you letter from White House Press Secretary Ron Ziegler.

Twice during my tenure in the anti-disinformation job, I was invited by the Army's psywar school at Fort Bragg, North Carolina, to talk to the school's officer students on what we knew about Soviet "dirty tricks." In spring 1984, I received an Agency award for my two years of countering Soviet disinformation.

But, the time had come for my next assignment to be set. I applied for and landed an assignment as Deputy Public Affairs Officer (DPAO) in Seoul, Korea. First, though, I had to take 10 months of Korean language and culture study.

Before starting that, one more Economic Summit for me, in London. The task this time was a little different—covering the Japanese briefings for their press contingent and then informing Ron Ziegler's office on what points they were stressing so that Ziegler would not be blind-sided should they toss him unexpected questions at his press briefings.

I used free time in London to visit the British Museum to see such rarities as the Rosetta Stone and the Elgin Marbles. I also went to the British Library, where I sought out a book Allan Burleson had told me about: a 17th century Latin grammar, *Grammatica Burlesa,* by a possible ancestor, Edward Burles. His preface in English contained remarks hinting he was unhappy with his situation. We have speculated that he later emigrated to the American colonies to become the Edward Burleson in Connecticut known as the progenitor of our Burleson line.

In July 1984, I began commuting to State's Foreign Service Institute in Arlington VA instead of to USIA headquarters. From the house I rode my bike two miles to the subway. A schoolboy again! The 10-month course consisted of one afternoon a week of Korean history, politics, etc., and 25 hours of language study. And lots of home study, of course.

Learning a new hard language at age 57 would have been too tough, but several factors gave me a boost. Paleolinguists (who trace languages back to their roots) believe the early users of proto-Japanese and proto-Korean were neighboring tribes in central Asia many millennia ago. The grammar of the two languages is very similar, and—allowing for phonetic change over the millennia—some of the vocabulary is similar. (E.g., "bear" in Korean is *kom* and in Japanese, *kuma*).

Greater similarities in vocabulary derive from the fact that, historically, Japanese and Koreans alike became literate through Chinese. Along with the difficult written characters, they adopted many Chinese words as their cultures gained sophistication under the influence of China. So, Chinese "loan words" in the two languages are similar.

In our class was a younger officer, Karl Chan, a naturalized Chinese-American originally from Hong Kong with whom I became fairly close during our Korea years. Often studying together, we would try to guess the pronunciation of a Korean word—Chan from his knowledge of Chinese and I from my knowledge of Japanese. He was more often right than I, because the Korean pronunciation is closer to the original Chinese than is the Japanese.

Also, one of our teachers was the Korean wife of a U.S. Foreign Service Officer who had lived in Tokyo for four years, studying Japanese while her husband was assigned there. So, when I had trouble understanding some aspect of Korean, she could suggest a Japanese parallel. Such factors helped me keep up with the younger officers and pass the course.

I had a few absences during that year that somewhat handicapped me. First, in November 1984, brother John died. Serving a parish in eastern Washington, he finally lost his lifelong battle with diabetes when, 10 days before his 60th birthday, his heart failed him.

Named as executor of John's estate, Hugh-ko immediately contacted me and asked that I come and help. So, I flew to Spokane, arriving in a light snowstorm. Allan Burleson had arrived earlier from Sandpoint and, with Hugh, met me at the airport. On our drive from Spokane into eastern Washington's wheat country, Hugh-ko reminded me that for several years he and John worked together making and selling signs at craft fairs around the state, and so had become quite close. With no offspring himself, John willed half his estate to Hugh-ko and left the other half to the Methodist Church. That bequest would make it possible for Hugh-ko and his family to move to the San Juan Islands, where 25 years before John had hosted 8-year-old Hugh-ko on that camping and fishing trip.

The church elders had scheduled a memorial service. One thing John had done in his short tenure there was to get a church bell donated to the church. It was not yet mounted in the steeple, but stood outside on a stanchion.

Mary flew up from California to represent the family also. The memorial service went smoothly and beautifully. The elders honored John's efforts by ringing the bell standing outside. Mary and I each spoke to the congregation. Still a counselor in the Berkeley school system, Mary had to return the next day. Sunday afternoon, Pat Burleson arrived in a rental truck with the two boys, then almost five and three. Most of John's things would go to charity or otherwise be dealt with by church members. Also, John had a library of several hundred books, which he had been loaning to church members in the small towns where he served. I kept a few that had some connection to our family.

Finally, we set off for Seattle. I drove the rental truck, with Saijo beside me, while Hugh, Pat and Kai in their car towed John's 17-foot aluminum boat. A memorable journey indeed and precious quality time with these offspring. The next day, I returned to Washington, D.C., and was back in class, having missed four days of school.

In my Christmas '84 letter, I wrote, "Near midyear we enjoyed the stage show 'Cats' at the downtown National Theater, and in December at the same theater saw Yul Brynner live in a farewell performance of 'King and I'." I also noted that "my lady with the magic hands and irrepressible spirit has been busy – chairing some of the cultural and social activities of the Washington-Tokyo Womens Club, constantly making art and craft objects for charity bazaars, friends, family, etc.; managing the home, keeping youthful with a daily half hour of stretching exercises and half hour on her exercycle, and generally gracing the world with her inner sunshine and sense of beauty."

My other absence from the Korean class was in February 1985 when suddenly I developed iritis again, this time in my right eye. I quickly went to an ophthalmologist for treatment, but could not read for 10 days while the condition persisted. After the first five days, I returned to class to keep up with what was going on, but still could not read.

In late June we all graduated. That meant packing up again in Chevy Chase. We decided Seoul would be our final overseas tour and so put our Susanna Lane home on the market. We sold it within about six weeks and otherwise cut our ties to the D.C. area, except for retaining a condo in Virginia where Sheila was then living.

# FINAL ASSIGNMENT: KOREA

## (1985-87)

In late June, we flew west, visited long-time friends in Berkeley, overnighting with sister Mary & Harry, now living in San Francisco, and enjoyed a great dinner with them and two of their daughters. We spent July 4th in Fort Bragg with Kitty and Louise's families and enjoyed the town's Frontier Days parade and lumbermen's hijinks there.

Then on to Seattle. We spent a weekend with friends from our 1981-82 Seattle sojourn, Ed and Verna Borup, whose home was just blocks from where we had lived before. Kimie and I had decided that when we retired it would be to the Puget Sound area and probably Bellevue, which we had found comfortable and congenial.

So, we began house-hunting there on Somerset Hill, with its great panoramic views. We did not really expect to find a suitable house in just two days, but soon had seen two that were possibilities. In the end, we put money down on one house, even though Kimie had doubts about it. I felt we should have our money invested in a house so that, presumably, our money from selling the Chevy Chase house could ride the market up and be protected from inflation. We authorized the realty agent to rent and manage the property.

We also visited with Hugh, Pat, their two boys and Pat's parents. Hugh & Pat took us up to the San Juan Islands to see their building lot on Orcas Island (purchased with part of John's inheritance) and visited Lopez Island, where Pat would later teach.

From SeaTac we flew to Honolulu, where we visited with Charley and Ruth James and the James children. I had briefings at the CINCPAC office dealing with Korean affairs. The USIA liaison office, headed by an old Tokyo friend, had set up my schedule in CINCPAC.

At that time, North Korea was regularly dropping propaganda leaflets on South Korea from balloons; and the psywar people at CINCPAC had a standard slide briefing on the unremitting tension between the two Koreas. The first slide: a big red "THREAT!" Heavy handed, but overall a useful introduction for my work in Seoul, where the U.S. Forces in Korea have their headquarters.

Of course we stopped (for 10 days!) in Tokyo and saw friends there and Kimie's family in Yokohama before proceeding to Seoul. Kimie's mother, then 89, had broken a leg about six months earlier, but was up and about again, even walking several blocks with us to see a shrine festival. At one point she got behind us and trotted a little to catch up!

We also took a side trip to the Science & Technology Expo at Tsukuba (70 miles NE of Tokyo), staying with Hank and Jeanne Gosho. Hank had been called out of retirement to handle the US Pavilion's public relations, because of his successful handling of the same job at the 1980 Expo in Osaka. One memorable item there: a single, huge 8-month-old tomato plant, grown hydroponically, that had borne 7,000 tomatoes.

As incoming DPAO in Seoul, I was met at Kimpo airport west of the city and escorted to the Embassy housing compound where we would be quartered. We had a temporary apartment, as the DPAO house was under renovation. Many houses in the compound dated from the Japanese era (1905-45) and so needed periodic maintenance and upgrading.

The compound was about half a mile from the Embassy and nearly a mile from the USIS offices, but the wide urban boulevards made those very walkable distances. About a half mile east and west from our housing compound were two well-preserved Yi Dynasty palaces 200 and 450 years old. Also nearby were the Korean National Museum, several great shopping streets, bookstores, etc. I found that my position would bring us free tickets to Korean concerts and other cultural events. So, besides the U.S. culture that USIS would be sponsoring, we would be exposed to much Korean culture.

My boss, CPAO Bernard Lavin (1924-2002), was an Asia hand who had earlier served elsewhere in Asia and seven years in Korea. An accomplished vocalist, Bernie, on a previous Seoul tour, had recorded a tape of his rendition of Korean songs in English and Korean. That and his natural gregariousness made him popular among Koreans.

Our ambassador was Richard ("Dixie") Walker. A Reagan political appointee, Walker had been a professor of Asian studies in South Carolina. Hence, the "Dixie" eponym. Quite conservative, he got along famously with our military in Korea.

Soon after we arrived, Lavin had me visit our branch posts: Taegu, Kwangju and Pusan. I had visited Taegu in 1970 (when our Information Officer, Bill Maurer, was BPAO there); but I needed an updating. My visits acquainted me with the BPAOs—very important as I was their supervisor and would be writing their annual evaluations. Also, I needed a feel for the situation in each region.

In ancient times, the peninsula consisted of several separate kingdoms, until the Yi kings united them into a single state about the time that Columbus sailed across the Atlantic. Even after some 500 years of political unity, local pride remained strong. That was especially true in Kwangju, once the capital of the pre-Yi state of Cholla.

A Japanese colony 1910-45, Korea was ruled with particular harshness by the Japanese military governors. So, anti-Japanese sentiment remained strong in Korea and had been fostered by Korea's postwar leaders.

Kimie felt she had to be constantly aware that Koreans of any age might be harboring enmity toward Japanese. In fact, her one encounter with anti-Japanese sentiment was vicarious. After a morning coffee party that she hosted for a group of Korean wives, one of the ladies lingered behind as the others departed. She then told Kimie in Japanese that her mother had been Japanese, "but please don't tell the others." Kimie was surprised, as she would not have guessed that. But, the incident alerted her to a psychological undercurrent in polite Korean society. At the opposite end of the spectrum was a USIS Korean employee whose mother lived in Japan in the early 1900s and attended an elite girls' school there. He felt no enmity and invited us to his home so that Kimie could meet and converse in Japanese with his mother.

Kimie herself never sensed any hostility toward herself. On the Seoul subway, indeed, she was pleasantly surprised always to be offered a seat when the trains were crowded—a custom that had long since disappeared on Japanese subways and an indication that the Confucian ethic of respect for age remained strong in Korea.

Since the early 1960s, military dictators had suppressed political dissent and civil rights, claiming national security required it. With a North Korean army of almost one million only 35 miles from Seoul on the other side of the DMZ, such arguments were not easily countered. Not long before we arrived, a North Korean soldier had defected across the DMZ and told Korean and U.S. commanders that the North had dug 10 or more tunnels under the DMZ to make a surprise invasion of the south easier. U.S. and South Korean searchers subsequently found and neutralized only three of these.

When the South exposed this perfidious violation of the 1953 truce, Pyongyang's brash propagandists claimed that the tunnels were merely old Japanese coalmines. Of course, there was no coal in the area, all the drill marks were angled from the north and the tunnels were just the size for running the North's jeeps through. So, the atmosphere at the DMZ remained palpably tense. In booming Seoul itself, North Korea was evident only from the occasional balloon-borne propaganda leaflets that drifted down into our gardens.

Meanwhile consumerism flourished in Seoul and other major cities. The East Gate, South Gate and Itaewon markets were warrens of countless shops selling all sorts of goods cheaply—mostly seconds and overruns of items ordered for the U.S. market. So, we loaded up on clothing, stainless-steel flatware, etc. (My hoard of excellent Korean cotton socks would last for the next 12 years.) Enterprising furniture dealers scoured the countryside for traditional Korean furniture, restored it and sold it to us eager Americans for about what we might have to pay for the cheapest particle-board furniture in the U.S.

Korean art students were copying old paintings to turn out well-executed folding screens and art scrolls. Korean ceramists had helped establish fine porcelain-making in Japan four centuries earlier when warlord Hideyoshi's troops took them forcibly to Kyushu. Heirs of potters who had avoided that fate still turn out beautiful work in Korea, some of which we bought—vases especially.

After I had been in Seoul just three months, Lavin and I faced a problem: An occupation of our cultural center in Kwangju by radical students. That was ended within 24 hours when the police moved in. Our problem was our American center director, who complained that the ambassador's okay for the police to go in had violated his (the center director's) "lifelong commitment to nonviolence." He later proved so emotionally volatile that we had to persuade him to end his assignment prematurely. He soon went back to academic life in California.

After six months in Seoul, Kimie and I took a weekend trip to Kyongju, the capital of the Silla Kingdom (57 BC to 938 AD—a millennium!). Tumulus tombs of Silla's royalty stand conspicuously in a 5-square-mile area of the city. Chambers inside those 30- to 40-foot mounds, like those in Egypt's pyramids, were stuffed with treasures for the rulers' afterlife. Many such items now fill museums in Kyongju and Seoul. Of special interest are the similarities between these burial mounds and the burial mounds of Japan's emperors from the 3rd and 4th centuries AD (Japan's "Tumulus Era"). In Kyongju are also stone structures from some 1300-1800 years ago, including a 30-foot astronomical observatory tower.

As in Japan, we had full access to US commissaries and PXs for food, clothing, etc. These were a huge draw also for Korean wives of U.S. servicemen. One amazing occurrence while we lived in Seoul showed that tunneling was a skill not limited to North Koreans: A tunnel was found running into a Korean neighborhood from a US commissary warehouse in south Seoul. We never heard how much inventory had "leaked" out that way.

Due to heavy-handed domestic security, popular resistance to the military regime was subdued—except by university students and some labor groups. Student demonstrations were common, and the police routinely suppressed them with tear gas and batons. A photo that characterized those years caught a riot policeman beating a handicapped student with his own crutch. We learned to avoid pedestrian underpasses the day after such events, for they still reeked enough of tear gas to sting one's eyes. Rising anti-Americanism among radical students led us in USIS to put out a monthly tabloid-size newspaper aimed at the more moderate students, to give them material for dealing with the radicals. Starting at 20,000 copies, it was popular enough that we had to increase the distribution to 30,000.

After we had been in Seoul about a year, Bernie Lavin retired, to be replaced by John Reid, who had been in Korean language training almost from the time of our arrival. Reid was different. A confirmed bachelor, he had previously served in Saigon, Thailand and Lebanon (at the time of the terrorist bombing of our Beirut embassy and the Marine barracks). In Southeast Asia, he developed an interest in houseplants. During his first few months, he asked me to guide him to Seoul's plant nurseries south of the Han River.

I soon found that John's botanical ardor was offset by a social coldness reminiscent of the herpetic nature I saw earlier in Brement in Jakarta and Saigon. Even his barhopping was pursued with cool intensity. At parties and receptions, he would chitchat, but never seemed to relax. He appreciated Kimie's charm and social skills; but I did not succeed in staying close to him. In the office, he often bypassed me to deal directly with the Information Officer, Cultural Officer and the branch-post PAOs.

Three times while we were in Korea, Kimie and I joined group tours—to a hot spring resort in the south, to the mountains and to the DMZ. Separately, I also escorted visiting Americans to the DMZ a few times, descending also into one of the North Korean tunnels. ROK officers led those tunnel excursions down a steep access path.

In August 1986, Kimie and I took Stateside leave to visit Hugh-ko and his family on Lopez Island in the San Juans. We were charmed once more by our two grandsons—Saijo, now 7 and Kai, 4. While there, we went with Hugh-ko's family to nearby Orcas Island for sightseeing and dinner at the Rosario Resort. Scanning the dessert menu after we finished the main course, Pat read the list to Kai. When she read "strawberry shortcake," Kai exclaimed, "Oh, I'll have that! I read about it in a book." (Meaning Pat had read to him about it.) And, when the dessert was set in front of him, in a stemmed goblet heaped with whipped cream, his eyes bugged out. I scrambled for my camera and barely got it out in time to catch his expression.

Returning from that trip, Kimie and I easily agreed that we had been overseas long enough. I had served under some very good CPAOs; but my luck now seemed exhausted. Now 67, Kimie had soldiered on for over a quarter century as a Foreign Service wife, not always living in places or houses she would choose to. Our visit to the San Juans, especially, made us sense keenly how much of our descendants' lives we were missing. Rits had been promoted in her stock brokerage office to a position that gave her a private office. Sheila was now in a career as a sales lady in office software. And. I was nearly eligible for a pension and "maxed out" on how much I could add to that pension. It was about time to say goodbye to the Foreign Service.

Returning to Seoul via Japan , we took a KAL flight from Narita. Only after boarding did we learn the plane would first stop in Pusan. As the plane prepared to land there, we were ordered to pull down the window shades "for security reasons," i.e., to keep passengers from seeing whatever defense facilities were there. Not long after that North Korean commandos from a submarine were detected landing north of Pusan and were hunted down over the next 10 days. Soon after our return, I told John Reid I would retire in late 1987.

We had many interesting experiences in that final 14 months of service to our country. We gave parties for up to 70 guests at a time. Kimie arranged for kitchen help and a bartender (a Mr. Kim) for such occasions. We had a new ambassador in Seoul: James Lilley, who would later be US ambassador to China. He had lived in China as a child while his father worked for Standard Oil. In the '90s, news programs sometimes carried his comments on Northeast Asia; and he recently published his memoirs, *China Hands*, recounting his career as a CIA agent and a protégé of George H.W. Bush.

Late in our tour, Kimie and I had a visit from Sumie and Hiroko and enjoyed showing them Seoul, Kyongju and other interesting places around Korea.

In our final year, Richard Nixon visited Seoul, part of his "rehabilitation" efforts. Of course, Ambassador Lilley threw a reception for him. I attended, but declined to join the embassy officers lined up to shake Nixon's hand.

I have not so far mentioned a duty that commonly falls on Foreign Service posts: assisting "Codels" (Congressional delegations) when they visit on fact-finding missions (or "junkets"). In one case, we had a Codel of senators and a Codel of congressmen arriving in Seoul within a day of each other. Almost all substantive officers (as distinguished from administrative officers, communication tech, etc.) were enlisted to assist.

As usual, USIS had to arrange a press conference for the visitors. An amusing episode there: One savvy Korean newsman asked, "What is the special significance for Korea of two such high-level delegations coming here at the same time?" Senator Allan Simpson looked around at his colleagues and then said, "No particular significance. In fact, we didn't know until we arrived that a House delegation was coming. On the Hill, we have separate travel offices; and I guess they don't communicate with each other."

Years earlier in Tokyo, I was assigned to assist a Codel that included Ed Muskie and served as his "control officer"—a decidedly good experience, for he and his wife were fine, undemanding people. A few years later when they came again, Mrs. Muskie was struck by phlebitis; and Kimie and I visited her and Senator Muskie at the Zama Army Hospital (where I was once a patient). Another time, I was control officer for a senior congressional staff member. When his official business was finished, he had me accompany him to a landscape supply company to buy a large stone lantern, and then finagled to have the Embassy pay the shipping costs.

In Seoul, I had contacts with Korean alumni of UC Berkeley, including a cultural anthropologist, Professor SOHN Pow Key, whom we had known in Berkeley as a grad student in the early 1950's. Another academic contact was Prof. LEE Tae Dong, who 30 years earlier had been a student of, and inspired by my cousin Mary Patterson when she and her husband were Fulbrighters in Korea. We became good friends with Professor Lee and his wife and have remained in contact with them ever since.

As the time neared for my departure, we gave parties for our closer Korean contacts, and were given farewell parties by CPAO Reid and our Korean employees. Those were generally fun, but I knew Reid was glad to see me go, so that he could name a deputy of his own choosing.

In Seoul, I completed the details of retiring from federal service—38 years altogether, including my brief military "career." At the Embassy consular section on December 3, 1987, we got our new non-diplomatic passports and winced as holes were punched in our black diplomatic passports to cancel them.

What had I accomplished since starting with USIA 31 years earlier? I had grown as a person, shaking out some weak spots in my makeup. I had played a small role in helping my fellow professionals and many visiting Americans better understand our Japanese ally. I had encouraged Kimie to continue developing her skills in many areas. And she had not only given many friends and others a very positive image of the modern Japanese, but had ably assisted several ambassadors' wives. From writing hundreds of reports and cables to the satisfaction of senior diplomatic officers, I had honed my writing skills. (Hope you readers agree.) We had seen many areas of the world. And, I believe that, as a team, we contributed to better trans-Pacific understanding, which we now hoped to continue doing at home in the USA.

*Rug cutters in Saigon - 1974*

*Partying on Saigon River - 1974*

*Kimie and her mother in Sendai - 1977*

*Sheila and friend in Mendocino - 1978*

*With Hugh-ko and Pat - 1980*

*With grandson Saijo - 1980*

*Agra - 1981*

*All aboard the QE2 - 1981*

*Grandsons Saijo and Kai - 1985*

*We two in Seoul - 1985*

*Seoul - with PAO Bernie Lavin - 1985*

*Seoul - with PAO John Reid - 1985*

# PART IV:
# SILVER RETIREMENT

# RETIRED CITIZENS

## (1987-1989)

From the time we left Berkeley in 1956, I had focused on advancing my career in USIA. We lived where the career took us. As the Foreign Service during those years did not permit wives of their Foreign Service husbands to hold real jobs while overseas, Kimie, despite her many talents, could not develop a career nor live where she wanted to. Now she was 68. So, as we arrived at SeaTac International Airport, I told my lady that now she would be my prime focus—the things she wanted to do, the way she wanted to live would be my top priorities.

She had performed magnificently in our 31 years with USIA. In dozens of ways, she had helped the diplomatic missions where we served and embodied the openness of America. She had become a multi-cuisine cook. She knew how to assure that our guests had a wonderful time and enjoyed themselves and her bright, engaging personality. And, she was a great money manager. I was confident we would have great "golden years" together.

Kimie followed her usual practice, when settling into a new home, of contacting the local Newcomers Club and joining in their social activities. She would walk confidently into a room of strangers with a big smile and cheery "Hi! I'm Kimie!" People could not but accept her warmly. They soon learned she had a great sense of humor, was an excellent bridge player, could play the Japanese or international versions of mah jongg and was a good bowler and fair golfer. The homes she created were always interesting to visit.

She still had a warm place in her heart for Berkeley, but was content to settle in Bellevue, where the cool climate and beautiful setting suited her well. Still, she remained negative about the house we bought in 1985 in south Bellevue. Its floor plan was a long rectangle, which she characterized as *unagi no nedokoro* (an eel's nest)—i.e., too long and narrow, even with its adequate 2700 square feet and excellent view—lake, city and mountains—(toward which the house was oriented).

So, I set about making it more to Kimie's liking. We had daughter-in-law Pat's brother help us repaint the interior. He was between jobs and recently divorced from a wife with whom he had run an interior decorating business. Over the next two years, I put some $40,000 in improvements in the house: new dual-pane windows throughout, vinyl siding outside, new wood paneling in the dining room, new carpets in the living room and dining room, and central air conditioning. I built finished storage space in the lower level with two walk-in closets, and had a forced-air blower installed in the downstairs fireplace to reduce heating costs. We had the kitchen totally done over. I dolled up the garage a bit, too. After all that, Kimie still disliked the house. Despite the panoramic views and despite its location in a prime Bellevue neighborhood.

We involved ourselves again in the activities of the Bellevue Sister City Association, the Japan-America Society and the World Affairs Council in Seattle. Kimie renewed contacts with her friends of 5-6 years earlier, occasionally played some golf and found friends with whom to pursue social interests and sports. She felt liberated not to have to give parties in our home for people she did not know, as she had during our 27 years in the Foreign Service. Now she gave fun parties for her friends and generally began enjoying retired life.

At perhaps the first party we held in our home after retiring, I was sitting and talking with friends when Kimie urgently signaled to me from the kitchen door.

"What's the problem?" I asked out loud without getting up.

"You are. Refill their drinks!" she ordered.

Mischievously referring to our practice in Seoul, I asked, "Where's Mr. Kim?"

"You are Mr. Kim!" she shot back. That brought down the house, and properly activated me.

I resumed translating for the government again, this time with the aid of a home computer whose 30MB hard drive now seems primitive—no color, slow, word-processing only, with a noisy daisy-wheel printer. But, it easily beat out my old manual typewriter.

We were just a few hours' drive from Hugh-ko and his family on Lopez Island, where Hugh-ko had his own sign-making company and had begun serious scuba-diving—some of it commercial, for *uni*—sea-urchin eggs for sushi. He found that the island waters also had delicious medium-sized abalone, oysters, bay scallops and of course Dungeness crabs. Fishing and clamming were fairly good around the islands. So, relying on his boat from Uncle John, he was reaping much of their seafood needs from the surrounding waters. And, he learned to smoke the salmon he caught, better than any store-bought smoked salmon (and without the saltiness of lox).

Seeing that many island fishermen were throwing away the roe of the salmon they caught, he arranged for them to bring it to him. He would freeze it and bring it down for Kimie to process into great salmon caviar whenever he came to Bellevue. Enough for all of us.

In 1989, a group of people, centering on Bellevue Sister Cities (BSCA), started a "Japan Week in Bellevue" with help from area businesses and the Japanese Consulate General. Exhibitors and people interested in Japan put on events and displays at Bellevue Square, the city's finest shopping mall. I got involved as a committee member. One way the Japan Week committee raised funds was by a raffle with the grand prize a round trip for two to Japan—upgradeable to business class. Well, Kimie won that. So, we had tickets, which we gladly used in March 1990 to visit the family in Yokohama and friends in Tokyo.

In about May 1989, a USIA couple we had known in Seoul—Doug and Pat Baker—invited us to visit them in Spokane, where they had settled after retiring. We had not been to the eastern side of the state since 1963 and so took them up on it. We took I-90 across the Cascades and into the farm country of the state's eastern half and the ponderosa country around Spokane. Finally, 270 miles from Bellevue, Spokane itself, a comfortable city of about 200,000 surrounded by hills and mountains. Doug and Pat's home was on a hill overlooking the Spokane Valley six miles east of the city proper.

Over supper at the Bakers' home, we were discussing houses—theirs and ours—and Kimie unloaded about her dissatisfaction with our home on Somerset Hill. "So, let us show you a very special house just up the street," Pat urged. We had no intention of moving to Spokane, but saw no harm in seeing the house.

Doug called their agent, Pat Porter, and arranged for her to show us the house. It was walking distance, and we met the agent in front of the house that same evening. Or rather, at the bottom of the house's driveway, for the house was set back from the road and some 25 feet above it, up a curving 2-lane 125-foot asphalt driveway flanked by trees, a lawn and rock outcroppings.

Pat Porter explained that this 5,600ft² house was 10 years old and sat on 2.6 acres, about half in ponderosa pines. We began to see that this was indeed as special as Doug and Pat had said. On a 25x35-foot concrete parking pad outside the house's built-in 3-car garage (three separate doors) Pat Porter told us more. The owners became rich from their gift shops in Anchorage, including the one at Anchorage airport which drew so many Japanese tourists when we were there. So, one could say the house was built with Japanese money.

We went in. The basic footprint was octagonal so that the house could wrap around a stunning indoor 43-foot swimming pool. Clear cedar planking lined the walls of the pool area from its tiled deck up to and including the ceiling two stories above the pool. I would later understand that this unfinished cedar helped absorb humidity when the pool's plastic cover was open.

Four large skylights, six ceiling-mounted floodlights, ten pairs of dual-glazed sliding doors and several 2nd-floor windows helped light the pool area, not to mention floodlights on the lower walls and an underwater floodlight. Two large exhaust fans in the ceiling helped remove any excess humidity when the pool was in use. On the walls at pool level were three sections of rough lava stone between the cedar plank walls. A walkway (or catwalk) 110 feet long encircled the pool area at the 2nd floor level. The pool itself was an elongated bean shape with light blue underwater surfaces, had a diving board over the 8-foot deep end and a separate soaking spa in one corner. The surrounding deck was patterned ceramic tile. The overall effect was stunning.

The rooms were large: upstairs a 25-foot living room with lava-rock fireplace, a dining room, a family room with wet bar and Franklin stove. The kitchen had a beamed ceiling, abundant cabinets, dinette space, brick alcove for the oven/stove, a large center island with a beverage sink and Jennair grill. A separate laundry plus lavatory opened off the kitchen.

On the other side of the upstairs: a guest bedroom with full bath and a 26-foot master suite with large walk-in closet, soaking tub, two washbasins, a lavatory and double shower. Off the catwalk was a wide space for a housewife's home office. Downstairs: two more bedrooms, a ¾ bath, a poolroom (with a 2nd wet bar and pool table), utility room (pressure pump, two furnaces, water softener and the pool's 2KW heater, water pump and sand filter), the 3-car garage and a shop, plus the pool area, which had a 3rd wet bar. All materials were good quality and the decor tasteful.

In front of the house was a large 3-tier redwood deck. A smaller side deck overlooked a large south lawn, while a third deck in back was designed for barbecue parties. Wrought-iron grills guarded all ground-floor windows and sliding doors. The front door had grillwork and double wrought-iron screen doors so formidable that cousin Allan Burleson later would call that the "portcullis," as if it were a castle gate.

Feeling some sensory overload, we asked about price, expecting a figure far out of our reach. Pat said it originally was $350,000, but had been reduced to $320,000. We were amazed. In the Seattle area such a house would have cost perhaps three times that. We guessed our current home (on which we had only a small mortgage) would fetch some $260,000-270,000. So, this fabulous Spokane mansion was not really beyond our means.

Kimie's eyes were sparkling. "I love this house!" she exclaimed. "But, I think we should see some other homes, too, for comparison." Pat Porter agreed to show us several other homes on the same hill and south of the valley the next day.

That night, I asked Kimie if she really would consider leaving Bellevue. "You know I don't like our present house," she said. "We never had a house I really loved. I love the house we saw tonight, if we can afford it."

The next day Pat Porter showed us four other houses in the $250,000-$320,000 range. None could hold a candle to the first house. We saw the house again in the daylight and were even more convinced we should bid on it. Kimie said, "If we can get this house, I wouldn't mind living here until I die." So, before returning to Bellevue, we asked Pat Porter to sound out the owners on price. We were thinking of offering $280,000. She doubted they would go that low. "Ten years ago, the construction cost was $275,000, and you know how much inflation we've had since then," she said, "but I'll ask."

So, we returned to Bellevue and our panoramic view on Somerset hill. A real estate agent estimated the selling price for our house: $280,000. Of course, commissions, our mortgage balance, moving costs, etc., would reduce our net from the house. So, we would still need a small mortgage, but decided to try for the Spokane house.

We expected the 4½-hour driving time from Seattle to Spokane would not be a big barrier to visits from Hugh-ko and his family. If they came visiting 2-3 times a year and we visited them 2-3 times a year, we would see them as often as we did in Bellevue. And, for Rits and Sheila flights to Spokane would not be significantly less convenient.

We reached a compromise of $300,000 on the Spokane house and got the owners to agree to take back a second mortgage of $60,000 to help cover our selling and moving costs. Then we plunged into selling the Somerset house and preparing to move.

After two months of intensive effort, we nailed a buyer—an accountant for Microsoft. That early in Microsoft's existence, he did not draw a great salary and so asked *us* to take back a second mortgage. As this was our first solid offer, we reluctantly agreed. The next day, when we were working out details with our agent, a young Chinese couple came to the front door. "We want to buy your house," the man said. We invited them in, but told them we already had a contract. "We will pay your asking price and all cash up front," the couple urged.

"But, you haven't looked at the house! How do you know you want it?" I asked. It turned out they had driven by the previous day with the man's mother; and she had *ordered* them to buy the house. Now she was in the hospital for surgery, but said they must return and buy the house. We consulted our agent, who said we could only accept that offer if we could get our current buyers to back out. After several days of maneuvering, our buyers were hanging on like bulldogs, refusing to give up. We were stuck with them and the disadvantageous sale.

# GOLDEN SPOKANE YEARS

## (1989-95)

In late September 1989 we moved to Spokane (elevation: about 2000 feet, but about 2200 feet at our house). Climate about like inland northern California's. Sister cities in Japan, China, Germany, the USSR and Ireland. Site of Gonzaga University, Whitworth College, the Community Colleges of Spokane and Eastern Washington University (actually about 15 miles to the southwest).

Spokane began in the 19$^{th}$ century as the hub of the "Inland Empire"— eastern Washington and its wheat fields and northern Idaho and its metal mines and timber. It grew up around Spokane Falls on the Spokane River—power for the city's nascent industries. Soon 4-5 major railroads came through. In the early 1970s, Spokane overhauled its downtown area in preparing for its 1974 world's fair. It ripped out abandoned rail yards, created an attractive riverside park and began making itself over as a modern city.

In Spokane and the valley, Kimie again joined in activities for newcomers and began building a network of friends: several bridge groups, a gourmet dining group, seniors' bowling, a poker group, the Northwood neighbors dinner group, Spokane Symphony Associates and Spokane Mushroom Society. We also joined the Spokane-Nishinomiya sister city organization, founded by one Ed Tsutakawa and a mayor of Spokane. Ed has often been called Spokane's "shadow mayor," as his network of contacts involved him in many civic groups. Ed is a Nisei, who spent some of his school years in Nishinomiya and so was well qualified to serve as a bridge between the two cities. I like to call him "Mr. Japan in Spokane," as that was a major role he played. He and his wife Hide (which she pronounces like Heidi) helped introduce us to Spokane's cultural and social scene.

In 1990, Ed also introduced me to a firm of Spokane patent lawyers, who began sending me Japanese patents for translation. Over the next 12 years, I probably translated over 200 patents for them plus about a 100 more for a client of theirs, MICRON Technologies of Boise.

In fall 1990, I read in the *Spokesman-Review* of a temporary teaching position coming open in the social science department of Spokane Falls Community College. I applied and landed the job: one year teaching a course on American politics three days a week, subbing for a professor on sabbatical. The following school year, I heard that Gonzaga University needed a teacher of beginning and 2nd-year Japanese. So, I took that one, too. I had about ten students in each class, and enjoyed leading them in the adventure of learning Japanese. Near the end of the first semester, a poli sci professor asked me also to teach a course in that department. I agreed to teach a semester course on US-Japan relations. This was the era of "Japan bashing," so that we had much new material to work over. In 1992-93, I taught courses on US-Japan relations and Japanese culture in the Community Colleges' seniors program (non-credit courses at community centers in the city), averaging 15 students per class. All this fitted well with our lifelong mission of contributing to better trans-Pacific understanding.

Kimie was making the most of our great Spokane home. Besides her usual daily half-hour stretching exercises and hiking about 20 minutes around our property (or, in bad weather, around the pool-area catwalk), she set up her exercycle in the family room, where she would pedal the equivalent of several miles while watching TV. We had discovered "TV-Japan"—a satellited TV service that helped us stay current on Japan (including sumo tournaments and cooking shows). Kimie often did water aerobics in our pool—jogging back and forth in chest-deep water—in lieu of her walking exercise. My Christmas letter in 1990 said: "The result is severely retarded aging. She looks gr-r-reat! If anyone is well described by 'she doesn't get older—she just gets better,' it is this lady."

That fall, mainly through Ed Tsutakawa's efforts, Mukogawa Women's University of Nishinomiya opened a branch campus in Spokane. The college bought the Fort Wright campus—an early 20th century Army base, later the Holy Names College for women. The site was somewhat run down, as the Catholic sisters had lacked funds for its upkeep. Mukogawa, incorporated as Mukogawa-Fort Wright Institute, did several million dollars of refurbishing and building during its first five years to create a beautiful campus on the bluff above the Spokane River just west of the city. Ed became its general administrator. Each semester, 150-200 girls majoring in English take intensive American studies and English classes there and find ways to interact with the community. (By 2005, 4,000 girls had studied there.)

The school also turned one of the original buildings into a Japanese Cultural Center for Spokane's general public, offering exhibits and courses in language, Japanese cooking, etc. Large meeting rooms in another building remained available for rental by community groups for parties and meetings.

About this time, Whitworth College in north Spokane initiated a series of Japan-related lectures and programs. There I chaired a panel on "Japanese Perceptions of America." Ed Tsutakawa, some others and I later persuaded Whitworth to expand that the following year into a "Japan Week in Spokane," with related activities at Mukogawa and the city libraries. This grew into a continuing citywide spring event, with support from many local groups, joined by the Japanese-American community and Japanese exchange students at local colleges and universities. Mukogawa provides the venue during that week for a family-oriented cultural fair where children can practice origami, calligraphy, etc., and visit the Cultural Center and its hands-on display of Japanese toys.

An amazing coincidence (besides my again being associated with Nishinomiya, where my Japan experience all began): The academic dean for MFWI, Dr. Hiroshi Takaoka, and his wife Michiko are former

Fulbrighters. She hails from Kobe, while he is from Nagaoka in Niigata Prefecture (where Hugh-ko and I witnessed the 3-foot firework fired off in 1962). Hiroshi was one of the students I helped screen for his Fulbright grant in 1962! Now three decades later we were meeting again.

Soon after coming to Spokane, Michiko Takaoka learned that the Cowles Museum there had a large Japanese doll that was presented to the city's school children in 1927 as part of a US-Japan doll exchange. Checking further, she found that this exchange had brought 58 such dolls to schools across the USA and had sent many American dolls to Japanese schools. Intrigued, Michiko almost single handedly, revived the exchange and made it a feature of Mukogawa's celebration of Doll's Day each year. So, dolls are again being donated throughout each country. Continuing her study over the years, Mrs. Takaoka has located 44 of the original 58 Japanese dolls and has published a book about them: *Ningyo Taishi*—Doll Ambassadors.

In 1992, another coincidence: Lopez School, where daughter-in-law Pat taught and which our two grandsons Saijo and Kai were attending, was selected to get two of the dolls from the revived exchange. Michiko-san did not know of the connection. Pat came to Spokane with Kai and two other students to attend the ceremony and receive the dolls on behalf of the school. Of course, they overnighted with us.

That summer, because she had long led teachers' workshops on teaching about Japan, Pat was chosen to join other social studies teachers from Washington state for an all-expenses visit to our Japanese "sister state," Hyogo Prefecture (capital: Kobe). She also visited Kimie's family in Yokohama. In subsequent years, she would return to Hyogo several times and serve on the Washington state committee planning the return visits by Hyogo teachers. In 1993 she, Hugh-ko and the two boys made a similar trip to Japan on their own. Good inheritors of the mission Kimie and I had set for ourselves decades ago.

In 1992 I was elected President of the Spokane-Nishinomiya Sister City Society, a position I held for 3½ years. So, my community involvements were expanding. That fall, our sister city group was invited to participate in the "Global Business Opportunities Convention," hosted by the Osaka Chamber of Commerce. Ed Tsutakawa put together an 8-person team to represent Spokane at the convention. He assigned me the task of presenting Spokane as a good destination for Japanese students wishing to study abroad. So, I visited all our local colleges and obtained their brochures and other materials relevant to exchange students. The other themes we would push were investment, trade and tourism. We planned to reserve just a single booth, but our friends in the Nishinomiya Chamber of Commerce kicked in enough to give us a double booth.

We each paid our own air fare and hotel charges; but our travel agent gave us a very sweet deal because Japan Airlines was ending its Seattle→Tokyo service: $700 for the round trip on JAL, upgraded to business class. Also, a $100 gift certificate. And, because JAL could not get us a connecting flight to Osaka on arrival, an airport hotel coupon including dinner and breakfast. We would be in Osaka two nights for the 3-day event and then spend one night in Nishinomiya. Kimie chose not to go.

The convention went very well for us. Few of the hundreds of people coming by our booth had ever heard of Spokane; and we were one of only two US cities there with its own booth. So, we helped make Spokane known. We sparked interest in Spokane as a sightseeing destination (golfing, fishing, skiing opportunities, etc.), but few queries about students matriculating in the Spokane area. So, I had many college brochures left over and took them to the USIS American Center in Osaka as future handouts.

On the side, we heard Sony president Morita give an inspiring speech on global trade. I roomed with Ed, and so got better acquainted with this man who was in many ways my mentor in Spokane. We had a great visit in Nishinomiya, touring Mukogawa Womens University, its affiliated high school and a Frank Lloyd Wright building now owned by Mukogawa. We also visited the Nishinomiya (Shinto) Shrine, where the chief priest was a former classmate of Ed's.

Afterward, I went to Yokohama to visit Kimie's family, including her mother, then living with Sumie's son. But, it was very good to get back to Kimie after an absence of 8-9 days. The lawns needed mowing, too.

In November '92, we had our first significant snowfall—8 inches. Through that winter we had repeated snows, with no thawing in between. All told, we got 83 inches of snow that winter, with a pack of about 28 inches by season's end. Lots of plowing for me with the heavy-duty snowplow that came with the house: 2500 square feet of driveway and parking space. Also, with a snow shovel, I cleared a path to the mail box (125 feet), around the house (240 feet), and shoveled the three decks (about 400 square feet). So, each snowfall meant a good two-hour workout for me.

Toughest was clearing our roof, a nearly flat expanse of about 2400-square feet. The attic below the roof was well braced, but I was not sure how much snow it could support. So, in February I went up with my snow shovel and began dumping snow over the edge. That took about 12 hours of heavy labor over the course of a week.

In early December '92, we visited Rits and her offspring in the Washington D.C. area. Sheila was doing well in her job and had bought a home in suburban Virginia, where we stayed. She also had re-established ties with her brother Ray, who was now married and whom we now could get to know. He and Sara had a 3-year-old son Brian and 16-month-old daughter, Amy, who already was displaying a feisty personality reminiscent of Kimie's. We were utterly charmed. Brian was (and is) quieter, and tended to concentrate on his models and electronic toys and games. One Saturday evening, Kimie and I baby-sat the kids while Ray and Sara went out. Trying to put Amy to bed, I seemed to do everything wrong, as she explained to me in great detail—in a quite unintelligible tongue while she threw a mighty tantrum.

Back in Washington State, we went to Lopez Island for Christmas with our West Coast offspring. A 650-mile round trip from Spokane, but worth every minute.

Each year, a sister-city delegation from Nishinomiya came to join in Spokane's May Lilac Festival, usually riding in the evening Lilac Parade. We hosted them individually in our homes during their 3-day stay, and our Sister City Society threw a Western party on the last night of their visits. We always had a local singing cowboy there and live music for dancing. And, we proudly showed them the Nishinomiya Garden in a major city park, the Mukogawa campus and other sights.

In spring 1993, I was asked by the Washington State Malt Commission to interpret for them for a few days. They explained that Japanese brewers buy most of their malt (made from barley) from Canada; but our Malt Commission wanted to introduce them to our local malt. I agreed to interpret. The Commission's guests represented Sapporo Beer, Asahi Beer and Kirin Beer. The first day, we visited farms growing barley and other grains in the greater Spokane area, so that the Japanese could get an idea of the state's productive capacity. The second day we visited Washington State University to see the experimental fields and research labs there.

That summer, I had a more unusual interpreting request, from a woman who, with her partner, held 4-day "vision quest" camps. They had been doing these vision quests for a decade or more, but this year had six Japanese clients. This is, of course, a Native American practice, where young Indians were coached to seek self-understanding by purifying themselves in a smoke house and then undergoing a period of fasting alone in an isolated wild place until they had a vision that brought them a kind of enlightenment.

The camp was outside of Spokane in hills where there were indications (petroglyphs) that local Indians had done vision quests there before white men came. Several buildings there provided us with decent living quarters. The two women leaders set up a tepee, though, for discussion sessions before sending the participants off by themselves. The Japanese all had had recent life crises, such as a divorce, job loss or simply doubts about the course of their life. My job was to interpret, not to fully participate in the quest.

In summer 1994, I again assisted at the vision quest camp. The evening of the concluding day a program was being held in Spokane that all at the camp were interested in: a *taiko* performance in one of Spokane's best theaters. The performers: Ondekoza (Devil Drum Troupe) from Sado Island off Niigata. To publicize the performance, they had paraded at noon through Riverside Park with their biggest drum (8 feet long, 4½ feet in diameter, 250 pounds).

Kimie and I met this unique troupe a year earlier when they came through Spokane and were put up for the night at the local Buddhist temple. They had no Spokane performance, but played a few pieces on small drums, a bamboo fife, etc. We sometimes attended the services at the temple and so were invited to the impromptu potluck dinner the temple held for them. There we heard the amazing story of their tour.

They had flown into Seattle and were headed for Carnegie Hall. They had a rented minibus and truck for transportation; but as part of their training some troupe members at all times were running, not riding. They had some performances scheduled across the northern tier of states and hoped also to line up performances down the East Coast. When we saw the troupe in 1994, we heard the full story. They indeed performed in Carnegie Hall, after doing several gigs en route. They had performed in Philadelphia, Washington and down the coast to Florida, then west across the southern tier, and finally all the way up the West Coast—a full circuit of the USA. With some members running the whole way!

It is difficult to describe such a taiko performance. Extraordinarily dynamic, usually with drums of all sizes in concert with a *shichiriki* (bamboo fife) and *shakuhachi* (bamboo flute). When the biggest drum is struck, you feel the impact in your gut. A never to be forgotten experience.

In 1994, our Group Health doctor, Dr. Kearney, diagnosed Kimie (75) with diabetes, but kept it controlled with oral medications. By then, she had seen two bridge partners die of old-age illnesses. We were well cared for medically, as Group Health could, as needed, refer us to the region's best hospital. In late '93 I had a hemorrhaging ulcer, caused by the aspirin I was taking to help keep my heart in shape. Had to have emergency surgery for, without my knowing it, I had lost a fair amount of blood.

So, Kimie began feeling we were physically vulnerable. Moreover, in the five years we had lived in Spokane, our visits back and forth with Hugh-ko and family were much less frequent than we had anticipated: They had come over just three times, and we been to Lopez only once or twice a year. Sheila had visited twice and Rits just once. Not enough! Also, we were feeling the financial burden of maintaining our beautiful big home.

So, despite our social and cultural involvements and a good circle of friends (including two War College classmates now retired in Spokane), we decided we should move back to Western Washington. We put our house on the market. For a whole year, Pat Porter tried in vain to sell it. Many people were put off by the pool—the feature we considered its key attraction. Or by taxes. A California couple came and were intrigued by the property; but when they heard that the annual property tax was about $4400, they backed off quickly. Their home in California was protected from tax increases by Proposition 13. So, they had unrealistic ideas about such taxes.

The pool should not have bothered prospective buyers. It needed very little attention, being indoors and covered by its plastic cover when not in use. The water was filtered "24/7" by a pump through a large sand filter. About twice a week I tested the PH and chlorine and added chemicals when needed. About every two weeks I unrolled a hose from the pump to the outdoors and flipped a switch to flush debris from the sand filter. Three times in five years, we drained the pool for repairs, cleaning and maintenance. In 1993, we replaced the plastic cover—all 900 square feet. So, it was nearly new. Humidity was no problem in the pool area as I have explained. But, potential buyers seemed to have a mindset that indoor pools are a problem and so found my explanations counterintuitive.

In 1994, Pat Burleson was named Washington State Elementary School Teacher of the Year. Hugh-ko was busy with his sign business and commercial scuba diving. He had joined the Lopez artists' co-op, was doing lapidary work, mostly with opals. And in season he joined a friend's "reef netting" crew. That last needs explanation.

Northwest Indians devised reef netting centuries (or millennia) ago for catching salmon migrating through Puget Sound. A V-shaped net is camouflaged with seaweed, etc., and spread out in a marine channel between three boats—two at the wings of the net and one at its base. The crews then wait passively for the fish to enter. That is detected by a lookout on the high mast of one boat. When the fish are into the V, the wing boats swing the net closed and the net is hauled in. The catch may be a few dozen to hundreds of fish. Today, the Fish and Game Service regulates this fishery, allotting licenses and fishing days depending on estimates of the salmon run. Now the runs have dwindled so much that some years the season never opens, or a single boat may get only a day or two of fishing and so not recoup the cost of the license and other expenses.

Kimie was still busy with social activities (some of which I joined in, too). In the senior bowling league in 1994 she twice bowled games of over 200 points, but had an average of around 145. She continued to give some great parties, from single-table bridge parties to sister-city events of nearly 40 persons. All her skills remained as sharp as ever.

On January 16, 1995, Kimie turned on TV-Japan (satellited) to catch a sumo tournament, but instead found NHK broadcasting news of a terrible earthquake in Japan's Kansai region, Kobe and our sister-city Nishinomiya especially. She called me to come and see. As soon as I realized how bad it was, I began contacting sister-city members and the Takaokas at the Mukogawa campus, for Michiko Takaoka is from Kobe. Our sister-city association was sending two English teachers each year to Nishinomiya; and we had two there at the time, as well as the daughter of one of our members, who was working for Japan's biggest saké brewer, Ozeki, headquartered in Nishinomiya.

Early reports indicated high casualties in Kobe and Nishinomiya; and soon the cameras were showing growing conflagrations in several areas of Kobe. So, many more casualties could be expected. Then we heard that the girl at Ozeki Sake had called home to report she was OK. Then, emergency services took over all lines, and we could not contact any Nishinomiya friends for about four days.

The day after the quake, we were watching NHK's nonstop coverage when the news media began calling us. A local ABC TV station and one from Seattle asked us to let them come to watch also, as so few reliable reports were coming in through normal channels. At the same time, we had the Takaokas come over to watch. NHK was listing the known dead when the Takaokas arrived. So, the Takaokas were sitting there, occasionally exclaiming when they saw the name of someone they knew. I was interpreting for the TV-station reporters, who were busily taking notes. Not an everyday kind of experience!

When we finally got a call through to Nishinomiya, we of course asked how we could help. Eventually, they said that medical supplies and money would be appreciated. On advice from a former member of Spokane's emergency response team, we contacted Sacred Heart Medical Center, where the team was located. They, in turn, contacted other local hospitals and clinics to ask for any excess medical supplies.

About then, Ed Tsutakawa, who was in Hawaii when the quake struck, arrived and began helping to make such contacts. In the Inland Northwest Trade Council we had a member who worked for UPS and whose boss had a Japanese mother. That led to UPS agreeing to truck the donated medical supplies gratis to any airport pickup point.

I recalled that JAL had a training facility at Grant County Airport, 100 miles to the west in Moses Lake. I called the Japanese manager there and asked if they could help fly the supplies to Osaka. He said they would get back to us. And, we got word out to the local media, schools, etc., to seek monetary donations and ask that volunteers come that Friday to Sacred Heart Hospital to help pack the medical supplies.

The reply from JAL: They had a plane leaving that weekend for Osaka and would take our shipment for nothing. Pure luck and fine cooperation! On Friday afternoon, about 30 people, literally aged eight to 80, showed up to help box the medical supplies, which filled the whole loading dock at Sacred Heart. When finished, we had 75 large cartons filled; and

UPS had to send a larger truck. So, it all came together. The estimated value of the medical supplies was $90,000. And, money donations from around the area totaled nearly $30,000. The bank electronically transferred that to Nishinomiya.

About that time, we heard from our two exchange teachers in Nishinomiya. They were okay, and their rooming house was only slightly damaged. One of them, an athletic Afro-American woman, had climbed into the wreckage of collapsed homes in the neighborhood and rescued several people. "They were our neighbors; we couldn't just stand by!" the teacher exclaimed when people insisted on treating her as a heroine.

In February 1995, Pat was to run a 3-day workshop on Lopez on teaching about Japan. Some 70 social studies teachers signed up—an ambitious project indeed! Pat called to ask if Kimie and I could help. In the end, I helped moderate one session, and Kimie undertook to prepare the Saturday night dinner. For 75 people! Moreover, she decided to make *makunouchi bento*—a complex, roughly 10-course meal.

So, on a Thursday we drove to Bellevue to pick up Japanese groceries at the Uwajimaya supermarket, then drove to Lopez to get started. Hugh-ko and Saijo (then working as a busboy at The Islander restaurant, where the dinner would be held) pitched in to help Kimie. The end result: she turned out a *great* dinner and won a standing ovation from the teachers. Even now, a decade later, some teachers reminisce to Pat about that meal. Kimie had unique ways of demonstrating her love.

In March, sister Mary called to invite us to a special event in Sacramento. Harry's son Adam, who had long been living in Fukuoka, Japan, was involved with artisans carving Noh masks; and he himself was then carving professional quality masks. In 1994 he took some of the group to the Bay Area for an exhibit and lectures at Oakland's Mills College. Now, he was bringing the group and some Noh performers to Sacramento. The masks would be exhibited at the Crocker Museum and Noh would be performed there, too. Intrigued, I flew (without Kimie) to Sacramento for that event. It was beautifully put on, and

I was delighted to meet the group, Adam and his Fukuoka bride, Motoko.

At the end of April, we had our fourth Spokane Japan Week—better than ever, with a visit by the Japanese Consul General from Seattle, and—now a regular part of this event—the entertaining "Japanese Speech Challenge" for high-school students of Japanese. I should have mentioned that two friends we met in Spokane Sister Cities were Atsumi Macauley and Akira Yoshida. They were employed in a most interesting activity: satellited Japanese language classes—programs that enabled students throughout the Pacific Northwest (and even as far away as Texas and Alaska) to learn Japanese from satellited lessons and correspondence with the two Spokane teachers. A big boon for students at schools that could not afford local Japanese classes.

In early May, after a year of no buyers, we took our house off the market, although we were not giving up on its eventual sale. A few weeks later, I was showing a Nishinomiya visitor, Mr. Moriyama, around Spokane; and he had an extra few hours before his next appointment. So, I took him to our home for tea.

In Japan, people are much less mobile than we are, have a strong sense of place or hometown and do not move as capriciously as we often do. So, Moriyama-san was amazed (1) that we would sell our home, (2) that just two people were living in so large a house, and (3) that the asking price was about what a small condo would cost in Osaka. As he left, he said he had a friend in Nishinomiya who might wish to buy our house. I agreed to send him photos and other information on the house to pass on to his friend.

The end result: The friend turned out to be a wealthy physician who owns a geriatric hospital in Nishinomiya. He already owned a home in Beppu (a hot spring resort in Kyushu) and certainly was interested in an overseas vacation home for his family and staff. So, with the help of Doug Baker, we produced a video on the house and sent it to the doctor. About a month later (July 2-3), the doctor and his wife arrived with Mr. & Mrs. Moriyama to see the house.

As we now had tried for so long to sell, Kimie was tense about the sale. She was doubly nervous because now we had an unexpected visitor: George's daughter Gillian, who was en route to southern California by Amtrak and was arriving about 1:30 AM of the day we were to show the house. (The plot was getting as thick as a Kabuki drama!) Gillian had not seen us since she was a little girl and naturally wanted to visit with us and sightsee. Kimie was focused on making the best possible impression on our Japanese guests.

Well, I juggled both situations: did some sightseeing with Gillian, hosted our Japanese visitors; and the sale went through like a breeze. The doctor was sold on the house as soon as he saw our video; but Kimie was not convinced until his signature was on the dotted line. An attorney helped us with the legal papers.

Another aspect of the sale: It turned out that the doctor or his staff would visit Spokane just a few times a year. They asked us to leave basic furnishings in the house so that they could come as tourists would. Kimie took on that project with her usual conscientiousness, buying such things as oak dressers and bureaus. When that was all done, we guessed we had left some $6000 in furnishings in the house, including beds for four.

Also, the house needed a caretaker. I arranged for Jeff Jones, a local teacher of Japanese and his wife Ann to occupy the house. They had taught English in Japan under a Japanese Government program. They had a home in Spokane, but were very receptive to the proposal that they live in our Spokane house. I also arranged for the Nishinomiya hospital to pay at least half of the monthly utility bill and for a gardener, thus minimizing the financial burden for Jeff and Ann. So, this turned out to be nearly ideal for all parties. Jeff and Ann lived in the house for six years and had two babies there. (By 2003, though, the house was on the market again and took 2 years to sell.)

After we first put our house up for sale, Kimie and I went to the Puget Sound area several times to house hunt. After several trips, we decided to narrow our search to Bellevue alone. Now we asked for help from our friend, Aiko Suganuma, whom we met in 1988 in Bellevue and who now had her own real estate agency.

# BELLEVUE RE-ENTRY
## (1995)

We finally zeroed in on a house Aiko showed us in northeast Bellevue. It had the lake view that Kimie wanted—Lake Sammamish instead of Lake Washington—and mountains: the top of 14,000-foot Mount Rainier, the Cascades and nearby Cougar and Tiger mountains. A special charm of our view appeared on clear nights when a full moon rose behind the firs below us, its beams turning the lake surface to shimmering silver and silhouetting the fir trees. So like a Japanese woodblock print.

We moved into the house about September 1, 1995, six years after we had moved to Spokane. The space is generous, though less so than our Spokane house. We have everything essential on one floor.

Soon we had a visit by Hugh-ko and family, as well as other family members from near and far. George's daughter Maria came to Bellevue with her husband to exhibit Bruderhof's Community Playthings at a major exhibition in Bellevue. Their visit coincided with one by Hugh-ko and family, for whom Kimie anyway was preparing another of her fantastic Chinese dinners. So, that worked out beautifully.

We now were just two miles from major shopping, two miles from the Uwajimaya supermarket and 2½ miles from Group Health. Very convenient indeed. Our neighborhood was ideal for exercise walks. We began at 1+ miles and within a few months had worked up to two miles, with some fairly steep hills.

We began re-engaging with the groups we had joined before: Bellevue Sister Cities, the Japan-America Society and the World Affairs Council. I became active in the Lake Washington Chapter of the Japanese-American Citizens League (JACL), courtesy of my membership derived through Kimie. She joined Eastside Newcomers, the Bellevue Women's Club and Overlake Service League, a charity that runs a thrift shop in Bellevue Square. And, she renewed her contacts with bridge-playing friends from six years earlier.

I volunteered in the Japan-America Society "Japan in a Suitcase" program—joining teams who visit primary schools and take the kids on imagined trips to Japan to visit a Japanese home and school. After a few years I switched to a similar program for high school students studying Japanese.

Late in 1995, Ed Tsutakawa called to inform me that I was to receive the 1995 Spokane Mayor's Award "for outstanding contribution to the Spokane sister cities program" in coordinating assistance to Nishinomiya after the quake. So, I went to Spokane to receive the plaque.

We went to Lopez that year for Thanksgiving, and back east to Rits's home for Christmas, riding comfortably in an Amtrak sleeper compartment. Our travel package included return by air. We of course also saw Rits's children and grandchildren. But, how could Kimie have three generations of offspring? She still looked so young!

In April '96 I had a little accident. In our backyard trimming an apple tree, I left the safety of the ladder and was perched atop the tree when I lost my balance and fell head first through the tree. Fortunately, half way down my head hit a branch, so that I flipped and landed on my behind. *Fortunately*, because I landed on a large flat rock that could have seriously scrambled my gray matter. Fortunately, too, a neighbor happened to be watching. He immediately called 911 and alerted Kimie. I regained consciousness half an hour later in the Group Health emergency ward. My only injury was a cut on the back of my head. But, about 16 months later the balance mechanism in my right inner ear went out. Doctors could not agree on a direct cause-and-effect tie to my fall, but I suspect the fall set me up for that.

Late at night on July 17, Kimie suddenly experienced severe pain below her rib cage. I rushed her to Group Health's emergency room, where doctors diagnosed pancreatitis and admitted her to the hospital. Her gastroenterologist, Dr. Ylvisaker, told us the next day it was a severe case that might keep her on IV tubes for as much as two weeks. Without such treatment to rest her pancreas, her life was at risk. I spent hours each day at her bedside and helped her exercise in the ward and greet friends coming with flowers and warm wishes. She actually stayed on IV feeding for 19 days and in the hospital for 22. Her strength returned quite slowly. She had lost about 14 pounds when she came home. Now she had to go onto insulin, as the illness had so damaged her pancreas. A few months later, she was back in the hospital to have her gall bladder removed—another five days in the hospital. She seemed to recover well from that.

That fall (1996), a group of us visited our sister city, Yao (part of Osaka). Kimie was still not strong enough to go; but I visited Kimie's family in Yokohama and friends in Tokyo.

1997 was a better year. Kimie could no longer do the 2-mile walking course, but handled well the less hilly 1-mile courses. In June, we went to Lopez Island for grandson Saijo's high-school graduation. In August, we quietly celebrated our 50th anniversary, but were lured to a surprise party the day before by some of Kimie's close friends. For the big "golden" day, Hugh & Pat came for a visit. I had designed a gold pendant and had a jeweler make it for my girl: a "50" with a heart-shaped zero adorned with three sapphires. When some of her friends, unaware of the anniversary, saw the pin, they asked, "Are you really 50?" She scarcely looked it, even at 78. For years, I had been calling her "miracle girl."

In September, at the request of City Hall, I took on the first of a several interpreting assignments with city hall staffers from Yao, our sister city: 15 days of almost daily interpreting as these visitors under the Bellevue-Yao staff exchange made the rounds of Bellevue to learn how our city handled city administration, relations with citizens, human services, etc. Very enlightening for me, too. I learned to greatly respect the efforts our city government makes to improve life here.

On the final day of that assignment, I took the staff exchangee to see "The Tale of Otokichi," a drama that a committee I served on had planned as the kick-off for Bellevue's 1997 Japan Week. Performed by a troupe from Nagoya, the drama was based on the true story of the first Japanese known to have set foot in what is now Washington state: three young castaways—survivors of a cruel saga.

In 1833, their small ship was sailing up Japan's coast to Edo (now Tokyo) with a cargo of ceramics and rice. Hit by a fierce storm that tore away the mast and rudder, the ship was left hopelessly adrift. For 17 months, the ship rode the currents across the north Pacific as the crew died one by one from scurvy and exposure. Washing up on this coast near the extreme northwest tip of Washington in 1834, the three survivors were picked up by Makah Indians and put to work to earn their keep. When the British Hudson Bay Company at Fort Vancouver, near the mouth of the Columbia River, heard of strange arrivals up the coast, it sent a ship and arranged to have the men turned over to them.

As the Japanese spoke no English, the British put them into school at the fort. One student there was Ranald MacDonald, half British/half Indian, who was intrigued by these men from across the Pacific. Years later, that interest led him to smuggle himself into a Japan still secluded from most outside contacts. Arrested and taken to Nagasaki, MacDonald won the friendship of one of his captors and began teaching English to several officials—men who would later serve as interpreters when Commodore Perry arrived with his Black Ship flotilla in 1853 to open Japan to Western contacts.

Meanwhile a Hudson Bay Co. agent devised a plan to use the castaways as bargaining chips for opening trade between Britain and Japan and had them sent to London. But, the London government was then preoccupied with the China trade. The three Japanese were sent on to Macao and put in the care of British missionaries. While others looked for a way to get the three men into Japan, the missionaries conceived of having them help translate the Bible into Japanese. Some progress was made in that; but what the devout men of God could not know was that the language used by these down-country sailors was too rough to suit their purpose. After an aborted effort to get the men into Japan, the three ended up employed by the British in the ports of East Asia. The youngest, Otokichi, did see Japan again from the deck of a British ship on which he was an interpreter. But, none of the three would ever set foot on home soil again.

A few decades ago, a Japan Bible Society publication told the story of that first effort in Macao to put the Bible into Japanese. When people in Nagoya read that the Japanese involved were from their area, they began checking and found the hometown, Mihama, of the castaways of 140 years before. Now the townspeople learned the true fate of the men they thought were lost at sea and had memorialized on headstones in a Mihama cemetery. That led to their story being written up and performed as a drama, first in the unfortunate men's home town, then elsewhere in Japan, in Singapore and finally in Bellevue.

The head of our committee recruited a half dozen Makahs to act in the rescue scene; and I recruited eight young students from a Bellevue dance/singing school to do the scene at the Fort Vancouver school. The two performances at Bellevue's Meydenbauer Center Theater were well attended. Some 50 Japanese from Mihama had timed a visit to this area to those performances and attended the matinee. They also took a bus to the Makah reservation to thank the tribe for their long-ago aid to their native sons.

In October 1997, we flew to Yokohama to see Kimie's siblings. Sumie's husband Takeo was fighting cancer, but was in remission. He went with us to look at new developments in Yokohama. Such as the development where the Mitsubishi Shipyard once was, now replaced by a 70-story commercial tower and a 40-story hotel/mall/cultural complex. Such as a posh restaurant/mall complex where the Navy PX and commissary once stood. And, Takeo joined us on a trip to Nikko, where we again toured our honeymoon site of a half century before. We also saw former colleagues in Tokyo and Yokohama, such as Fujita (from our Niigata era), Sen Nishiyama (from our 1963-69 tours) and Mizutani-san (secretary during the '60s and '70s).

You may by now have picked up on our credo "there's no friend like an old friend." So, Kimie also spent an afternoon with her chum from high school days, Mochizuki Yasuko-san. With Sumie and Takeo we also visited the Tokyo grave of Kimie's mother, who had died that March at age 99, outliving her husband Kojiro by two decades.

Back home, we spent Thanksgiving with Hugh-ko and family at Pat's parents' home on the Olympic Peninsula—a very heart-warming time. As if we had not sufficiently quenched our travel thirst that fall, we flew east for Christmas with Rits and her offspring. From there we made a side-trip to southwest Pennsylvania to visit brother George, then in the 5th year of his fight against cancer. He was confined to a motorized wheel chair, but was in good spirits. Besides George and Vonnie, we also met many of their offspring at the same Bruderhof. George would succumb to the cancer 15 months later.

So, in three months we made a road trip to the Bay area, a journey by air to Japan, a short trip to the Olympic Peninsula and flight to the Middle Atlantic States, with a 200-mile side trip to Bruderhof. Also notable for 1997: Daughter-in-law Pat became president of Washington State's Social Studies Teachers Assn. for the year.

In 1998, the group that had sponsored nine years of "Japan Week in Bellevue" went out of existence due to debts; but several of us who felt that educational activity must continue rallied to create a new body, Eastside Nihon Matsuri no Kai (Eastside Japan Festival Assn.). We met monthly through June, and more often during the summer as the time neared for the Festival—the first of what would be annual weekend fall festivals of exhibits and stage performances presenting many aspects of Japan's culture.

In July, our sister-city group hosted and entertained a visiting delegation from Yao, our Japanese sister city, over three fully packed days. So, I remained a "Pacific citizen" heavily involved in promoting trans-Pacific understanding.

Now Kimie began to feel less energetic than normal, but continued our daily mile-long walks through our neighborhood, now choosing the flattest route. Through 1997-99 Kimie had periodic blood tests and CAT scans at Group Health to check on the condition of her liver and pancreas.

We again visited Ritsuko and family for Christmas '98; but unhappily Ray and Sara were now divorced. The year 1999 went about the same for us. Kimie and I joined a Bellevue Sister Cities delegation on a three-day visit in October to our sister city in Osaka. Then we again went to Yokohama to see her family. With sisters Sumie and Hiroko, we took a two-day trip by train to Niigata to visit that city for the first time in over 20 years. And, Kimie turned 80. No stopping the clock. She was beginning to say, "I've lived long enough." Lacking her usual get-up-and-go and limited by her diabetes in what she could eat, she was beginning to feel that life was now less fun.

# CRISIS

## (2000-2001)

In early 2000, a dark cloud appeared in Kimie's medical picture: She began having pain in the pancreas area again. Dr. Ylvisaker diagnosed it as partial blockage of the bile duct, and in February she had laparoscopic surgery to clear that out. She was to be an outpatient; but the procedure induced another bout of pancreatitis—five more days in the hospital on IV feeding. During that time, the doctor ordered an X-ray and MRI scan to get a better picture of conditions in Kimie's midriff. With the results in June, he saw shadows in her liver that would need further analysis in several months. Meanwhile, my girl bounced back some, resuming her social activities and, in June, going with me to Lopez for grandson Kai's high school graduation.

So, I decided to attend a convention in Monterey in late June. I had been active in our local Japanese American Citizens League (JACL) chapter since 1997, on the board since 1998 and chapter president from 2000. Each of the JACL's 112 chapter presidents was supposed to attend if possible. That was my first visit to the central California coast since Kimie, Hugh-ko and I were there in 1966.

It proved very instructive, for the convention was wrestling with some hot issues. Such as, trying to resolve differences between Nisei vets who had volunteered in WWII and Nisei men who resisted being drafted from the internment camps until their civil rights were restored. Also we passed a resolution supporting a Hawaiian request that our government admit that their queen was illegally ousted and Hawaii was illegally annexed, and that Hawaiians should get the same special treatment that Native Americans have. As the oldest Asian American civil rights body, JACL's stand on such issues carries weight.

Also, as the Pacific Northwest District representative on JACL's US-Japan relations (USJR) committee, I was able to get the convention to adopt language on the committee's mission and to allocate a minimal budget for the USJR. So, attending the convention was well worth my time.

Home again, I spent a quiet summer with Kimie—doing more translations and otherwise carrying on normally. On September 7, Kimie saw Dr. Ylvisaker again, for a follow up on her spring illness. He ordered a blood test. A week later, he told us the test showed a positive indication of liver cancer. He ordered an ultrasound scan. Too soon, we had the diagnosis: untreatable liver cancer.

The doctor had us consult an oncologist in Seattle, who confirmed the diagnosis in a matter-of-fact manner. He said he doubted that any surgeon would be willing to attempt surgery on Kimie's tumor, given her age and other factors. He said that if we were lucky, Kimie might live two years without serious discomfort, as the liver has no nerves for pain.

We looked at each other. Two years! We tried to take this philosophically, but... We had been married 53 years and deeply in love since spring 1946. We knew all fine things come to an end eventually; but the death sentence seemed unreal. Maybe we could find something at least to halt the cancer or delay its progress.

Since August, we had been communicating with Kimie's sisters about their plan to visit us in October. Kimie decided not to tell them about the cancer, lest they cancel their trip. Of course, we told our family here in the U.S. Our offspring all decided they must come to see Kimie and meet their three Japanese aunts.

So, in the second week of October, our house filled up with relatives: Kimie's sisters Fusae, Sumie and Hiroko, our children Rits and Hugh-ko (with Pat), our grandchildren Sheila, Ray, Saijo and Kai and two great grandchildren Brian and Amy. It was a great time for re-warming family ties and for our offspring to get acquainted with Kimie's sisters. Brian's origami skills charmed his aunts, as did Amy's lively personality and big blue eyes. Yet, we knew this could be scene one of the last act.

I treated the group, except for Kimie (who wished to conserve her strength), to a trip to Blake Island in Puget Sound to enjoy the Indian dances and a salmon barbecue. After the eastern contingent had left, Kimie, her sisters and I took a catamaran cruiser to Victoria on Vancouver Island for a two-day visit. We sampled the British aura of the place, with afternoon high tea at the Empress Hotel, and toured the city and Bouchart Gardens north of the city, where Kimie gamely walked the entire 1+ mile route.

Of course, on the day they arrived from Japan, Kimie told her sisters about her cancer. Fusae, a nurse by training, was not ready to admit that no treatment would help. In the weeks after they returned to Japan, Fusae, as well as brother Toshio, sent medicines (mainly vitamins and minerals) touted in Japan as a boon for cancer patients. Sumie sent a tincture of the Brazilian *agaricus* mushroom—a very expensive substance.

In early December, Kimie had MRI imaging again. That showed the hematoma's growth had accelerated. Dr. Ylvisaker had to back away from guessing how much time Kimie might have. She was by then beginning to feel some pressure on her diaphragm from her swelling liver and the resulting edema.

We were blessed at Christmas by visits from Hugh-ko and family, Rits and Sheila. But, just then we were having trouble adjusting the level of Kimie's new medications. She slept much of the time and so could not join fully in the yuletide activities.

In January, more pancreatitis and another five days in the hospital on IV tubes. Instead of losing weight this time, she emerged with severe edema—20 pounds of fluid that her liver no longer could filter from her blood. Dr. Ylvisaker recommended halting non-essential medications.

Late that month, both her GP and Dr. Ylvisaker independently urged that we enroll Kimie in Group Health's in-home hospice program. That meant they believed she had no more than six months to live. We swallowed hard and filled out the forms, but still had our fingers crossed that the agaricus might halt or even reverse the cancer.

Dr. Ylvisaker had warned us that Kimie would experience increasing nausea as the disease progressed. Now that started. She began eating much less and very selectively. We had trouble controlling her blood sugar. She slept poorly, as her new medications often made her extremely restless, causing her pace the house for hours at night. To avoid waking me, she sometimes slept on a living room sofa or family-room recliner and then napped during the day or evening to make up for her broken nights. Her mood became more variable, with some depression—most unusual for my normally cheerful descendant of the sun goddess, but understandable in those circumstances.

During February, we got rid of her edema with extra diuretics. Her weight came down to 110 pounds. She had not been that light since 1951; but of course that also meant she was losing muscle and fat.

We now appreciated all that the hospice program could do for her. Two or three times a week a visiting nurse, came to check Kimie's vital signs and general condition. A social worker came sometimes to see what she might need besides medical help, and arranged for a volunteer to stay with Kimie when I had to attend meetings. Some of our neighborhood friends had volunteered already, but this gave us another option.

A spiritual adviser, Maria Hoagland, came to see my Kimie many times. Maria had been a child of Lutheran missionaries in Japan and so could, as needed, converse with Kimie in Japanese. Kimie told her she wanted to see a Nichiren Buddhist priest (Nichiren Buddhism having been the religion of her parents). Maria found a young priest in Seattle and referred him to us. Over the next months, he came perhaps five times

405

to counsel Kimie and recite prayers over her (in Japanese, Sino-Japanese and Sanskrit!).

As the tumor continued to grow, the pressure on Kimie's lungs made her short of breath and she needed oxygen at least several hours a day and sometimes through the night. Angela had a health equipment supplier bring an oxygen machine for home use and a portable tank for times when Kimie could go out for minor shopping (driving herself until March) or for her doctor appointments. Despite all she was going through, she remained resilient physically. She often got up to work in the kitchen, prepare her favorite dishes or even cook something for me.

A JACL friend whose brother runs a cancer center near San Diego urged that we contact him. I sent him information on Kimie's condition. When he read it was liver cancer, he ceased communicating. Another friend touted a treatment center in Tijuana and obtained literature on that for us. One brochure listed cure rates they had achieved—from 40% on some cancers down to 0% for liver cancer. Other friends also spoke of treatments they had heard of and people who had beaten "the big C," but none were liver cancer cases.

On April 8, Rits came again for 10 days—a big help for Kimie's morale. (Rits was able to continue her work from her agency's local office, but had to go in when Wall Street opened—6 AM Pacific time.) About then, Kimie's edema returned with a vengeance, and she decided she was not going to recover. Now she wanted to clear the spiritual ledger—to quit "sweating the small stuff" that had so preoccupied her in the past.

Sadly and sincerely, she apologized to Rits and Hugh-ko for having been "such a bad mother" and said, "I never realized what wonderful children I have!" She asked us to forgive her for being so self centered all her life. She apologized to me for her fib about Rits's parentage and not correcting that for the first six years of our marriage. I told her I long ago understood she had made up that tale before she came to trust my commitment to her, because she then loved me so much that she feared the truth might drive me away. So, I instead felt blessed to have received such love from her when I was a mere 19-year-old. Now she said she felt she did not deserve to have had "such a good husband." I knew, of course, that her often perverse ways had led her to show her love in her own idiosyncratic way, often goading us to improve ourselves just as she constantly pushed herself. Her mind now relieved of such preoccupations and her true feelings bared, her love for us became a most beautiful thing to behold and to accept with deep gratitude and sadness.

In mid-April, the nurse ordered a rented hospital bed to help her sleep better, installing it in the family room where she could watch TV. In March, another volunteer worker started coming—a young professional masseur, who coincidentally had a Japanese grandmother. He returned about weekly and did help to relieve some of Kimie's discomfort.

The amazing thing was that most of these services under the Hospice program—nurses, counselors, equipment, etc.—were cost free for us. Our medical expenses plummeted to near zero.

As spring set in, I made sure that Kimie saw our cherry blossoms and irises, as she loved flowers so. She saw her GP monthly into April and Dr. Ylvisaker just occasionally. On such visits to the doctor, the lady who had first entranced me with her feather-light dancing now was weak enough that she leaned heavily on my arm. By late spring she was getting only palliative care and complained that "my doctors have given up on me." That was essentially true, as the doctors could do nothing more for her. We found that Tylenol and oxycodone with chamomile tea at bedtime best helped her irregular sleep problem.

In May, the nausea came more frequently, and her edema was increasingly uncomfortable, with her lower body more swollen. The nurses called this ascides, a symptom of liver decline. On June 4, Dr. Ylvisaker tried to relieve the swelling by draining fluid from her stomach, but could take very little. That was the last treatment a doctor would try. She was so weak when she went in that time that I had to take her in a wheelchair to the doctor.

With that failure and the constant discomfort of the edema, Kimie really began to despair. Once she asked the nurse if she could go to Group Health's Kelsey Creek hospice unit to get an overdose of oxycodone. We were only partly successful in cheering her up. To Marie Hoagland, Kimie admitted that she had one fear about dying: She had always had no sense of direction and so might not know where to go when the time came.

Despite zero appetite, Kimie continued to eat solids, but in ever smaller amounts. She felt she had little time remaining; but knew Sheila and Rits would want to come see her again. So, she wanted to sustain her strength by eating.

On Monday, June 11, she got up early to change the water for the flowers on the memorial shelf for her parents, but then went back to bed, complaining of being very weak. At 6:30 she arose again and checked her blood glucose. 88! Dangerously low. I called the hospice nurse, who advised taking glucose tablets quickly. Kimie did; and soon her blood glucose was 123. I reported that to the nurse, who advised giving Kimie a reduced dose of insulin. (I had helped Kimie inject her insulin since early May.) But then Kimie could not bring herself to eat, feeling it would not stay down. She took oxycodone at 9:30 AM, but that made her very agitated. She asked me to get a doctor to come and to call Hugh-ko to come and help me. She was concerned that I needed a break.

At 11:15 AM she finally slept. An hour later a hospice helper came to bathe her; but we could not rouse her. So, she just applied some lotion. Kimie felt nauseous, but was fast asleep when the helper left. Next, the Nichiren priest came to pray over her, but she never seemed aware he was there. At 2:30 she felt nauseous again, but nothing came up. Soon after, she became very dopey. I checked her glucose level again. 54! Perilously low. I gave her some fruit juice and a glucose pill. About then, the nurse came and checked Kimie's "vitals." She turned to me and said, "This looks like insulin shock. I'm sorry, but I think it's time for her to go to Kelsey Creek."

Now it was my time to despair. I felt so defeated. I should have double-checked about giving her the insulin that morning; only I knew how little she was eating. Still hoping it would be a temporary stay, I agreed. The nurse called an ambulance. As Kimie was rolled out of our front door on a gurney, she said gamely, "Well, I guess I have to say goodbye to this house." The house her magical touch and fine aesthetic sense had turned into a warm, beautiful home. She left it at 4 PM, Monday, June 11, showing her normal indomitable spirit.

I followed the ambulance to the Care Center and saw that Kimie was made comfortable in a private room. The hospice staff and a social worker were very helpful and arranged for me to overnight on a daybed in Kimie's room. But, first, I went home to get my things, eat supper and call our children and grandchildren. Hugh-ko and Pat arranged to come down the next day. Rits and Sheila would arrive a few days later.

That first night, Kimie slept poorly. The night nurse checked her about 11 PM and found Kimie fairly alert. The nurse told us she had a son in college, a 6'11" basketball player. She said, "He was a Prairie Dog at the University of Minnesota, but now he's a Timber Wolf at the University of Wyoming, so I guess he's coming up in the world." Kimie got a good laugh out of that. That was the last time my Kimie, beloved by all for her sense of humor, would laugh.

Over the next few hours, I was up every three or four minutes as she called me constantly to do one thing or another. The nurse gave her more oxycodone. That quieted her and I got some sleep.

Hugh-ko and Pat arrived about mid-morning. I went home for breakfast, some sleep and to check out the house. Over the next several days, we continued that pattern: I stayed in Kimie's room overnight while Hugh & Pat slept at our house.

Rits and Sheila arrived on Wednesday; and Saijo and Kai came to visit for several hours. Kimie seemed aware of their presence, but gradually became less alert and scarcely spoke. The damned poisons were building up. The nurses assured us, however that, she could hear and understand most of what we said to her. So, we told her the news that Ray would be arriving on Saturday. That afternoon—Thursday—when I offered her some pine-nut soup that she had made earlier and kept in the freezer, she avidly ate about 6 ounces plus some yogurt, as if desperate to sustain her strength until Ray came. My hopes began rising, and I dared to think we might be able to take Kimie home again.

Yet, when I returned to the hospice from home Friday afternoon—bad news. While I was gone, Kimie had begun experiencing severe pain, as Dr. Ylvisaker said she would at the end; and the nurse had started a stronger pain medication. Hugh-ko said the hospice doctor had told them he did not expect Kimie to live past the weekend. Final defeat. I broke down at that news.

Ray arrived Saturday afternoon. Kimie seemed to know he was there. Some friends visited Sunday afternoon; and on Monday Kimie's onetime golfing partner, Verna, dropped by. Kimie was unresponsive to either visit and had become so weak that she no longer could clear her lungs. The "death rale" began.

About 5PM on Monday, we were in Kimie's room talking, all except Hugh-ko and Ray, who had gone out to the lounge. Suddenly Pat got up and left the room. When she came back with Hugh and Ray, she was crying and told us a totally amazing thing:

"I was just sitting there when suddenly I saw Uncle John's face on the wall. I could not believe what I was seeing. Then he was there standing at the foot of Kimie's bed, smiling at me and at her! He was wearing his favorite jacket, and made that sound with his lips that he often made when he was going to speak. I saw him clearly, not ghostly, but just like he always was. Then he was gone. I didn't know what to say and was so amazed that I felt like weeping. So, I went to get Hugh and Ray."

As we discussed this, Rits, who had been near the foot of Kimie's bed, said she had felt a presence, but had discounted it.

I went to Kimie, took her dainty hand and whispered into her ear, "Darling, Pat just saw John. He came here with a smile on his face to guide you across. So, you don't have to keep hanging on. We'll miss you terribly; but it's okay to let go now."

Within moments, her breathing changed to a kind of gasping. The rattle of phlegm in her lungs quieted. Her beautiful eyes opened one brief moment, seeming to look beyond this world, and then closed again. She was quiet.

I called out for someone to call the nurse. The nurse came, checked her pulse and eyes. "She is gone," she said. The time: 6:05 PM, Monday, June 18, 2001.

I had lost my treasured soul mate of 55 years. Her face still was serene, beautiful, ageless. She had lived on at the hospice for seven days. She had fought the cancer for nine months. Three months is more common. We might be comforted to know that the care given her had extended her life for a half year, except that her final two or three months were so physically uncomfortable. I am grateful that we had the extra time to resolve so much and help bring her peace of mind.

The literature that the hospice counselors shared with us contains accounts of people near death indicating that they see long-dead friends or family members who seem to come to help them through the death process. When I told Allan Burleson what Pat had witnessed, he said Grandma Burleson (Solomon Burleson's wife) had seen her son Guy in the room with her after he drowned, at age 38, in Lake Cayuga and before the news of his drowning reached her. "So, we have a family history of this," Allan said.

And, what more appropriate guide for sense-of-direction-challenged Kimie than Pastor John, who had served parishes in this state for three decades and passed on 17 years before? He knew the way.

Careful readers of this memoir may recall that Kimie, as a girl, saw her grandmother coming to visit after she had died. And, that Kimie had sensed the disturbed soul of the man who originally owned our north Berkeley home, even grasping that he killed himself with much loss of blood in that basement laundry. You may believe or disbelieve. These experiences and now my late brother's appearance as Kimie was about to pass over have forced us to re-think our past beliefs about an afterlife. We know Pat is level headed, down to earth and not strongly religious. We believe she did see John's spirit, which she said was in no way like a religious "vision." John simply appeared in that hospice room and stood at the foot of Kimie's bed. We feel this is convincing evidence that there indeed is something after death.

Elsewhere I have noted that the fear of death is one of our strongest emotions and our capacity for self-deception is nearly infinite, especially when motivated by a fear of death. I believe that, combined with the survival instinct, helps explain our primordial impulse toward religion and belief in an afterlife. Yet, we have much personal evidence and testimony from many others that something we call a soul or spirit seems to survive the death process. In trying to adopt a fully "modern" mentality and explain all phenomena through science and rational logic, have we perhaps suppressed some modes of human consciousness because science cannot explain them? Just as we stress the separation of church and state, we often insist on separating the scientific and religious realms, perhaps at the expense of understanding aspects of our being that some experiences tell us are real, even if not understood.

Since Kimie left us physically, I often feel her spirit with me. Wishful thinking? Perhaps. I choose to believe she is often close. I look at her photo and she seems to be in the room with me. I often hear her voice, sometimes chiding, sometimes encouraging me. I answer or simply chuckle at how strongly her personality still comes through. That helps to ease the abiding grief of losing her physical presence.

When that grief surges up, I make myself recall all the bright times we shared; and the grief is submerged in a flood of joy. For, she was an unfailing source of sunshine, humor, excitement and beauty for me for 55 years. So, I continue this new form of communion with her and in my heart treasure this shining gem, ever the fire opal glinting with surprising lights. She inspires me to sustain the commitment we made long ago to work for ever better understanding between our two nations. I am indebted to Japanese culture for producing so fine a person, to my own nation for all it has given me and gave to her.

So, how do I tell others about a girl I alone knew so well? A woman/girl, forever youthful, adored through years of vigorous health and sickness, joy and sorrow, ecstasy and anger and all conditions and feelings in between. We knew each other so well that one word, one look, one touch resonated with meaning that bound our souls together through 20,000 days of sharing. As, in 1997 when she saw me cut my hand and instantly cried out in distress, "You did it again!" Meaning it gave her total recall of a similar incident 50 years before.

Her voice, high and ringing in her green years, slowly mellowed to mid-range as the decades slipped by, but never lost its capacity to make my heart sing, or seize my full attention if her mood was disturbed. A clear, high soprano until high school, they tell me, so that she sometimes soloed at school music festivals. In high school she seemed to lose confidence in her ability to carry a tune and thereafter would only sing when a whole group was singing and over-riding the sound of her voice. Standing beside her, I could hear it and revel in its sweetness.

The wonder of her dainty hands, fingers tapered, fine instruments for a dozen arts, and with skin so smooth and soft, even at 80, that I could imagine only a cloud would feel softer. She used few cosmetics. After 60, she put moisturizing cream on her face at night, but lightly. And, waking in the morning, she was always serenely beautiful.

Yet, she had samurai steel in her spirit, a will so strong that even after the rebel cells in her liver began their destructive course, she continued her exercises, walked for strength and (until 3 months before her passing) drove her own car, defying the fate those cells were plotting. Mushy feelings she almost never displayed, maintaining a tough-love approach to us all, until the last two months, when she decided she could not cross over without letting us know how she really felt. Then she phoned old friends from years and decades past, across the state, in California, Maryland and Japan to say goodbye in a way that they would know how special they were to her. She disliked writing letters, much preferring direct communication.

In our later years, I felt uncomfortable using any categorical or generic terms in referring to her, such as wife or woman. She was purely and simply Kimie.

She liked to criticize my appearance: nose "too big," ears and eyes "too small," etc. After we had been together maybe 45 years, she finally said, almost reluctantly, "Well, you do have a pleasant face." By then, life with her had made it so.

She kept a list of the birthdays of family and friends, marking them on the calendar at the start of each year and then sending birthday greetings – by card or phone to each one. She cared.

We are left with these indelible memories of our shining Kimie. So talented, but always modest about her skills, a down-to-earth aesthete in tune with life's beauty and so able simply to express the beauty in her soul.

I used to say to her, "God made one mistake when he made you: he should have made you immortal." I was wrong. The many wonderful things her friends have said about her or written in their sympathy cards show that her spirit will be present so long as anyone who knew her, or knew *of* her, still lives. Also, some of her offspring clearly have inherited some of her traits. That may be immortality enough.

I remain cheered and motivated by her bright example of how to live life with verve and joy and love for our fellow humans—expressed in the many things she loved to do for people she cared about: beautifully cooked meals, artificial flowers made faster than Mother Nature's, the simple giving of herself and her time. I am infinitely grateful to have shared life with this special girl/woman. And so, I need to alter my pledge "to love and to cherish" her "till death do us part." It must now be "*though* death do us part."

# LATER YEARS

Without Kimie's physical presence but always inspired by her example, I continue our mission of promoting cross-Pacific understanding by staying active in the same non-profit organizations as before. Our annual Japanese Fall Festival (Aki Matsuri) in Bellevue draws thousands of visitors from all over the Puget Sound region. I continue to help plan and carry it out.

I continue to be active in the JACL at the chapter and district level; and by 2006 I will have served at three consecutive JACL conventions on the resolutions committee.

In 2002 I translated my first full book—on a technique for making Japanese dolls and on their costumes from Japan's Kyoto court era. In 2003 I quit doing translations on technical subjects, but help sometimes with shorter translations or interpreting work.

Since 2002, I have joined Hugh-ko in Yokohama after he and Pat had finished guiding a groups on study tours of Japan (which are fully funded by a foundation). We have good visits with Kimie's family and with friends, and work out our own study tours in Japan so that we can help others understand that country better.

I have traveled quite a bit each year, visiting family and friends in California and on the East Coast. I have joined sister city delegations to Bellevue's two East Asian sister cities and to the two in Europe. In 2004 I became president of Bellevue Sister Cities Assn.

In 2003, we all were thrilled to see Pat Burleson receive an award from the US-Japan Foundation for excellence in teaching about Japan; and then, about 10 days later, saw her honored also by the Seattle World Affairs Council as 2003's "World Educator" in front of 400 guests and Governor Locke, who praised her for setting an inspiring example for other social studies teachers in the state.

On October 2, 2004, (Kimie's birthday!) a *very* special event: Sheila's wedding to Frank McClaughlin on the New Jersey shore. Our whole West Coast contingent attended, except for Kai, who had just begun a new job. Later in October, I took a real nostalgia trip to Southern California, for the 60$^{th}$ reunion of my high school class of 1944. I allowed myself an extra day before the reunion in order to drive south to Escondido and Vista, which I had not seen in 60 years. On the street where we lived in Escondido in the early 1930s, all buildings were new, *except* the church and the rectory that was once our home.

Going on to Vista, I nearly missed the turnoff. For, the town seems now to be little more than a suburb of Oceanside. With difficulty I found the hill and street where we lived in the late '30s. Our former home stood little changed, except for being partly hidden by more mature trees and vegetation. Moral: when you've been gone for over half a century, you really can't go home again.

Back in Claremont, the reunion at Webb was interesting; both for meeting the old men who had been my classmates and for seeing how the campus has changed. Now co-located there is the Vivian Webb School for girls; and the student body—once all white—now is multi-ethnic and includes students from around the world, especially Asia.

I have gone to see cousin Allan, now in his 90's in a retirement home in Sandpoint, about every six months. Of course, I have the joy of watching population growth in the family: grandson Ray has three children now and one more on the way. Sheila and Frank's son, Franklin Bernard McLaughlin IV, was born in January '06. So, by mid-2006 Kimie will have five great-grandchildren. But, she will always look much too young!

# EPILOGUE

Reflecting on this life, I am struck by the irony that my first exposure to Japan, off Kyushu and in Nagasaki Bay on the "General Weigel," led me to write a poem. The simple error that, in November 1945, misdirected our ship there, instead of to Nagoya, cost our country perhaps a few thousand dollars in fuel oil. Under the situation prevailing while I was in Texas learning the infantryman's deadly skills, our leaders in Washington expected to launch—that November—a massive invasion of Kyushu, at a cost of millions of dollars and hundreds of thousands of lives. Instead, triple blows against Japan—the two atomic bombings and the Soviet entry into the war during its final 10 days—finally forced Japan's leaders to accept the surrender terms laid out at Yalta and Potsdam.

For me, that meant I would be saved to fight, four or five months later, the bloodless "battle of Yokohama"—the often intense arguments Kimie and I waged as we two strong-willed and very stubborn people began meshing our personalities. The bond between us was annealed in the heat of such "battles," under the late 1940's pressure of official and legal hostility to our union and cemented in place by our overcoming other trials of life in the next five decades.

Together with her and inspired by her, I was able to have a micron-scale role in building the new edifice of the US-Japan alliance that now supports the broad range of ties bridging the Pacific. And so, after a life whose course was fundamentally altered by the war in the Pacific and by my unforgettable Kimie, I can be very comfortable in continuing to work as a "Pacific citizen" and, indeed, as a *pacific* citizen.

*Sheila and Ray at his wedding - 1987*

*Saijo and Hugh-ko - 1990*

*We two in Spokane - 1994*

*Great-grandchildren Amy and Brian - 1995*

*Kimie's siblings in Yokohama - 1999*

*Kimie and her sisters - Vancouver Island - 2000*

*Family group at Sheila's wedding - 2004*

*With Rits on Jersey shore - 2004*

Printed in the United States
106437LV00003B/70-168/A